When the Soviet Union Entered World Politics

When the Soviet Union Entered World Politics

JON JACOBSON

University of California Press

BERKELEY   LOS ANGELES   LONDON

University of California Press
Berkeley and Los Angeles, California

University of California Press, Ltd.
London, England

© 1994 by
The Regents of the University of California

Library of Congress Cataloging-in-Publication Data

Jacobson, Jon, 1938–
    When the Soviet Union entered world politics / Jon Jacobson.
        p.   cm.
    Includes bibliographical references and index.
    ISBN 0–520–08332–6 (alk. paper). —
    ISBN 0–520–08976–6 (pbk. : alk. paper)
    1. Soviet Union—Foreign relations—1917–1945.   I. Title.
DK266.45.J33   1994
327.47–dc20   94–4959
                                                       CIP

Printed in the United States of America
9 8 7 6 5 4 3 2 1

Contents

Maps

Acknowledgments

As the mutual hostilities of the Cold War era were finally effaced, first with the advent of "the new political thinking" fostered by Eduard Shevardnadze and Mikhail Gorbachev in what was then the Soviet Union, and then with the end of Communism as a force in world politics, I became increasingly interested in the prospects for thinking of Soviet foreign relations as a thing of the past. That project entailed, it seemed to me, transcending concerns and assumptions that had strongly influenced foreign policy within the nations of both NATO and the Warsaw Pact during the era of the Cold War, matters that had also contributed heavily to the bipolar historiography of twentieth-century international relations that prevailed during much of that same period. I found the basis for a fresh historical examination, first of all, in the scholarly reinterpretation of the early Soviet Union that had been underway in North America, the United Kingdom, and Europe during the previous two decades or more and, second, in the new appreciation of pre-Stalinist models for Soviet politics and economy that flourished in the USSR during perestroika. As I proceeded, two things became evident to me. On the one hand, the politics, economy, society, and culture of the USSR during the 1920s had been researched much more extensively than had the foreign relations of those same years, and on the other hand, the reconsideration of Soviet society was taking place in Russia, Europe, and America apart from any comparable examination of foreign relations. My project became therefore one of both reexamining the situation of the Soviet Union in the world politics and economy of the post-Revolution decade and one of integrating the study of foreign policy with research into the domestic economy and politics of the early USSR. This work thus spans the gap between those two research areas, examines Soviet foreign relations in the context of the international history of the 1920s, and restores to them their crucial place in the story of the early Soviet Union.

My debt is to those scholars who have engaged in the study of the early USSR, who have increased our understanding and altered our conceptions of the period, and on whose writings this work relies. I am especially thankful to Ronald Suny, John Hatch, and posthumously, Kendall Bailes, for sharing with me their knowledge and for generously giving me counsel at various stages of this work. Donald Raleigh, who read the manuscript for the Press, has earned my gratitude for his probing insights and helpful suggestions. Lynn Mally unstintingly provided her assistance and erudition, and I owe her much both as a colleague and a friend. Patrick Morgan, Keith Nelson, and Sergey Plekhanov have made the Foreign-Domestic Nexus Project of the Center for Global Peace and Conflict Studies at the University of California, Irvine, into an invaluable environment for the exchange of information and ideas between Russian and American scholars. Led by Anthony Adamthwaite, the Political Relations and Institutions Group at the Center for the Study of Germany and Europe at the University of California, Berkeley, has become a significant forum for discussion among historians and political scientists of contemporary Europe. This work has benefited from the dialectic within both organizations.

My deepest gratitude goes to Georgi Derluguian of the Fernand Braudel Center at State University of New York-Binghamton and the Peace and Security Center at Cornell University for his guidance, insight, patience, and wonderful sense of humor; I learned more from him about both the Soviet Union and world politics than I can describe here. Carolyn Johnston-Viens assisted me in the preparation of this work, and Corinne Antezana-Pernet, Lynn Sharp, and Katherine Turley each contributed their great efforts, exceptional talents, and unfailing good will to its completion. My younger daughter Margreta not only assisted me in the research for this book but also teased me unmercifully lest I take myself too seriously. Pamela LaZarr and the staff of the Interlibrary Loan Service at the UCI Library efficiently located and obtained a multitude of sources. Eleanor Gates edited the manuscript both skillfully and expeditiously, and Dore Brown produced this book from it.

I am fortunate in knowing Sheila Levine and Monica McCormick at the University of California Press; I am grateful for their confidence in this work; and I probably owe them more than they will ever tell me. My friend and colleague Robert Moeller gave to me of his unfailing wisdom and his fine cuisine often and without constraint. William Hamilton cooked for me many more meals than I for him and has sustained me with his constant friendship as well. My elder daughter, Kirsten, and my son-in-law, Benjamin Boyer, supported this project with their interest while reminding me of the importance of both the preservation and the cultivation of the earth. Most of all, Patricia O'Brien, my wife, encouraged me throughout, read drafts of this work, and suggested revisions. It was she who courageously rescued the final copy of the manuscript and the computer disks on which it was entered from the onrushing Laguna Beach firestorm of October 1993, an inferno that was halted thirty feet from our front door by firefighters who came to our street from throughout California. It is for this and much more that this book is dedicated to her.

Introduction

In the late 1950s, George F. Kennan set out to explain to his fellow Americans how Soviet Russia's place in world politics had been transformed, as he stated it, from "the initial weakness of 1921 to the pinnacle of power and success it occupies in the wake of World War II." In doing so, he gave a major share of the credit for that transformation to the effectiveness of Soviet diplomacy and to what he termed "Soviet resourcefulness and single-mindedness of purpose."[1] In this work, I examine the beginnings of the Soviet Union's historic rise to world power in the twentieth century and explore the role that diplomacy and other instruments of foreign relations played in that ascent. I consider the formative years of Soviet foreign relations, from the time Soviet Russia first entered world politics in 1920–21—following the Russian Revolution, the Paris Peace Conference, and the Civil War—to "the great turning point" in Soviet history in 1928–29, when the economy, politics, and foreign relations of the Union of Soviet Socialist Republics (USSR) were cast in the form they were to retain for decades. The 1920s take us from Lenin's domination of Soviet politics up to Stalin's emergence as the new leader with increasingly dictatorial powers. It is in these years that the foreign relations of the USSR took on their characteristic features. In examining this period, I hope to clarify the terms on which the USSR entered world politics, to contribute to an understanding of how Soviet foreign relations were originally formulated and conducted, to estimate how much credit can be assigned to diplomacy in making the USSR a world power, and to identify some of the fundamental tendencies of Soviet foreign relations.

Within Euro-American scholarship, the interpretation of early Soviet foreign relations began with Louis Fischer's *The Soviets in World Affairs* (1930), the work of a historian with direct knowledge of the events of the

1

time, with personal access to important Soviet diplomats, and with strong sympathy for Georgii Chicherin, the people's commissar for foreign affairs (1918–30), and his efforts to find for the USSR a place of equality, respect, and stability among the major world powers. Interpretation continued with three monumental achievements of perceptive and thoughtful scholarship completed at various stages of the Cold War—Theodore von Laue's "Soviet Diplomacy: G. V. Chicherin, Peoples Commissar for Foreign Affairs" (1953), George F. Kennan's *Russia and the West under Lenin and Stalin* (1961), and Adam Ulam's *Expansion and Coexistence* (1968).[2] It was further advanced following the détente of the 1970s by Teddy J. Uldricks in his article "Russia and Europe: Diplomacy, Revolution, and Economic Development in the 1920s" (1979), which analytically integrated early Soviet politics, foreign relations, and strategies of economic development, and which transcended the "totalitarian" and "Communist ideology" models of Soviet foreign relations that had prevailed since the 1950s.[3] Each of these works considered the foreign relations of the 1920s comprehensively and within a framework of concepts. Each advanced the analysis of policy to a new level of sophistication.

The concept of early Soviet foreign relations informed by the totalitarian and Communist ideology models was highly complex and nuanced; specific aspects of it varied with time, circumstance, and proponent; however, it also had a basic logic, consistency, and coherence. As synthesized briefly, it included the following concepts: (1) the USSR's foreign relations were driven primarily by revolutionary ideology during this period; (2) the destruction of capitalism by direct insurrectionary offensive was the central intention of the first Soviet leadership cohort and the ultimate aim of their regime; (3) the conduct of normalized political and commercial relations was not genuinely representative of Soviet foreign policy and amounted to no more than a facade and a temporary expedient to be adopted only until proletarian revolution (aided by the Red Army if necessary) destroyed democracy and capitalism everywhere; (4) Soviet foreign relations were completely coherent and under the highly centralized control of the Politburo, which directed them by means of a coordinated set of foreign policy instruments; (5) the diplomats of the Foreign Affairs Commissariat played no influential role in the actual formulation of policy; and (6) the Bolsheviks, their mentality, and their diplomacy were exceptional in the history of world politics, not readily comprehended by observers untrained in the ways of the Kremlin and not to be analyzed in the same categories and terminology as were the foreign relations of the liberal democracies of the free world.

By the late 1970s the explanatory power of these hypotheses had sharply diminished. The totalitarian and Communist ideology models did not stand up well to the close investigations and the changed perspectives that had been incorporated into historical scholarship since the 1960s. Beginning at that time, an ever-increasing body of documentation available from government, business, and personal archives in Germany, England, France, the United States, and Eastern Europe enabled scholars to reconstruct some of the contacts made between the diplomats, politicians, and trade representatives of these nations and their Soviet counterparts during the 1920s.[4] By utilizing these records, often in conjunction with published sources from the USSR, diplomatic historians in Canada, the United States, Europe, the United Kingdom, and Israel defined and analyzed the policies of the governments of Europe and America toward the USSR. Along with some Soviet historians, they arrived at a more complete understanding of early Soviet diplomacy itself and of Russia's role in the international relations of the pre-Stalin era. Much of this scholarship was based on primary research. It assiduously avoided overinterpretation and eschewed the assumptions of Cold War history writing. Meanwhile, other scholars working primarily in the United Kingdom and America undertook a reevaluation of the economy, society, politics, and culture of the USSR during the 1920s.[5] Much of this scholarship depended on a continually increasing flow of documentation from the USSR. Together with work done by Soviet historians during the period of "the Khrushchev thaw" (1956–1964),[6] it transformed the interpretation of early Soviet history. These two research endeavors—one directed to foreign relations, the other to early Soviet society—developed simultaneously. For the most part, however, they were undertaken without reference to one another, a condition which by the late 1980s had come to be deplored by experts in the field, Soviet and non-Soviet alike.[7]

From the advances made in the study of early Soviet foreign relations, the outlines of an interpretation that differs significantly from the one influenced by the totalitarian and Communist ideology models can be discerned and defined. The assumption that a revolutionary offensive in Europe remained the distinguishing characteristic of Soviet foreign policy after the end of the Civil War is giving way to three closely related notions: (1) that the survival and consolidation of the revolution in Russia became the paramount concern of Lenin's foreign relations sometime between 1917 and 1921; (2) that the security of the early Soviet state depended on preserving the status quo in Europe that had been established by 1921; and (3) that Soviet foreign policy was based on this precept. The view that post–Civil War foreign policy was ideologically driven is being replaced by a picture of Lenin as a political realist second to none and by a discussion of foreign relations conceived in terms of power politics and conducted by conventional means. The notion that the formulation of policy was completely centralized in the hands of a monolithic elite and guided by an all-encompassing and unifying purpose is giving way to a view of policy as initiated from a diversity of sources and to a picture of Lenin's associates and successors as people who disagreed widely over policy objectives and whose conduct of foreign relations was frequently improvised, disjointed, and incoherent. Their haphazard efforts to inspire, to supply, and to advise revolutions in Germany, England, and China during the 1920s, rather than being seen as posing a serious threat to capitalist Europe and its dependencies, are increasingly regarded as a series of disasters for both international Communism and Soviet foreign relations.

Glasnost and *perestroika* (1985–91) evoked a largely conservative response from the Soviet historical establishment. In an article entitled "The History of the USSR's Foreign Policy; the Search for New Approaches" (1990), L. N. Nezhinskii, the department head of the Institute for Russian History of the Soviet Academy of Sciences, stated that the "tremendous and arduous job of working out a new balanced view of history requires much caution, responsibility, and competence," and that the effort to do so "may not be done in a hasty and sensationalist-media-manner." "The time-tempered practical recommendations and approaches of V. I. Lenin," he added, remained the solid basis for a correct interpretation of foreign policy issues.[8] Important work that had been in preparation for some years was published at this time—Zinovii Sheinis's biography of Maksim Litvinov being one example[9]—and there were some important "revelations." However, much of the discussion of "new approaches" was limited to upgrading the reputations of some figures from the past and downgrading others. As A. A. Galkin stated during a discussion of the future of the historical study of the Comintern held at the Institute of Marxism-Leninism in June 1988, "We are still at the stage of giving marks to historical personalities and events, not analyzing them."[10] On the other hand, not all the scholarship published in the USSR before 1985 can be dismissed as valueless because of the constraints imposed by "party line" conformity; some remarkable works were published during the era of the Khrushchev thaw. The findings of Soviet scholarship from both the Khrushchev and the Gorbachev eras are essential to this study. They have influenced significantly the discussion of matters ranging from Soviet policy toward the Saudis of Arabia, to policy options available at "the great turning point," to the covert military collaboration between Soviet Russia and Weimar Germany.

The historic events of 1989–91 have transformed both the task of writing Soviet history and the methods by which it is researched. The dissolution of the Soviet Union into its component republics, the end of Russian hegemony in Eastern Europe, and the demise of Communism on an international scale require new assessments both of the foreign relations the USSR conducted for more than seventy years and of how the international history of this period was shaped by Soviet Russia. As the USSR recedes into the past and as the twentieth century comes to an end, the task of historians becomes one of estimating its place in the world politics of the century. The end of the Cold War gives to scholars on both sides of the former Iron Curtain perspectives on the past that lie outside the framework of East-West antagonism. Access to the records of bodies such as the Central Committee's Foreign Office (subsequently International Department), the Comintern's Presidium and Political Secretariat, and the Collegium of the Foreign Commissariat (subsequently Foreign Ministry), if made available fully, can form the evidentiary basis of this project.

These developments offer historic opportunities, and the study of the formative period of Soviet foreign relations is a project that is likely to occupy graduate students and their dissertation directors for years to come. They also present challenges. For example, during *perestroika* Soviet scholars recognized that one of the major problems with the histories of foreign relations written in the USSR up to that time was the "depersonalization," *obezlichivanie*, of both the formulation and the execution of foreign policy.[11] In its most extreme form this meant that Soviet achievements in international relations were credited without differentiation to "Lenin," to "the followers of Lenin," to "the Central Committee," and to "the Comintern." Other leading Bolsheviks—except for Trotsky, who was always wrong—were not mentioned, and failures were not discussed. Under conditions of open investigation and access to archival material, the repersonalization of historical writing on Soviet foreign relations can flourish, and the many "blank spots" in the record can be filled in.

Archive-based studies of Soviet foreign policy will continue the project of writing the international history of the period between the two world wars that began when the records of the German Foreign Ministry, captured by the Allies at the end of the Second World War, were made generally accessible to scholars in the early 1960s. It continued later in the decade when the British adopted a thirty-year rule for their state papers, and the Americans, the French, and other nationalities subsequently followed suit. With each new stage of access, there were exciting revelations, important articles and monographs, revisions of earlier interpretations, and new rounds of debates among scholars. Predictably, research in the archives of the former Soviet Union will open a new stage in the historical study of interwar international relations. Will this stage follow a pattern similar to previous ones? What do Russian archives hold? Did Soviet diplomats of the interwar years make carbon copies of everything and carefully file them in several different places, as did their German counterparts? Did they record revealingly candid statements, as did British politicians and Crown servants, never suspecting that historians would be reading them only thirty years later? Were papers of importance intentionally burned with the advance of the Wehrmacht on Moscow in 1941, as happened in Paris a year earlier? Will copies of Politburo minutes be available on microfilm for sale to any library with the funds to purchase them, thereby permitting intricate studies of policy making, or will the study of Soviet foreign relations remain a history of grand strategies for some time to come? What is certain is that research at each stage has facilitated that which followed. Earlier research has raised questions to which subsequent projects have responded, and it has served as a springboard for the conception of new projects and as a basis of comparison for the new results yielded. One purpose of this book is to give focus and direction to further investigation by defining significant interpretative issues in the study of early Soviet foreign relations and by assessing the status of research and writing in the field up to 1991.

My interest in the early history of the Soviet Union is that of an international historian. This work is premised on the assumption that Soviet studies can contribute to an understanding of international history and that international history also has something to say to Soviet studies. To that end, I explore here the territory where research into Soviet diplomacy and foreign relations borders the reevaluation of early Soviet society, economics, and politics undertaken by scholars since the 1960s, and I integrate these heretofore largely separate projects into a unified discussion. In doing so, I hope to clarify not only the international relations of the 1920s but also some of the central interpretative issues of early Soviet history. In particular, I stress the problems and dilemmas confronting the Bolsheviks as they sought to promote the national security and economic development of the USSR while at the same time internationalizing the October Revolution in Asia and institutionalizing it in Europe. And I aim to show the significance of the international situation both for the formulation of their plans to industrialize the USSR and build socialism there and for the struggle among them to succeed Lenin in the leadership of the party and the state.

The task of international history, as I have suggested elsewhere, is to combine an expanded conception of the politics and economics of international relations with an integrated analysis of policy and to do so within an international context.[12] In this work the imperatives and strategies of national security, of economic development, and of socialist revolution, both within and beyond the frontiers of the USSR, are treated as the materials from which foreign policy was constructed during the years between the Civil War and the First Five-Year Plan. Along with the statements and actions of diplomats and the contacts between the Soviet government and the governments of other countries, both the strategies of the Communist International and the high politics of the Russian/Soviet Communist Party are taken as material for study. The two modes of early Soviet foreign relations—revolution and diplomacy—are integrated into a coherent discussion. The project of repersonalizing early Soviet history is advanced by giving agency, whenever possible, to individual members of the party/state leadership, to Comintern figures, and to diplomats of all ranks. In that relations between the USSR and Europe, Asia, and America are all included in my field of view, preparation of this work has involved an investigation of both primary sources and the scholarship of historians and political scientists emanating from the United States, Canada, Europe, the United Kingdom, and Russia.

I argue that foreign relations were central to the political imagination of the Bolsheviks and to their actual political behavior from the day they came to power—even during the era of "socialism in one country." Party and Comintern congresses began with an assessment of the international situation and of Russia's world position. Geopolitical estimates and even diplomatic considerations influenced what manner of revolution the Soviet leadership promoted in Europe or Asia. Sponsoring revolution abroad could both augment Soviet national security or, to the contrary, put it at risk. Soviet Russia's integration into the world economy or isolation from it mandated one or another strategy of socialist industrialization. In turn, the choice between integrationist and autarchic economic foreign policies had repercussions on the internal political development of the USSR and on the outcome of the leadership struggle. The crisis which resulted in "the great turn" in Soviet history toward the administrative-command economy and the advent of Stalinism had its inception in the diplomatic crisis and war scare of 1927. No full scheme of early Soviet history can be set forth without accounting for the interrelationships among the economic and political development of the USSR, world politics and economy, and the continuation of the revolution in Russia, Europe, and Asia.

The reason international relations occupied a position of such importance was that the challenges confronting the Bolsheviks in the twelve years following the October Revolution were international in dimension. The first such challenge was posed during the years 1917–21 when, contrary to their expectations, successful proletarian revolutions in Central and Western Europe did not follow forthwith from the revolution in Russia. Soviet Russia was left in a relatively isolated position as the first and only socialist state in an international system dominated by capitalist powers whose governments pursued policies toward the USSR ranging from strict nonrecognition, to willingness to deal with the USSR only on terms that undermined the results of the revolution there, to acceptance of the Soviet regime as a legitimate government despite its persistent encouragement and support for revolutions in Europe and Asia. Only slowly and unevenly did these governments establish normal relations with Soviet Russia. Not until 1929, when the government of Great Britain renewed diplomatic relations with the USSR after a two-year break—and exchanged representation at the ambassadorial level for the first time—did the Soviet Union have functioning diplomatic relations with all the major countries of Europe.

The second challenge came in the years 1924–1926, when the capitalist powers of Europe and America stabilized their relations with each other with a series of agreements on military security, intergovernmental indebtedness, international trade, and transnational inter-industrial relations that did not include the USSR. By means of these arrangements, the governments of England and France reconciled their most outstanding differences over how to implement the Treaty of Versailles; Germany managed a rapprochement with the victors of the World War; and the United States underwrote this Western European stabilization with considerable international lending. By this time the USSR, in contrast, had achieved favorable and stable diplomatic and commercial relations only with Germany. The evolution of this "international capitalist stabilization," as it was termed in the language of the Comintern, posed a fundamental challenge to the very basis on which Lenin had premised Soviet foreign relations in 1917, namely, that conflicts among the "imperialist powers" could be counted on to keep Soviet Russia safe from the numerous and various dangers feared from a united coalition of capitalist powers.

The third challenge became evident by late 1926. By this time the economies of the industrialized nations of Europe had recovered from the devastation of the World War and from the dislocations of the postwar inflation. Industrial production in the United States had greatly expanded through the extensive introduction of new technologies. Both Europe and America had surpassed their prewar production levels. Russian industry by the same date had barely recovered to its 1913 levels of production.

The implications of these three challenges for Soviet foreign relations were directly pertinent. How long could a revolutionary socialist country be safe in a world dominated by powerful capitalist states that were not being transformed by proletarian revolution, that were becoming both relatively and absolutely more prosperous and powerful, that were being integrated into an increasingly stable international system, and that were not forming relations with the USSR of the kind that were vital to its security and its economic development alike? It was in this uncertain environment that the basic assumptions, precepts, and institutions of Soviet national security were formed. The sources of the most durable features of Soviet foreign relations are found in the international experience of the Soviet regime during the years between the Bolshevik and Stalinist revolutions as the Soviet Union entered the order of world politics that emerged from the wars, revolutions, and treaties of 1914–21.

The position of Soviet Russia in that order was an anomalous one. The Bolsheviks ruled an empire covering one-sixth of the globe, but the prewar Triple Entente that tsarist Russia had formed with the imperial governments seated in London and Paris could not be reconstituted following the revolution, the Civil War, and the abeyance of the current German threat. Although Lenin and Wilson each proclaimed a new world order in 1916–17, neither they nor their successors found a common purpose. While Russia and Germany shared a "community of fate" as nations against which the World War peace settlement was made, the "special relationship" they formed expired as each found a broader range of diplomatic options. In this situation of relative isolation, one which they termed "capitalist encirclement," those who had made the October Revolution sought security not only in conventional diplomacy, but also in distinctive measures of ideological certitude, economic self-sufficiency, and military preparedness. The shield formed of these components remained in place until the advent of "the new political thinking" of Eduard Shevardnadze and Mikhail Gorbachev in the late 1980s. By that time, however, the shield could be lowered, and the foreign relations with which Soviet Russia had entered world politics in the 1920s relinquished only at the expense of the Union itself.

In the account that follows, the role of ideology in both the formulation of Soviet foreign policy and the methods by which it was conducted is examined in Chapter 1. The "revolutionary" mode of Soviet foreign relations, as opposed to the "diplomacy" mode, is treated in Chapter 2. Chapters 3, 5, and 8 focus on Russian relations with Asia, and Soviet policy there is analyzed in global terms and in relation to crucial diplomatic developments in other regions. In Chapters 4, 6, and 7, the strategies and tribulations of the Commissariat for Foreign Affairs as it strove to secure a place for Soviet Russia among the world powers are discussed. The succession of crises during the years 1927–1929, which decisively shaped the future of Soviet foreign relations, politics, economy, and society, are examined in Chapters 9 through 11.

1 The Ideological and Political Foundations of Soviet Foreign Policy

Lenin, International Relations, and Revolution in Russia

By the time he led the Bolsheviks to power in Russia in 1917, Lenin had developed a highly sophisticated concept of international relations.[1] In a number of works written in the years immediately before the October Revolution, most prominent among them *Imperialism, the Highest Stage of Capitalism* (1916), Lenin identified what he regarded as the most significant features of the political economy of the early twentieth century. In its imperialist stage, the capitalist mode of production became monopolized on a global scale; financial and industrial capital merged; a powerful oligarchy of "finance capital" appeared; the further development and survival of the world economy depended on the export of capital as well as of commodities; global monopolies appropriated the world's markets; and imperialist states completed the territorial division of the globe.[2] Once they had taken over the less developed areas of the world economy as colonies or semicolonies, the imperialist powers could continue their competition for resources, markets, and investments only by taking them from one another. An interimperialist war of redistribution, the ultimate contradiction of capitalism, would then weaken the imperialist system to the point of collapse. In this, Lenin's social theory of history, the crisis of capitalist development, was not confined to contradictions within the domestic economy, as it was in classical Marxism. It was a matter of global economics and world politics.

So too was Lenin's theory of revolution. Because monopoly-finance capitalism developed unevenly from country to country, socialist revolutions would not start simultaneously everywhere in the world. Instead, capitalism would fail at a single point, or perhaps at several points—at the weakest link or links in the imperialist chain. Revolution would begin in several countries, or even in one separate country; it would not be instantly international. For this reason, different states with opposing social systems would exist at the same time after the inception of proletarian revolution. Here Lenin's theory is significant in two ways. With it he made national differences a crucial element in the causation and inception of socialist revolution, and he created theoretical space for postrevolutionary relations between socialist and capitalist countries.

Lenin's critique of imperialism (much of which he shared with the German Social Democrat, Rudolf Hilferding), his theory of the unevenness of capitalist development (which he shared with Trotsky), along with the importance he attributed to the global economy, to the state, to national diversity, and to conflict among nations, represented significant contributions to socialist thought. Karl Marx had left an ambiguous legacy to his ideological heirs. While in his more journalistic writings he tended to be "state focused, politically oriented, and open ended," Marx's more theoretical work was "class-oriented, economics-grounded, and determinist."[3] In the latter, he located the main contradictions of capitalism in the internal workings of developed industrial societies. In his inaugural address to the First International, he called upon workers to "master the mysteries" of international politics,[4] but Marx himself did not do so. It was Lenin's adaptation of Marxism that placed distinct national societies and global relationships alongside class conflict within advanced capitalist countries at the core of revolutionary theory. Thus, the Bolsheviks came to power with a leader who was ideologically predisposed to think in terms of international relations.

As it happened, those who led the new Soviet state engaged intensively in international relations from the moment they came to power. "From the very beginning of the October Revolution," Lenin later stated, "foreign policy and international relations have been the main questions facing us."[5] During the months from October 1917 to November 1920, the Soviets made peace with the Central Powers; Finland, the Baltic states, and Poland became independent nations; much of the remainder of the former Tsarist Empire was reconquered; the Red Army defeated the forces of counterrevolution in a long civil war; the military intervention of the Allied powers was turned back; and a war with Poland carried the Red Army to the gates of Warsaw.[6] Only in October–November 1920, with the preliminary Treaty of Riga terminating the Soviet-Polish War, and with the defeat of the forces of Baron Wrangel, the last of the White generals, did three years of violent, international, ethnic, and class warfare come to an end. As civil war and international relations merged to present the new regime with its major problems, Lenin and the Bolshevik leadership of necessity gave considerable attention and thought to foreign affairs. This period of conflict also left an indelible mark on their concept of foreign relations.

The Bolsheviks had come to power with two central expectations. They believed, first of all, that the imperialists would attempt to overthrow the revolution in Russia and that, with their combined forces, they were capable of doing so. The revolution in Russia would therefore not be secure until the threat of imperialist intervention had been eliminated by the spread of proletarian revolution to several, if not all, of the major powers of Europe. Second, they expected that the Russian Revolution would detonate a chain reaction of socialist revolutions that would spread throughout Europe and the world in a single movement, putting an end to socialist-capitalist opposition and rendering nations and national institutions obsolete, thus obviating the need for conventional interstate relations. None of them were certain how long the entire process would take, but they were convinced that the October Revolution could not survive in isolation. Its fate depended on what happened in Europe. Ultimately, socialist revolution and a system of capitalist states could not exist side by side. Either proletarian revolution would spread to Europe or the revolution in Russia would be defeated by international action.

In the months after the end of the World War in November 1918, revolution *did* sweep through Central Europe. By the spring and summer of 1919, the Bolshevik leadership from Lenin to Zinoviev was predicting that a European Soviet Republic lay only months, a year at the most, in the future. However, local security forces and foreign intervention crushed the Soviet elements in the Central European revolutions. And the Soviet-Polish War of 1920, which General Mikhail Tuchachevskii—but not most of the party leadership—regarded as a revolutionary war and an opportunity to establish soviets in Poland by military force,[7] ended without victory. Neither a Soviet Germany, nor a Soviet Hungary, nor a Soviet Poland—much less a European Socialist Republic—became established. And by November 1920, just after the end of the Soviet-Polish War and the defeat of Wrangel, the last prospect of proletarian revolution in Europe—factory occupations conducted by workers in Italy—died out. On the other hand, revolution in Russia was not extinguished. The Red Army defeated its class enemies, divided its opponents along ethnic lines, and turned back the intervention of the British, the French, and the Americans. (The Japanese remained at Vladivostok until October 1922.) These three years of revolution and civil war confirmed the Bolsheviks in their basic beliefs that the leading capitalist powers were fundamentally hostile to Soviet power and at the same time highly vulnerable to it.

Revolution and war also left an international situation that sharply contradicted the initial expectations of the party leadership. The revolution in Russia was surviving in isolation without the support of successive proletarian revolutions in Central Europe, and this situation seemed likely to continue for the next few years at least.[8] For this situation the Bolsheviks were prepared neither by Lenin's prerevolutionary theory of capitalist crisis nor by the initial expectations of the party leadership regarding relations between revolutionary Russia and the imperialist powers. It necessitated an agonizing reappraisal of the world political situation and the formulation of a foreign policy for the new Soviet state. Both took place from November 1920 to July 1921, the first nine months of peace following the three years of revolution, civil war, and intervention.

The central feature of the post–Civil War situation was, as Lenin stated it during these months, an equilibrium between the forces of capitalism and socialism, a balance that he termed "temporary" and "highly unstable," "but one that [was], nevertheless, certain, obvious, indisputable." "Our predictions have not materialized," he admitted candidly. "Neither side . . . has gained victory or suffered defeat." "It is very strange for those of us who have lived through the revolution from its inception . . . to see how things have now developed. . . . Probably none of us expected or could have expected that things would shape out like this." There existed, he determined, "a highly protracted situation, without any final decision one way or the other." Nevertheless, a significant objective had been achieved, he believed. The capitalist powers had been forced to abandon armed intervention without defeating the Soviets and without extinguishing the flame of socialist revolution. Proletarian rule and the Soviet Republic survived although "world revolution" was delayed. The result was, Lenin concluded, that

> without having gained an international victory, which we consider to be the only sure victory, we are in a position of having won conditions enabling us to exist side by side with capitalist powers. . . . We have won the right to an independent existence. . . . Today we can speak, not merely of a breathing spell [*peredyshka*], but of a real chance of a new and lengthy period of development. Until now we have actually had no basis in the international sense. Now we have this basis.

The Russian Communist Party (Bolshevik), or RCP(B), led what could exist as a viable, independent state within the capitalist world system. This, Lenin affirmed, was "something much more significant" than the "breathing spell" won in March 1918 with the Treaty of Brest-Litovsk ending the war with Germany.[9]

The defeat of counterrevolution and military intervention was one of two essential elements in the international equilibrium of 1921, as Lenin saw it. The demise of European proletarian revolution was the other. Following the suppression of the Communist revolutions in Munich and in Hungary in mid-1919, he began to express doubts about specific revolutionary situations in Central Europe, and by the spring of 1920 he was attacking the "infantile disorder" of "leftism" within the German Communist Party (KPD). However, Lenin continued to speak and write confidently and often of the imminence of world proletarian revolution through November 1920, until the last prospects for immediately extending proletarian revolution to Europe had died. He did so for the last time on 6 November, at the celebration of the third anniversary of the October Revolution. Thereafter he acknowledged in his public speeches that he had given up the expectation that revolution would soon spread to Europe. Beginning on 21 December 1920, when he spoke of "world revolution," it was to say that it would not come in the near future.[10] By March 1921 he was informing the Tenth Party Congress that "it would be madness on our part to assume that help will shortly arrive from Europe in the shape of a strong proletarian revolution. . . . In these past three years, we have learned to understand that placing our stake on the world revolution does not mean relying on a definite date."[11] It remained for Trotsky to justify what he would soon call "the strategy of temporary retreat" to the assembled Communists of Europe, America, and Asia at the Third Comintern Congress in June–July. "At that time, in 1919," he said in a statement that was to become famous, "we said to ourselves: 'It is a question of months.' Now we say: 'It is a question of years.' "[12]

In the context of this emergent international equilibrium the Bolsheviks took actions in February and March 1921 that proved to be of major consequence for the foundation of Soviet foreign relations and the formation of the Russian Socialist Republic. Treaties of mutual recognition were signed with Persia (26 February), Afghanistan (28 February), and Turkey (16 March)—the latter being the first treaty between Soviet Russia and a state of major importance in the international system. Negotiations leading to the first commercial treaty with a capitalist power, Great Britain, were concluded on 16–21 March. On 18 March the Treaty of Riga with Poland was finalized. These agreements, all of which had been under negotiation for months, were important steps in the adoption of a foreign policy of diplomacy and commerce, as opposed to a foreign policy of revolutionary offensive, either by means of insurrection or conquest. During the same weeks, the Tenth Party Congress (8–16 March) heard Lenin propose the abandonment of War Communism and the adoption of what would be called the New Economic Policy (NEP), and it approved measures to discipline the workings of the Russian Communist Party by forbidding intraparty factions.

Taken together, these measures have been referred to as Lenin's "new course." It has been argued that they were inherent in his political strategy from the time the Bolsheviks seized power, that, beginning at that moment, he made a series of deliberate compromises in foreign affairs by which he sacrificed international socialist revolution for the survival of the Russian Socialist Republic as a state.[13] The more conventional argument maintains, however, that the steps taken in the spring of 1921 represented a retreat from previous policies and "a single integrated pull-back executed on . . . different battlefields in the same war."[14] There can be little doubt that these actions were interrelated, although there is ample reason to question whether they were the result of a fully coordinated decision-making process at the highest levels of the party leadership.[15] Open rebellion against the regime among both the famine-ridden peasantry of the Volga and the original supporters of the revolution at the naval station at Kronshtadt made reform necessary; the end of Allied military intervention and the new international equilibrium made it possible. The New Economic Policy, and in particular the restoration of market relations in the countryside, was aimed both at fostering relations of "peaceful coexistence" with the bourgeois states and at restoring the economy. Its purpose was, Lenin stated later, "to give the capitalists such advantages as will compel any state, however hostile to us, to establish contacts and to deal with us."[16]

In these measures both sides of the legacy of Leninism to the development of the Soviet Union can be discerned. In the Lenin of NEP and "peaceful coexistence" historians have discovered a "farsighted and flexible genius" and "the grandfather of *perestroika*."[17] In the Lenin who prohibited intraparty factions, who suppressed political dissidence and diversity, who persecuted the Social Revolutionary Party, and who deported two hundred professors (the "philosophers' ship" to Germany), they have seen the founder of the authoritarian, single-party state incapable of reforming itself. Upon reflection it seems that one necessitated the other and that they were joined in a single dynamic. The retreats from prerevolutionary expectations in economic and foreign policy to positions previously occupied by anti-Bolshevik revolutionaries such as the Mensheviks and the Social Revolutionaries necessitated that the party be disciplined and the alternatives to it repressed.[18]

As this work will demonstrate, the new international situation of 1920–21—the survival of proletarian revolution in Russia without the support of similar, successful uprisings in Europe—had fundamental implications for the theory and practice of Soviet foreign relations. Insurrectionary initiative in Europe was officially postponed until a majority of the working class there was brought under the influence of communist parties. Antiimperialist revolt in Asia became the ultimate assurance of successful global socialist revolution. The security of Soviet Russia was made to rest on the capabilities of its diplomats and on solidarity with the European proletariat. The needs of what came to be called "the world revolutionary process" were coordinated with the requirements of Soviet national interest—the security and reconstruction of the socialist homeland, a supportive international communist movement made in the image of Bolshevism, and conventional foreign relations conducted within the norms of the international diplomatic community. These developments are considered in the remainder of this chapter and the three that follow.

Beginning "Peaceful Coexistence"

When he issued the Decree on Peace shortly after coming to power in October 1917, Lenin did not expect that a lengthy period of "peaceful coexistence" would follow the outbreak of proletarian revolution in Russia. Because he expected the existing governments of Germany, England, and France to be unable to accept the Soviet peace offer, the new leaders of Russia would be obliged to "prepare and launch a revolutionary war," as he had written in 1915, and "to systematically incite all those peoples now downtrodden by the Great Russians, all the colonial and dependent countries of Asia (India, China, Persia, etc.), and also . . . call to insurrection the socialist proletariat of Europe against their governments. . . ."[19] However, when the German High Command did not accept the Bolshevik peace offer, both Lenin and Trotsky recognized the impossibility of transforming Russia's war with Germany into a European-wide war of revolutionary proletarians against their capitalist oppressors. Instead Lenin gathered support within the party for a separate peace with Germany while Trotsky conducted an all-out campaign of propaganda directed at the peoples of the Central Powers and the Allies alike. It was in the context of this nonmilitary struggle against imperialism, which took place during the negotiations with Germany leading to the Treaty of Brest-Litovsk in March 1918, that Trotsky—in the first public use of the term—called for "peaceful coexistence" among all peoples.[20] Lenin, during the same period, associated the concept of peaceful coexistence with a respite from military conflict, with *peredyshka*, a brief "breathing spell," or, perhaps more aptly, a "peace break," during which proletarian revolution would be preserved in Russia while it spread to Europe. Thus "peaceful coexistence" between revolutionary Russia and the rest of the world, the initial foreign policy stance adopted by the Bolshevik leadership, began as a measure of revolutionary security, as a policy designed to protect proletarian revolution from the superior forces of the German army.

Beginning in late 1919, what was then called the People's Commissariat for Foreign Affairs (Narkomindel or NKID) conducted what it termed a "peace offensive" directed at the peoples of Europe and, in particular, at the more progressive and pacifist segments of the populations of the Baltic states and Great Britain. The objective was to put an end to the economic blockade, the diplomatic isolation, and the military intervention to which the new Soviet state was subjected. The first breakthrough came when Estonia requested peace negotiations in November and concluded a treaty of peace with Moscow in February 1920. Lenin called the conclusion of this agreement—Soviet Russia's first permanent arrangement with a European state—an event of "gigantic historical significance" and shortly thereafter employed the phrase "peaceful coexistence" for the first time. He does not seem to have meant the term to denote a stable and durable settlement between the two states but rather stated instead that "we do not want to shed the blood of workers and Red Army fighters for the sake of a piece of territory." More diplomatically, Georgii Chicherin, Trotsky's successor as people's commissar for foreign affairs, called the Estonian treaty "the first experiment in peaceful coexistence with bourgeois states" and "a dress rehearsal for understanding with the Entente." Soon afterward he began to call for "peaceful coexistence with other governments no matter what they are."[21] Agreements followed with Lithuania in July and Latvia in August. All three treaties were negotiated by Leonid Krasin, who more than any other Bolshevik at the time favored forgoing revolution in Europe and ending the state of war with the bourgeois states in order to repair, restock, and revive the Russian economy.[22] Thus, Trotsky initially used the term "peaceful coexistence" to refer to relations among oppressed peoples; Chicherin employed it to mean normal interstate relations between the Soviet government and the governments of the capitalist states; while to Krasin "peaceful coexistence" meant trade agreements and commercial relations as a means of rescuing the Russian economy.

By the spring of 1920, Lenin's concept of peaceful coexistence was evolving from that of a short "peace break" in the imperialist war to something more developed. With the defeat of the forces of General Anton Denikin and his evacuation from the Crimea on a British destroyer in March, Lenin envisioned an end to the Civil War; following the failure of insurrectionary soviets in Hungary and Bavaria, he called for the disciplining of "infantile leftism" within the international communist movement in April; with the lifting of the Allied naval blockade in January, he aimed at a trade agreement with England. Thereafter he seems not to have wavered from a policy of stabilizing the Soviet regime in Russia and improving relations with capitalist states, although the diversity of policy preferences within the party leadership compelled him to speak and act ambivalently.[23] The crucial debate among the leadership took place at the Ninth Party Congress in September over whether the Red Army was to be utilized to support proletarian revolution in Europe, with Trotsky, Kamenev, Dzerzhinskii, and Bukharin in favor, and Lenin, Radek, and others opposed.[24] When the Red Army was driven back from Warsaw and the Civil War came to an end—marked by the withdrawal of Wrangel's forces in November, escorted from the Crimea by the French—Lenin determined that what the international situation offered to the revolution in Russia was no longer a "peace break" but what he called "a new and lengthy period of development." During the months that followed, as he reevaluated the international situation, he concluded that Soviet Russia had won the right to an independent existence within the capitalist world system, and his concept of peaceful coexistence took on the form it would retain for the remainder of his active political life.

The historic purpose to which the "new and lengthy period" was to be put, as Lenin saw it, was the restoration and development of the infrastructure of the Russian economy, for which he thought it necessary to acquire the investment, the machinery, and the expertise of the industrialized economies of Europe and America. The new leaders of Russia wanted to establish economic relations with the advanced capitalist economies of Europe and America, Lenin told the Eighth All-Russian Congress of Soviets in December 1920, "because we realize [their] necessity—our chief interest is in obtaining as quickly as possible, from the capitalist countries, the means of production (locomotives, machines, and electrical equipment) without which we cannot more or less seriously rehabilitate our industry, or perhaps may even be unable to do so at all, because the machinery needed by our factories cannot be made available." "We must turn all our efforts to achieving this." Lenin's stated objective was to close the gap between Russia and the advanced capitalist states by 25 to 50 percent. Without machine purchases from abroad, he concluded, "we shall be in a very difficult position indeed, and shall be unable to overtake them without superhuman effort."[25]

Thus in late 1920, Lenin announced the readiness of the party to take on the task of economic reconstruction. However, five years of the World War, Civil War, and War Communism had left the Russian economy near collapse. And by February 1921, destruction of the economic infrastructure, diminished resources, shortages of goods, lack of services, and, above all, low farm production and famine threatened the survival of the regime itself. The peasantry was in open rebellion against the grain requisitions of War Communism, and even the navy, the vanguard of the October Revolution, was in revolt. In response to this crisis, Lenin formally introduced what came to be called the New Economic Policy at the Tenth Party Congress in March.

As the New Economic Policy developed over the next two years,[26] it constituted first and foremost an effort to revive agricultural production by ending government grain requisitions, allowing a legal market in agricultural commodities, and eliciting grain sales from the peasantry by providing consumer merchandise for purchase. Limited private enterprise in retail trade and small manufacturing employing less than twenty persons was restored, while the "commanding heights"—major industry, transportation, banking, and foreign trade—remained nationalized, and the economy stayed under government supervision.

Foreign technology and capital were invited to participate in the Soviet economy on a concessionary basis, for NEP was intended to promote the conditions in which Soviet Russia could conduct foreign trade and gain access to the technology of Europe and America. In the words of a resolution of the Executive Committee of the Communist International (ECCI) passed subsequently (in 1922), the New Economic Policy was "the expression of the solution of the task of incorporating the proletarian state in the chain of international relations."[27] To this end, Russia concluded a commercial agreement with Britain the same month NEP was announced, and this was followed by similar agreements with Germany (May), Norway (September), Austria and Italy (December), Sweden (February 1922), and Czechoslovakia (June).[28]

The prospects for obtaining "the means of production" from Europe looked favorable at this time. Trade between Russia and Europe had developed rapidly since early 1920 in what amounted to a foreign trade explosion. In 1920 Russian foreign trade was ten times larger than in 1919, albeit only one percent of what it had been before 1914. Made possible by the lifting of the Allied naval blockade, this revived trade involved primarily purchases of equipment and materials for the Russian railways. It was financed by expending some of the gold reserves accumulated by the tsarist regime which were reminted in Sweden to escape the restrictions placed by the United States and Britain on the acceptance of Russian gold.[29] Purchases of heavy machinery from abroad continued to be funded with gold until mid-1922. Eventually Soviet economic planners would look to grain exports and to foreign loans to pay for imports from Europe and America. However there was no question of grain exports in 1921, for the proclamation of a new economic policy coincided with one of the worst famines in modern history.

The famine was centered in the drought-prone Volga region and extended east into the Urals, west into the Ukraine, and south into Caucasia. The regions affected contained 37.5 million persons; however, no reliable figures exist for the number of persons directly affected.[30] Reports of drought and crop failures brought the famine to the attention of the party/state leadership in November 1920, and again in the following January with reports of large-scale peasant migration from the Volga. By early 1921 it was apparent that government grain reserves would be inadequate and that the railway system was so badly devastated that what food supplies existed could not be delivered. This situation raised critical political problems. To acknowledge the extent of the famine would encourage "the enemies of Soviet power," as anti-Bolsheviks at home and abroad could lay responsibility for the disaster at the door of the regime itself.[31] Consequently the seriousness of the problem was publicly acknowledged and brought to the attention of the world only in July. At that time the Central Committee admitted that the situation was desperate, and, in an effort to attract foreign assistance, it appointed an All-Russian Famine Relief Committee composed of well-known non-Bolshevik personalities as well as of party members such as Kamenev and Krasin. Urgent appeals for international aid were issued first through the writer Maxim Gorky (13 July) and then by Chicherin (2 August).

The famine undermined the basis on which NEP was premised—a free market in grain. It also made peaceful coexistence a matter of life or death for the people of the Volga. To the Soviet regime the famine posed a dilemma of survival. On the one hand, foreign famine relief seemed indispensable; on the other, intervention conjured bad memories for the Bolsheviks. Allied food relief had been deployed on the side of counter-revolution during 1919, both in Central Europe and in the Russian Civil War. Russian émigrés spoke of transforming the All-Russian Famine Relief Committee into a new provisional government. Assistance would be accompanied, the Soviet leadership believed, by the danger of renewed intervention—what Lenin called "new plans for further invasions, interventions, and counter-revolutionary conspiracies."[32]

In the spring of 1921 news of economic difficulties in Russia sent the international standing of the new regime into a severe decline. By August, however, there occurred what the NKID subsequently referred to as "a turnabout."[33] The regime was rescued from its dilemma by Herbert Hoover, the American secretary of commerce, who, ignoring the All-Russian Famine Relief Committee, quickly offered directly to the Soviet government the assistance of the American Relief Administration (ARA) in return for the release of all American prisoners and full freedom in administering relief. Hoover promised that the ARA would not engage in political activities. He himself hoped that this action would increase the influence of the United States in Russia and eventually induce transformations in the Soviet system that would go beyond those of NEP. American farmers were inundated by a huge grain surplus due to the end of wartime demand, the end of price controls, and the resumption of foreign competition. Supplies arrived quickly. Eventually, at the height of its efforts in 1921–22, the ARA sustained 10 million people, and Congress appropriated $20 million for the project.[34] At the same time, the line put forth by the foreign press shifted 180 degrees, from one predicting that the famine would bring an end to the Soviet regime, to one that saw in famine relief the beginnings of closer economic relations between Russia and America and Europe. Lloyd George discussed the famine in the House of Commons, where he linked up relief and an economic rapprochement with the Soviets. The Supreme Allied Council, meeting in Brussels in early October, approved private philanthropic assistance but linked famine relief to a comprehensive reconstruction of the Russian economy, and it made government credits dependent on the willingness of the Soviet government to reverse its cancellation of the foreign debts of previous Russian regimes.

In response, Chicherin announced in a note to the Allied powers on 28 October the willingness of the Soviet government to recognize the prewar debts of the tsarist regime "as part of a system of agreements" providing for economic aid to Russia, for full recognition of the Soviet regime as the legal government of Russia, and for an international conference to settle differences between the two sides and to effect "a final reconciliation" between the Allies and Soviet Russia. We know little about what debate may have taken place within the Politburo and the NKID regarding the decision to take this step. The report of the NKID for the year, made to the Ninth Soviet Congress two months later, and published only in 1990, states only that "recognition of the debts of the Tsarist regime followed from the current policy of the Russian government, which is aimed at cooperating with capitalist countries in the economic sphere, tackling the economic rehabilitation of Russia as a priority task, and using Western capital to this end."[35]

With this demarche, "peaceful coexistence" reached a new level of importance in Soviet policy. By October 1921 it had become a means of exploiting the prospective benefits of the new international equilibrium for two interrelated purposes. One was to normalize relations with Europe and America, to put an end to the diplomatic isolation that had persisted after the end of the Civil War, to reduce the potential for further anti-Soviet coalitions, and thereby to provide the security necessary for the consolidation of Soviet power in the lands of the former Russian Empire in Asia. The other was to obtain the technology, the machinery, and the expertise necessary to reconstruct and develop the war-torn Russian economy. With this security and these resources, the RCP(B) would be able to stabilize Soviet power in Russia and to prevent a relapse into capitalism and a restitution of bourgeois rule. A policy of such historic importance deserves full analysis.

Lenin consistently rejected autarky as an economic objective of the New Economic Policy. "It would be absolutely ridiculous, fantastic, and utopian," he stated, "to hope that we can achieve complete economic independence."[36] There is every indication that he and other economic "integrationists" among the party/state leadership expected the concessions granted to foreign capitalists along with the New Economic Policy to last for decades, perhaps half a century.[37]

However, the interdependence of the economy of socialist Russia and the capitalist economies of Europe and America, on which the strategy of economic recovery and reconstruction propounded by Lenin in 1921 was premised, was partial. The projected integration of Russia into the global economy was limited by the nationalization of foreign trade decreed in April 1918 (as a measure of War Communism) and by a foreign trade monopoly that took a definitive form in March 1922. By controlling imports through this monopoly, the Foreign Trade Commissariat could and did limit the import of consumer goods and allocate foreign exchange to the purchase of the machinery and raw materials necessary for economic reconstruction. Controlled exports prevented foreigners from buying up cheaply national treasures, natural resources, and agricultural produce. More broadly, the foreign trade monopoly was designed to eliminate profiteering foreign middlemen and to prevent outside capitalist interference in the socialist development of Russia. In London, Paris, Berlin, New York, and elsewhere, special trading companies were formed that operated as branches of Soviet trade delegations. So that no questions could arise regarding the enforceability of the contracts they negotiated, the trading companies were incorporated under the laws of the countries in which they operated.[38]

Among the top party/state leadership, Lenin stood as the main advocate of the foreign trade monopoly and as the main supporter of the strategy of limited integration into the capitalist world economy, although on neither issue was there complete agreement. Other consistent supporters of integration among the Bolsheviks included Rykov, Krasin, and Sokolnikov. Aleksei Rykov became head of the Supreme Economic Council in 1923–24 and when Lenin died he replaced him as chairman of the Council of People's Commissars. As a member of the Politburo from 1922 to 1930 he was the most persistent spokesman for economic integration within that body. Grigori Sokolnikov, a Central Committee member since 1917, became commissar for finance in 1922, a position in which he remained until 1926. He was mainly responsible for framing the integrationist strategy, and he was its major proponent during the years 1921–1926. The financial reform he engineered in 1922 made Soviet currency convertible and thus the whole New Economic Policy possible. For this "economic miracle" the foreign press referred to him as "the Bolshevik Count Witte."[39] He subsequently became ambassador to London (1929–32) and deputy commissar for foreign affairs (1933–34). Leonid Krasin, a fervent supporter of the foreign trade monopoly, saw long-term low-interest development loans from the capitalist powers as the solution to the problems of economic development.[40] He was commissar for foreign trade from 1920 to 1924 and as such negotiated the Anglo-Soviet Trade Agreement in March 1921 and attended the international economic conferences at Genoa and The Hague in 1922. The Bolshevik most respected by European governments, he handled the sensitive negotiations with Britain following the "Curzon ultimatum" in 1923 and represented the Soviet government in Paris in 1924–25 and in London in 1925–26.

The program of the integrationists—to grant concessions to Russia's natural resources, to conclude trade treaties, and to integrate partially the economy of Russia with those of Europe and America—had political purpose. Indeed Lenin represented the benefits of economic relations with capitalist states as primarily political. Commercial relations would win over a section of the capitalist world "to our side," he stated, and would serve to accentuate the antagonisms among them and to prevent them from "forming an alliance among themselves for the struggle against us." The Japanese, he thought, could be divided from the Americans, the Americans from the Europeans, and the Germans from the Entente. All the conflicts among the capitalist states generated by the World War could be used to protect Russia while the technology acquired from them was used to restore and develop the Russian economy to the point where it could resist future efforts by its enemies to overwhelm it.[41] Foreign trade became the means to the security of an isolated and militarily vulnerable Socialist Republic in a postwar world.

By what means would the aims of the integrationists be attained? "Before the October Revolution," Chicherin later stated, "no attempt was ever made to work out a program of the foreign policy of the socialist state in the midst of capitalist states."[42] However, Soviet foreign relations came to be guided by a complex set of coherent and interdependent expectations that can be discovered in the statements of Lenin and the other integrationists. By late 1921 Lenin had come to expect that commercial transactions with the capitalist powers, whether explicitly approved by the governments involved or not, would lead to a diplomatic breakthrough and to recognition of the Soviet regime as the government of Russia. Normal diplomatic and commercial relations would in turn provide access to the industrial technology necessary to restore and reconstruct the Russian economy as well as reduce the likelihood of resumed military intervention. Military security and economic reconstruction would then promote the further political consolidation of the new regime. Economic exchange was presumed to lead to diplomatic recognition; both were prerequisite to security and to reconstruction required for regime stability. Military security, political consolidation, and economic reconstruction were in turn linked to the advance of international proletarian revolution. The economic development and political consolidation of the first socialist republic would both inspire by example the working classes of the capitalist, colonial, and semicolonial countries and make possible economic assistance to proletarian revolutions abroad.

In the context of these expectations, what did "peaceful coexistence" mean? The term became a part of the vocabulary of Soviet foreign relations at a time when it was believed that the capitalists would find no relief from proletarian revolution and that the revolutionaries of Russia would have but a short "peace break" in which to catch their breath before the military onslaught of the imperialists resumed. However, with the Red victory in the Civil War and the revolutionary recession of 1920–21, the term gained new meaning. Chicherin perhaps spoke too candidly, if he did indeed state in November 1921 what has been attributed to him, when he said: "Our foreign policy is a mere expression of the new economic policy, which is as a matter of fact a proletarian Thermidor."[43] As Lenin explained it in his programmatic statements of 1920–21, "peaceful coexistence" described the status of relations between Russia on the one hand and Europe and America on the other at a specific moment in history, when the forces of socialism and capitalism had come to the point of equilibrium with neither able to overcome the other. Looking at that equilibrium, he perceived something much more significant than the Brest-Litovsk "peace break" in the midst of the imperialist onslaught; he envisioned "a real chance of a new and lengthy period of development." This notion of a lengthy period was stated more fully in a resolution adopted by the Central Committee in May

1922, following the Genoa Conference: "the whole course of international relations recently bears witness to the inevitability, at the present stage of historical development, of the temporary coexistence of the communist and bourgeois systems of property."[44] Thus, after 1921 the notion of peaceful coexistence was associated with something other than a short "peace break" or a simple tactical expedient. It did not, however, imply international reconciliation or a policy of "live and let live." In the Bolshevik theory of foreign relations, socialist and capitalist systems remained antagonistic; neither would nor could be transformed by coexisting peacefully.[45]

Strictly speaking, "peaceful coexistence" referred to relations between socialist and bourgeois systems of property. In actuality, however, the NKID and Lenin himself used the term to refer to relations between states within an international system and, in particular, to normal, stable, and favorable diplomatic relations with the industrialized capitalist states and mutually beneficial trade and economic relations with them. Peaceful coexistence was a *state* of international relations, however, and not a policy. The policy conducted in the state of peaceful coexistence came to be called either "the struggle for peace" or "the struggle for peace and disarmament." The process by which both peaceful coexistence and the struggle for peace and disarmament became the central notions of Soviet foreign relations began in 1922, when Chicherin and Deputy Commissar Maksim Litvinov first put them forth in international settings at the Genoa and Hague economic conferences and then at the Moscow disarmament conference. There and thereafter the phrases served a variety of purposes. They linked Soviet Russia's foreign policy toward the capitalist powers with Marxist-Leninist ideology; they integrated the public presentation of foreign policy; they sloganized the interests of Soviet Russia within the international system; and they exposed "the hypocrisy of bourgeois statesmanship" in polemical form. In 1927 they became fixtures of Soviet foreign relations, when "peaceful coexistence" was installed as official party doctrine and Litvinov issued the Soviet plea for universal peace and disarmament at the Preparatory Commission on Disarmament at Geneva.[46]

Ideology and the Foreign Policy of the Early Soviet State

Thirty years later, at the Twentieth Party Congress in 1956, Nikita Khrushchev revitalized the term "peaceful coexistence" within the vocabulary of Soviet foreign relations and made it the centerpiece of a new post-Stalin bundle of socialist doctrines. In his usage "peaceful coexistence" no longer referred to a "peace break" from the imperialist onslaught or even to "a new and lengthy period of development." Instead it became the *only* alternative to the destruction of both socialist and capitalist society in total thermonuclear war. In the Khrushchevian doctrine, a third imperialist war was neither desirable nor necessary to the collapse of capitalism; socialism would triumph through economic and ideological competition.[47] This doctrine amounted to a significant departure from the doctrine of war—stated by Lenin during World War I and reconfirmed by Stalin in 1928–29—that global imperialist warfare was inevitable and advanced the world revolutionary process. To lend authority to the introduction of this notion, one with which Mao Zedong and the Chinese Communist Party would disagree strongly, Khrushchev stated that "peaceful coexistence" had always been the basic principle of Leninist foreign policy.

For the thirty years after that, the omnipresence of "peaceful coexistence" throughout Soviet history remained the official line of the CPSU and the Soviet Foreign Ministry: Peacefulness was inherent in socialism, and the "struggle for peace, disarmament, and cooperation among nations" was the central feature of the Leninist course that Soviet foreign relations had always followed. Lenin had conceived "the struggle for peace" even before the October Revolution, and he and his successors pursued it unceasingly. "Lenin's concept of peaceful coexistence" and "Leninist principles of Soviet foreign policy" continued to be as valid "in the present-day world" as they were in Lenin's time. "The Leninist policy of peace" had been, was, and always would be the basis of all Soviet foreign relations.[48]

In the era of "the new political thinking" fostered by *perestroika*, the meaning of Lenin's legacy for the foreign relations of the Soviet Union was reconstructed. In a work on the history, theory, and politics of "peaceful coexistence" published in 1988, Alexander Bovin, a former speech writer for Khrushchev and Andropov and one of the ideologues of the détente of the 1970s, dramatically rejected the thesis that an elaborate preconceived concept of "peaceful coexistence" guided Lenin's diplomacy. In so doing he attacked the standard work on the topic written during the Brezhnev years by the prominent historian of foreign relations A. O. Chubarian.[49] Moreover, in publications supported or authorized by the Foreign Ministry of Eduard Shevardnadze, what was esteemed in Lenin's foreign policy was not "meaningless theorizing" but rather Lenin's ability to abandon the theoretical positions assumed by the Bolshevik Party before 1917. An editorial in the May 1990 issue of the official Foreign Ministry journal affirmed "the special value" of the practical experience in "building foreign political relations" that Lenin had acquired as he "simply addressed himself to every problem that arose as the revolution went on." The significance of Lenin's legacy was found not in his theory building but in his method for understanding the problems of foreign relations and in his approach to their solution. That approach was identified as "political realism." Lenin did not regard himself "as an enunciator of everlasting truths"; "he resolutely revised his own conclusions, especially when theoretical concepts formed earlier clashed with life."[50] The same year, N. V. Zagladin, professor at the Academy of Social Sciences of the Central Committee of the CPSU, published a full-scale reexamination of the entire history of the Soviet foreign policy—both its successes and its failures—which began from the premise that Lenin never formulated "a system of Soviet foreign policy."[51] Thus by 1991 "peaceful coexistence" was regarded no longer as a well-developed feature of a Leninist theory of international relations nor was it a special form of the class struggle; it was something improvised by Lenin and Chicherin in response to the events of the years 1917–1921.

Among Western scholars, Barrington Moore, Jr., writing in the 1950s, put forth the view that a significant change took place in Soviet politics in 1921, once the majority of the leadership of the RCP(B) acknowledged that the socialist revolution that had broken imperialism's weakest link in Russia would not sweep to victory in Central and Western Europe in a unitary movement. Thereafter, according to Moore, thoughts of global proletarian revolution ceased to play a motivating role in Bolshevik foreign relations, and the security of the state became the exclusive goal of their foreign politics. The primary means to that end, Moore added, were traditional power politics and normal diplomatic relations that were conducted with considerable skill.[52] Although this thesis found considerable support among American and European scholars, it has also been subjected to significant qualification.

One qualification is found in that body of historical scholarship which, questioning how homogeneously ideological Bolshevik foreign relations were prior to 1921, has discovered a diversity of foreign policy opinion among the party leadership. The Bolsheviks disagreed with each other from the day they came to power, and they altered their views, sometimes from week to week, as the vicissitudes of proletarian revolution in Europe encouraged or discouraged them, and as they responded to the requirements of national security under ever-changing international circumstances. By the spring of 1921 the practice of foreign relations had become a synthesis of Leninist realism, power politics, and ideology.[53]

The second qualification is made by those who have argued that ideology played a more vital and creative role in the politics and foreign policy of the USSR during the twelve years following the October Revolution than the Barrington Moore thesis suggests.[54] Marxism, they have contended, was central to the worldview of the Bolsheviks; it structured their orientation to social questions; and they made a serious effort to state their most important operational political beliefs in theoretical form. In the formulation of policy, Leninist Marxism—although it offered no direct answers to political questions—outlined the broad principles from which a diversity of positions on issues under consideration were generated. This was particularly true of the vigorous debates over strategies of economic development and foreign relations that took place during the 1920s. Paradoxically, however, it was this very conflict among the party/state elite over these alternative strategies that, by 1929–30, finally put an end to open discussion of policy and to free ideological development, and installed in its place an orthodoxy of Stalinist Leninism defined by the leader and those who did not disagree with him.[55]

That those who made the October Revolution did not eradicate ideology from their concept of international relations as Soviet Russia entered world politics is evident in their post-1921 conception of foreign relations.[56] They continued to believe that the entire system of imperialist interstate relations would inevitably disappear, to be replaced by a global community of socialist proletarians, probably within their lifetimes. The violence, the conflict, and the disequilibrium of the postwar order indicated its eventual collapse. Until then, socialist Russia and capitalist Europe would remain antagonistic. Relations between them were a zero-sum game; any benefit to one side disadvantaged the other; there could be no permanent compromises with imperialist states. Because capitalism sought profits, the imperialists could be enticed into a mutually beneficial cooperation with Soviet Russia. However, this peaceful interrelationship was possible only during a defined historical period. Capitalism was innately aggressive; in its imperialist phase it was inevitably warlike; "peaceful coexistence" would end with the resumption of interimperialist warfare. The imperialist oligarchy strove to dominate the world; capitalist governments were presumptively hostile; the paramount objective of bourgeois statesmanship was to defeat proletarian revolution by defeating the first socialist republic. Proletarian movements and worker organizations could play a decisive role in international politics, and in particular, the world proletariat could and should protect the first socialist republic from the aggressions of its enemies. Because the interests of Soviet national security were identical with those of world revolution, the resources of foreign communist parties could be expended as the survival and consolidation of the regime in Russia required it. All politics were connected and were determined by social relations. Changes in the terms of international relations could take place only as a result of a shift in class relations; diplomacy and decision making had a limited capability to change international conditions.

Thus, ideology played a demonstrably significant role in the conception of Soviet foreign policy during the 1920s, and the influence of the ideological formations of the early Soviet period was lasting. As was the case with the American republic, which also took on a project of creating a new world order in 1917, the foreign relations doctrine of the Soviet regime was expressed in terms of a global mission. The idea of "the anti-imperialist struggle" as the most fundamental doctrine of Soviet foreign relations was born in the Civil War and came of age in the crucial years of relative isolation during the 1920s. It remained fundamental to the conception of Soviet foreign policy until 1986, when, for the first time, the influence of "the world revolutionary process" on international relations went unaffirmed at a party congress. Until then the terminology of "the anti-imperialist struggle" was the language in which foreign policy was promulgated, even during efforts at détente with the West. The doctrine served as the means by which "the exploited proletariat" of Europe, "the oppressed nations" of Asia, and "the peoples of the USSR" were identified with the revolution in Russia, the Soviet regime, and the leadership of the RCP(B)/CPSU. It was the regime's primary measure of political integration, of "solidarity" in Leninist terms, and it gave purpose to policy and justified the regime itself. At the same time, "the anti-imperialist struggle" limited accommodation with the capitalist camp to the ideological and diplomatic stalemate termed "peaceful coexistence."

Ideology also complicated policy making significantly during the 1920s. The Bolshevik doctrine of war introduced one such complication.[57] In various works written between the outbreak of World War I and the February Revolution, Lenin catalogued three types of warfare, each an inevitable feature of international relations during the imperialist phase of capitalist development: interimperialist military conflict over the distribution and redistribution of colonies; wars of national liberation occurring as colonies resisted imperialism; and wars between capitalism and socialism. The latter might take two forms, Lenin thought, although he did not elaborate on either of them. One form was wars of revolution occurring as the proletariat, victorious in one state, rose up, attracted to itself the oppressed of other countries, and employed armed force against the exploiters on an international scale. The other was counterrevolutionary attacks by the capitalist states on the socialist republic(s) taking place as the international bourgeoisie attempted to crush the proletarian revolution. The Civil War and the intervention of the Allies only confirmed Lenin and other Bolsheviks in their belief in the inevitability of socialist-capitalist warfare. And even after 1921, while Narkomindel proclaimed the doctrine of "peaceful coexistence" and pledged Soviet Russia to "the struggle for peace," statements about the inevitability of war continued to occupy a place of importance in resolutions on the international situation adopted by congresses of the RCP(B) and the Communist International.

In doctrinal terms, the contradictory relationship between peaceful coexistence and inevitable war could be resolved: Capitalism was inherently aggressive; in its imperialist phase it was inevitably warlike. "Peaceful coexistence" defined the international situation during a specific historical period distinguished by an impermanent peace among the imperialist powers and by unfavorable prospects both for proletarian revolution and for counterrevolutionary wars of intervention. "The struggle for peace and disarmament" guided Soviet policy toward Europe and America during that period. In the actual conduct of foreign relations, however, "the inevitability of war," "peaceful coexistence," and "the struggle for peace and disarmament" created significant problems for the presentation and reception of foreign policy. How could representatives of the capitalist powers respect the integrity of Soviet policy, and of those who formulated and conducted it, when the latter stated simultaneously that peaceful coexistence was possible but that war was inevitable? This contradiction between the ideological foundations of foreign relations and the conduct of diplomacy continually complicated Soviet foreign affairs during the 1920s. At the same time, the creation of a permanent institution for perpetuating and internationalizing the Bolshevik Revolution and extending it to Asia frustrated the efforts of the NKID to normalize relations with the capitalist powers. Why and how that happened is discussed in the next two chapters.

2 Internationalizing the October Revolution

Formation and Organization of the Communist International

In January 1919, as the wave of proletarian revolution in Central Europe crested, Lenin issued an appeal—by wireless—for an international congress of revolutionary socialists to be held in Moscow. The congress met in March, announced the formation of the Communist International (abbreviated as Comintern, or CI), and elected its Executive Committee (ECCI).[1] Successive congresses were convened each year until 1924 (except for 1923). Thereafter they were held only on occasions when a new "general line" was to be propagated, for example, "class against class" in 1928 and "popular front" in 1935. However, when the general line shifted again in 1939 with the Nazi-Soviet Non-Aggression Pact, and again in 1941 after the German attack on the Soviet Union, Comintern congresses were not convened. Stalin "dissolved" the organization in May 1943 to remove international Communism as a factor in foreign relations once Churchill and Roosevelt announced that Britain and the United States would join the Soviet Union in the war against Germany on the European continent.[2] What was initiated as the organization of independent parties of revolutionary socialists ended as the manipulated tool of Soviet security interests.

During the fourteen years that it existed no party affiliated with the Communist International succeeded in seizing power—whether in Europe, Asia, Africa, or the Americas. In this respect the Comintern was an obvious failure, as many non-Soviet scholars, representing various political persuasions—non-Marxist, Marxist, ex-Marxist—have pointed out. On the other hand, the CI can be credited with certain successes. In the 1923–1927 period it advised and assisted a revolution of national liberation and unification in China. In the 1930s it coordinated the sympathies of the European and American Left—trade unionists and intellectuals, Communists and noncommunists alike—for the Soviet Union, for its effort to build socialism, and for the struggle against Fascism. Moreover, to state that no Comintern-affiliated party "seized power" is to examine too narrowly the problem of how the October Revolution was internationalized. Historically, the Communist states that emerged within the world system of capitalist nations were of three types: (1) the original great world empires, Russia and China, which were directly and heavily influenced by contact with the modernizing and expanding West, but which successfully resisted complete conquest, and which underwent revolutions of anti-Euro-American modernization; (2) those states that became Communist by conquest, the "tank socialist" states, of which Georgia (1920), Poland (1945), and North Korea (1948) are examples; and (3) states such as Cuba and Mozambique, which "dropped out" of the capitalist world system and sought help from, and adhered to, existing Communist states to escape domination by the major colonizing powers. The Communist International functioned in all three patterns of emergence. Parties associated with the Comintern produced the leaders who took power in the "tank socialist" states of Eastern Europe from 1944 to 1948, in the modernizing anti–Western Chinese empire in 1949, and in Cuba in 1959. In these ways the movement organized by the Communist International did have a significant impact on twentieth-century world politics. It also affected the security and the insecurity of the USSR.

The role the Communist International played in world politics and in Soviet security was written during the decade following the October Revolution,[3] and it was shaped by the outcome of the three fundamental contradictions in which the CI operated during those years: (1) the contradiction between the theory of impending international proletarian revolution propounded in theses adopted at Comintern congresses, on the one hand, and the historical reality of the failure of proletarian insurrection in Europe, the restabilization of capitalism, and the recasting of bourgeois civil society, on the other; (2) the contradiction between the centralized control, the organizational discipline, and the doctrinal orthodoxy necessary to preparing and coordinating a worldwide movement for revolutionary action and the ecumenical latitude and strategic flexibility required if local Communist parties were to maintain contact with the masses and to win the support of a maximum number of followers; and (3) the contradiction between the ever-increasing subordination of the CI to the national security imperatives of Soviet Russia and the requisites of socialist revolution in the two dozen nations represented in the Communist International.[4] Within these three contradictions, the course of Comintern politics and policy developed from 1919 to 1928. The affiliated national parties became increasingly subordinated to a centralized Comintern structure, which in turn became increasingly subject to the requirements of Soviet foreign policy. At the same time, continued Comintern adherence to the language of class confrontation and social upheaval and the ideological, advisory, and financial support given to the revolutionary activities of the Communist parties of Europe, Great Britain, and Asia undermined the efforts of the Soviet government to reach one of its primary foreign policy objectives—substantial, reliable, and stable diplomatic and commercial relations with Europe and America.

The Communist International was founded at a time when the Bolsheviks believed that the sparks of revolutionary conflagration would jump from Russia to Germany in the immediate future and the blaze they ignited then sweep through Europe. During the months that followed, Lenin concluded from the defeats of the revolutions in Berlin, Munich, and Budapest that "the vanguard of the working class" had been won over to revolutionary socialism, but that additional effort would be required "to awaken the dormant masses." He also concluded that the successes of the October Revolution in Russia demonstrated the means by which that task was to be achieved. "The experience of the victorious dictatorship of the proletariat in Russia has clearly shown," he wrote in *"Left-Wing" Communism, an Infantile Disorder* (April 1920), "that absolute centralization and the strictest discipline of the proletariat are one of the fundamental conditions for victory over the bourgeoisie."[5] The universal application of the lessons of centralization and discipline learned in Russia required a document, and this was duly supplied in the "Twenty-one Conditions of Admission into the Communist International," drawn up by Grigorii Zinoviev, who chaired the Second Comintern Congress in July–August 1920 and then served as president of the ECCI until 1926. After some additions made by Lenin, by Jules Humbert-Droz, who subsequently assumed any number of important Comintern functions, including the direction of its Latin Secretariat, and by Amadeo Bordiga, who cofounded the Italian Communist Party the next year, the document was adopted by the Second World Congress as a whole.[6]

The central purpose of the "Twenty-one Conditions" was to distinguish the parties of the Communist International from the social democratic parties of the Second International. To make that distinction clear, parties entering the Comintern were to adopt the name "Communist," to break absolutely with all reformist movements and leaders, including noncommunist left-wing socialists, and to stand openly for the revolutionary overthrow of capitalism and for "the dictatorship of the proletariat." Affiliated national parties, or "sections," were to be organized on Leninist principles of centralism and discipline and governed undemocratically from above. Each party was to prepare for civil war by establishing an underground organization, by conducting revolutionary propaganda among the proletariat, peasantry, and armed forces, and by setting up cells in trade unions and other worker organizations. Party programs were to be approved by the CI; the decisions of the Comintern Congress and its executive committee were binding on the national parties; and those parties that disobeyed Comintern theses and resolutions could be expelled. All in all, national Communist parties were to be based on the Bolshevik model and to meet Leninist standards of orthodoxy in principles, aims, organization, and strategies.

The implementation of the "Twenty-one Conditions" during the fall and winter of 1920–21 was the first in a series of steps by which intracommunist relations took on the form that would characterize them throughout the twentieth century.[7] Over the next seven years, the affiliated national parties were recast in the disciplined image of the RCP(B). The Communist International became bureaucratized, and authority was concentrated in the ECCI and its Presidium rather than in the congresses.[8] ECCI emissaries intervened directly in the affairs of the national "sections," often without the knowledge of the local leadership.[9] The entire movement came under the control of the Russian party, which played an increasingly dominant role in determining policy. By the time of the Sixth Congress in 1928, the Comintern was organized on the model of the RCP(B); Bolshevik doctrine and tactics were those of the international movement; and the diversity of revolutionary initiatives that had existed in 1919–20 was replaced by a centralized conformity. As E. H. Carr concluded, the international Communist movement had one policy, and it was directed by the RCP(B) in accordance with Soviet national interests.[10]

The "Twenty-one Conditions" evidenced the place the October Revolution would then occupy in world politics after 1920. With their adoption, the Bolsheviks closed the door on the complex configuration of revolutionary possibilities present in the European situation between 1917 and 1923—the years extending from the collapse of the old imperial regimes to the restabilization of capitalism. They thereby divorced their revolution from a potential left majority in Europe that looked beyond a return to the parties and politics of the prewar Second International, but whose sympathies for the Bolshevik Revolution and potential solidarity with it did not extend to an acceptance of a harsh, disciplined centralism.[11] And they separated themselves irrevocably from those social forces that would become the dominant movements for political emancipation and progressive social transformation in twentieth-century Europe—movements of democracy in its classical meaning and form as opposed to authoritarian "democratic centralism," movements of national diversity as opposed to internationalist conformity, and movements of collaborative and incremental reform as opposed to social polarization and insurrectionary confrontation. Moreover, the Bolshevik model for revolutionary organization was transferred to Europe at high cost to the international Communist movement—and to the detriment of Soviet foreign relations. In the first instance, Communism was deprived of genuine and dependable alliances with other socialists, and the Communist International was doomed to cynical and unstable "united fronts" as its sole means of capturing a mass following. In the second instance, the homeland of the Comintern was left ideologically isolated, and this isolation posed a formidable problem for Soviet diplomacy as Soviet Russia entered world politics.

The First Foreign Relations
of Proletarian Internationalism

From 1920 to 1928, relations between those who had made the October Revolution in Russia and those who led the Comintern-affiliated national Communist parties of Europe and Asia developed in three phases. First, during the summer and autumn of 1920, hopes of promoting proletarian revolution throughout the world, and the influence, authority, and repute of the Comintern among revolutionary socialists were as great as they would ever be. In this situation acceptance of the "Twenty-one Conditions" represented independent commitments made by national Communist parties to a unified revolutionary offensive and to common Leninist principles, aims, organization, and strategies.

Second, when the Third Congress in June–July 1921 acknowledged that European-wide revolution was a matter of years rather than of months, the terms of international Communist solidarity changed accordingly. By the time of the Fourth Congress in November–December 1922, the unifying principle of proletarian internationalism became support for the Soviet Union as the source of international proletarian revolution and as the bastion from which the struggle waged by the proletariat of the more advanced countries of Europe was supported.[12] Soviet Russia no longer depended on "world revolution"; "world revolution" depended on the Soviet Union. The definitive failure of proletarian insurrection in Germany in November 1923 finalized this transformation. Thereafter, at least until the victory of the Chinese Revolution in 1949, the defeat of revolutionary socialism everywhere was assured if it were extinguished in the USSR. The task of the parties of the Communist International was therefore to support the consolidation of "the dictatorship of the proletariat" in Russia.

Third, in the months following the Fifth Congress in June–July 1924, the construction of "socialism in one country" became "the essential determining factor of the 'world revolution.' "[13] By 1926 the purposes of international proletarian solidarity were redirected once again, this time to the defense of the security of Soviet Russia from the military attacks allegedly being planned within the ruling circles of European imperialism. These shifts in the doctrine of proletarian internationalism thus corresponded with changes in the political relations between the RCP(B) and the other parties of the Comintern.[14] And each of them indicated the increasing predominance of the Russian party within the international movement.

When the Comintern was founded and the conditions of admission defined, it was not intended as an organization through which the RCP(B) would exercise dictatorship over the international movement. Although the Bolsheviks held a dominant position, gained from having actually executed a proletarian revolution, the Communist International might have developed as a forum in which non-Russian Communists could have challenged the notion that the leaders of the Russian party had a monopoly on determining what was in the best interests of international revolution.[15] Instead the CI became a place where Zinoviev criticized the organization and strategies of every Communist party except the Russian one.

The mechanisms through which the Russians exercised an ever-increasing predominance during the years 1921–1928 are known in general but not specifically.[16] The Communist International took on permanent organizational form following the Fourth Congress in 1922, and by the time of the Fifth Congress in 1924 that organization was fully defined and implemented. Thereafter congresses met only twice (in 1928 and 1935); the Executive Committee (ECCI) carried on the work of the CI and met in plenary session at least once a year from 1919 to 1933. By statute, the Russian delegation on the ECCI was more than twice the size of any other. The Executive Committee began with nine members; after the 1928 congress it had fifty-seven. Immediate control over actual situations—and the supervision of clandestine activities in particular—was concentrated in what began as the Small Bureau and became the Presidium (of the ECCI). The membership of this body was selected by the ECCI and was dominated by the RCP(B) leadership and representatives of illegal Communist parties based in Moscow.[17] Between 1919 and 1928 Grigorii Zinoviev, Nikolai Bukharin, Karl Radek, Leon Trotsky, and Josef Stalin—all prominent members of the RCP(B) since before the revolution—were members, although not all at the same time. It pronounced and conducted policy until 1926, when some executive functions were shifted to a new body created by the ECCI and elected by the Presidium—the Political Secretariat (of the ECCI). It was initially a group of eight with three candidates, its most prominent members being Bukharin and a number of permanent, career Comintern officials—Iosif Piatnitskii, Otto Kuusinen, Dmitrii Manuilskii, and Jules Humbert-Droz. From 1919 to 1926 Zinoviev was president of the Communist International and the ECCI, and during that period both Trotsky and Radek played important roles in it too. All three became involved in the "United Opposition" within the RCP(B) leadership, and when they were initially defeated in late 1926, Bukharin became titular leader of the CI. Neither he nor any of his successors assumed the title of president, however. When Bukharin was forced out of this position in 1929, with the defeat of the "Right Opposition," his place was taken over first by Viacheslav Molotov, a close associate of Stalin and subsequently minister of foreign affairs (1939–49, 1953–56), and then by Manuilskii, who acted on Stalin's behalf.

Why did this growing Russian predominance become acceptable to the leaders of the other national Communist parties? Certainly the status the Bolsheviks enjoyed as successful revolutionaries was the most important reason. When strategies and organization were discussed in the ECCI, national Communists found it difficult to oppose those who had participated in the revolution of 1905 and the revolutions of February and October 1917. The historic significance of the Bolshevik achievement, and consequently the level of their prestige within the international Communist movement, increased over the years, particularly after the failure of the German Communist Party to seize power in November 1923. As it became increasingly apparent that a revolution would not quickly transform Europe into one socialist republic, the international Communist movement took on a permanent apparatus to maintain a regular flow of instructions and subsidies to the separate national parties. Within this permanent organization, the RCP(B) held a logistical advantage over the other parties because the CI was headquartered in Moscow where the Russian party controlled the resources of a state.

Increasingly, the Bolsheviks controlled decision making, the apparatchiki implemented their decisions, and the national Communists found themselves unwilling to oppose what they regarded as legitimate international socialist discipline, something never attained by the Second International.[18] Russian delegates and Comintern emissaries were able to impose their notions of organization, their analyses of revolutionary situations, and their designated strategies on often-divided and hesitant "section" leaders. Persistently the Presidium encouraged those foreign Communists who were most consistently loyal to the ECCI, people who were referred to in public declarations as "the best representatives of the working class,"[19] and whom Kuusinen privately called "the best friends of the Russian party."[20]

There remains much to learn about the history of the Comintern—about the apparatus and the operations by which diverse revolutionary initiatives were channeled into a single international "general line," by which national parties became subordinated to a centralized organization, and by which the concerns of the RCP(B) leadership came to prevail over all others. The history of the Comintern that was constructed out of the documentation available prior to the years 1987–1991—largely theses, resolutions, and manifestos published at the time they were issued[21]—is a story of revolutionary strategy, Marxist ideology, and prescriptions for political organization. Much of it revolves around discussion of "united fronts" from "above" and "below," of "Right deviations" and "Left oppositions," of an ideology-infused struggle among the leadership of the Russian party, and of loyalty and orthodoxy enforced under the slogan of "bolshevization." Research into the actualities of intracommunist politics, as opposed to the rhetoric of resolutions, depends on access to internal documents.[22] It would seem, therefore, that the study of the apparatus and operations of the Communist International should be near the top of the agenda for scholars as access to archival sources is extended.[23]

The Postwar Crisis and the Foreign Relations of Late Leninism

Although the October Revolution had overthrown bourgeois power in a territory covering one-sixth of the earth's surface, it was evident by the time of the Third Comintern Congress in 1921 that the immediate effects of the imperialist war had not established proletarian revolution in Europe, that revolutionary socialism was confined within a national context, and that capitalism was now stronger in America and in Japan than it had been before 1914. Nevertheless, the official view put forth by the Comintern during the years 1921–1924 did not question the theoretical-historical prognostication for capitalist collapse and "world revolution" propounded before 1917 by Marx, Engels, Lenin, Trotsky, and other revolutionary socialists. Instead, the theses adopted by Comintern congresses proclaimed that what was inevitable would take longer than earlier expected.

At the center of the 1921–24 Comintern "general line," with its sustained expectation of proletarian revolution, was the notion that the crisis of capitalism would emerge directly out of the postwar international situation. As defined in Comintern theses and analyzed by Fernando Claudin, there were three major elements of that crisis:[24] First, the system of imperialist states was moving toward another world war, and this would generate a great new revolutionary crisis. The principal contradictions that would cause this war were the conflicts emerging between the United States and Britain, on the one hand, and between America and Japan, on the other. Second, the initial revolutionary breakthrough would occur, as it had in 1917, in the country where the concentration of contradictions, internal and external, produced the greatest explosive charge. Germany, defeated in the World War, weakened economically, oppressed by the Treaty of Versailles, and possessing the second-strongest Communist party affiliated with the International, would perform the role Russia had played in 1917. Third, following this breakthrough, socialist revolution would spread to the other links in the imperialist chain—the industrialized nations, the dependent countries, and the colonies. This time the revolution could from the beginning count on the support of a proletarian state, a state moreover with military resources at its disposal. Protecting, conserving, and strengthening the Russian bastion of socialism was therefore fundamental to the success of "world revolution" while the proletariat of industrialized Europe would remain the front line troops in accomplishing international revolution.

This "general line," for which Zinoviev was mainly responsible, was introduced in the "Theses on the World Situation" and "Theses on Tactics" adopted by the Third Comintern Congress in June–July 1921. The Fourth Congress in November–December 1922 placed the Treaty of Versailles at the center of its analysis of the revolutionary situation, and member parties were directed to work for its abolition.[25] The anti-Versailles analysis was then worked out fully by Karl Radek, the chief Comintern tactician and a member of the ECCI Presidium (1921–25), in his report to the Third ECCI Plenum in July 1923 following the crisis of the Ruhr occupation. This line persisted through the Fifth Congress of June–July 1924.[26] The Fifth Plenum of the ECCI in March–April 1925 assimilated the full effects of failed uprisings in Germany, Bulgaria, and Estonia, and the general line took on a much more pessimistic tone. The use of the term "partial stabilization of capitalism" was an acknowledgment that Europe had made a definite recovery from the postwar crisis. The Sixth ECCI Plenum in February–March 1926 introduced the notion that this capitalist stabilization was "temporary" and "precarious," a line that persisted essentially unchanged at the Seventh ECCI Plenum of November–December 1926, when Bukharin and Stalin assumed leadership of the organization. However, no reference to capitalist stabilization was made in the resolution on

"The Tasks of the Communist International in the Struggle against War and the Danger of War" adopted by the Eighth ECCI Plenum in May 1927. This resolution stated, rather, that the "relative equilibrium" that had existed up to that time had given way to an international situation in which a major war could break out at any moment, and one in which "open military conflict" had already begun in China.[27]

Lenin was the first Bolshevik to dissent from the reassuring reassertions of 1921. At the Fourth Congress, the last he attended before becoming physically incapacitated, he responded to the report made by Zinoviev as president of the ECCI by insisting that previous congresses had not solved the problem of how to internationalize proletarian revolution. In particular, he denounced "the monster resolution" adopted by the Third Congress that was aimed at microimplementing the "Twenty-one Conditions" by transferring Bolshevik organization and tactics to the Comintern-affiliated parties. The resolution was, Lenin stated, "almost entirely Russian"; "everything in it is based on Russian conditions." This was "a big mistake," he decided; "we have ourselves blocked our own road to further success." To this he added: "We have not yet discovered the form in which to present our Russian experience to the foreigners." The immediate task facing Russian and foreign Communists alike, Lenin concluded, was to use the respite from imperialist war to undertake a fresh and serious study of the methods and content of revolutionary work. "I submit that after five years of the Russian revolution, the most important thing for all of us to do is to study. . . . We have only now gained the opportunity of studying. I do not know how long this opportunity will last; I do not know how long the capitalist powers will allow us to study in peace. But we must use every moment of respite from fighting and war to start learning from the beginning."[28]

Bukharin—a member of the ECCI Presidium (1920–29), a candidate (1919–24) and full member of the Politburo (1924–29), and an editor of *Pravda* (1917–29)—came to Lenin's support by advancing the theory of "national types of socialism" in which he complicated the problem of internationalizing the revolution by asserting that the advent of socialism would be subject to national conditions and that each proletarian revolution would require a different NEP-type transition period. "Even if we take the most developed countries in the industrial sense, do you really think they won't face the same problem [as Russia does]? Absolutely yes, they will face it immediately after the take-over. How can you, for instance, in the very first moment subordinate the economy of the American farmers to an organized economic scheme? No way. Each stratum needs some economic freedom. The same is true for Germany."[29] The notions of separate national revolutions and of gradual transitions to socialism would, of course, be developed further in Bukharin's thinking in the years that followed. But for the time being, the opinions of both Lenin and Bukharin were set aside, and the Fourth Congress not only confirmed the decisions of the Third but strengthened them.[30]

Lenin took a different tack from that of Bukharin. During the next few months he outlined the elements of the study he recommended in what were his last writings, five short articles composed in January–February 1923, between his first and second strokes—a body of work now referred to as his "Political Testament."[31] In the last of these articles, "Better Fewer, but Better" (March 1923), Lenin turned his attention to the future of global international relations. He began by dividing the world into two groups of countries. One group was composed of the prosperous nations that had emerged victorious from the World War. The other group included the colonial and semicolonial countries, revolutionary Russia, and those European nations that had succeeded the empires defeated in the World War. The nations of Group I held the stronger position, both militarily and economically, Lenin thought. The victorious imperialist countries could dominate their colonies militarily and exploit them economically, and by utilizing the profits to compensate their urban proletariat thereby delay revolution within industrialized capitalist society. Among the nations of Group II, Germany was at the mercy of the victor powers, while Russia was in economic ruin and without large-scale industry. For these reasons Lenin regarded the immediate prospects for successful international proletarian revolution with extreme caution and prudence—even pessimism.

In his final formulation of the problem, Lenin did not construe world revolution as the inevitable consequence of the postwar crisis, as set forth in the Comintern's general line. Nor was he able to define clearly, either in theory or in political detail, the process that would lead to that end. By 1923, international revolution was for Lenin an eventuality that lay somewhere beyond the immediate future. The cataclysm of capitalism would come, he decided, in a "military conflict between the counter-revolutionary imperialist West and the revolutionary and nationalist East." Although the circumstances of that conflict were indeterminate, the outcome was beyond doubt. Group II would prevail because it was united against imperialism, whereas the advanced capitalist nations competed among themselves for markets and raw materials and could not harmonize their economic relations. Moreover, the countries of Asia were becoming radicalized as capitalism itself brought them into the imperialist system and educated them for the struggle against itself. Adding the population of Russia to that of the colonies and semicolonies of Asia resulted in a geopolitical entity that Lenin called "Russia, India, China, etc." It comprised the vast majority of the world's demographic resources and thereby assured the success of Group II. The major task confronting the revolutionaries of Russia, Lenin asserted, was *proderzhatsiia,* "holding out," "prevent[ing] the West European counter-revolutionary states from crushing us," until that great battle between the East and the West took place.[32]

As it became evident to him that the 1917 breakthrough in Russia had exhausted the revolutionary potential of the world imperialist war, Lenin came to a conception of world revolution that differed sharply from his idea of five years earlier. The completion of the world revolutionary process involved not only the "international victory" that would be won when the proletariat in several of the mature industrial societies of Europe seized power, but it also entailed the maturation of the peoples of Asia into a revolutionary force preliminary to a major armed conflict between the forces of European imperialism and those of Asian revolution. Finally, it involved the achievement of "genuine communism" in Russia, which required, Lenin believed, both the industrialization of the Russian economy and the "civilization" of Russian society.[33] Postwar imperialism was in crisis, Lenin thought, because it had enemies on three fronts—the oppressed peoples of Asia, the exploited workers of Europe, and the revolutionary proletariat of Russia. In his last thoughts, the complete victory of socialism on an international scale had three dimensions, and it was a complex and protracted process.

How would the revolutionaries of Russia "hold out" while the October Revolution was fully internationalized? Doubtless, by coordinating the international Communist movement in both Europe and Asia and by consolidating the position of the Communist Party in Russia.[34] But "holding out" meant also entering into the relations of the existing international system and thereby standing off the imperialist states, avoiding military engagement with them, accentuating the conflicts among them diplomatically, and finding allies among the postwar Group II countries, Germany in particular. Meanwhile, the major impact Soviet Russia would have on the international situation, Lenin maintained, was not as a detonator of socialist revolution but as a model economy. As early as May 1921 he stated: "We are now exercising our main influence on the international revolution through our economic policy." The working people of the world looked to Russia as an example. In Lenin's mind, socialist Russia and the capitalist states were engaged in a kind of proto-Khrushchevian competition of economic systems. "That is why for us questions of economic development become of absolutely exceptional importance," he stated. "Once we solve this problem, we shall certainly and finally have won on an international scale."[35]

As the Bolshevik Revolution's way out of the postwar/postrevolution international stalemate, Lenin advocated following three directions at once: support for the struggle of the oppressed peoples of Asia; exploitation of the contradictions among the imperialist states; and the socialist industrialization of Russia, in other words, the roads of revolution, diplomacy, and economic development. Bolshevik relations with Asia are discussed in Chapter 3. Analysis of Soviet relations with Europe and America begins in Chapter 4, and discussion of the international imperatives and consequences of economic development are taken up in Chapter 6. First, however, we will consider how revolution and diplomacy interacted in early Soviet foreign relations.

International Revolution and National Security

During the first three years of the Soviet regime in Russia, the Bolsheviks developed not one but two foreign policies. With one of them they coordinated and assisted the efforts of national Communist parties in both Europe and Asia in their revolutionary opposition to the metropolitan and colonial governments of the imperialist powers. With the other they pursued conventional diplomatic and commercial relations with those same metropolitan governments. The latter policy became generally known as "peaceful coexistence"; the former was subsequently termed "the world revolutionary process." To those who had made the October Revolution, both policies seemed essential;[36] for the first and only socialist republic could survive only under conditions of peaceful coexistence, and it was only by means of world revolution that it would reproduce itself. Solidarity with the European proletariat under the slogan of "the anti-imperialist struggle" and divisions among the capitalist states fostered under conditions of "peaceful coexistence" both contributed to the survival and consolidation of the Soviet regime in Russia. By 1921 the Bolsheviks were committed to both and could renounce neither.

Consequently, while the NKID announced that socialism and capitalism could exist side by side to their mutual benefit, Comintern manifestos proclaimed the end of capitalism and the coming triumph of proletarian revolution in Europe. Such contradictory statements created difficulties both for the conduct of Soviet diplomacy and for the propagation of revolution. How could the governments of Europe and America feel confident about the reliability of diplomatic relations with Soviet Russia when they knew that the ruling party affirmed the doom of the present system of international relations? On the other hand, how could Communist Party members in Russia and Europe maintain faith in the approach of socialist revolution when the Bolsheviks reinforced capitalism with offers of industrial concessions, access to natural resources, and even payments on prewar tsarist debts?

American and European political scientists and historians have frequently referred to this simultaneous search for a place for Soviet Russia in the international system of capitalist states and the coordination of efforts to overthrow that same system as the "dual policy." They have characterized it as the most fundamental of the contradictions present in early Soviet foreign relations and placed it at the center of the problematic on which scholarly discussion and interpretation are based. For this "dual policy," two basic explanations have been suggested. During the most intense period of the Cold War, some scholars represented the revolutionary drive of the Communist International as the central intention of Soviet foreign relations and regarded diplomacy and foreign trade merely as facades behind which the USSR retreated temporarily at a time of vulnerability and weakness. This view has been largely supplanted by subsequent scholarship that has emphasized Lenin's realism and pragmatism, depicted the security of the Soviet state and the survival of Bolshevik control in Russia as the principles to which all forms of Soviet foreign relations were subject, and emphasized the ineptitude of the Comintern organization and the failures of its efforts at sponsoring seizures of power both in the imperialist countries and in their colonies and dependencies.[37] Both interpretations suggest that the pursuit of revolution on the one hand and of security on the other were successfully integrated within early Soviet foreign relations, an integration achieved by prioritizing one or the other of the two elements. I would argue that whatever integration was attained was achieved more in theory than in actuality.

The foreign governments that entered into recognition treaties and trade agreements with Soviet Russia were assured therein that the Soviet government would not interfere in their domestic affairs, and when these governments subsequently protested against the propaganda and subversive activities supported by the Communist International, they were informed through the NKID that the Soviet government and the Comintern constituted separate organizations. Meanwhile, Communist Party organizations in Russia and abroad were informed in resolutions adopted by Comintern and RCP(B) congresses that there was no distinction between the interests of Soviet Russia and those of the European working class. The purposes of international proletarian revolution were formally and definitely subordinated to the imperatives of Soviet national security and economic reconstruction. The Third Congress of the Communist International in June–July 1921 resolved that "unconditional support of Soviet Russia remains as before the cardinal duty of Communists in all countries. Not only must they vigorously oppose any attack on Soviet Russia, but they must fight energetically to clear away all the obstacles which the capitalist states place in the way of Soviet Russian trade on the world market and with other nations."[38] This notion—that foreign Communist parties were to protect Soviet Russia—continued as a central tenet of both proletarian internationalism and Soviet foreign relations doctrine for decades. It was based on the belief that support from the proletariat of the major capitalist states (along with the ability of Soviet diplomacy to exploit the contradictions among the imperialists) had prevented the success of Allied intervention during the Russian Civil War, despite the vastly greater military capabilities of the intervening countries. "The massive sympathy of the working people all over the world," Lenin stated in December 1921, was "the decisive reason for the complete failure of all the attacks directed against us."[39]

If the RCP(B) counted on international proletarian solidarity to thwart future military interventions and to promote Soviet foreign trade, what obligations did the Russian Communist Party assume toward the proletariat of Europe? At the Second Comintern Congress in 1920 Lenin took the position that the country in which socialist revolution had already succeeded would be required to make the greatest sacrifices in support of the international Communist movement.[40] However, that obligation was implicitly and incrementally renounced beginning in 1921.

In that renunciation the "March Action" in Germany played a crucial role. In the spring of 1921 Bolshevik foreign policy was pulled in two directions. One element of the party, the one for which Lenin spoke, was pointed in the direction of peaceful coexistence and *peredyshka*—trade treaties with European states, a new economic policy, and the repression of popular political dissension. The other element supported "the theory of the (revolutionary) offensive," developed by Bukharin, embraced by Zinoviev, and adopted by the ECCI. The latter element had considerable support among the leadership of the German Communist Party. Its Central Committee persuaded the mine workers of Mansfeld and the chemical workers of Halle to call a general strike, which they believed would serve as the beginning of a nationwide proletarian insurrection. They acted with the avid encouragement of Béla Kun, the veteran leader of the revolution in Hungary and a member of the inner circle of the ECCI to which Bukharin and Zinoviev also belonged. In March, Kun had recently arrived in Germany as ECCI emissary, probably without clear directives from his associates as to how far to go in promoting insurrection.[41] The decision in favor of action was taken on "impulse and faith, without benefit of either organization or preparation,"[42] and resulted in a disastrous defeat for the KPD. Although masses of armed workers did not take to the streets, more than 150 of those who did were killed. Many party members were jailed. Party membership subsequently dropped from 350,000 to 180,000 persons.

In the aftermath of the "March Action," Zinoviev and Bukharin defended the decision of the KPD Central Committee. So did Radek, who, although he was the chief ECCI strategist and expert on German affairs, was apparently not informed of the action in advance. Lenin had been unenthusiastic about the project, and its failure did not surprise him. Along with Trotsky and Kamenev he interpreted the outcome as part of a general, although temporary, revolutionary recession. However, confronted by the impending Third Comintern Congress in June, the Bolsheviks settled the differences among them and closed ranks behind a new general line. The complicity of Zinoviev and Radek in the action was excluded from discussion, but the right of the ECCI to intervene in the affairs of member parties was upheld. The KPD was criticized for overemphasizing the importance of the offensive in the revolutionary struggle. The new line was incorporated in the theses and resolutions adopted by the Third Congress: "The first period of the postwar revolutionary movement . . . seems in essentials to be over." "It cannot be denied that the open struggle of the proletariat for power is at the present moment slackening and slowing down." "The world revolution . . . will require a fairly long period of revolutionary struggle."[43]

This delay in "the open struggle of the proletariat for power," along with the imperatives of accommodation with the major capitalist powers, formed the basis of a profound change in the strategy of the international Communist movement. The "revolutionary offensive" was renounced in favor of the "united labor front," or, as it was more commonly known, the "united front." The theses on the "united front" adopted by the ECCI in December 1921[44] indicated clearly that the immediate purpose of the Communist parties of Europe was no longer to launch armed insurrections and to seize power on their own. Their tasks were to build up the structure and membership of the national parties, to create mass organizations, to accomplish proletarian unity under Communist leadership, and to counteract anti-Soviet campaigns by means of propaganda and agitation.

Karl Radek formulated the tactics by which these purposes were to be pursued largely out of Lenin's writings, particularly *"Left-Wing" Communism*.[45] As Radek, Lenin, and Zinoviev conceived them, "united fronts" were temporary alliances with the trade unions, political parties, and other proletarian organizations of the social democratic Left concluded at a time when the prospects for successful revolutionary insurrection were remote.[46] In Lenin's words, they were "a necessary evil in an evidently non-revolutionary situation."[47] They were the ECCI's reaction to what was termed "the offensive of capital"—the postwar ebbing of the revolutionary tide and a decline in real wages. They were also a response to the less than completely successful results of implementing the "Twenty-one Conditions"—a split in the international socialist movement in which the majority of Europe's proletarians remained affiliated with reformist parties and trade unions. Speaking in retrospect, Zinoviev described the rationale for the united front best: "The tactics of the united front were in reality at the beginning an expression of our consciousness, first, that we have not yet a majority of the working class, secondly, that social democracy is still very strong, thirdly, that we occupy defensive positions and the enemy is attacking . . . fourthly, that the decisive battles are still not yet on the immediate agenda."[48]

Lenin did not regard the security of the Soviet state and the advance of international proletarian revolution as contradictory goals. Speaking and writing during the thirty months from the end of the Civil War in late 1920 to the completion of his "Political Testament" in early 1923, he developed and articulated a concept of foreign relations with the capitalist powers in which security and revolution operated dialectically. Although he did not expound it systematically, his foreign policy concept can be constructed historically from an analysis of his statements on international relations during these months. Without necessarily attributing to him a coherent program of foreign relations, one can discern the rudiments of a foreign policy that advanced the class struggle under conditions of peaceful coexistence. It was based on the belief that the aggressions of the imperialist states could be checked by exploiting diplomatically the contradictions among them, particularly if European workers demonstrated to prevent their governments from launching a second war of intervention or putting into effect another economic blockade against Russia. A Soviet state secured and defended in this manner, with access to the industrial technology of America and Europe, would restore and develop the Russian economy. With economic recovery, "the dictatorship of the proletariat" could be consolidated in Russia, and the example of successful socialism would encourage and inspire the workers of Europe. With the Russian economy reconstructed, the Soviets would in turn aid the newly victorious proletarian states "and protect them from strangulation by American capital," as Lenin phrased it.[49] In the foreign relations of late Leninism, international proletarian revolution and the national security of the Soviet state were not incompatible—at least theoretically.

In the actuality of Soviet foreign relations, however, the dialectic of "world revolution" and "peaceful coexistence" was a clumsy one, both in Lenin's time and afterward. At times, pursuing normal relations with the capitalist powers and preparing the proletariat of Europe and the oppressed of Asia for revolution complemented one another. But, for the most part, efforts to sharpen social conflicts in Europe and nationalist conflicts in Asia in order to promote the global revolution on which the security of the Soviet Union ultimately depended actually increased the insecurity of the Soviet state in the short term.

The examples are many. The strategy of revolution in Europe articulated in Comintern theses and resolutions was designed to increase the contradictions among the imperialists by supporting Germany in ideological opposition to the victors of the World War, and to sharpen class antagonism in Germany by encouraging the German proletariat in revolutionary opposition to the bourgeoisie both of the former Allied powers and of Germany as well. In both instances, Comintern rhetoric was deployed against the Treaty of Versailles, which was represented as the instrument by which the working class of Germany was exploited and the entire German people oppressed. This attack could not but undermine the peace settlement, encourage nationalist and revanchist forces in Germany, and diminish the prospects for international stability in Europe—thereby putting the national security of Soviet Russia at risk.

Moreover, Comintern strategists failed to recognize and therefore to grasp the opportunity for strategic, as opposed to tactical, "united front" collaboration with the forces of social democracy in Europe against the threat posed by Fascism. Instead, from 1924 to 1934, Comintern spokesmen from Radek, Trotsky, and Zinoviev to Stalin and Bukharin associated the two forces within the doctrine of "social-fascism."[50] Again the effect was to undermine the political forces most favorable to the durable peaceful stability in Europe that was essential both to Soviet national security and to the construction of socialism in Russia.

In Asia, Comintern strategy vested the Nationalist Revolution in China with momentous expectations. However, the ideological encouragement, the political advice, and the military assistance given to that revolution from 1923 to 1927 was delivered at the expense of stable diplomatic and commercial relations with Great Britain. Britain was the major foreign power in China; it was also the state from which most of the other governments of the world took their lead in their relations with the Soviet Union. Therefore Comintern coordinated revolutionary activities in China created difficulties for the NKID in Europe.

From the beginnings of the NKID's efforts at détente with Europe and America in 1921 until the eve of his retirement in 1930, Chicherin petitioned the Politburo to disjoin the two levels of Soviet foreign affairs and to separate the activities, the personnel, the instruments, and the policies of the Comintern from those of the Soviet government. Lenin supported him by insisting in 1921 that the Politburo adopt an official ban on foreign policy statements by party leaders unless they had Chicherin's prior consent. Lenin himself ceased to couple the policies of the government and those of the Comintern in his public speeches. And he directed that Soviet diplomatic representatives not engage in propaganda and agitation: "We have the Comintern for such purposes." Trotsky, however, was openly derisive of such principles on several occasions, especially at the Fourth Comintern Congress in 1922.[51] As it was, Politburo members sat on the ECCI; leading diplomats had Comintern connections; and embassies abroad housed Comintern emissaries throughout the 1920s—all of which undermined the credibility of the campaign for peaceful coexistence conducted by the NKID in London, Paris, and Rome.

Most of all, the rhetoric of Comintern leaders troubled Soviet diplomacy, and did so not only with the victorious Allies but with the "defeated and oppressed" nations as well. The foreign relations the NKID conducted during the period of Chicherin's leadership were based on favorable relations with Weimar Germany and Kemalist Turkey. These successor states to two of the defeated Central Powers were the anchors of his foreign policy in Europe and Asia respectively, and promoting good relations with them was the major achievement of his career as foreign commissar. He was therefore particularly sensitive to damage caused by the CI to diplomatic relations with either country, and he expressed this most vehemently following a series of statements made in late 1926 and early 1927 by Bukharin, then leader of the Comintern. Addressing a letter to Bukharin directly, Chicherin stated: "Would you please stop equating Chiang Kaishek with Kemalism. This is absolutely ridiculous and spoils our relationship with Turkey. Isn't spoiling our relationship with Germany enough for you? . . . Now you are definitely spoiling our relations with Turkey!"[52]

3 Revolutionary Russia and Islamic Asia

The Theory and Strategy of Global Revolution

The foreign relations with which Soviet Russia entered world politics in 1920–21 were based on several propositions. One was that the revolutionary potential of the imperialist war had been exhausted and that proletarian revolution would be delayed until Communist parties could mobilize mass movements. Another was that reconstructing the infrastructure of the Russian economy depended on three factors: protection from further foreign intervention, the technology of mature industrial capitalism, and a secure place for the Soviet state alongside the capitalist world order. The third was that, for the immediate future, the anti-imperialist revolution begun in Russia could be continued among the Muslim peoples of Asia. Each proposition gained its appropriate slogan—"united labor front," "peaceful coexistence," and support for "national revolutionary" movements.

Of all the leading Bolsheviks, Lenin and Stalin had the longest-standing and deepest appreciation for the potential of revolutionary movements in Asia.[1] From his study of the uneven development of capitalism, Lenin concluded that worldwide social revolutions bringing the proletariat to power would not occur everywhere at once. "World revolution" would happen in phases, differ from region to region, and take the form of both social and national revolutions. In the fully developed industrial economies of Western Europe and North America, where bourgeois democratic revolution was completed, and where capitalism had reached its imperialist stage, the proletariat would struggle for power and fight for the independence of the colonies and dependencies dominated by their country. In the multiethnic countries of Eastern Europe, where the development of capitalism was not complete, the struggle for worker solidarity and national independence would take place simultaneously. In colonial and semicolonial

51

areas, where capitalism was underdeveloped and supported by native "feudalism," and where the conditions for socialist revolution had not matured, it was the first duty of socialists to support the bourgeoisie in its struggle for democracy and national independence. This notion of a regionalized and phased global revolution, set forth in Lenin's "April Theses" (1916),[2] strongly influenced the formulation of the Bolshevik revolutionary program and the concept of revolution in Asia in particular.

From Lenin's pre-1917 theoretical considerations, two major implications for postrevolutionary strategy followed. One was that the overthrow of imperialism required the combined efforts of the workers of the developed capitalist countries of Europe, the peoples of the multiethnic Russian Empire led by the victorious proletariat there, and the oppressed populations of colonial and semidependent Asia led by nationalist revolutionaries.[3] Appeals to all three revolutionary constituencies were featured in Bolshevik rhetoric following the October Revolution. The second implication, one that has not been so widely recognized as the first, was that when Lenin and Stalin thought of the breakup of the international imperialist order, they thought of it in territorial terms as well as in terms of social conflict. The end of imperialism was not a simple matter of proletarian insurrection, just as the overthrow of the autocracy of the Russian tsar was not. Both required the liberation of self-identified national entities, which Bolshevik rhetoric referred to as "peoples." In 1917 the power of national self-determination had disintegrated the Russian Empire; a similar disintegration of the international imperialist system would follow. From these two strategic premises the Bolsheviks deployed a number of policies aimed at promoting the territorial breakup of the imperialist world order during the years 1917–1923. They are the subject matter of this chapter.

At Lenin's insistence, the Sixth Party Congress, held between the 1917 February and October revolutions, recognized the right of all the "peoples" of the Tsarist Empire to secede and to form independent states.[4] By November 1918, however, the party's position had changed and Bolshevik national-colonial policy in Asia bifurcated and traveled down two separate paths. In the Muslim world of the eastern Mediterranean and southwest Asia—tied directly or indirectly to the British and French empires—support for national independence and social revolution became the centerpiece of an anti-imperialist foreign policy. By contrast, secessionist movements within the lands of the former Tsarist Empire both in the Caucasus and in Central Asia were labeled counterrevolutionary. They would be crushed, Stalin, the commissar for nationalities, announced in *Pravda*, between the military power of the Red Army advancing from without and the revolutionary agitation rising up from within.[5]

In rejecting political independence for the Asians of the former Russian Empire—Bukharin suggested that the term "national self-determination" be reserved for colonial regions[6]—the Bolsheviks stood in direct opposition to the theoreticians of national communism, a movement of Muslim members of the RCP(B). Their theory of revolution originated in the 1919 writings of Sultan Galiev, who argued that the proletariat of Europe would never overthrow the bourgeoisie and that revolution there had died and was showing no signs of revival.[7] However, because Asia was on the verge of revolt, "world revolution" continued to be both necessary and possible. The strategy by which it should be perpetuated, he maintained, was to transfer revolution beyond the borders of the Tsarist Empire to include the masses of oppressed Muslim peoples of Asia. Thus, Sultan Galiev argued not for an alliance between the proletariat of Europe and the oppressed of Asia but rather for a purely Asian strategy, for an alliance there of the peasantry and the nationalist bourgeoisie, composed mainly of merchants and progressive members of the clergy. He developed the notion of "proletarian nations" to buttress his argument that entire nationalities were oppressed, that all oppressed peoples were proletarian, and that in the oppressed countries of Asia was located the potential for continued and self-sufficient revolution. The leading exporters of that revolution would come, Sultan Galiev added in 1920, not from European Russia, not from those who were "ignorant and afraid of Asia" (a phrase often used by national communists at the time), but from the Islamic regions of the Middle Volga, the Urals, the Caucasus, and Central Asia—from those who shared the languages, the religion, and the culture of their neighbors to the south. Finally—and this was perhaps his ultimate departure from strict Leninist orthodoxy—in order to transport revolution organically to colonial and dependent Asia, the Muslims of the Urals, Turkistan, and Azerbaijan needed to be free from ethnic Russian domination because only fully independent Muslim states, liberated from European control, could unleash revolution in Asia.

From the precepts of Sultan Galiev's national communism emerged a direct challenge to Russian control of the October Revolution and to the ideological hegemony of Lenin, Trotsky, and Stalin. This may well have been what inspired or provoked Lenin into insisting that the problem of revolution among those whom he and the other Bolsheviks called "the peoples of the East" be considered and strategized in an organized, unified, and systematic manner. In advance of the Second World Congress of the Communist International held in July–August 1920, Lenin prepared and distributed a set of propositions, or theses, to structure a consideration of what was called "the national and colonial question."[8] The first full debate among Communists on the theory and strategy of revolution on a global scale followed.

As had been the case at the First Congress the year before, the Second Comintern Congress was occupied with the problems of revolution in Europe; two of its ten sessions, however, were devoted to discussion of Asia.[9] The most serious debate revolved around two sets of issues.[10] One pertained to the place of Asia in the grand strategy of global socialist revolution. Was revolution in Asia more or less crucial than revolution in Europe? Would it precede or follow revolution in the capitalist states? To which area should the major share of the attention and resources of the Communist International be directed? The second set of issues related directly to tactics. What social classes in Asia were ready to engage in revolutionary activity? Should Communist parties support or form alliances with nonproletarian political forces in a joint struggle for liberation in Asia? Could soviets be formed in agrarian societies?

There arose no disagreement among the delegates to the Second Congress regarding the theoretical and strategic importance of Asia. Just how and why Asia was important, however, were issues on which a diversity of opinion was expressed. Manabendra N. Roy, voicing an opinion held by himself and other Marxist-informed Asian revolutionaries, maintained that the liberation of Europe depended on social revolution in Asia, that revolution in the colonies would precede revolution in the metropolitan areas, and that the Comintern should therefore divert the major share of its attention and resources to supporting revolutionary activity there. "It is," he argued, "necessary to channel energy towards developing the revolutionary movement in the East, toward its ascent, and to adopt as our basic thesis that the fate of world communism depends on the triumph of communism in the East."[11]

Roy was a professional revolutionary from Bengal who had converted to Marxism while in the United States during the World War. He knew Indian conditions, Marxist dialectics, and revolutionary organization. Along with Mikhail Borodin, he served as Comintern representative in Mexico, and at the Second Comintern Congress represented the Mexican Communist Party. His challenge to Lenin's position on the national and colonial question[12] launched a debate with Lenin and other Europeans at the congress that would make him a major figure in Comintern affairs.[13] Where Roy argued for the "Asian road" to world revolution, some Europeans, most prominently Giacinto Serrati—a delegate of the Italian Socialist Party, a member of its "maximalist" wing, and subsequently a leading militant in the Italian Communist Party—responded that revolution in Asia was impossible until it was completed in Europe. Therefore, it was irrelevant to Marxists.[14]

Here as elsewhere, Lenin arbitrated the dispute, and his view, something of an intermediate position, prevailed. Asia was important, he told the congress, because national liberation movements there undermined the imperialist world order and because Asia was of such enormous demographic size. While admitting that the parties of Europe had neglected Asia, Lenin was nevertheless unwilling to divert support from revolution in Europe.[15] Zinoviev, the entire Russian delegation, and most of the Europeans at the congress supported Lenin. In response, Roy backed off from his assertion that revolution in Asia must precede revolution in Europe and acceded to Lenin's position: Revolution in the colonies was a matter of urgency because it would accelerate the rate of revolutionary change within the imperialist camp.

On the issue of with what class or classes in Asia revolutionary Marxists should ally, Lenin maintained that the strongest anti-imperialist forces, and the best potential allies for Communists, could be found among the movements of national liberation that had been awakened in Asia in the years before and during the World War. These movements were of necessity bourgeois, he admitted, since the majority of the population of Asia was composed of peasants rather than of proletarians; however, in the absence of a large proletariat, they had a much greater chance for success against imperialist control than did nascent and weak Communist parties acting alone. The task of the Comintern therefore was to enter into temporary alliances with what Lenin called "bourgeois democratic national movements in the colonies and backward nations," as well as with anti-colonial movements within the imperialist states. However, proletarian elements were to remain organizationally and ideologically independent of these nationalist movements so that they could be educated by Communists in their special tasks—fighting for radical solutions to the problems of bourgeois-democratic revolution and struggling against the very movements with which they allied. This strategy for revolution in Asia was designated in the resolutions of the Fourth Comintern Congress (November–December 1922) "the united anti-imperialist front." A. B. Reznikov, the leading Brezhnev-era expert on the history of the Comintern in Asia, called it "a great scientific discovery" and an idea of "immense theoretical and practical significance."[16]

Roy rejected it. Bourgeois democracy, he stated, was opposed to the interests of workers and poor peasants; it had no popular support; it was not a revolutionary force; sooner or later it would collaborate with imperialism and oppose revolution. The task of Communists, Roy contended, was to form parties from among the emergent proletariat and the poor peasants, create and lead mass movements, and campaign directly for power. Such parties represented the only viable revolutionary force in Asia, he maintained, and the only authentic challenge to imperialism.[17] In opposition, Serrati rejected both Lenin's position and that of Roy. Unless the proletariat was strong enough to stand alone, he insisted, no socialist revolution was possible; only by means of proletarian revolutions and soviet regimes could nations be liberated. Zinoviev attacked Serrati's position as nothing more than a summary of Marx and Engels, and Lenin supported him, telling the congress that the *Communist Manifesto* had been written "under completely different circumstances."[18] Nevertheless, Lenin compromised with Roy. In the text of the theses he submitted to the congress, the term "bourgeois democratic" was changed to "national revolutionary."[19]

How large was Lenin's compromise? A comparison of the text of the original supplementary theses submitted by Roy with the text of those adopted indicates that Roy's underwent drastic alteration during the course of the proceedings,[20] whereas only minor changes were introduced into those of Lenin. The concession Lenin did make, the substitution of "national revolutionary" for "bourgeois nationalist," was probably not unwelcome to him either rhetorically or strategically. Both the theses devised by Roy and those written by Lenin were discussed, revised, adopted unanimously by the full congress, and published accordingly—indicating that the delegates did not regard any contradiction between the two of them as serious. The historical outcome of the double adoption was, however, strategic ambiguity. The exact nature of the conditions and terms of cooperation between Communists and nationalists in Asia was not predetermined. Within months, the course of events in Persia and India would clearly show the difficulties involved in relating actual revolutionary situations to preconceived strategy.

Embedded in the study of Comintern Asian policy are interpretative issues of major relevance to the historical study of twentieth-century global politics. How much significance did the first Communists attribute to Asia in their grand strategy of global revolution? What did they consider the place of nationalism in the crisis of imperialism and in the inception of socialist revolution? Did they develop a coherently conceived grand strategy of global revolution once the prospects for continuous revolution in Europe had faded?

Among the Bolsheviks there was a diversity of opinion regarding the relationship between revolution in Europe and revolution in Asia following the October Revolution, and they proposed a variety of revolutionary strategies. Individuals were not consistent in their views—Lenin least of all—and no coherent debate on global revolution took place subsequent to the Second Comintern Congress. By the time the matter was debated again within the Communist International—in 1927, during the Nationalist Revolution in China—open debate on strategy and free ideological development had been stifled by the struggle for succession within the Russian Communist Party.

Trotsky and Bukharin seem to have been the most convinced that national liberation in Asia depended on successful proletarian revolution in Europe. In the manifesto of the First Congress of the Communist International, authored by Trotsky, freedom for colonies was regarded as something that depended strictly on proletarian revolution in Europe: "The workers and peasants not only of Annam [a region in Indochina with its capital at Hue], Algeria, and Bengal but also of Persia and Armenia will obtain the possibility of independent existence only on the day when the workers of England and France will have overthrown Lloyd George and Clemenceau and taken the state power into their hands."[21] Zinoviev shared this opinion, although he momentarily became emotionally enthusiastic about the prospects for uprisings in Islamic Asia at the time of the Baku Congress in September 1920. Stalin, who attributed greater importance to revolution in Asia than did any other major Bolshevik, including Lenin, consistently saw the two revolutions as strongly interdependent: Socialist revolution could not triumph in Europe without revolution in the colonies, but colonial revolution could not succeed without the destruction of capitalism at its center.[22]

Western scholars have insisted that Lenin never gave to the revolutionary potential of Asia the same attention he devoted to Europe—either before or after October 1917.[23] He considered Asia systematically only around the time of the Second Comintern Congress in the summer of 1920, and his interest at that time was, as it continued to be, almost exclusively theoretical. That is to say, he never adopted an Asian strategy. On the other hand, party historiography in the USSR during the years prior to 1987–1991 attributed to Lenin an almost divine omniscience in revolutionary strategy. His analysis of national liberation movements, the result of "long years of practical experience, painstaking study, and theoretical analysis," yielded "a set of ideas consonant with the major socio-economic and political trends in the changed world." He "constantly anticipated great battles and revolutions in the colonial East. All his works and speeches dealing with the East attest to his full combat-readiness to meet these great battles equipped with a thorough knowledge of the scientific principles and strategy and tactics of the world socialist revolution."[24]

One cannot agree. Lenin's speeches and writings during the last thirty months of his politically active life do not disclose a highly articulated theory of global revolution for the postwar/postrevolutionary world into which was integrated the development of both capitalist Europe and agrarian Asia, and in which social, national, and colonial questions were represented as components of a unitary revolutionary process. A definite strategy for advancing the cause of international revolution on a global basis eluded him. In speaking to the Third Comintern Congress (June–July 1921) he was overtly indefinite regarding the particulars of the Asian situation, stating that revolution in Asia "may break out . . . sooner or later, and very suddenly too," and that in the decisive battles of world revolution the populations of Asia "will perhaps, play a much more revolutionary part then we expect."[25] It seems that as the revolutionary effects of the World War exhausted themselves without yielding a Europe of soviet republics, Lenin became increasingly open to alternative scenarios of world revolution.

There were nevertheless matters about which Lenin was definite. For instance, he was convinced that colonial revolt and revolutionary nationalism could powerfully undermine imperialist domination of the global political economy. He reassured his party that the enormous population and revolutionary potential of the Asian continent guaranteed that, ultimately, global socialist revolution could not fail. He was not cynical about the principle of national autonomy. To the contrary, he vehemently criticized the centralizing policies followed by Stalin, Grigorii Ordzhonikidze, and Feliks Dzerzhinskii in bringing Soviet rule to Georgia as being "Great-Russian chauvinist," and he warned against the adoption of "imperialist" attitudes toward national minorities in Central Asia.[26] He did not believe that European-style class struggle could be induced artificially in agrarian Asia or that revolution there could be installed by military force. He was confident that the struggle for national liberation in the colonial and semidependent world both could and should proceed autonomously, and he was very cautious about identifying national particularism and nationalist insurgence too quickly, too easily, and too closely with the proletarian cause. "Don't paint nationalism Red," he admonished in 1920.[27] To comprehend how and why Lenin came to these conclusions, it is necessary to understand the revolutionary initiative undertaken by the Bolsheviks in Islamic Asia in the years 1919–1921.

A Soviet Republic in Persia

Within weeks of the October Revolution, the Bolsheviks issued a revolutionary appeal to the Muslim peoples of Asia, both to those living within the frontiers of the former empire of the tsars and to those residing beyond. It was entitled "To the Muslim Toilers of Russia and the East." The Muslims of Russia, the proclamation stated, would be granted cultural autonomy under the protection of the Soviets. Those of "the East"—the "Persians, Turks, Arabs, and Indians"—were encouraged to drive out "the European imperialist robbers," "the oppressors of your countries."[28] Addressing all of Islamic Asia in a single statement was no mere convenience. As was true of other such revolutionary proclamations made during the early months of the new regime, it indicated that the appeal of the October Revolution was intended to be universal. As Ronald G. Suny has reminded us, the Bolsheviks aimed a common rhetoric of self-determination and national liberation at the empires of the Europeans in Asia, at the semi-colonial periphery of Turkey, Persia, Afghanistan, and China, and at the Muslim former subjects of the tsar.[29] In the remainder of this chapter, I will examine the appeal of the revolution in Russia to the Muslim peoples of the former Tsarist Empire and to those on the southern periphery of the Russian Federation.

The reconquest of Transcaucasia began in April 1920 when Mikhail Tuchachevskii, Grigorii Ordzhonikidze, and the troops of the Eleventh Red Army reoccupied Baku, the major port on the Caspian Sea and the center of the Caucasian petroleum industry. Ordzhonikidze was chairman of the Military Revolutionary Council on the Caucasian front, Tuchachevskii was temporarily military commander in the area, and most of the troops were ethnic Russians. The reason for the operation had been stated by Lenin the previous February: "We are in desperate need of oil."[30] The conquerors toppled the nationalist Musavatist government of Azerbaijan and replaced it with a commission of Muslim Bolsheviks who formed the Soviet Republic of Azerbaijan.

The large Armenian state created by the Treaty of Sèvres, concluded in August between the Allied powers and the Ottoman government in Constantinople, was disassembled. Turkish nationalist forces invaded formerly Ottoman western Armenia in September, reassuring Chicherin that they would avoid infringing on Soviet interests in eastern Armenia. The Russian government in Moscow attempted to mediate the conflict, hoping to defend its strategic interests in Transcaucasia without becoming involved in hostilities. When their efforts failed and the Armenians accepted Turkish peace terms, Ordzhonikidze organized a regiment of Armenian troops and Communist Party members, most of whom came from the industrial and cultural centers of Baku and Tiflis. They proclaimed themselves the Revolutionary Committee of Armenia, appealed by radio for a national uprising, and asked the Eleventh Red Army for assistance. Soviet troops blocked any further advance by the Turks but made no attempt to expel them. The Turks meanwhile refused to withdraw and massacred some of the Armenian population.[31]

RUSSIAN SOVIET
FEDERATIVE SOCIALIST REPUBLIC

CAUCASUS MOUNTAINS

CASPIAN SEA

BLACK
SEA

GEORGIA

Derbent

Tiflis

Batum

Ardahan

Kars

Lake Sevan

Erivan

AZERBAIJAN

Baku

ARMENIA

TURKEY

Lake Van

Tabrīz

Lake Urmia

Enzeli

Resht

PERSIA

Qazvīn

to Tehran

SYRIA

IRAQ

0   50   100   150 Miles

0   100   200 Kilometers

1.   Transcaucasian Soviet Federative Socialist Republic in 1923

In late January 1921, Stalin asked the Central Committee to authorize Ordzhonikidze to organize an insurrection in Georgia, to be supported by the Red Army if necessary. Lenin hesitated, and while communications with Moscow were mysteriously disrupted, Ordzhonikidze acted on his own and authorized an armed uprising, which was supported by elements of the Eleventh Army. After two weeks of hard fighting, the Bolsheviks entered Tiflis, deposed the Menshevik government, and proclaimed the Georgian Soviet Republic.[32] The Turks responded by occupying the southwestern districts of the country. The Caucasian "Iron" Cavalry Division commanded by D. P. Zholba secured Batum, but under the terms of the Soviet-Turkish treaty of 16 March the Soviet government made considerable territorial concessions to Turkey—the Kars region of Armenia and Artvin and Ardahan in Georgia.

In Central Asia the reconquest of the key border territories of formerly tsarist Russia was assured in July 1919 when the Red Army gained control over the entire 1,600-km-length of the Orenburg (Chkalov)-Tashkent railway. Military units arrived at Tashkent (the capital of present-day Uzbekistan) in November, and a five-man Commission for Turkistan Affairs was installed there. It was led by Mikhail Frunze and Valerian Kuibyshev, both of whom played leading roles in the reconquest of the two former tsarist protectorates, the Emirate of Khiva, on the steppes of what is today northern Turkmenistan, and the Emirate of Bukhara, in present-day southern Uzbekistan and western Tadzhikistan. Both emirates were riddled with conflict between the central authority and nomadic tribes on the periphery, and between reactionary emirs and groups of enlightened-statist "Young Khivans" and "Young Bukharans." The latter were movements of young, radicalized Turkistani intellectuals and merchants influenced by indigenous radicalism and Young Turk ideology, both of which had developed independently of Russian socialism. In December 1919, elements of the Red Army invaded Khiva, which was declared the People's Republic of Khoresm the following April. In August–September 1920 a "popular revolution" in Bukhara led by "Young Bukharans" was supported by, and perhaps staged by, Bolsheviks from the Turkistan Commission. Red Army units commanded by Frunze intervened, captured the city, destroyed the famous minaret and the public mosque, and seized the state treasury for shipment to Moscow. So transparent was the Bukharan operation that even Moscow was embarrassed and scolded the local Bolsheviks for "appearing imperialist" and for their "colonial attitudes."[33]

With the military and revolutionary reconquest of Caucasia and Central Asia, relations between the Soviets of Russia and the Muslims of Asia became matters for decision and action. Would the October Revolution be continued, internationalized, and directed southward beyond the borders of the former Russian Empire? If so, would it be transmitted by those of similar religion, languages, and culture, or would it be controlled by Europeans from Moscow and Petrograd? Muslim national communists like Sultan Galiev had an answer to this question. Just as Soviet Turkistan was "the revolutionary lighthouse of Chinese Turkistan, Tibet, Afghanistan, India, Bukhara, and Khiva," he wrote, so will Soviet Azerbaijan "become the Red lighthouse for Persia, Arabia, and Turkey."[34] Muslim national communists wanted the October Revolution activated in Asia, and wanted it led by Muslims and accomplished forthwith—a purely Asian strategy of continuous revolution. But the leadership of the RCP(B) within the Comintern was not convinced.

Within five months of Azerbaijan's coming under Bolshevik control, and at about the time the Red Army entered Bukhara, the Comintern proclaimed a major revolutionary initiative in Islamic Asia. Ordzhonikidze and RCP(B)-Central Committee member Elena Stasova arranged a "Congress of the Peoples of the East" and convened it in September at Baku, the capital of Azerbaijan. To this congress were invited "the enslaved masses of Persia, Armenia, and Turkey" as well as the "more distant peoples" of Islamic Asia and India.[35] Almost 2,000 delegates from twenty-nine nationalities, one-half of them from the Caucasus and most of these from Azerbaijan, attended the congress, where they heard Zinoviev call for "a holy war above all against British imperialism."[36] Although the delegates gave vent to much uncomplicated anti-European nationalism, those who attended the congress at Baku did not constitute a cadre of disciplined, dedicated, and devout activists sophisticated in Marxist theory and skilled in revolutionary tactics; nor did the congress transform them into one.[37] And those who represented the highest levels of the Comintern at the congress did not commit themselves to an Asian strategy. Zinoviev and Béla Kun disparaged the idea of self-sufficient revolutions of national liberation in Asia. They insisted that the class struggle and the alliance between the peoples of Asia and the proletariat of Europe and Russia were the indispensable elements of international socialist revolution.[38]

Thus, as the Civil War ended in Russia, disparate strategies for continuing the October Revolution and for extending it to Asia were being articulated, and these the Comintern could not fully coordinate and direct. As a result, the beginnings of the NKID's efforts to introduce "peaceful coexistence" into the relations between the new Soviet state and the major powers of Europe and to normalize relations with the countries on the southern periphery of the soviet republics were seriously complicated. Nowhere was this more true than in Persia.

With the revolution in Russia and the withdrawal of tsarist armed forces from northern Persia in 1917, Great Britain occupied a position of almost complete domination in a region close to the new soviet republics and of vital strategic significance to them. British forces occupied Persia and Mesopotamia and Turkish Armenia to the west. British naval units controlled the Caspian Sea. The Anglo-Persian agreement (signed in August 1919 but never ratified) represented the highest achievement of Lord Curzon, British foreign secretary (1919–24) and former viceroy and governor-general of

India, in his efforts to found a post–World War British Empire in the eastern Mediterranean and southwest Asia.[39] It would have given to British advisers control over the Persian treasury, army, and railroads. The governments of both France and the United States lodged protests against the treaty; Persian nationalists were outraged; and the assembly (*majlis*) in Tehran refused to ratify it. The NKID also objected to it, particularly in that the Persian government refused to open even minimal diplomatic relations with the new Soviet state—despite the fact that the Soviet government renounced the Anglo-Russian agreement of 1907 dividing Persia into spheres of influence, denounced the secret wartime treaties between Russia and the Entente calling for partition of the country, canceled the debt incurred by Persia with the tsarist regime, surrendered tsarist concessions there, and handed over to the government in Tehran the assets of Russian-owned banks.[40]

A squadron of eighteen ships formed the northernmost tip of British influence in Persia; these were the remnants of the navy the British had organized for counterrevolutionary General Anton Denikin, commander in chief of the Armed Forces of South Russia (1919–20). With Denikin's defeat and the Bolshevik advance into Transcaucasia in March–April 1920, local Persian authorities interned the ships and placed them under the protection of British Indian forces. The ships were based at Enzeli (subsequently Pahlavi and then Bandar Anzali), the best Persian port on the Caspian and the center of the lucrative prewar Russian caviar industry. Since 1918, British and White forces had repeatedly used Enzeli as a base from which to launch attacks on Baku and on Krasnovodsk across the Caspian in Russian Turkistan. In April 1920, Trotsky cabled Lenin and Chicherin: "The Caspian must be cleared of the White fleet at all costs. If a landing in Persian territory is required, it must be carried out." Before forwarding the memorandum, Lenin noted in the margin: "I fully agree."[41] On 18–19 May 1920, Soviet naval forces in the Caspian under the command of Fedor Raskolnikov captured the ships, landed 2,000 marines, surrounded the British garrison, and took the city of Enzeli. British forces retreated to Qazvīn, 90 miles northwest of Tehran. The government in London declined to reinforce them, and Prime Minister Andrew Bonar Law (1922–23) made clear in the House of Commons that His Majesty's Government was under no obligation to defend Persia. British prestige in Persia thereupon suffered a blow from which it never recovered.[42]

Following the attack on Enzeli, Soviet policy in Persia ran on two tracks. Proceeding on one track, Chicherin warned Ordzhonikidze and Raskolnikov not to extend Soviet military force beyond Enzeli, and Russian forces were withdrawn from Persia within three weeks as part of the

Soviet Russian effort to establish relations with the government of Persia in Tehran. On the other track, the Soviets undertook a major revolutionary initiative beginning with the contacts Raskolnikov established with leaders of the revolutionary nationalist movement in northern Persia.[43]

The densely forested mountains of the Gilan and Mazanderan provinces in northwestern Persia, along the shores of the Caspian Sea, had been beyond the control of the authorities in Tehran for some time. Local chiefs, who headed bands of guerrillas called *jengheli* (from the Persian, "of the jungle") effectively controlled the countryside. One such chief was a minor landowner, cleric, and military adventurer named Mirza Kuchik Khan, who was allied with radical bourgeois intellectuals from both Resht, the capital of Gilan province, and Tehran. His movement was anti-Western, Pan-Islamic, and socially radical, and it was directed both against the existing regime in Tehran and against British presence in Persia. In May 1920, Kuchik Khan addressed a letter to the Soviet commanders at Enzeli asking for assistance against the troops of the Persian government, which had recently expelled his forces from Resht. And on 4 June, two days before they evacuated their forces from Persia, Raskolnikov and Ordzhonikidze met Kuchik somewhere on the road between Enzeli and Resht and apparently persuaded him on the spot to proclaim himself president of the "Soviet Republic of Gilan." Thereby was created the first Soviet "satellite" beyond the frontiers of the former Russian Empire.[44] Kuchik Khan then personally directed a message to Lenin requesting the help of all socialists belonging to the Comintern "in liberating us and all weak and oppressed nations from the yoke of English and Persian oppressors."[45]

In Moscow and Petrograd the news from Persia evoked an outburst of jubilation. As leader of the Red Army, Trotsky immediately sent to Kuchik Khan a message stating that "the news of the formation of the Persian Red Army has filled our hearts with joy."[46] The head of the Eastern Department of the NKID announced that revolution would spread from Persia to Afghanistan to northern India. A Persian branch of *Adalet*, a revolutionary Social Democratic party formed in 1916 of workers in the Baku oil fields, moved to Resht and there founded the Persian Communist Party. It was in the midst of these events that the Second Comintern Congress convened in July 1920. When Lenin informed those assembled that "the Soviet movement in the whole East, in all Asia has already started," he was in all probability referring to the Persian situation.[47]

Behind the scenes, however, party leaders like Trotsky were much more skeptical regarding Soviet power in Asia.[48] The Gilan adventure was sponsored by Ordzhonikidze, Stalin, and Sergei Kirov, then a leader of the Communist Party of Azerbaijan and subsequently its general secretary

(1923–26). It was an embarrassment to Soviet diplomacy. Chicherin angrily opposed the whole operation, never calling it anything other than "Stalin's Gilan Republic,"[49] and fought with the supporters of the Gilan Soviet for Lenin's backing. Typically, Lenin supported both positions. He agreed not to grant the Gilan Republic formal diplomatic recognition, but he asked the NKID to give an official reception to a Gilan mission that arrived in Moscow in August 1920.[50] He also sanctioned military assistance to the Gilan Soviet, an action he may have seen as an implementation by military means of the doctrine of alliance between Communist parties and revolutionary nationalist movements that he had propounded at the Second Comintern Congress. Eventually a division of Red Army troops, mainly from Azerbaijan and Georgia, was dispatched to northern Persia to aid the Gilan Soviet Republic, the first and last time that organized combat units of the Red Army were directly involved in operations assisting a nationalist-communist coalition beyond the borders of the soviet republics.[51] The aid program was undertaken semi-independently by the Azerbaijan Soviet Republic, which thus gave the Russian government in Moscow the capability of "plausible denial" and allowed it to adopt an official policy of noninterference in the conflict between Gilan and Tehran.

Conflict within the government of the Gilan Soviet Republic itself strengthened Chicherin's hand in the policy dispute over Persia. The Gilan regime was composed of followers of Kuchik Khan, Kurdish chiefs, "anarchist" followers of the Tehran bourgeois intellectual Eksanullah Khan, and Communists. Some of the latter were important party personalities, both Persian and Russian, one of whom openly declared that it was the intention of Soviet Russia to liberate all Persia. Others were Persian migrant workers from the Baku oil fields who were inept at politics and who more than once stated openly that the Comintern had instructed them gradually to subvert and overthrow the power of the tribal leaders.[52] A. Sultan-Zade, the founder of the Persian Communist Party and a member of the ECCI (1920–23), was true to the program he had articulated in support of Roy at the Second Comintern Congress, namely, immediate socialist revolution and establishment of Soviet institutions. Not unexpectedly a struggle for control of the movement erupted between Kuchik Khan, on the one hand, and the Communists on the other. In July the government split, and Kuchik withdrew into the forest with his troops. Sultan-Zade formed a new government in Gilan dominated by the Persian Communist Party which attempted to implement a full-scale program of proletarian dictatorship, including nationalization of enterprises, closure of the bazaars, removal of the veil from women, and attacks on the clergy. With the Gilan Soviet involved in open conflict, the government in Tehran sent the Persian

Cossack Brigade under the command of Colonel Petr Storroselskii, a counterrevolutionary Russian officer, to "pacify" the area. Resht fell in August
and Storroselskii's forces marched on Enzeli, but Soviet troops held them
off and drove them back from the port city.[53]

At this juncture the correlation of forces within the Bolshevik leadership
tipped away from support for insurrectionary initiative in Persia. The
Second Comintern Congress defined the strategy for situations such as
those at Gilan: Purely Communist regimes could not be immediately
introduced in semicolonial Asia; Persia must first go through a stage of
bourgeois revolution; national revolutionaries were objectively progressive and were to be supported. In Gilan the Persian Communist Party, with
a new Central Committee, resolved to adopt the tactics of the "united anti-
imperialist front," to avoid "revolutionary adventurism," to form a class
alliance extending from the proletariat to the middle bourgeoisie and the
intelligentsia, and to support a program of bourgeois democratic reforms.[54]
The following spring the Persian Communist Party and Kuchik Khan
reallied in a "united front" government.

After the Persian Cossack Brigade was driven back from Enzeli, it was
reorganized by British advisers. They dismissed Storroselskii and the other
Russian officers of the brigade, and at its command they placed the energetic, nationalistic, and ambitious Reza Khan, subsequently prime minister
(1923–25), and then shah (1925–41) of Persia/Iran. In February 1921,
Reza and his force of 3,000 Cossacks marched on Tehran and installed a
new government in which Reza was appointed minister of war and commander in chief of the army. The first actions of the new government were
to renounce the unratified Anglo-Persian agreement of 1919 and to sign
with the Russian Federation a treaty that had been under negotiation since
the previous October.[55]

The Soviet-Persian treaty was a document without strong precedent in
international law. It went into effect from the moment it was signed; it had
no expiration date; and there was no mechanism for renunciation. The
Soviet government agreed to freedom of navigation on the Caspian Sea and
to the presence of a Persian fleet there. It renounced all debts incurred
by Persia with the tsarist regime, returned offshore islands seized by
the tsarist government, and surrendered every concession Russia held or
claimed in Persia, with the exception of the Caspian Sea fisheries. What
Soviet Russia gained in return was the reaffirmation of the border of 1917,
the reduction of British influence in Persia, and special military rights.
Regarding the latter the Persian government consented to allow Russia to
"advance troops into the Persian interior for the purpose of carrying out

military operations necessary for its defense" in the event that a third country (Britain) used Persian territory as a military base or threatened the Soviet frontier.[56] Over these provisions, contained in the notorious Articles V and VI of the treaty, there was vigorous debate in the Persian parliament. And only the strength of anti-British feeling in the country prevented the Tehran government from demanding of Moscow that the text of the treaty be revised to delete the two clauses. In 1941 they served as the basis for Soviet occupation of northern Iran. The Khomeini regime repudiated Articles V and VI in 1979; otherwise the treaty remained in effect.

Throughout the treaty negotiations, the objective of the NKID was to protect Transcaucasia, Baku in particular, from British military power. The oil center was vulnerable to attack from northern Persia; twice in 1918 British forces had occupied Baku from their base there. The RCP(B) Central Committee authorized Chicherin to agree with Tehran that if British troops were completely withdrawn from Persia, Azerbaijani troops would be evacuated from Enzeli. In this regard, the treaty was a triumph for Russian diplomacy. Tehran formally renounced the one-sided Anglo-Persian agreement of 1919, and British troops were withdrawn in May 1921.

Soviet forces remained, however, and in conjunction with the forces of Kuchik Khan they marched on Tehran in June. They were held off by Reza Khan's Persian Cossack Brigade while the Tehran government protested strongly. Moscow was persuaded thereby to abandon all support for the Gilan Republic and stated that it would recall and punish those officials responsible for terrorizing the Gilan people. Chicherin was even able to get the Central Committee of the RCP(B) officially to admonish the "undisciplined" Bolsheviks of Transcaucasia.[57] Red Army troops were withdrawn in September. Thereafter Kuchik Khan disputed the direction of the movement with his Communist allies which he settled by inviting them to a lavish feast at which he slaughtered the entire Central Committee of the Persian Communist Party. The Persian army "restored order" in Gilan, and the Gilan Soviet Republic expired in October. Kuchik Khan fled to the mountains of the Talysh district along the Persian-Azerbaijan frontier, where he froze to death.[58] The Persian Communist Party lost three-quarters of its membership, and by 1924 it had but 600 adherents.[59]

The Gilan Soviet Republic had been launched as the Red Army was achieving its final victories over the forces of counterrevolution. The incursion into Persia was an extension of the Civil War at a time when the international boundaries of southwest and Central Asia were being redrawn amidst the turmoil of the collapse of the Turkish and Russian empires, and when conflicting territorial claims abounded. The means by which the October Revolution was to be internationalized in Asia were still being defined, and coordination of "the world revolutionary process" by the Communist International was just beginning. The Communist parties in the territories of the former Tsarist Empire had not yet been worked into the disciplined unitary organization; decentralized initiative remained possible. For those who had fought and won the Civil War, revolution, reconquest, and security went hand in hand.

War and Diplomacy in Afghanistan

At the beginning of the twentieth century, the territory of Afghanistan was occupied by a loose confederation of disparate Tajik, Hazara, and Pushtun tribes and principalities. The emir in Kabul was little more than the chief of one of them, and many tribal leaders, rather than paying tribute to him, received payments from him, allegedly for guarding the frontiers. Since the 1860s, control of Afghanistan had been the main prize in "the Great Game" played between the British and Russian empires as the Russians extended the security of their region by subduing one central Asian tribe after another, and as the British moved north from India seeking ground on which to anchor the defenses of the North-West Frontier Province of India (in present-day Pakistan). In 1907, confronted with a common German threat, Russia and Britain suspended the struggle, concluded the Anglo-Russian Entente, and settled their rivalry in Central Asia as well as in Persia. Afghanistan was placed within the British sphere of influence, and Afghan foreign relations, including those with Russia, were conducted by the government of British India in Delhi.

Ten years later, two events changed the terms of Russian and British relations with Afghanistan.[60] The October Revolution brought to power a government which, unlike the Tsarist Empire, proclaimed its respect for Afghan independence, and the faithfully pro-British emir of Afghanistan (since 1901), Habibullah Khan, was assassinated under mysterious circumstances in February 1919. The new emir Amanullah Khan (1919–29) was associated with an enlightened and reformist-minded group of intellectuals in the Young Afghan movement. He was the son-in-law of Mahmud Tarzi, a man who had spent years in exile, who had strong Young Turk associations, who was well known outside the country as a leading Young Afghan anticolonialist, and who served as his foreign minister. Within months of coming to power, Amanullah adopted a program of radical reforms (which eventually resulted in a traditionalist revolt that drove him from power in 1929), declared Afghanistan an independent country, denounced existing treaties with Britain, opened negotiations with Soviet Russia, and declared a "holy war," calling on Indian Muslims to rise against British rule. In general, he displayed what Lord Curzon termed, with classic British understatement, "a truculent attitude."[61]

2. Soviet Turkistan and Afghanistan in 1922

Following a brief, three-week conflict, called the Third Anglo-Afghan War, Amanullah sued for peace. The Indian Army had confronted him within a few miles of the border, and the ability of British forces to bombard Kabul and Jalālābād from the air impressed him. Under the terms of the treaty of Rawalpindi (August 1919), Amanullah recognized British authority over the Pathan tribal belt of the North-West Frontier Province. The government of India recognized the independence of Afghanistan and surrendered control of Afghan foreign relations while at the same time cutting off the subsidy the emir received. The Indian government had little choice but to surrender its strategically significant position. Although the Indian Army had repulsed the Afghan invasion, its military campaign had collapsed completely when the long-established practice of defending the Peshawar district of the North-West Frontier Province with local tribal troops failed disastrously. So many men deserted from the Khyber Rifles that the commanders found it necessary to ask each man individually whether he wished to remain in British service or to be discharged. Six hundred of seven hundred men opted for discharge, and the unit had to be disbanded.[62] In the aftermath of the war, the government of India reevaluated its whole frontier policy, and the British Indian Army was permanently redeployed in the area.[63]

The Red Army meanwhile had given support to the Afghan war effort, turning back a British Indian attack in Turkistan and forcing the enemy to give up the idea of opening up a second front against Afghanistan in the north.[64] The basis for continuing Soviet-Afghan collaboration was then laid in April 1919. As tensions mounted between Kabul and London, Amanullah addressed two letters to Moscow, which did not arrive until six weeks later, having been passed with enormous difficulty through the military fronts of the Civil War.[65] One letter, addressed to the NKID, requested formal diplomatic relations. The second was a personal greeting from Amanullah to Lenin calling him "the greatest hope of the Afghan people." Lenin responded promptly by praising the Afghans for their heroic defense of their freedom, calling Afghanistan "the world's only independent Muslim state," agreeing to an immediate exchange of diplomatic representation—making Afghanistan the first country in the world to recognize the Soviet government—and suggesting the possibility of "mutual assistance against every encroachment on the part of foreign plunderers."[66] Soon thereafter, a second dispatch announced the impending delivery of "a completely outfitted radio-telegraphic station which represents the latest achievement of technology."[67] Indications of Soviet-Afghan collaboration had a decisive effect on the terms of the Anglo-Afghan peace negotiations taking place at the same time.

Yakov Surits, who subsequently had a long career of ambassadorial posts in Turkey, Germany, and France, was appointed "extraordinary and plenipotentiary representative of the RSFSR in Central Asia with residence in Kabul"—suggesting to one scholar that his duties included directing subversive activities from northwest India to Chinese Turkistan.[68] He was succeeded in March 1921 by Fedor Raskolnikov, the mastermind of the Gilan Soviet Republic, and the man who made Kuchik Khan a world revolutionary figure.

A dynamic and charismatic personality,[69] Raskolnikov took his name from the protagonist of Dostoevskii's *Crime and Punishment,* and while a student he had worn his hair long, wrapped himself in a long, dark coat, and affected a typical "nihilist" stance. His Bolshevik credentials went back nearly to the foundation of the party—he had been editorial secretary of *Pravda* when it first appeared in 1912. Drafted for the World War, he attended the naval academy, and by the time of the October Revolution he was a junior officer and an important revolutionary organizer among the sailors of Petrograd. His bravery and achievements during the Civil War were legendary. Raskolnikov was married to Larissa Reisner, who was well known before the revolution as a decadent-leaning poet and subsequently as a prominent "aesthetic revolutionary." A man of letters himself, he organized literary magazines and authored books following his service in Kabul. His presence in Kabul contributed significantly to the romanticization of diplomatic representation in Afghanistan that characterized numerous "diplomatic novels" published in the USSR and, eventually, the film *Mission to Kabul.* During his posting in Kabul, Raskolnikov and Reisner separated and then divorced. She returned to Moscow in early 1923, and the following autumn accompanied Karl Radek to Germany, where she acted as liaison between the KPD leadership in Berlin and the Comintern delegation in Dresden during the abortive "German October" revolution. After Raskolnikov's appointment to Kabul ended in 1924, he held important positions in the NKID and in the Communist International, including the directorship of the Eastern Division of the Comintern Secretariat. While abroad at a diplomatic post during the purges of the 1930s, and knowing the fate of ambassadors who returned to Moscow when recalled, he declined to go back and instead published a bombshell "open letter" to Stalin in the French press, accusing him of betraying the revolution and becoming a despot. For this he was rehabilitated during the Khrushchev thaw, and during *glasnost* he became the object of admiration among reformers.

In Kabul, Soviet diplomacy could operate without the embarrassment of the Comintern. No socialist or Communist party existed in Afghanistan, and the CI displayed little interest in inspiring and supporting one. With Afghanistan, the Comintern employed the rhetoric of bourgeois nationalism rather than of proletarian revolution, and aimed it directly at the Pan-Islamic proclivities of the Young Afghan nationalists. As Afghanistan was the only independent state in the Muslim world, so Lenin told the new Afghan ambassador, the "great historical task befell it of unifying around itself all the enslaved Muslim nations, and of leading them on the path of freedom and independence."[70] Moreover, Afghanistan was of great strategic significance both to the military security of the soviet republics and to the cause of global anti-imperialist revolution. An independent and neutral Afghanistan, like an independent and neutral Persia, diminished British predominance on the southern rim of the socialist republics and formed the basis for a possible anti-British nationalist movement on the frontiers of India. These prospects, rather than the hope of creating a socialist revolution there, attracted the Bolsheviks to Kabul.

It was primarily the need for assistance from Soviet Russia in the event of a renewed Anglo-Afghan war that brought Amanullah into treaty negotiations with Moscow. He seems to have aimed at a comprehensive offensive-defensive alliance, a step the NKID was not prepared to take. However, the Soviet government was willing to grant financial and military assistance, and a formal Soviet-Afghan treaty of recognition and friendship was initialed by Surits and Mahmud Tarzi in September 1920 and signed the following February.[71] Both governments promised to refrain from entering into agreements with third parties against the interests of the other—a provision of much greater potential benefit to Russia than to Afghanistan. In exchange, Moscow promised Kabul, in addition to the radio station promised in the summer of 1920, a telegraph line from Kabul to Kushka via Kandahār, a yearly subsidy of one million rubles in gold or silver, and technical specialists. No mention was made of the military aid Surits had promised the previous spring—airplanes with crews, an air force training school, antiaircraft guns, and 5,000 rifles with ammunition.[72] The agreement strengthened Amanullah's hand in maintaining Afghan independence from Britain, and after 1921, Afghanistan was no longer the extension of the British Empire it had been in 1914. Lenin and Chicherin believed moreover that the treaty would accelerate the liberation of the oppressed peoples of Asia,[73] and the Foreign Office in London feared that Kabul would become the instrument of a Bolshevik campaign to overthrow British rule in India. Neither happened.

Instead, major tensions developed in the new Soviet-Afghan friendship, largely as a result of Russian efforts to sovietize the former Tsarist Empire in Central Asia and of Amanullah's ambition to incorporate part of it into a confederation of Islamic states in Central Asia. The confederation he imagined included the emirates of Bukhara and Khiva and entailed direct Afghan sovereignty in the Turkmen districts of Kushka, Panjdeh, and Merv. Persia, regarded as too weak to oppose or rival Afghan aggrandizement, was expected to accept Kabul's domination. In the event that the former Russian Empire disintegrated further, all of Turkistan would be included. If British power in India receded, Amanullah would lay claim to the lands of the Pushtun tribes to the south and to the maritime province of

Sindh Sind with its port at Karachi. As might be expected, Moscow looked with favor upon Afghan claims made at the expense of British India and Persia, but not upon Amanullah's claims to Soviet Turkistan.[74]

The Afghan-Soviet rivalry in Turkistan was intensified by the *basmachi* rebellion, which Amanullah sought to win over to his Pan-Islamic movement, and which the Soviets were intent on suppressing. The *basmachi* (from the Uzbek term for bandit) were armed bands organized around local chiefs, called *kurbashi*, who exercised both military and political authority over their followers. They had begun as improvised self-defense organizations during the period of semianarchy that existed in the region from early 1918 to late 1920. The sovietization of Turkistan, the nationalization of cotton and vine growing, famine, and unemployment swelled their ranks and transformed them into a loosely organized, counterrevolutionary, anti-Soviet resistance in the defense of their independence and their traditional way of life. The rebellion of the *basmachi* began in, and was centered in, the Fergana Valley of what became Soviet Tadzhikistan, where it had strong support from the local population. With the Soviet takeover in Bukhara and Khiva, it spread to those areas too. By December 1921, *basmachi* forces numbered 20,000, and the movement was growing into something approaching an Islamic revolt against Soviet power. The *basmachi* were Muslim and Turkistani and identified themselves as *mujahedeen*. The forces opposing them—mainly ethnic Russians—closed Muslim religious schools and curtailed the activities of the clergy. Muslim units of the Red Army proved to be unreliable and deserted to the *basmachi;* important Muslim figures in the Bukharan government defected; and the Central Committee of the Russian Communist Party had to take over coordination of the Communist parties of Turkistan, Bukhara, and Khoresm. The *basmachi* rebellion became the most formidable mass anti-Soviet revolt prior to the Afghan resistance of 1978.[75]

The conflict reached its most intense level with the arrival in Bukhara of Enver Pasha, former war minister of the Young Turk ruling triumvirate of the Ottoman Empire. Ultra-ambitious and opportunistic, Enver had dreams of a Pan-Turanian Islamic federation in Central Asia. He signed his documents as "Commander-in-Chief of all Forces of Islam, son-in-law of the Caliph [he was married to the daughter of the last Turkish sultan], and Representative of the Prophet." Along with other Young Turks, he stood accused of organizing the 1915 genocide of the Armenian people, and at the end of the World War he was sought by the Kemalist nationalists of Turkey as a traitor and by the Allies as a war criminal. In the summer of 1920, Enver and another leading Young Turk, Djemal Pasha (subsequently shot on the steps of the Tiflis Cheka by Armenian *fidai* nationalist guerrillas), arrived in Moscow, after having earlier contacted Karl Radek in Berlin, and offered their services to the revolution. Although Lenin distrusted Enver, he was prepared to use him in the cause of Islamic anti-imperialism.

Together Enver and Djemal participated in the Baku Congress, and Enver was sent to Turkistan in November 1921. There he was expected to act as a pro-Bolshevik leader of well-known nationalist and Pan-Turkic reputation, consolidate Soviet control over the Turkmen of Central Asia, and promote anticolonial rebellion against British influence throughout the region. However, instead of winning the Muslims of Central Asia to the cause of world revolution, Enver assumed a Pan-Islamic program, defected to the anti-Soviet *basmachi* rebels, and joined with Ahmed Zeki Velidi (Torgan) in an effort to bring unity to the movement. The deposed emir of Bukhara named him commander in chief of Bukharan resistance forces, and by the spring of 1922 he had gathered together some independent tribal chiefs, acquired about 7,000 supporters, and captured Dyushambe (subsequently the capital of Tadzhikistan). Enver rejected the efforts of the NKID to negotiate a truce with him, stating: "Peace is only acceptable after the withdrawal of Russian troops from Turkistan soil. The freedom fighters, whose commander I am, have sworn to fight for independence and freedom until their last breath." In return he dispatched an ultimatum to Moscow in May demanding national independence for the "peoples of Bukhara, Turkistan, and Khiva."[76]

Moscow responded angrily, temporarily suspended the Soviet-Afghan treaty, and sent Ordzhonikidze and the Third Red Army to Turkistan, where they took ruthless punitive measures. Crops and wells were destroyed and hostages were taken and executed. Aerial bombardment and, allegedly, poison gas were used. Entire villages were wiped out in what became known during the *glasnost* era as "the most unknown Soviet war." The Russians deployed a relatively small force (estimates of troop strength vary) but one far superior to the *basmachi* in size, training, and especially in firepower. When Enver insisted in fighting open battles against superior forces, he suffered major defeats at the hands of the Red Army. His supporters drifted away, and he was killed in a skirmish with Russian troops near the Afghan frontier in August 1922.

Enver had never succeeded in fully uniting the *basmachi* chiefs and the British had rejected his pleas for military assistance. Amanullah gave up the struggle in November in order to turn his attention to the south, where British Indian forces were gaining control of the relatively independent tribal areas along the Indo-Afghan frontier. He abandoned his project for an Afghan-led Central Asian Islamic Confederation. Enver's successor kept the struggle alive among the *basmachi* in the hope of massive British and/or Afghan military assistance that never came. In the end a combination of military operations and the economic and social concessions that accompanied the New Economic Policy extinguished the revolt. The *basmachi* rebellion in the Fergana Valley was defeated by a Red Army offensive in 1923 that employed cavalry, artillery, armored cars, and airplanes. A hard-core but incoherent anti-Soviet resistance persisted in the mountains of southern Bukhara until 1928 and on the steppes of Turkmenistan until 1935. Thus the *basmachi* resistance was tenacious, but the most remarkable story of the conflict may be the ability of the young Soviet state to win a significant guerrilla war in one of the most inaccessible regions of the world.

The *basmachi* war clearly demonstrated the limits of Amanullah's rapprochement with Soviet Russia. Following the September 1920 Soviet revolution-invasion in Bukhara, the emir and his entourage had escaped into the mountains to the east, and from there the advance of the Red Army drove him to take refuge in Kabul. Amanullah considered himself the protector of the emir. He granted diplomatic recognition to the People's Republic of Bukhara only under intense pressure from Moscow, and as the anti-Soviet resistance in Central Asia intensified after the arrival of Enver, Amanullah gave to the exiled emir of Bukhara and to the *basmachi* direct and covert military assistance and also allowed them to use northern Afghanistan as a base of operations. Nadir Khan, the war minister and Amanullah's successor as emir of Afghanistan (1929–33), personally coordinated military operations from northern Afghanistan. At one point (July 1922), he took up a position with a considerable force on the Afghan-Soviet frontier and addressed a message to Chicherin making his intentions clear: "I have the honor to warn Your Excellency that unless the Bolsheviks stop their unfriendly activities against Bukhara, the government of Afghanistan will be forced to annex it. This is the only way to help the Islamic state of Central Asia against treacherous Bolshevik plotting."[77]

These tensions did not, however, disturb the essential geopolitical basis of Soviet-Afghan affinity—their mutual desire to turn back the efforts of the government of British India to gain control of the independent Pushtun tribes of the Peshawar district of the North-West Frontier Province. When this "forward policy" resumed, Amanullah visited Peshawar in 1923 and met with tribal leaders. Together they concluded that the situation was dangerous for the security of Afghanistan as well as for the Pushtun tribes, and Kabul distributed sizable amounts of money. With the connivance and encouragement of Amanullah, some tribes conducted raids against British forces and then took refuge in Afghanistan. This constituted an opportunity for the Soviet government, in the words of Larissa Reisner, to "remind the British, particularly after Lausanne, of their weak spot in the East."[78] It was also a chance to renew collaboration with Amanullah following the *basmachi* war.

To support Amanullah and the Pushtun against the "forward policy," Raskolnikov in February 1923 recommended to the Commission for Turkistani Affairs in Tashkent that arms and money be distributed to tribal leaders. Both were forthcoming; the radio transmitter promised in 1920 was constructed; preparations were made to deploy eleven military aircraft; and the NKID authorized Kabul to import arms from Italy across Soviet territory.[79] Anglo-Afghan tensions mounted in this latest continuation of "the Great Game," and by the end of the year a "Fourth Anglo-Afghan War" seemed imminent. The British openly threatened to bomb Kabul from bases in India, but were deterred by the presence of Soviet aircraft. Only Amanullah's surrender to demands that tribesmen who resisted British Indian authority be arrested prevented war.

Soviet support for Amanullah's regime continued in the face of a conservative rebellion against the emir that erupted in March 1924. Centered in the mountainous eastern province of Khost, the revolt prefigured the opposition to Amanullah that would force him to abdicate in 1929. The rebels opposed the landslide of progressive reforms Amanullah had introduced beginning in April 1923—centralized administration, constitutional government, development of education, encouragement of trade and industry, legal recognition of private property in land, direct taxation, suppression of slavery, and a formal penal code.[80] The rebels came within 80 km of Kabul, where they were stopped when Soviet (and German) planes and pilots, in a remarkable feat of contemporary aviation, crossed the Gindikush mountains and bombed, strafed, and dispersed them.[81]

The direct military assistance rendered to Afghanistan from 1919 to 1924 indicated the extent to which Soviet Russia was willing to go to protect an independent and intentionally progressive regime against its enemies, both those within and those without. By establishing and maintaining normal and friendly relations with internally and externally stabilized regimes in Afghanistan, Persia, and Turkey, the Soviet government largely restored the prewar borders of the Russian Empire along the southern perimeter of what would become the Soviet Union and reinforced "anti-imperialist" regimes against British control and influence. In Afghanistan the objectives of Soviet policy were consistent with the principles of conventional international relations. The ECCI made no effort to promote social revolution among the tribes of Afghanistan, and no attempt was made to create an Afghan Soviet Republic or even to inspire a Communist party.[82] No dual policy was conducted in Kabul. The purposes of global revolution were not absent from Soviet-Afghan relations, however, for Afghanistan occupied a place of importance in the Comintern's project for revolution in India.

The Comintern and the Indian Revolution

India was at the center of the struggle between revolutionary Russia and the British Empire. In the Bolshevik geopolitics of revolution, a blow struck at British India would inflict a decisive defeat to British power in Asia, inspire anti-imperialist revolts from Syria to China, and so "set the East ablaze."[83] Calculations such as these formed the basis of an audacious scheme to ignite a revolution among the Muslims of India launched under Comintern auspices in late 1920.[84]

The project was planned in the Small Bureau of the Comintern Executive Committee and approved by the ECCI, the Politburo, and Sovnarkom in the early fall of 1920 during the period following the Second Comintern Congress and about the time of the Congress of Asian Muslims at Baku. The central element of the plan, which was premised on the active support of Emir Amanullah, was to train and equip an army of Indian liberation in Afghanistan. Troops, recruited from among the Muslim population of India, would join with the forces of the anti-British resistance among the Pathan tribes of the North-West Frontier Province. This "Army of God" would occupy territory in northern India, set up a government there, and extend the Indian liberation movement from this base. The central figure in the scheme was M. N. Roy, then a leading member of the Central Asian Bureau of the Comintern. In late 1920 he was dispatched to Tashkent to organize the Indian revolutionary army. With him he took two trains with twenty-seven wagons loaded with weapons, ammunition, and military supplies, ten wagons of dismantled airplanes, a supply of gold coins, bullion, and pound and rupee notes, and the staff of a military training school.[85]

Those recruited by Roy in Tashkent were young Muslim zealots, *mujahedeen*, members of the Pan-Islamic Khilafat movement in India who regarded the preservation of the Ottoman Empire and the temporal authority and spiritual leadership of the sultan to be essential to the unity and welfare of all Muslims.[86] They were incensed at the partition of the Ottoman Empire, at the terms of the Treaty of Sèvres (August 1920) in which it was codified, at the treatment nationalist Turkey received at the hands of the Allied powers, and at infidel rule in India. In the summer of 1920, 18,000 of them left India for Afghanistan, some of whom intended to travel to Turkey to join the army of Mustafa Kemal Pasha, organizer of the Turkish Nationalist Party. On their way some fifty of them were captured by Turkmen tribesmen in Afghanistan and then liberated by the Red Army. Taken to Tashkent, some became enthusiastic Communists. Of these, the most important was Shaukat Usmani, who was to become a leading figure in the Indian Communist Party. Others, amused at being designated "representatives of the Indian revolution," resisted political education.[87] Only a few eventually became Marxists.

The Indian Military Training School at Tashkent lasted only a few months before it was disbanded in May 1921 along with the Central Asian Bureau of the Comintern. The task of directing revolutionary activities in Central Asia was transferred to the newly formed Eastern Commission of the ECCI in Moscow. Roy returned to Moscow, where he was placed in charge of coordinating Communist activities in India. With him went twenty-two graduates of the Indian Military School who received further training at the Communist University of the Working People of the East established in April. A year later, Roy and his activities were transferred to Berlin, where he published a journal and wrote books that were then smuggled into India, probably via the Soviet diplomatic mission in Kabul.

Just as Roy withdrew from Tashkent, Raskolnikov arrived in Kabul as *polpred,* or diplomatic representative. Chicherin formally instructed him to "categorically avoid the fatal mistake of undertaking artificial attempts to plant communism" in Afghanistan.[88] Instead Raskolnikov's considerable talents and efforts were expended on persuading Amanullah to permit the organization in Afghanistan of revolutionary activities directed at India. His immediate task was to induce the Kabul government to allow Moscow to open the consulates provided for in the Soviet-Afghan treaty concluded the previous February. Three of them were located in the north of the country (at Herāt, Meimen, and Mazār-i-Sharīf), but two were located in the south near the frontier with India (at Kandahār and Ghazni), where Moscow had no commercial interests and in which no Soviet citizens resided. (The joke making the rounds of the Kabul bazaar at the time was that Afghanistan would claim the right to open consulates in Siberia.)[89] The only conceivable purpose of the consulates in southern Afghanistan was to maintain points of observation, propaganda, and infiltration on the borders of the North-West Frontier Province of British India.

British intelligence correctly recognized the intended purpose of the consulates. In the terms of London's note of protest to Moscow, it was "to secure facilities for attacks through Afghanistan against the peace of India."[90] The Foreign Office warned both Kabul and Moscow against establishing the consulates. For months, Surits and then Raskolnikov avoided making an explicit and binding declaration that the consulates would not be opened, and the Afghan foreign ministry delayed assuring London pending official notification from the Soviet government. The notice from Moscow arrived on 21 November 1921; the next day the governments of Afghanistan and Great Britain signed a treaty normalizing relations and exchanging diplomatic representation.[91] Thereafter, Amanullah refused to allow Afghanistan to be used as a base for revolutionary operations against British India, requiring that all arms sent through Afghanistan be placed under the control of the Afghan government, that all Indian revolutionaries entering Afghanistan be disarmed, and that the Soviet-supported "Provisional Government of Free India," which was headquartered at Kabul, leave the country.

The Muslim Indian revolutionaries trained in Tashkent and Moscow began filtering back into India in late 1922. Some of them traveled on foot across the mountainous Afghan-Indian frontier in apparent contradiction of Afghan restrictions. Many were promptly arrested by British authorities on passport violations and immediately forswore Communism. Others augmented the several small groups of party members in India supported by Comintern funds. The government of India responded by tightening censorship and increasing surveillance. Roy's newspapers were confiscated; his confidential dispatches were intercepted by British intelligence; and the chief courier between Roy in Europe and India was apprehended. Shaukat Usmani was tracked down and arrested, and the government in Delhi notified its provincial governments that "prompt and definite steps must be taken to counter M. N. Roy's organization and propaganda and to terminate the activities of his principal followers."[92] Nine of the latter were tried in the Peshawar conspiracy case in 1923. The next year in the Cawnpore Bolshevik conspiracy case, additional members of the Indian Communist Party, including Usmani, were convicted of conspiracy to organize a revolution to overthrow British rule in India. A court of appeal upheld the convictions but found the notion of a conspiracy "absurd and unbelievable."[93]

With the trial and conviction of the cadres of the Indian Communist Party, the authorities of British India effectively suppressed what there was of the small, irresolute, and undisciplined invasion force mobilized by Roy. The leadership structure of the Communist Party of India was destroyed at least temporarily, and potential followers were discouraged. Within two years, the Indian Communist Party had but fifteen to twenty members, and the Bolshevik revolutionary offensive among the Muslims of southwest Asia and India ended for all practical purposes. In the months between Roy's withdrawal from Tashkent and the Cawnpore Bolshevik conspiracy trial, Soviet foreign relations developed in other directions. In October 1921 the NKID undertook a major initiative aimed at concluding a comprehensive postwar settlement of outstanding problems affecting Soviet relations with the victors of the World War. In April 1922 the Rapallo agreement was signed, sealing the Soviet-German "special relationship" that would be the lodestar of Soviet diplomacy in the years to follow. And, at the end of 1923, the first Soviet political and military advisers arrived in Canton to assist in a revolution of national liberation and unity in China. These developments are considered in the next two chapters.

4 First Détente

The Russian Economy, German Industry,
and Lloyd George's Grand Design

In September 1921 the Politburo decided that some of Russia's foreign debts might be recognized, and in a major diplomatic demarche on 28 October, Chicherin informed the member governments of the Supreme Allied Council (Great Britain, France, Italy, the United States, and Japan) that the Soviet government was prepared to pay back the loans the tsarist government had contracted prior to 1914—provided the capitalist states of the West assisted the economic reconstruction of Russia with long-term low-interest loans, accorded the Soviet regime full, de jure diplomatic recognition, accepted the inviolability of Soviet Russia's frontiers, guaranteed noninterference in Soviet internal affairs, and concluded a general treaty of peace.[1] The proposal stipulated that any financial settlement must be reciprocal—in other words, that the Soviet government be compensated for damage done by Allied forces during the Civil War. Finally, Narkomindel suggested that an international conference be held in the near future to arrange a settlement along these lines and to conclude a formal peace treaty.

Six months later, in April–May 1922, representatives of the governments of thirty-four nations, including the principal allies of the World War (with the exception of the United States), Soviet Russia, and Germany, met at Genoa on the Italian Riviera.[2] The Genoa Conference was the largest of the many post–World War I intergovernmental conclaves and the first to which Germany and Russia were invited. It was also the most comprehensive and wide-ranging in purpose. On its agenda was not only a peace settlement between the Allies and Soviet Russia but other large issues concerning European economic reconstruction and political stabilization. The conference was the central event in a tentative and contentious postwar détente between Soviet Russia and the Allied powers. The issues involved in that détente are defined in this chapter, and why no settlement between Soviet Russia and the capitalist powers was concluded is explained systematically.

One element of the projected settlement between Russia and the West that prompted the Genoa Conference was the initiative taken by the Soviet government in October 1921. That initiative was aimed at ending Soviet diplomatic isolation, at establishing conditions of security on the European frontiers of the socialist republics, and at expanding economic relations between Russia and the capitalist world. It was the most serious attempt made by Lenin and Chicherin to implement the policy of "peaceful coexistence" and partial economic integration. However, it was inherently problematic for many reasons. Primary among them was the disagreement that developed between the Soviet government and those who held the Russian debt over what constituted Russia's financial obligations.

There was much room for dispute. The prewar debt of tsarist Russia was the largest foreign debt of any country in the world at that time. It amounted to 4 billion gold rubles. Eighty percent of it was owed in France and held primarily by small investors. It was this debt on which the Soviet government proposed to make payment. This was not the entirety of the Russian debt, however, at least in the opinion of the governments of the Allied powers. The Russian war debt composed primarily of credits from the Allied powers to both the tsarist and provisional governments for the purchase of war materials increased the total indebtedness to 12 billion rubles. It was owed primarily to the governments of Great Britain and the United States. Finally, claims resulting from property nationalized in the revolution, claims held largely by Belgian and French owners, increased the total debt by approximately 2 billion gold rubles more.[3]

Another source of a possible East-West settlement in 1921–22 lay in the designs drawn up by German big business for the future of the Russian economy. Since the end of the war some prominent representatives of large-scale commerce and industry in Germany had come to think of Russia as a potential colony, and during the second half of 1921 they became obsessed with opening the German market. The introduction of the New Economic Policy somewhat alleviated their fears of Bolshevism and raised their hopes that capitalism could be reintroduced in Russia. Although their plans included rebuilding the Russian transportation network and reconstructing some manufacturing, they had no intention of making Russia industrially self-sufficient or even of restoring the industries developed in the 1890s. Men like Felix Deutsch of the German electrical cartel

AEG considered that industry to be economically "artificial," as having been introduced for "political reasons." He intended, as did other business leaders whom he consulted, for Russia to remain a vast source of raw materials and a huge market for German manufactures. Postrevolution Russia was for Deutsch a land of 150 million peasants who lacked the everyday necessities of life and who represented a gigantic business opportunity. In exchange for the products of their industry, German businessmen expected to have complete freedom to export out of Russia not only raw materials but treasures as well—gold, rugs, paintings. "Everything which Russia can no longer afford," Walter Rathenau said, "comes out."[4]

Rathenau was German minister of reconstruction and foreign minister in 1921–22. He was also general director of AEG and the first prominent German capitalist to call for closer economic ties with the new Soviet regime following the World War. He believed that Russia would be compelled to restore capitalism fully and to accept foreign assistance on any terms it was offered—so grave was the economic situation there, and so unworkable the principles on which Communism was based. He maintained moreover that Germany was locked in a postwar economic struggle to the death with Britain and France. In that struggle, the loss of Germany's prewar trade with the victors of the World War required that Germany find new markets and raw materials—above all, in Russia. If the Russian economy fell under the control of the British and French, Rathenau believed, Germany would lose the postwar struggle. If, on the other hand, Germany participated in the reconstruction of Russia, and perhaps even controlled it, the Reich could weather its postwar economic problems, recover successfully from the war, and emerge again as a world economic power. For this reason Rathenau's minimal goal was to prevent the loss of the Russian economy to the British and French; his maximum goal was to establish a German dominion over it.

The chief obstacles to German participation in Russian reconstruction were financial. Famine-stricken Soviet agriculture could not provide the grain that Russia had exchanged for manufactured goods before the war, and German banks could not furnish sufficient credit to Russia on favorable terms. Indeed, the massive capital requirements of Russian reconstruction were beyond the resources of any one country. Confronted with this problem, Rathenau and coal and iron baron Hugo Stinnes developed a solution to it in May 1921. In November–December, they proposed their solution to representatives of the British and French governments and industry, who in turn modified it somewhat. The result was a project for an international consortium that would combine the financial resources of the industrialized capitalist West and devote them to the reconstruction of

Russia.[5] With financial backing from Britain, France, Italy, and possibly the United States, Germany would rebuild the Russian railway system. As that reconstruction proceeded inland from the coastal regions to the sources of raw materials, the natural resources exploited would be exported to finance the construction of further railroads and manufactures. In this project, German business would control the commercial penetration of Russia and would reap the benefits therefrom. The Soviet government would retain ownership of the reconstructed enterprises and would compensate foreign owners of property nationalized in the revolution. To entice the ex-Allies into joining the consortium, Rathenau pointed out that German exports would be directed toward Russia, where Britain had few established trading interests, and he stipulated that one-half of the profits earned by Germany would be allocated to the payment of war reparations to the Allies.

The third element of a possible Soviet peace treaty issued from the efforts of David Lloyd George, the British prime minister (1916–22), and his advisers to restructure the World War peace settlement in a manner that would revive international trade, stimulate the British economy, and set strict limits on any commitment by London to enforce the Treaty of Versailles.[6] At various times in 1921–22, Lloyd George proposed (1) a ten-year European nonaggression pact aimed specifically at Soviet Russia and the states of eastern Europe, (2) a general disarmament agreement to reduce the burden of weapons procurement on the finances of France and Britain, (3) a new structure of peace to supplant the League of Nations from which both Soviet Russia and Weimar Germany had been excluded, and, as a reassurance to the security-dependent French, (4) a promise that the whole new structure would be centered on Anglo-French collaboration.

In all these measures, Lloyd George's intention was to eliminate from the agenda of postwar international politics any provision for military action, either to enforce the Versailles Treaty or to fulfill obligations to the covenant of the League of Nations, without prior consultation and negotiation taking place. Central to his concept of international relations were the ideas that armaments, alliances, and efforts to attain military predominance inevitably led to war and that measures providing for collective security, for the enforcement of the Treaty of Versailles, for the application of sanctions, and for the ratification of the status quo would not in fact provide security for Europe. To the contrary, they were the source of Europe's insecurity, he thought. The solution, Lloyd George believed, lay in eliminating any threat to peace originating either with potential aggressors or with treaty enforcers, in dissolving hostile blocs, in reestablishing a balance among the powers of Europe, and in achieving general disarmament.

This project for political stabilization based on a reconciliation of victors and vanquished and on a renunciation of force and coercion was one-half of Lloyd George's proposed reconstruction of European international relations in 1922—his Grand Design. It amounted to a new European order that would enable those who governed Great Britain to resume the relationship to the Continent to which they were accustomed and which they preferred—that of leading Europe from the edge. The other half was aimed at the economic reconstruction of Europe, the revival of international trade, the stimulation of British exports, and the relief of unemployment in the United Kingdom. To these ends he hoped to bring the United States—attracted by the promise of European disarmament—back to Europe both as a generous creditor, ready to forgive or reduce war debts, and as a guarantor of peace.

However, having no scheme of his own to implement economic reconstruction, Lloyd George combined the consortium project of Rathenau and Stinnes with Chicherin's proposal for an international conference on Russian and European reconstruction. In doing so, he became the chief architect of the Genoa Conference—a daring diplomatic enterprise directed at both economic revival and political stability and based on a peace resettlement revised in accordance with the post-Versailles international situation, as well as on coexistence and collaboration between Soviet Russia, Europe, and America. All this was to be achieved by an international conclave held at one of the Continental resort cities Lloyd George enjoyed visiting, a conference with an imperative to succeed placed on it by a public opinion whose expectations had been raised by the advance publicity given it by an attentive newspaper press.

Inherent in the conglomeration of schemes advanced by Lloyd George and his advisers, by Rathenau and German industry, and by Lenin, Chicherin, and the Politburo integrationists is what might be called a Genoa composite project. In the months of negotiations that culminated at the conference itself, the project was elaborated on and modified, but it was not realized. Had it been accomplished in its most elaborate form, Soviet Russia would have received full and immediate diplomatic recognition as well as Western technology and capital, either in the form of long-term loans and credits or through a consortium led by Germany and financed by the victors of the World War. A portion of German profits from trade with Russia would have been pledged to reparations payments, and until those proceeds were available there would have been a payment moratorium. The Soviet government would have acknowledged as its obligation both the prewar tsarist debt and the Russian war debt, and it would have agreed to compensate the foreign owners of property nationalized in the revolution, although the actual form and amount of payment and compensation would have been subject to negotiation and adjustment. The security of France would have been maintained by a consultative pact with Britain and by a European-wide treaty of nonaggression. The United States would have joined in this guarantee of the peace in some manner and either scaled back or forgiven the debts of its wartime allies.

Thus, the Genoa composite project was unparalleled as a framework for a comprehensive post–World War peace agreement. It was aimed at fundamentally reshaping the European order, at ending both the war and the war-after-the-war, at leveling the ground on which the victors and the vanquished played, and at bringing both Russia and the United States back into the European system. Contained within it was the potential for a comprehensive postwar East-West settlement following years of war, revolution, and civil war and for an alternative form of East-West relations— relations based on recognition of the sovereignty of both socialist and capitalist states and on reciprocally beneficial economic exchange.

The Making of Soviet Diplomacy

Soviet preparations for the Genoa Conference were premised on the belief that normal relations with bourgeois states would constitute Soviet Russia's first line of defense against capitalist hostility. While commercial relations would provide Russia with the materials for economic reconstruction, formal legal recognition and full diplomatic relations, as well as the profits capitalists expected from trade with Russia, would hinder them from resuming military intervention. By the time the Soviets launched their initiative in October 1921, they had made only small progress in the direction of stable relations with the world's major powers. Although they had established commercial relations with England and Germany, Turkey was the only power of international significance with which Moscow had full diplomatic relations. Diplomatic recognition by the Allied powers and reconstruction loans obtained from them were therefore the primary objectives at which Soviet policy aimed in late 1921.

Lenin's personal contribution to the conceptualization of Soviet foreign relations has been recognized by Soviet and non-Soviet scholars alike. He identified three sets of interlocking contradictions within postwar international politics. They were the contradictions between capitalist states and socialist Russia, the contradictions between imperialist states and the national liberation movements in colonial countries, and the contradictions among the capitalist powers themselves. The first of these sets of contradictions indicated that peaceful coexistence would not last forever. The last of them were valuable assets to be utilized by Soviet diplomacy both to prevent the imperialist states from uniting against the Soviet regime—diplomatically, militarily, or economically—and to win from them favorable terms of trade and credit. The most important contradictions within the capitalist state system, Lenin thought, were the potential rivalry between Japan and the United States over Japan's postwar position in China and Korea; the antagonisms between the United States, which had emerged from the war solvent, financially independent, and enriched, and its new war debtors Britain and France; and the conflicts between a defeated Germany and the victorious Allied powers over implementing the Treaty of Versailles. The task of Soviet diplomacy, as he identified it, was to exacerbate these contradictions and to play off one side against the other in order to strengthen the position of the young Soviet state within the postwar world order.[7]

The international situation of 1921–22 offered to Soviet diplomacy significant opportunities in keeping with Lenin's concept of foreign relations. The morass of postwar international indebtedness, which he termed "the imperialist confusion," had entangled the victors of the World War more and more deeply in contradictions from which they would not be able to extricate themselves. This "world economic crisis," as Lenin termed it in December 1921, "has created an intolerable situation from which there is no escape." Specifically, in the financial and economic system created by the Treaty of Versailles—the reparations and war debt problems—and in the postwar monetary inflation and the recession in international trade, Lenin perceived an opportunity to exploit what he considered the most important of the contradictions of the imperialist system—namely, the hostility between Germany and the victors of the World War perpetuated by the Paris peace settlement. "The conditions obtaining in Germany in consequence of the Treaty of Versailles make her existence impossible," he had stated months earlier. "Naturally, her only means of salvation lies in an alliance with Soviet Russia, a country towards which her eyes are turning."[8]

Not only did Lenin set forth the fundamental strategies of early Soviet foreign relations, and appreciate the possibilities of a Russo-German anti-Versailles alliance, he also impressed on Soviet diplomacy his own realistic and calculating political style. As early as the negotiations with the Germans that led to the Treaty of Brest-Litovsk, he had delineated what he termed the process of "flexible amalgamation"[9] that he thought crucial to foreign policy making and participated directly in the execution of foreign affairs on a day-to-day basis. However, for reasons of personal security, Lenin decided that he could not attend an international conference outside the country, and Trotsky and Zinoviev were precluded from going to Genoa for the same reason. Lenin did nevertheless take a strong interest in the preparations for the conference. He personally recruited members of the delegation, including the thirty-two-year-old veteran Latvian Bolshevik Jan Rudzatak and Aleksandr Bekzadian, then people's commissar for foreign affairs for Soviet Armenia and subsequently Soviet representative in Norway and Hungary.[10] (The other delegates were Chicherin, Litvinov, Krasin, Waclaw Vorovskii, and Adolf Ioffe.) A new communications station was constructed in Moscow so that Lenin could maintain contact with Chicherin and the delegation in Genoa, and he asked Trotsky to make arrangements for the "most reliable" possible communications with the conference site, suggesting that a Soviet frigate with a powerful radio be dispatched to the Italian coast.[11]

The conference at Genoa was the first major diplomatic venture undertaken by the NKID. The staff prepared for it enthusiastically as Litvinov coordinated their efforts and Chicherin chaired lengthy meetings three times a week at which he read long memoranda from Lenin in which every possible contingency of the projected negotiations was considered as if the conference were to be an international game of chess.[12] Lenin also instructed Chicherin to make no reference at the conference to the inevitability of imperialist wars, to the violent overthrow of capitalism, or to any other of what he called the "terrible words" of revolutionary prognostication. Instead, he stated, the NKID should formulate a "broad pacifist program," the purpose of which was to achieve what he called the "chief political task" of the delegation, namely, to isolate "the petty bourgeois, pacifist and semi-pacifist" wing of the bourgeoisie from the "crude," "aggressive," and "reactionary" wing, to flatter them, and to convince them that agreement with Soviet Russia was both possible and desirable.[13] If, however, as Lenin expected, the other delegations at Genoa refused to discuss the pacifist program and limited the conference agenda to a discussion of debts and trade, then the strategy of the Soviet delegation should be to "divide among themselves the bourgeois countries that have united against us" in order to attain the best possible economic agreements.[14] Thus the Soviet delegation went to Genoa prepared with not one but two strategies of "divide and conquer," one based on class relations, the other on international relations.

In the "broad pacifist program" devised by the NKID and then revealed to the world in Chicherin's opening address to the Genoa Conference, the Soviet government proposed that the Russian Federation and the other states represented at the conference agree to a full agenda of measures to reform postwar international relations. According to Chicherin's program, they would grant each other diplomatic recognition; make mutual pledges of nonaggression, of complete equality in relations, and of noninterference in each other's internal affairs; agree to settle disputes by peaceful means; assent to a general reduction of armaments and a ban on submarine, aerial, and chemical warfare; and convene a world congress on economic reconstruction. At Lenin's specific direction, the Soviet program called for the cancellation of all war debts and for the revision of the Versailles and other treaties of the postwar settlement. In preparation for the discussion of war debt cancellation and treaty revision, Lenin urged Chicherin to read John Maynard Keynes's *The Economic Consequences of the Peace.*[15]

In presenting this program, the Soviet delegation at Genoa adopted what might be called the "peaceful coexistence negotiating stance": Fundamental economic and political differences between socialist Russia and capitalist Europe existed and made relations between the two sides difficult. Nevertheless, the two opposing systems could collaborate to their reciprocal benefit, particularly in the area of economic reconstruction. The Russian Federation would not, however, tolerate interference in its internal economic or political development, and the New Economic Policy was not to be misconstrued as the beginning of a transformation toward capitalism. General disarmament was by far the most important issue on the agenda of international politics. Soviet Russia had taken the lead in proposals for more progressive and humanitarian international relations. Indeed, it was the only country that truly spoke for, and acted in the interests of, world peace. Pronouncements such as these, which were formulated to define the basic orientation of Soviet policy toward Europe and America during the period of the Genoa détente, continued to shape Soviet foreign policy during the post–World War period and for years afterwards. In part, the effectiveness of Narkomindel diplomacy in overcoming Soviet diplomatic and economic isolation and in achieving diplomatic recognition by every major country in the world except the United States by 1924–25 may be attributed to the effectiveness of this negotiating stance. Its appeal was comprehensive. For the center-right of the European and American political spectrum of the 1920s, it seemed to offer opportunities for commerce and profit; for the center-left it proposed disarmament and peace.

The Genoa-Rapallo Impasse

Each part of the Genoa composite project proved attractive to one or more of the governments attending the conference. In particular, Soviet willingness to pay tsarist debts and the possibility of exploiting both Russian natural resources and the huge peasant market elicited sufficient interest in Europe to make possible the convocation of the largest and most elaborate of the post–World War I international meetings. Nevertheless, the conference at Genoa and the successor conference held at The Hague soon afterwards ended in failure. Tsarist debts were not repaid; the owners of nationalized property were not compensated; no investment consortium was formed; and no Russian peace treaty was ever concluded. The United States did not rejoin its wartime allies in augmenting European security. The problems of war debts and reparations were not resolved in 1922; they sent the armies of France and Belgium into the Ruhr in 1923 and the national finances of Germany and then France into crisis. In 1924 the world powers (except for the United States) began granting diplomatic recognition to the Soviet government without having first obtained from Moscow agreements regarding the payment of Russian debts. In 1925 the Locarno Conference in effect divided the security of Europe; it reinforced that of Western Europe, but left unresolved the security of the USSR and of the nations of Eastern and Central Europe. Following the reparations, war debt, and loan settlements of 1924–26, the economies of Europe and America prospered unevenly without participating significantly in the reconstruction of Russia. Industrial production in the USSR was restored to prewar levels by 1926–27, and a drive to build a socialist economy was launched without substantial long-term credits from the capitalist powers. All this being so, what happened to the prospects for a great East-West settlement following the Great War?

The United States was invited to Genoa as one of the five principal Allied powers but declined to attend. America had decisively influenced the outcome of the World War and the framing of the peace settlement, and it possessed the financial resources to make a significant contribution to Europe's economic reconstruction. Policymakers in Washington, however, recognized that the governments of Europe were not prepared to accept the "American solution" to the problems of postwar economic reconstruction. In articulating that solution, Secretary of Commerce Herbert Hoover set forth three political prerequisites to economic recovery.[16] The Allied powers would have to agree to lower the amount of reparation payments to what Germany could afford both financially and politically. America's war debtors would have to arrange to make reasonable payments on their obligations. And the nations of Europe would have to reduce their expenditures on armaments just as the Pacific powers had concluded a naval arms limitation agreement at the Washington Conference in February 1922. These measures, American policymakers maintained, would restore balanced budgets in Europe, reduce inflation, and revive trade through market mechanisms without the necessity of "artificial schemes" such as those proposed for consideration at Genoa. Genoa they saw as a "political" conference, one at which Europeans were likely to try to impose sacrifices and obligations on the United States that would benefit neither America nor Europe. To the Americans the Genoa project looked like a British scheme to get other countries to finance Russian purchases of British machinery.

The NKID thwarted the investment consortium. Chicherin summarized the Soviet attitude toward it when he called it "an international capitalist front for the exploitation of Russia." He also devised the strategy for destroying it—detach Germany from the consortium by intimidating Berlin. In a series of negotiations conducted from October 1921 to January 1922, Soviet negotiators threatened to cancel orders for German manufactures unless German-Soviet economic relations were expanded; at the same time, they held out the prospect of large purchases should orders be forthcoming.[17] Moscow's primary weapon in the negotiations was the threat to reach a separate agreement with France. In a series of articles in *Pravda* and *Die Rote Fahne*, Karl Radek, the Bolshevik expert on German affairs, stated that if Germany did not abandon the consortium idea, Russia would enter into an alliance with France, recognize the Versailles Treaty, claim reparations from Germany under Article 116 of the treaty, and use the proceeds to settle the tsarist debt.[18] These threats gained some credibility from Moscow's announced willingness to make payments on the tsarist debt and by the start of negotiations between Russia and France in Moscow in October. In Berlin formal discussions between a Russian delegation led by Radek and Krasin and a German delegation consisting of Rathenau, Chancellor Joseph Wirth (1921–22), State Secretary Ago von Maltzan of the Foreign Ministry, Stinnes, and Deutsch commenced in January 1922. On the 25th, the Soviets set forth their opposition to the consortium; the next day Wirth told the Reichstag that the German government opposed any policy that would treat Soviet Russia like a colony.

Potentially, France had much to gain from the Genoa project. Germany might be able to pay reparations to the French government out of the proceeds of its trade with Russia; Soviet finances might be better able to sustain debt payments to France if the Russian economy were reintegrated into European trade patterns; and an international consortium would preclude independent economic ventures in Russia by Germany. However, French policy was, as the expert on the topic has stated, "poorly coordinated and hesitatingly implemented."[19] Officials in the ministries of Trade and Finance wanted to bypass the multilateral preparations for the Genoa Conference in favor of reestablishing the bilateral economic relations France had maintained with Russia before the war. At the same time, however, Jacques Seydoux at the Ministry of Foreign Affairs drafted a plan to implement the consortium project. According to his plan, France, Britain, and Belgium together would agree to divide the Russian market geographically into separate areas of enterprise before discussing the consortium idea with the Germans. (France would get the Donets Basin and the Ukraine.) Meanwhile, Raymond Poincaré, who became premier in January 1922, held out for a global financial solution within the context of multilateral negotiations. He made that solution difficult, however, by insisting as a matter of principle that the issues of private debts, war debts, and new credits be resolved before diplomatic recognition of any sort was granted the Soviet government and that discussion of reparations, disarmament, and schemes to supplant the League of Nations be excluded from the agenda.

Lloyd George and his advisers did not represent a political consensus in London. Lord Curzon and Winston Churchill, foreign secretary and colonial secretary respectively, were intransigent and outspoken opponents of the Soviet regime, and the two of them led the British cabinet to adopt a position that prevented the prime minister from granting diplomatic recognition to the Soviet government unconditionally or unilaterally, that is, independently of France, and then only at the level at which chargés d'affaires would be exchanged. Representation at the full ambassadorial level, they insisted, must await a probationary period, during which the Soviet leadership would be required to demonstrate a sincere willingness to fulfill the terms of whatever agreements they concluded.[20]

Thus, because of the preconference positions adopted in Washington, Moscow, Paris, and London, the basis for a comprehensive postwar settlement leading to the political stabilization and economic reconstruction of Europe was undermined thoroughly even before the Genoa Conference began. For this reason, much of the conference centered on the negotiation of a more narrow and limited East-West settlement involving Russian debts, diplomatic recognition, and possible Western assistance to Soviet reconstruction. However, no agreement was reached on this more narrow range of issues either, and the question of assistance was never discussed formally. Why not?

The best way to comprehend the lack of agreement on debts, credits, and recognition at Genoa, I think, is by introducing the concept of a "hypothetically most feasible postwar/postrevolution East-West settlement." By considering what the most feasible settlement would have looked like, and by reconstructing the positions taken by the major powers at the conference on the issues most crucial to its successful conclusion, we can understand why no agreement was reached between Russia and the Allied powers. Moreover, we will be able to discover what real possibilities for a settlement existed in 1921–22 and to discern the significance of the abortive détente of those years for the condition of East-West relations during the years after the World War and the Russian Revolution.

The principles underlying the settlement with the greatest potential for acceptance can be discerned through an analysis both of the very complex negotiations that led to the Genoa Conference and of the proposals made by each side at the conference itself.[21] The principles that emerge from that analysis were as follows: The Russian war debt, incurred by the tsarist and provisional governments, would be recognized in principle only. It would be substantially reduced, and Russia's creditors would grant a moratorium on both capital and interest until all the nations involved, including the United States, settled the entire question of the intergovernmental indebtedness incurred as the result of the war. The prewar tsarist debt would be assumed by the Soviet regime; the capitalist states would generate substantial long-term loans for the benefit of Soviet Russia; and some portion of the interest paid on those loans would offset payments on the tsarist debt. The Soviet government would relinquish its demand for compensation for damage done by the Allied powers during the Civil War. Foreign-owned property nationalized during the revolution would not be restored, but the former owners would be given preferential rights to long-term concessions to it or, where that was not possible, compensation in the form of bonds or shares in mixed companies. This complex financial settlement would be dependent on diplomatic recognition. Mutual de jure recognition would be granted forthwith, but ambassadors would not be exchanged until later. The bilateral recognition agreements and the ten-year European nonaggression pact proposed by Lloyd George would include provisions forbidding the dissemination of revolutionary propaganda by the Soviet regime.

A postrevolutionary settlement between Soviet Russia and the capitalist powers of Europe based on these principles could and did win approval from those who were most favorable to restoring an integrated international economy, for instance, exporters and investors in Britain and Germany and the more convinced integrationists among the Bolshevik leadership. Most strongly opposed to it, on the other hand, were debt holders and die-hard anti-Communists in Europe and ideological noncompromisers in Moscow. Moreover, a settlement such as this was not acceptable to all the governments involved, nor was it fully acceptable to any one of them. Belgian investors were unwilling to accept long-term concessions as compensation for their nationalized private property and insisted on a full restoration of ownership rights. Owing to their recent experience with Russian bonds, French property owners resisted accepting them as compensation for their losses. Lenin categorically refused to restore nationalized property because the exploitation of industrial property by foreign capitalists represented a deviation from socialist development. The French delegation insisted on full recognition of both prewar and war debts and of debts assumed by both the tsarist and the provisional governments. Paris could do no less at a time when the United States was refusing to renegotiate the French war debt and the German government had announced that it would have difficulty making its next reparation payment. Meanwhile, the Soviet delegation refused on principle to recognize any debts incurred as a result of the imperialist war. And if prewar debts were to be paid and foreign property owners compensated, the Soviets insisted on what they regarded as equality and reciprocity—in other words, offers of specific loan agreements by the creditors. In response, the representatives of the creditor powers, who were very precise in discussing Russian obligations, made no concrete proposals regarding reconstruction loans or credits.

Their unwillingness to make such proposals is explained in part by the fact that throughout the conference the Allied powers held to two contradictory principles on which they wished to base the reestablishment of relations with Russia. Both were adopted before the conference opened. One principle—expressed in the Cannes Resolutions adopted by the Supreme Allied Council in January 1922—was that no country had the right to dictate to another regarding its form of property ownership, domestic economy, or government. This amounted to an implicit recognition of the principles of "peaceful coexistence" and equality of rights among nations. The other principle was that no assistance to the reconstruction of the Russian economy could be undertaken without assurances that foreigners would be able to conduct business in Russia "under conditions of freedom," a principle elaborated at length in the London Experts Report issued in March and written by expert delegates from Britain, France, Belgium, Italy, and Japan.[22] In the statement of the London experts, the term "conditions of freedom" encompassed freedom in Russia for the operations of Western entrepreneurs, for their property, and their capital, freedom to import and export, freedom of movement and communication, guarantees against arbitrary arrest, and freedom to hire and fire workers subject only to the regulations governing employment in effect in other countries. All these conditions were to be guaranteed by the institution of an impartial system of justice in Russia. From the Soviet point of view, the London Experts Report looked like an effort to reinstitute individualism and capitalism in Russia and to defeat collectivism and socialism. In the words of one conference memorandum of the Soviet delegation, it amounted to "the complete enslavement of the Russian working people by foreign capital."[23]

However, some members of the Soviet Foreign Affairs and Foreign

Trade commissariats were willing to make significant concessions in order to gain foreign loans and credits.[24] Most prominent among them were Krasin and Litvinov, the two men among the Bolshevik leadership most experienced in relations with the capitalist West. Krasin in particular was prepared to undertake a "realistic" economic foreign policy, that is, to recognize both war debts and the claims of the former owners of nationalized property. They were joined by Chicherin, who, even before the conference began, had pressed for recognition of all prewar debts, including not only those of the tsarist government but also those of municipal, railroad, and private corporations. Then, at the critical juncture of the Genoa Conference—following the disruption caused by the signing of the Treaty of Rapallo with Germany on 16 April—he joined Krasin and Litvinov in a willingness to acknowledge Russian *war* debts. The three of them thereby went a considerable distance toward accepting "the hypothetically most feasible East-West settlement"[25] and well beyond the directives given to the Soviet delegation by the Central Committee. They did so because they were pessimistic about the possibility of reconstructing the Russian economy without foreign assistance and because they were convinced that if a foreign reconstruction loan was to be secured, the delegation would have to depart from the preconference directives given to it. They informed Lenin of their position during the last week in April.

The delegation's appeal to Lenin was premised on the belief that Lloyd George's willingness to conclude agreements assuring Soviet security and providing assistance for Russian reconstruction constituted an opportunity that might not recur and therefore had to be seized. Lenin, however, was not disposed toward rushing into agreements with capitalist states. In early March, before the conference began, he had taken a public stand against any concessions to capitalism, either at home or abroad, that went beyond those taken up to the time of the October 1921 initiative.[26] He continued to do so during the conference itself, intervening decisively in the negotiations despite the fact that his health had deteriorated significantly since the last months of 1921. He tired easily, had trouble sleeping, and worked less well than previously. Direct oversight of the work of the Politburo was turned over to L. B. Kamenev. Then, on 23 April 1922, Lenin was operated on to remove the bullet that was lodged three millimeters from his carotid artery, the result of the attempt on his life in 1918.[27]

Emboldened by what he regarded as a new diplomatic situation following the dramatic conclusion of negotiations between Russia and Germany and the signing of the Treaty of Rapallo with Germany on 16 April, Lenin took a tough and inflexible negotiating stance in response to the appeal of the Soviet delegation: there could be no full recognition of Russian debts (even if only in principle), no assumption of private debts, no restoration of nationalized property to foreign capitalists, and no agreement of any kind unless the creditors offered an immediate loan on highly advantageous terms. Complaining of the "unspeakably shameful and *dangerous* vacillations of Chicherin and *Litvinov* (not to speak of Krasin)," he sought and received Politburo approval for his position and sent a series of reprimands and instructions to the Soviet delegation in late April and early May.[28] He warned the delegation against being coerced or panicked into a settlement, assured them that the Socialist Republic need not fear ultimatums, blockades, or isolation, stated that Soviet foreign policy would be based over the near term on the new relationship with Germany, and instructed them to break up the conference accordingly.

Why Was There No Postwar East-West Settlement?

It has been said that the Genoa project was designed for a world that had ceased to exist. It envisioned a Russia reintegrated into a Europe restored on the model of the pre-1914 world—"an affluent, stable continent led by six great powers in virtual balance that dominated the world with their arms, wealth, and culture."[29] An alternative interpretation finds the significance of Genoa not in its past but in its future, as the first instance of one of the two fundamental policy orientations adopted in Europe and America toward the USSR. One of these policy orientations was intransigence, the other détente.[30] The détente orientation assumed that Soviet foreign policy was a search for security rather than a drive for revolutionary expansion; it recognized the Soviet regime as sovereign and legitimate; it sought to promote economic exchange and the negotiated regulation of differences; and it strove to incorporate the USSR into arrangements for a durable and peaceful stability. In the terms of this latter interpretation, the Genoa project was part of the first of several détentes that occurred in relations between Russia and the West during the seven-decade history of the USSR. Both of these interpretations are insightful and valid.

I would add a third, namely, that the historical significance of the Genoa project and of the Genoa Conference is to be found in what they indicate about the condition of East-West relations as Soviet Russia entered world politics. Genoa clearly indicates the lack of consensus among the capitalist powers and factions of the bourgeoisie regarding the place of revolutionary Russia in the political stabilization and economic reconstruction of Europe.[31] The leaders of the governments of Britain and Italy were prepared to recognize the Soviet government and to "do business with the Russians." By doing so they hoped to revive trade and industry, to lower unemployment, to win the electoral support of both workers and employers, and to gain parliamentary backing both on the left and on the right. On the other hand, the largest proportion of the total Russian debt was held in France, much of it by 1.2 million small bond holder-voters while Belgian investors had ventured heavily into Russian natural resources, public utilities, and manufactures. Neither group had much new capital to invest in Russia or many goods to export. Together they defended the principle of debt payment and the rights of private property and insisted that the Soviet government fully acknowledge its international financial obligations before being granted diplomatic recognition. Remarkably, the contradictions within imperialism on which Leninist foreign relations were premised did not simply prevent the capitalist powers from uniting against Soviet Russia; they also prevented the capitalist powers from agreeing on a settlement with Soviet Russia.

Such conflicts within the capitalist camp constitute one major reason that no postrevolution, postwar settlement was concluded. Another reason is that statesmanship on both sides fell somewhere short of greatness. The policy positions adopted by the Genoa delegations of the major European powers were based on serious misjudgments—on an underestimation of the durability of the changes introduced by the October Revolution, on a lack of appreciation for the cohesion within the Soviet party/state leadership, and on an overestimation of their collective willingness to make large concessions to capitalism. Lloyd George's analysis of Soviet politics was typical of that of many Anglo-American liberals of the immediate postrevolutionary era. He believed that there were two contending political elements in Russia. One was fanatically Communist; the other was prepared to give up Communist principles in dealing with foreign governments and willing to respect private property, the rights of individuals, the security of investments, and the inviolability of debts. To the appeasement-minded Lloyd George this meant that one could negotiate with the Russians as they partially reinstated capitalism and that one could encourage what he called "the anti-communist elements in Russia" by assisting in the economic development of their country.[32]

Winston Churchill took the intransigent position.[33] He and other intransigents believed that the Soviet regime lacked popular support and legitimacy, that the economic principles on which it was based were both irrational and unworkable, and that Soviet politics and the Soviet economy were of dubious viability for these reasons. The economic situation was so serious, and the need for aid from Europe and America so desperate, they believed, that the Soviet leaders would change their policies and broaden their government in order to attain it. Until they did, the best strategy was not to enter into either diplomatic or economic relations with them. The

Bolsheviks were, after all, inherently aggressive and dishonest, had no respect for the norms of international conduct, and represented an immediate and serious threat to "civilized" interests.

Thus, at the center of the capitalist world, two contradictory approaches to relations with postrevolutionary Russia opposed each other. One of them suffered the Soviet regime and sought to profit from economic relations with it; the other aimed at isolating the regime in order to induce it either to change or to collapse. In capitalist Europe as well as socialist Russia, policies of "peaceful coexistence" coincided with those of ideological confrontation; "dual policies" were sustained in both camps. And it was this dialectic of détente and intransigence on both sides that first inspired the Genoa Conference and then cut the ground from beneath it.

Lenin's policy was also founded on misconceptions. He believed that the system of imperialist states—before it self-destructed from its inherent contradictions—would be forced by the objective requirements of capitalist development to revive the Russian economy and that the governments of the bourgeois states would make the political compromises necessary to do so. Therefore, the future held more opportunities for trade and loan agreements, and the capitalist powers, he believed, would only grow more eager to conclude them. As he said to the Eleventh Party Congress on the eve of Genoa, agreements would be reached "through Genoa, if the other parties to the negotiations are sufficiently shrewd and not too stubborn; bypassing Genoa if they take it into their heads to be stubborn. But we shall achieve our goal."[34] At the conclusion of the conference, Chicherin articulated this policy stance in diplomatic terms for the world press. "The system of conferences has failed for the time being," he stated. The Socialist Republic still needed "permanent economic relations with all countries"—trade, capital, and technology. But it was not desperate; "we can afford to wait."[35]

Viewed critically, the Lenin-Chicherin strategy of expectation seriously misjudged the eagerness of European banks to grant long-term credits to a regime unwilling to acknowledge *fully* the debts of the Russian past. It underestimated the political persistence of the intransigent conservatives in London. And it depreciated the capacity of European capitalism to survive its postwar crisis and to achieve stabilization. As it turned out, there would be no further opportunities for a comprehensive East-West settlement that incorporated promoting Soviet security and reconstruction once the opportunities present in the international situation of 1921–22 were exhausted.

Neither Lenin nor Chicherin was discouraged by the collapse of the Genoa Conference, however; both assumed that diplomatic and economic relations with the states of Europe could be established piecemeal. Indeed, in the Leninist theory of diplomacy, bilateral agreements best advanced Soviet interests; by negotiating with the capitalist powers individually, the Soviet government could more readily exploit the antagonisms among them. In April–May 1922 the prospects for bilateral agreements looked favorable. Chicherin and the Soviet delegation to the Genoa Conference succeeded in preventing the European powers from exploiting Soviet economic weakness, from forming a consortium/coalition for the reconstruction of the Russian economy, and from imposing upon Soviet Russia a settlement based on capitalist principles. Instead, they were able to exploit the disunity of the European states and conclude with one of them a separate agreement on debts and recognition—the treaty signed between Russia and Germany at Rapallo on 16 April.

Under the terms of the Rapallo Treaty, the Soviet government renounced all claims to war reparations from Germany, and the German government, for its part, acknowledged the validity and legality of the decrees that expropriated and nationalized German state and privately held assets on Russian soil. The two nations established full diplomatic relations and agreed to mutual most-favored-nation commercial relations. It was these highly favorable terms that encouraged Lenin to adopt a tough stance against concessions to the West European powers and to torpedo the Genoa Conference. The draft telegram he submitted to the Politburo on 9 May and then sent to the Soviet delegation at Genoa read in part: "Considering the significance of the Russo-German treaty . . . we are coming to the conclusion that the right thing for us to do is to start building our entire foreign policy so that for a period of no less than several months all and sundry is based solely on the Russo-German treaty, which shall be declared the one and only model to be departed from only and exclusively for the sake of big advantages. Try to prepare this in the form of a rupture."[36] Litvinov publicly announced this new Soviet position a few weeks later, after the breakdown of the Genoa follow-up conference at The Hague. The principle of collective agreement, he stated, would now give way to separate negotiations and bilateral settlements.[37]

The Treaty of Rapallo quickly took on a variety of meanings in Russia and Europe. In official statements of Soviet foreign policy, the NKID presented it as a model treaty, as an example of the basis on which relations between the Socialist Republic and the capitalist states were to be established.[38] The Executive Committee of the Communist International meanwhile made clear that normalizing relations between Berlin and Moscow did not preclude the advance of proletarian revolution in Germany. Karl Radek proclaimed Rapallo to be exactly what bourgeois Europe feared most: an alliance of Soviet Russia and Weimar Germany against the powers of the Western entente and against the Paris peace settlement. For the victors of the World War, the treaty took on almost mythical proportions. In 1922 and for decades thereafter, "Rapallo" denoted a Russo-German conspiracy against the peace made at Paris and a threat to the West, a menace that combined the industrial and organizational capabilities of the Germans with Russian demographic power and the ideological antagonism of the Soviet regime.[39] None of these contemporaneous views of the treaty suffices as historical explanation, however.

What is the significance of the Rapallo Treaty for the history of Soviet foreign relations? Historians subsequently came to regard it as *the* great Soviet foreign relations victory of the 1920s—whether achieved by diplomatic or revolutionary means—and a triumph for Chicherin, for the NKID, and for the conduct of foreign relations through normal channels. Rapallo did confirm, at least partially, the validity of the policy of peaceful coexistence, a policy based on the rationale that Soviet Russia had the right to organize its economic life on socialist principles within a capitalist system of nation states. And the treaty did end the threat posed by a possible international consortium to the Soviet foreign trade monopoly, and it precluded the capitalist powers from forming a united front of debt collectors against Russia. Moreover, the sanctity of intergovernmental indebtedness was undermined; the antagonisms between Germany and the Western entente were accentuated; and both ends were achieved without renouncing the possibility of future bilateral debt/loan agreements with the former Allied powers. Finally, Soviet Russia simultaneously dissociated itself from the "rapacious" and "imperialist" Versailles system and broke out of its complete diplomatic isolation from the world powers, what was in Bolshevik terminology called "capitalist encirclement."

In the context of international relations in 1921–22, Rapallo was indeed a great success for Soviet foreign relations. However, the treaty did not become the model on which relations between the USSR and the major capitalist powers were established. After 1922 the NKID continued to strive for full diplomatic recognition on the Rapallo model, for trade agreements, and for long-term reconstruction loans, and to attain these ends without compensating the owners of nationalized property and without agreeing to make payments on *war* debts. But as we shall see, although Britain, Italy, and France did recognize the Soviet regime in 1924, subsequent negotiations did not get beyond the impasse reached in 1922. The USSR never paid any of the debts of the Russian past, and during the NEP period only Germany and Austria made significant long-term loans to Russia. What Euro-American technology was imported for the industrial development of

Russia was largely acquired on a pay-as-you-go basis or by means of short-term credits. Rapallo had no sequel, and neither did Genoa. There was no comprehensive East-West settlement of postrevolution, postwar international relations. When Germany and the victors of the World War met at the Hague Conference in 1929–30 to arrange what was called at the time "the final liquidation of the war," the USSR was not present. Russia and the West would not meet at another European megaconference until the Helsinki Conference convened fifty years later.

Russia and the West after 1922

The Genoa Conference has provided historical scholarship with a unique glimpse into how Soviet foreign policy was formulated in the 1920s. Less is known about policy making in the period that followed, particularly about the direction the party leadership may have given to the NKID. In late May 1922, Lenin suffered the first of a series of strokes. His health deteriorated severely and his speech was impaired. By October–November he had recovered sufficiently to participate in the preparations for the Lausanne Conference. This was his last direct involvement in foreign affairs, however. A second stroke in December left his right side paralyzed and rendered him incapable of writing. After a third stroke in March 1923 he was completely unable to participate in political decision making of any kind. He died in January 1924.[40]

It has been hypothesized that with Lenin's involuntary withdrawal from foreign policy deliberation, and with the party leadership involved in a prolonged struggle to determine his successor or successors, the Politburo gave less direction to foreign affairs, and the NKID took on a greater degree of responsibility for policy preparation. It has not been possible to verify this hypothesis without access to Soviet archives, and the memoranda and memoirs of non-Soviets are not informative regarding relations between the Politburo and the NKID because neither Chicherin nor Litvinov discussed with foreign diplomats the content or the structure of foreign-policy decision making among the Bolsheviks. This is obviously a matter on which archival research can be of the greatest importance.

With the evidence available to them, non-Soviet scholars have defined the role played by the NKID in policy formation from the end of Lenin's direction of foreign affairs to the beginnings of Stalin's uncontested leadership in terms of a distinctive set of policies associated with Chicherin personally. Sometimes called the "Chicherin line," these policies rested on a set of Leninist assumptions which held that conflict among the imperialist powers (Britain, France, the United States, and Japan) was inevitable, that the Versailles settlement contained the seeds of its own destruction, that the German problem could not be solved within the Versailles system, and that Europe was in the throes of a postwar crisis that would directly benefit both the international proletarian revolution and the security of the Soviet state. From these assumptions two foreign relations precepts devolved, namely, that the Socialist Republic was most secure when the capitalist powers were disunited and, consequently, that Soviet Russia was best off involved in, rather than isolated from, the system of capitalist international relations. For it was by entering world politics that Russia could exploit the contradictions among the capitalist states and thereby advance Soviet security interests and establish and maintain diplomatic and commercial relations with those powers on the most advantageous terms possible. It was in accordance with these precepts that Chicherin aligned Soviet Russia with Weimar Germany in a "special relationship," antagonized the British Empire, and condemned the Paris peace settlement and the League of Nations as tools of the victors of the World War for preserving bourgeois hegemony in Europe and imperialist rule in Asia. Chicherin's policies have been contrasted with those of his successor, Litvinov, who, as foreign affairs commissar during the 1930s, pursued a policy featuring improved relations with Britain and the United States, membership in the League of Nations, and treaties of mutual defense with France and Czechoslovakia—all measures directed at containing the German power Chicherin had courted.

Thus, much of the analysis of Soviet diplomacy during the twenty years between the two world wars has depended on placing Chicherin and Litvinov at opposite poles in the field of Soviet foreign relations. The analysis has been extended further with the hypothesis that, as deputy commissar from 1921 to 1930, Litvinov regarded Germany with deep suspicion, accepted the Rapallo policy only grudgingly, and harbored a design for reorienting Soviet foreign affairs. The foreign policy he is believed to have favored at this time resembled to a large extent the one he conducted beginning in 1934. It was a policy based not on the Rapallo relationship with Germany but on an Anglo-Soviet rapprochement, on improved relations with France, and on a conciliatory line toward the United States.[41] Remarkably, there is some evidence that Litvinov had begun to rethink the basic principles on which relations with Europe and America were based as early as 1925. In a public but little known speech made to a group of peasant administrators that year, he enunciated the concept that came to be known as "peace is indivisible." The purpose of Soviet diplomacy, he stated, was to conduct a struggle against all war, even against wars among bourgeois states, because, as the recent history of the twentieth century had demonstrated, a war between any two countries could develop into a general European war, and that war would undoubtedly involve Russia.[42]

Litvinov's pronouncement directly contradicts the doctrine of "peaceful coexistence" associated with Lenin and Chicherin. In the "peaceful coexistence" doctrine, the slogan asserting that the USSR led "the struggle for peace" was put forth as part of an effort to prevent the imperialist states from attacking the USSR while it was restoring the Russian economy following the Civil War and, later, while it was undertaking industrial development. In the "peace is indivisible" doctrine, "the struggle for peace" slogan was aimed both at preventing war among the capitalist powers and at preventing war between the capitalist and socialist camps. In both cases, "the struggle for peace" slogan was a way of propping up Soviet security in times of vulnerability.

However, the "peace is indivisible" version of Soviet foreign policy doctrine fundamentally challenged the Leninist concept of inevitable war. Lenin, and those who subsequently doctrinalized his views, maintained that international conflict was inherent in the highest and final stage of capitalism and asserted that war among the world powers was the ultimate contradiction of the imperialist system. The implications of the "peace is indivisible" doctrine, on the other hand, were that war among the bourgeois states and war with them were both preventable. In this way, Litvinov's 1925 pronouncement ran directly counter to the first principle of Leninist diplomacy by implying that the task of Soviet diplomacy was not to perpetuate the antagonisms among the capitalist states but rather to reduce them. Aggravating them would only intensify the insecurity of the young Soviet state by increasing the likelihood of a general and total war that would envelop Russia. Thus the "peaceful coexistence" and "peace is indivisible" doctrines each drew from the World War different conclusions for Soviet security. The former found confirmed in it the promise that the imperialist system from which socialism would emerge would inevitably destroy itself. The latter doctrine was at once less sanguine, regarding a future general European war as a direct and immediate threat to Soviet Russia, and more optimistic, asserting that peace could be constructed within the existing international system.

Although an analysis of Soviet foreign policy based on a Chicherin-Litvinov polarity is attractive, it remains somewhat problematic. First of all, the argument that Chicherin and then Litvinov were able to conduct foreign policies bearing their personal stamp depends heavily on the hypotheses—both as yet unconfirmed—that the collective leadership did not intervene decisively in foreign relations during the struggle to succeed Lenin, and that Stalin likewise avoided intervention during the years after 1930 except at certain crucial junctures. Moreover, the problem of linking separate policy conceptions to discrete personalities is complicated by what we know of the method by which the Soviets formulated and conducted foreign policy during the 1920s. In his biography of Litvinov, Z. S. Sheinis reports that during the period after 1922 "fundamental differences of opinion" emerged between Chicherin and Litvinov in the twice-weekly meetings of the NKID Collegium. Issues would be argued democratically, he states, and, if not resolved, whoever was in the minority—sometimes Litvinov, sometimes Chicherin—would have his objections recorded by the secretary and then address a letter to the Central Committee stating his views. The final decision would be made by the Politburo, and often the diplomat against whom the decision went would be assigned to execute the policy.[43]

Information such as this suggests that the NKID did not operate autonomously and that the post-Lenin party leadership played a greater role in determining foreign policy than has heretofore been assumed in some non-Soviet historical scholarship. On the other hand, it indicates that the NKID was more than a mere front for the Politburo and that Chicherin was not simply the executor of its commands, as assumed by other non-Soviet scholars. At the same time, the method by which policy was formulated and conducted renders much more difficult any effort to trace the origins of policy to a single individual. This is particularly so in that Soviet diplomats did not discuss their policy differences with representatives of foreign governments, and in that Litvinov, the probable dissenter in many cases, placed great importance on confidentiality.[44] Whatever policy differences there may have been between Chicherin and Litvinov will most likely be defined only through access to the minutes kept by the secretary to the NKID Collegium and the correspondence of the Central Committee.

On the other hand, the personal rivalry and mutual antipathy that existed between the two men is well documented, and the contrast between them in working style, personal manner, and political background was readily apparent at the time. Chicherin was raised in an aristocratic and pietistic family in which he and his sister were required by their parents to say grace in English at each meal.[45] He was educated at St. Petersburg University and entered the service of the tsar in the Foreign Ministry's Department of Archives in 1898. There he wrote a study of Aleksandr Gorchakov, the Russian foreign minister (1856–83) under whom his father, also a career diplomat, had served. When Trotsky's revolutionary appeal for peace failed in 1917 and it became necessary to negotiate a peace treaty with the Germans, Lenin appointed Chicherin to the position of commissar for foreign affairs. He was well suited to the position, being a revolutionary socialist, a trained diplomat, and a man of considerable intellectual talent.[46] Chicherin had an excellent memory and could talk for hours on politics and history in perfect English, French, or German, as well as in Russian. Nevertheless, to Western European professional diplomats he seemed shy, nervous, and often ill at ease, and he gained notoriety for not keeping normal hours. He arose around 11:00 A.M., worked, lunched, napped, and then labored until early in the morning in his apartment at the Foreign Commissariat building. To relax he played the music of Mozart on the piano next to his study. He also played to celebrate. When he learned in October 1922 that Japanese troops had evacuated Siberia, meaning that the last of the forces of foreign intervention had left Russian soil, he rushed to his piano without saying a word and began playing at 4:00 in the morning.[47]

By contrast, Litvinov grew up in all the uncertainty and insecurity of life in the Jewish pale of tsarist Russia at the end of the nineteenth century. He spent eight years in the Bolshevik underground and then ten years in England before returning to Russia in 1917 to continue his service to the revolution. He was appointed deputy commissar for foreign affairs in 1921, with Europe and America as his special responsibility. In his diplomatic work Litvinov was precise, orderly, methodical, and punctual. He arrived each morning at the same time, read the incoming correspondence from the missions abroad, and then received colleagues and visitors, once again at the same time each day. He worked at night only under unusual circumstances, spending that time with his family.

In the years after 1922, Chicherin and Litvinov, along with Krasin and Christian Rakovskii, negotiated postrevolutionary Russia's entrance into world politics without in turn recognizing the legitimacy of the capitalist world system or agreeing to pay any of the debts of previous Russian regimes. To this project Chicherin contributed a rhetoric of Soviet respectability and international morality which convinced a significant segment of world opinion that Soviet foreign policy was progressive and humanitarian, that bourgeois diplomacy was hypocritical, and that capitalist foreign relations were laden with dangers to world peace. Litvinov meanwhile contributed his organizational skills, his exceptional talents as a negotiator, and what Anastas Mikoian described as his "knack for winning the hearts of Western statesmen."[48]

5 Soviet Russia and the British Empire

Commerce and the "Curzon Ultimatum"

In explaining the Bolshevik grand strategy for internationalizing the October Revolution, a favorite device of Western scholarship has been what might be called "the East-West alternation thesis." It can be stated as follows: Those who made the Russian Revolution turned to Asia as they lost confidence in revolution in Europe. After the defeat of proletarian revolutions on the Continent in 1919, the Bolsheviks, switching targets 180 degrees, promoted anticolonial rebellions in Asia. Lenin's theses on the colonial question at the Second Comintern Congress, the convocation of the Baku Congress of the Peoples of the East, and revolutionary involvement in Islamic Asia followed. Later, after the abortive 1923 revolution in Germany, an increasingly bolshevized Comintern turned eastward a second time and channeled resources toward China. In both instances the revolution in Asia was supported to redress an unfavorable correlation of forces in Europe. Promoting revolution in "the East" compensated strategically for defeats in "the West."

A different pattern of events, perceptions, policies, and strategies is presented in this study. During the initial phase of "world revolution" in Europe (November 1918–August 1919), the common assumptions regarding proletarian insurrection held by Lenin, Trotsky, and Zinoviev in 1917 were first confirmed and then contradicted. In the second phase (April–October 1920), the victories of the Red Army in its reconquest of the borderlands of the former Tsarist Empire in Central Asia, Transcaucasia, and Eastern Europe provided the basis for establishing and protecting revolutionary regimes in Bukhara, Persia, and, prospectively, Poland. In the third phase (October 1920–May 1921), the center of revolutionary initiative shifted to the ECCI and its Small Bureau, which authorized operations to be conducted by trained cadres in India and Germany. Heavy opposition and disappointing results in both instances seem to have led to a more institutionalized and easily controlled mode of internationalizing revolution, one that utilized the apparatus of Soviet diplomatic missions in places like Tehran and Kabul, not always with the approval of the NKID in Moscow or of the *polpred* on the scene. Initiatives along these lines on the southern rim of the socialist republics evoked the "Curzon ultimatum" in May 1923. The acquiescence of the Soviet government to this ultimatum did not mark the end of support for "world revolution" in either Asia or Europe, however. In the summer of that year, projects were conceived (presumably in the Politburo and the ECCI) that culminated in an abortive revolution in Germany in November and in the dispatch of political and military advisers to the nationalist revolutionary movement in China at almost the same time. What seems most remarkable about the pattern of revolutionary insurrection during the five years from 1918 to 1923 is not the alternation of attention between Europe and Asia but the simultaneity of advance, withdrawal, and advance in both regions.

The British counteraction against Soviet/Comintern revolutionary activity in Islamic Asia that culminated in the Curzon ultimatum was formulated first in the spring of 1920, at the time British forces were withdrawn from the Caspian and northern Persia. The policy on which the government settled at that time would constitute the primary counterrevolutionary strategy of the British government for the next seven years. It was to tie diplomatic and commercial relations to the cessation of revolutionary activity. On the eve of the arrival of a Russian trade delegation in May, the Cabinet agreed that the pending trade negotiations would be an occasion "to effect an all-round settlement which would include the East." It was time to drive "a good bargain," Lord Curzon thought. The Soviet government was willing to "pay almost any price for the assistance which we . . . are in a position to give," and that price, he recommended, was best "paid in a cessation of Bolshevik hostility in parts of the world important to us."[1]

Revolution in Asia became an integral part of the negotiations that led to the conclusion of the Anglo-Soviet Trade Agreement in March 1921.[2] The opening phase of these negotiations coincided with the meeting of the Second Comintern Congress, and the attention given to Asia in CI grand strategy did not go unnoticed at the Foreign Office's listening post at the British embassy in Copenhagen. It reported that "a general revolt in the East next autumn" was being planned in order to "hurry up the World Revolution, for which the chiefs of Soviet Russia have still great hopes."[3] From the first meeting between the two trade delegations in London until the day the treaty was signed almost ten months later, British negotiators—Lloyd George, Lord Curzon, and Sir Robert Horne, president of the Board of Trade (1920–21)—repeatedly charged Soviet Russia with activities hostile to Britain, first in Transcaucasia and Asia Minor and then in Persia, Afghanistan, and India. As evidence of these activities, Curzon specified, in notes dispatched to Moscow in October, "a revolutionary conference of Asiatic peoples at Baku," which was "clearly directed against British interests," and a school at Tashkent that was organizing forces for an attack on them.[4] The preamble to the trade agreement signed in London stated that both parties would refrain "from conducting outside its own borders any official propaganda direct or indirect against the institutions of the British Empire or the Russian Soviet Republic respectively."[5] And a letter from London to Moscow that accompanied it listed the conditions on which continued Anglo-Russian commerce depended. All pertained to revolutionary agitation and propaganda in Afghanistan and India. Among the items specified in the letter were Roy's school in Tashkent, "a forward base for work in India," the money, ammunition, and airplanes provided to the government in Kabul, and plans to establish consulates in eastern Afghanistan adjacent to the North-West Frontier Province.[6]

The trade agreement negotiations raise interesting questions. Why were the Bolsheviks willing to negotiate the end of support for revolutionary operations in Asia at the very moment the Communist International was initially developing an Asian strategy and the ECCI was beginning to make it operational? Why was the British government willing to grant trading rights to a country that was intent on bringing revolution to the heart of the Empire? How did they know Soviet/Comintern revolutionary activities in Afghanistan and India in such full detail? The answers to these questions are to be found in a consideration of Anglo-Soviet relations in the years 1921–1923.

The policy adopted by the government of Great Britain toward Soviet Russia was influenced from two directions. Lloyd George believed that the way to alleviate postwar unemployment in England was through the restoration of prewar world trade patterns, and the orders placed by Krasin with British factories were crucial to his hopes. At one point in the trade treaty negotiations, the only textile mills in Yorkshire working full-time were those with Russian contracts. Krasin was able to threaten Horne with a cancellation of these contracts should negotiations fail, and he did so.[7] On the other hand, Curzon was obsessed with the Russian threat to the British Empire in Asia, and he and Churchill would agree to a trade treaty only as a way of ending revolutionary activity there. Therefore the foreign policy on which the Lloyd George government resolved was one that deployed a counterrevolutionary strategy combining both détente and intransigence and promoting both foreign trade and imperial security.

To counteract what was referred to in Cabinet minutes as "Russian hostility and anti-British propaganda in Afghanistan and elsewhere,"[8] the Foreign Office drew up a list of complaints that the British representative in Moscow delivered to Chicherin on 7 September 1921. The Soviet government was not threatened with cancellation of the trade agreement, something the Cabinet agreed "should at this stage be held in reserve." However, the note did demand that the complaints listed be remedied forthwith. The most serious complaints were directed at the Soviet-Afghan treaty concluded the previous February, and specifically at the provision for consulates in eastern Afghanistan, which appeared to be intended, the note stated, as "prospective centers of propaganda." The present aim of Soviet policy in Asia, the note concluded, was to form a "powerful united Muslim movement which would deal a final blow against the power of capital" by destroying the colonial base on which it was believed to rest.[9] However, although the Foreign Office rightly recognized the purposes of Soviet policy, many of the particulars of the charges leveled were incorrect, half correct, or could not be substantiated. For this, the organization of the British intelligence services was at fault.

During the years 1920–1927 British intelligence was able to intercept and decode much of the diplomatic traffic of the government in Moscow with its posts in London and the Middle East. The Foreign Office paid close attention to these intercepts and eventually took over direct responsibility for the activities of the organization that provided them, the Government Code and Cipher School. "GC & CS," as it was called, had in its employ one of the leading cryptanalysts of tsarist Russia, and intelligence from decoded Soviet diplomatic correspondence began to flow in late May 1920, at the very time the Soviet trade delegation arrived in London.[10] Soon the Foreign Office learned on what issues Krasin was given latitude to negotiate and what Lenin thought of Lloyd George ("That swine Lloyd George has no scruples of shame in the way he deceives. Don't believe a word he says . . .").[11] The intercepts did much to discredit Chicherin at the Foreign Office during the trade negotiations. When he denied Soviet involvement in Bukhara, Persia, and Tashkent and on the northwestern frontier of India, intercepted messages conclusively proved otherwise. "With so colossal and finished a liar," Curzon wrote to the Cabinet, "it is useless to cope."[12]

Additional information came through other sources. Colonel F. M. Bailey, a daring intelligence officer, reported directly from Soviet Central Asia.[13] The intelligence bureau of the Home Office of the Government of India, known as the Delhi Intelligence Bureau (DIB), and headed by Colonel Cecil Kaye, kept track of Roy and other Indian revolutionaries through intercepts and an extensive network of informers. The Secret Intelligence Service (SIS) in London collected information on subversion in India through its post in Berlin.[14] The latter was the source of the information—much of it unreliable—that was used to substantiate the charges lodged in Moscow in September 1921. The NKID spotted the inaccuracies and informed the Foreign Office that its charges were "either unfounded or based on false information and forgeries."[15] A Foreign Office check confirmed that much of the information did indeed come from a tainted source—a publication issued by a White Russian intelligence organization in Berlin—and concluded that only two or three of the charges could be verified. Curzon was enraged. His only recourse with Moscow was to reaffirm his original charges feebly and to refuse to specify the source of his information.[16]

The Foreign Office protest was badly timed as well as badly informed. Soviet/Comintern-sponsored revolutionary activity in southwest Asia was dramatically cut back following the friendship treaties concluded with Persia and Afghanistan in February and the trade agreement signed in London in March. The treaty with Persia bound both parties to "strictly abstain from intervention in the internal affairs of the other," while the treaty with Afghanistan merely pledged respect for "mutual independence."[17] Accordingly, the Soviets closed down the Indian Military School in Tashkent and informed Indian revolutionaries that they would no longer receive funds previously allocated to them. In June, Chicherin instructed the Soviet representatives in Kabul and Tehran to "categorically avoid the fatal mistake of undertaking artificial attempts to plant communism" in Persia and Afghanistan and to maintain the "strictest non-interference in internal affairs."[18] The activities of the Council of Action and Propaganda based in Baku were curtailed, much to the dismay of its members who regarded the trade agreement as a "fatal blow" to their work.[19] In July, at Chicherin's request, the Politburo reined in the Communist Party of Azerbaijan—the spearhead of the Soviet revolution in northern Persia. Ordzhonikidze, the party chairman, was instructed "to in no instance violate the Soviet-Persian treaty and the directives of the Central Committee [of the RCP(B)] and the NKID." Similar instructions were issued to other party and Soviet organizations in Caucasia.[20]

British intelligence attributed this cutback in revolutionary activity to the famine and the financial difficulties in which Russia found itself following the Civil War. When they observed what seemed to be a resurgence of revolutionary activity in the summer of 1922, they correlated it with a new aggressive confidence given to Soviet foreign relations by the conclusion of the Rapallo agreement with Germany in April—apparently overlooking the impact of the better harvest in 1921. What GC & CS reported at this time was that large amounts of money and propaganda were being distributed to nationalist, anti-British movements in Persia and on the frontier of India through the Soviet missions in Tehran and Kabul.[21] This perceived renewal of revolutionary activity may have been the result of the newly acquired capability of GC & CS to intercept and decode telegrams between the NKID in Moscow and its posts abroad as well as of renewed revolutionary aggressiveness projected from Moscow.

In any case, the intelligence was accurate this time. The Kabul mission was dispensing weapons and ammunition, and in Tehran a major propaganda organization was operating out of the Soviet mission. The *polpred* there was Fedor Rothshtein, a prominent journalist and former editor of the *Manchester Guardian* and a secret Comintern emissary in Great Britain. The mission staff was unusually large; it directly financed several nationalist, anti-British newspapers; occasionally it sponsored pro-Soviet articles in anti-Western, clerical Islamic publications. During Rothstein's tour in Tehran (1920–22), the mission there also became a center of almost constant intrigue in Persian politics. Among its endeavors were efforts to organize a body of pro-Soviet opinion within the Persian merchant class and to prevent the growth of American economic influence over what were formerly Russian concessions in northern Persia.[22]

Of all the intelligence received at the Foreign Office, news of revolutionary activity directed at India and the North-West Frontier Province disturbed Curzon most. When the Lloyd George government fell in November 1922, and a Conservative Cabinet was installed with Andrew Bonar Law as prime minister, Curzon was able to operate with less constraint than before. Thereafter, in the absence of the détente-oriented Lloyd George, Curzon's own intransigent policy toward Russia played an increasingly significant role in British foreign relations. His aim in 1922–23 was to sever the relations with Russia into which Lloyd George had led the government. His policy found ready support from John D. Gregory, head of the Northern Division at the Foreign Office and its expert on Russian affairs, who weighed the tactical considerations. Gregory calculated that a break in relations with Russia was a weapon that could be used only once, and then only "if and when there is a reasonable chance of upsetting the Soviet government or at least dealing an effective blow to its stability." And when the Cabinet accepted the idea of sending an ultimatum to Moscow in the spring of 1923, Gregory called it a "great opportunity for us who would like a break anyhow . . . I cannot believe that we shall ever get so good a one again."[23]

What has generally been called "the Curzon ultimatum" was delivered to the NKID in Moscow on 8 May 1923.[24] It complained of a wide range of offenses to British interests and to British citizens. The most important of them were termed the "pernicious activities" conducted by Soviet authorities in Asia—the financial support given to revolutionary anti-British movements channeled through the diplomatic missions in Tehran and Kabul and the infiltration into India of revolutionaries trained in Tashkent and Moscow. Unless these and the other actions were apologized for and repudiated, Curzon's ultimatum stated, unless those responsible for them were "disowned and recalled," and unless the terms of the note were "fully and unconditionally complied with" in ten days, the Anglo-Soviet Trade Agreement would be terminated and British representatives in Moscow would be withdrawn. To substantiate the charges contained in the note, the Foreign Office relied exclusively on GC & CS decodes of intercepted diplomatic correspondence. The ultimatum made repeated and specific reference to them, although to do so risked revealing to the Soviet government the sources of British intelligence.[25]

The Foreign Office apparently took the NKID by surprise, and the in-house reaction was one of outrage. Litvinov found the ultimatum generally offensive. Chicherin objected particularly to the demand for the recall of the Soviet representatives in Afghanistan and Persia[26]—Raskolnikov at Kabul and Boris Shumiatskii, who had played an important role in organizing the Comintern Secretariat for the Far East in Irkutsk and attended the Third Comintern Congress in 1921 as a delegate, and then replaced Rothstein in Tehran in 1922. Nevertheless, it was the skill of Soviet diplomacy that made it impossible for the British Cabinet to hold to the demand for unconditional compliance within ten days, and its skill that succeeded in removing the element of ultimatum from the situation, thereby preventing a break in Anglo-Soviet relations. The response transmitted by the NKID was prompt and conciliatory and contained a minimum of what Robert Hodgson, the British representative in Moscow, called "communist verbiage."[27] It appealed deliberately and directly to the most "reasonable" elements of British politics: Curzon's note was unnecessarily hostile; ultimata and threats were inappropriate to the situation; Anglo-Soviet trade benefited both countries; the matters at issue were insignificant when compared to the contribution that peaceful relations between Great Britain and Soviet Russia could make to the peace and prosperity of Europe.[28] Krasin, who had been in Moscow, returned to London, where he succeeded in getting the ten-day time limit lifted.[29] This gave to Soviet diplomacy the time and the opportunity needed to work.

Both the NKID and the Foreign Office recognized Soviet/Comintern support for revolutionary activities in Persia and Afghanistan as the crucial issue at stake. Narkomindel attempted to make this the topic of separate negotiations and suggested that Chicherin come to London to conduct them. The Foreign Office both rejected this proposal and advanced a definition of the term "propaganda" that extended its meaning from that contained in the 1921 trade agreement: The Soviet government was "not to support with funds or in any other form persons or bodies or agencies or institutions whose aim is to spread discontent or to foment rebellion in any part of the British Empire . . . and to impress upon its officers and officials the full and continuous observance of these conditions."[30] Given the firmness of London's position, the crisis was resolved only when Moscow gave way in notes dispatched on 4 and 9 June, in which they agreed both to the demands made in Curzon's ultimatum and to the expanded definition of propaganda.[31] Curzon claimed what he called "a considerable victory over the Soviet government";[32] Stanley Baldwin, who was appointed prime minister during the crisis, agreed, and so did the London press. But the outcome was a success for Russia too. The NKID's skillful, cautious, and conciliatory diplomacy thwarted the primary intention of Curzon and the Foreign Office—either to break off relations or to inflict a humiliating defeat on Soviet policy in Asia.

Authoritarian Modernization, Nationalist Revolution, and Socialist Internationalism

Despite the deliberations of the Second Comintern Congress, the rhetoric of Baku, and the plans made in the Small Bureau of the ECCI, those who made the October Revolution proved willing to bargain away support for revolutionary insurrection in Persia and India in order to establish and maintain normal relations with the leading nation of the capitalist world. Following the Curzon ultimatum, the NKID directed diplomatic personnel in Afghanistan to have nothing to do with revolutionary elements, and ordered embassy officers in Persia to cease temporarily all political activities and work with secret agents.[33] Although the content of the discussions among the leadership of the RCP(B) is not known in any detail, these choices seem to have been made with consciousness and foresight. Trotsky, a consistent "Westerner" when it came to revolutionary grand strategy, stated most clearly the advantages to be gained from promoting and then restraining the forces of revolution in Asia. "A potential Soviet revolution in the East is now advantageous for us," he wrote to Chicherin six weeks before the Second Comintern Congress, "chiefly as a major item of diplomatic barter with England." He rejected the idea of military support for

Asian revolution and urged the NKID to "continue in every way to empha-
size through all available channels our readiness to come to an understanding with England with regard to the East."[34]

Chicherin, meanwhile, strongly opposed accepting any limitations on
Soviet/Comintern activity in Asia unless and until the problems of the
region were discussed and resolved at a full-scale Anglo-Soviet peace
conference. He was, however, unable to control the negotiations that led to
the conclusion of the trade agreement with England in March 1921. They
were in the hands of Krasin, who adopted a flexible stance. In July 1920 he
put the matter of a quid pro quo directly to Lloyd George: "If we promise
not to make trouble for you in the East, will you promise that France will
not make trouble for us [in Poland]?"[35] Lloyd George responded by rejecting the idea of a general Europe-Asia security trade-off. Curzon was
unwilling to delete the prohibition against propaganda from the agenda for
negotiation. The matter was settled by Lenin. In January 1921, faced with
the impending collapse of the Russian economy, he sided with Krasin and
"categorically insisted," as Chicherin wrote later, that the agreement be
concluded.[36] The Central Committee apparently gave Krasin full power to
conclude the negotiations and sign the treaty, and at the same time authorized Chicherin to attempt to modify the preamble to the agreement in
which the prohibition against propaganda was included. He succeeded in
deleting mention of Asia Minor and Persia from the text of the preamble,
and the British undertook a reciprocal promise not to interfere in the affairs
of the territories of the former Tsarist Empire. But Chicherin was by no
means satisfied. His major concern was that the British were gaining so
much from the treaty that they would have no incentive to proceed further
with political negotiations with Moscow. Consequently, he predicted in one
dispatch to Krasin, "our Eastern policy will suffer a heavy blow."[37] This did
not happen, for while Krasin negotiated in Europe, Chicherin laid the basis
for long-term Soviet relations in Asia by treaties with Persia, Afghanistan,
and Turkey.

Why then were the Bolsheviks willing to withdraw assistance for revolution among the Muslims of Asia in order to achieve a trade agreement
with England? First of all, the negotiations with London were expected to
yield full diplomatic recognition and a subsequent Anglo-Soviet political
conference and peace agreement—an agreement that would resettle the
international relations of southwest Asia so as to account for Soviet interests there—and win for the new Soviet state a place of legitimacy among
the great powers of Europe. The prospective rewards of relations with the
premier imperialist power were tempting enough to compensate for a
retreat from revolution in Islamic Asia, particularly in that both Lenin and

Krasin expected the commercial agreement to open the way to similar agreements with the more technologically advanced United States and Germany. And in fact, Germany and many other European states, with the exception of France, did sign commercial agreements with Soviet Russia in 1921.

Second, support for revolutionary activity in Central and southwest Asia became a strategic liability rather than an asset once the prospects for proletarian revolution in Europe faded and anti-Communist regimes were consolidated there. In the post–Civil War global political situation, insurrection, subversion, and propaganda on the southern perimeter of Soviet sovereignty could only attract the attention of the imperialist states and invite diplomatic, if not military, intervention. Such activities put at risk the foreign policy on which Soviet security was based, one aimed at the prevention of "capitalist encirclement" and the end of diplomatic and economic isolation.[38]

Third, the leadership of the RCP(B) was very hesitant about employing the considerable Muslim forces that had joined with the Red Army against the counterrevolution during the Civil War as a means of exporting revolution to the southern periphery of the Russian Federation. Those Muslim national communists within the RCP(B) who called upon the party to do so were removed from positions of influence within the party organization.[39] Hostility toward all religion, including Islam, and a fear and distrust of independent and uncontrollable local revolutionary movements, it has been suggested, were the major reasons for this unwillingness to deploy "the Islamic weapon." Very likely, the Russians among the party leadership understood that to use Soviet Muslims to promote national self-determination in Islamic Asia, even if it seriously dislocated the British Empire, would only encourage a Muslim desire for national self-determination within the reconquered Russian Empire.[40] Consequently, the revolutionary movement in Islamic Asia was brought increasingly under the control of the Euro-Russian leadership in Moscow and Petrograd. This control was constructed, beginning at the Second Comintern Congress and culminating at the Fourth, by defining the revolutionary movement in Asia as nationalist, as bourgeois-democratic, as anti-imperialist, and as the ally of the proletariat of Europe and Russia. While the Baku Congress was a dramatic expression of uncomplicated, anti-European Islamic nationalism, the Communist International under whose auspices it was convened remained the domain of Europeans and Russians who asserted the theoretical and strategic primacy of proletarian-based class struggle within advanced capitalist society.

Finally, Muslim culture was stronger and more impervious, and the

social structures of Central and southwest Asia more complex and hetero-
geneous, than was recognized by those who argued within the Comintern
for the immediate and integral internationalization of the October Revolution to Persia and India.[41] These conditions dimmed the prospects for a
rapid social revolution in Islamic Asia. From a historical perspective, therefore, the decision to restrict support for revolution there seems well taken.

The twelve-month period from the declaration of the Gilan Soviet Republic
in May 1920 to the withdrawal of Roy from Tashkent and the disbandment
of the Comintern's Central Asian Bureau in May 1921 was *the moment* of
international socialist revolution in Central and southwest Asia. Thereafter the expectation that the October Revolution might be continued in
these areas was decreasingly present as a factor either in Soviet foreign
relations or in Comintern affairs, and insurrection ceased to be the primary means of "anti-imperialist struggle" in the Middle East. Instead
Moscow supported neutralist-nationalist and modernizing regimes on the
southern perimeter of the Russian Federation, and did so through normal
relations conducted by the NKID. The drive for friendly relations with
stable neutralist regimes based on a mutual anti-imperialism was incorporated into the treaties concluded with Persia, Afghanistan, and Turkey in
February–March 1921.[42] Each of these agreements explicitly expressed
mutual solidarity against British imperialism. They also guaranteed the
right of self-determination to the peoples of Asia, precluded interference in
their internal affairs, and strictly forbade direct or indirect conduct of
revolutionary agitation or propaganda. Together the treaties established a
model of insurrection renunciation that was continued in the commercial
agreement signed in London during the same period. In Asia as in Europe
the price of normal and stable political and economic relations was the
promise to halt revolutionary activities.

In actuality, revolutionary socialism did not do well in the formally
independent or semidependent states of Central and southwest Asia and
the eastern Mediterranean.[43] In Afghanistan there was no Communist or
socialist party, and the Comintern made little effort to encourage one. Elsewhere, nationalist-minded authoritarian modernizers persecuted Communist parties while they railed against British imperialism. In Egypt, the
nationalist Wafd Party achieved power for the first time in January 1924
when a decisive electoral win resulted in a government led by Saad Zaghlul
Pasha. Although the Wafd stood for the independence of the Egyptian
economy from foreign domination, it represented landowner and em-
ployer interests domestically and was hostile to the labor movement and,
in particular, the Egyptian Communist Party. Within a month of coming to

power, Zaghlul took advantage of a series of strikes and factory occupations in Alexandria to forbid Communist gatherings, and by October he had decimated the party leadership by imprisoning some and forcing others into retirement. When the Comintern attempted to reconstitute the party Central Committee with foreigners—primarily Jews from Palestine—who were dispatched to Cairo for the purpose, the government arrested the entire CC membership. By 1928 the Egyptian Communist Party had disappeared as an organization and was represented at the Sixth Comintern Congress by the Communist Party of Palestine.[44]

In Persia, Colonel Reza Khan emerged as the ambitious and energetic commander of the Persian Cossack Brigade. Created in 1879 as a bodyguard for the shah, it was composed of 6,000 Persian troops and noncommissioned officers led by 237 Persian officers, 56 Russian officers, and 66 Russian noncoms. The Persian Cossacks, along with the British Indian South Persian Rifles, comprised the only effective military forces in the country. General William Edmund Ironside, commander of British forces in north Persia, manipulated the dismissal of the Russian commander of the Persian Cossacks, Colonel Petr Storroselskii, in October 1920, and in his place promoted Reza Khan.[45] Reza in turn engineered the dismissal of Russian military advisers in Tehran, led a successful coup d'état, and established himself as minister of war and commander in chief of the army the following February. The new government immediately concluded the treaty with Soviet Russia—and put down the Gilan revolution. Reza Khan, whom the British minister in Tehran called "an honest and capable officer without political ambitions,"[46] ousted the old elite associated with the Kadjar dynasty and reformed state finances. He distrusted the British, recognized the dangers of Russian power, and was intent on effecting greater central authority and national unity. The Soviet government assisted him by crushing the semiautonomous Talysh and Khalkhahli principalities on the Soviet border, by turning a blind eye to the repression of leftist movements in Persian Azerbaijan, and by lending direct assistance to Reza's suppression of pro-British Baludji tribal chiefs in southern Persia.[47] After being proclaimed shah in December 1925, Reza suppressed the independent press, disbanded independent trade unions, arrested 800 leading Communists, and forced the party organization underground.[48]

Mustafa Kemal Pasha formed his Turkish Nationalist Party in 1919 intent on rejecting the Treaty of Sèvres and preventing the partitioning of Anatolia among Greeks, Armenians, and Kurds. The first foreign policy action of his nationalist government was to send a high-ranking delegation to Moscow empowered to open relations with Soviet Russia. Kemal was unconcerned with the ideological differences between the two regimes. As he subsequently told members of the Turkish National Assembly, "Our impoverished and distressed Fatherland, besieged by enemies on all sides, need not care about the inner beliefs of the enemies of our enemies."[49] Under the terms of the April 1920 military agreement with Moscow, the Turkish army received light weapons and munitions, and three ships of the former Ottoman navy were armed in Russia. Communism in Turkey was another matter. When the Comintern founded the Communist Party of Turkey, Turkish authorities created their own police-sponsored "Zubatovite" communist party, assigned it an annual budget of 15,000 lires, and decreed that no person could call himself a Communist without registering in this party.[50] And in January 1921, Mustafa Subhi, the leader of the Communist Party of Turkey, and the entire membership of its Central Committee were drowned while in the hands of Turkish authorities as they were entering Turkey from Batum. No note of protest arrived from Moscow.

Turkey was the keystone of Chicherin's policy in southwest Asia. Lenin believed that the "mad oppression" (*beshenoe ugnetenie*) of Turkey by the Entente powers would promote favorable Soviet-Turkish relations despite the fact that the country was led by "Kadets, Octobrists, and nationalists,"[51] and Chicherin saw a nationalist Turkey as protection against Allied-sponsored interventionists showing up again on the Transcaucasian "underbelly" of the new Soviet republics.[52] (The armies of both Denikin and Wrangel had been supplied through the Straits and the Black Sea.) The Soviet-Turkish treaty of March 1921—the first treaty concluded by either country with another state that was a major player on the international scene—made the Straits the concern of the Black Sea powers. And Chicherin went to the Lausanne Conference (November 1922–July 1923) to gain international recognition for the principle that the Straits should be closed to all warships other than those of Turkey. There he found himself isolated and without bargaining power. The Turkish delegation agreed to a modified form of the Allied position, which demilitarized the Straits and put them under international control. Following the conference, Kemal was elected president of the newly founded Turkish Republic. He consolidated his rule, abolished the caliphate, and introduced reforms. He also banned Communist newspapers and demonstrations, suppressed the Communist-controlled labor federation, arrested more than three hundred members of the Turkish Communist Party, and banned it. It has been illegal ever since.

Observing these events from within the Communist International, the delegates of the Russian Communist Party—from Zinoviev and Radek to Bukharin and Stalin—insisted that "the anti-imperialist struggle" was advancing in Asia. The authoritarian modernizers there were objectively revolutionary, the RCP(B) leadership reported to both Comintern and party congresses. The nationalist reformers undermined both indigenous "feudalism" and global imperialism, even if their movements did not have a proletarian base or a socialist program. For this reason and because the time for emancipatory class struggle had not arrived in Asia, Asian Communists should continue to support movements of national liberation in "united anti-imperialist fronts."[53] This line was opposed by M. N. Roy, who argued that the revolutionary setbacks in Asia testified to the unreliability of the nationalist bourgeoisie there. His view was supported intermittently by delegates from the Persian, Turkish, and Chinese parties.[54] They did not prevail.

By the time of the Fifth Comintern Congress in June–July 1924, revolutionary strategy and tactics were premised on a different set of beliefs from those on which the CI was founded six years earlier, when it was thought that global revolution would be a single continuous process, taking place on many fronts at the same time, and that proletarian insurrections in Europe were only days or weeks from success. One of the new premises was that the forces of nationalist revolution arrayed against local "feudalism" and foreign imperialism were as important to "the world revolutionary process" as was conventional class struggle. Another was that differing national conditions would produce a succession of revolutions in separate countries rather than a unitary movement. Still another was that revolutionary breakthroughs would come where and when the power of the state was least strong and least able to suppress them, that is to say, in the least developed rather than in the most developed regions of the globe.[55] The remarkable implications of these strategic turnabouts are seen most vividly in the instructions issued by the ECCI to the various "sections" of the Communist International throughout the colonial and semidependent world in 1924–25.

The primacy of anti-imperialist nationalism at the expense of the conventional class struggle was obvious in the Comintern theses that sanctioned the support given by the Soviet government to authoritarian nationalists in Egypt, Turkey, and Persia while at the same time neither opposing nor criticizing the Communist-bashing of all three regimes. Elsewhere, long-standing religious, ethnic, and racial differences were to be submerged in the struggle against the British Empire. The Communist Party of Palestine was composed almost exclusively of Jewish Social Democratic émigrés from tsarist Russia. The ECCI instructed them to draw the Arab masses into their organization and to support Arab nationalists in the struggle against the British mandate over Palestine on the one hand and against bourgeois Zionism on the other. Jews and Arabs were to unite in a single movement aimed at an independent Palestine. Equally remarkable was the action taken by the Communist Party of South Africa. In the spirit of anti-imperialist national liberation, it decided to form a trade union that would incorporate whites, blacks, Coloreds, and Indians in a common struggle against British imperialism.[56]

China: Comintern and Guomindang

According to the "East-West alternation thesis," Soviet/Comintern involvement in China began as a reaction to the failure of the KPD to seize power in Germany in 1923. In fact, both the motivation and the timing of Soviet and Comintern participation in the Nationalist Revolution in China were more complex and more interesting than is suggested by the notion that revolution in Asia was a form of compensation for disappointments in Europe. Soviet involvement there is also of great historical significance, for it was in China that revolutionary Russia posed its most substantial challenge to the British Empire.

At the beginning of the twentieth century, China, like Russia, was a great land empire; again like Russia, it was not fully incorporated into the system of colonies and dependencies controlled by Europe and the United States. With its strong civilization and cultural traditions, China resisted European political control, and although the Chinese economy was penetrated by Euro-Americans, with its immense hinterland China was geographically unconquerable in a way that India and Africa were not. However, the Chinese state did come near collapse as the pressures for incorporation into a global system increased—just as did the Russian state.

Although the Chinese Revolution of 1911 preceded the upheaval of 1917 in Russia, the October Revolution did have a powerful demonstration effect for Chinese revolutionaries. It showed the possibility of escaping conquest and dismemberment by Europe and America, of transforming an empire and a national identity without relying on the old bureaucracy and state apparatus controlled by the traditional aristocracy, and of resisting Euro-American domination and control by means that were Westernized, modern, and nationally particular. By the beginning of the third decade of the twentieth century, Russia and China seemed to be in similar positions with respect to the world economy and geopolitics. Was this similarity not the basis for strong bonds between those who had made the Chinese Revolution and those who had made the one in Russia? Were they not "natural allies"? In June 1919, as the victors of the World War were settling their affairs with the defeated Central Powers in Paris, an editorial in *Izvestiia* recognized China as Soviet Russia's potential partner against

Great Britain, Europe, and America: "Revolutionary Russia will find in China a faithful ally in the struggle against the imperialist predators who are now busy in Versailles soaping the rope for the peoples of the East!"[57]

In the Bolshevik calculus of anti-imperialist resistance, world socialist revolution, and international power politics, China was an integral of great significance. European, Japanese, and American concessions and privileges in China were, along with British rule in India, the most crucial links in the postwar "imperialist chain." A revolution of national liberation expelling foreigners and their capital from China would disrupt the imperialist world system, critically wound the British Empire, make global politics safer for the new Soviet state, and constitute a first big step toward a revolution of class emancipation in Asia. Ultimately the vast population of what Lenin called "Russia, China, India, etc." guaranteed that the cause of global socialist revolution could not fail. Not surprisingly, the revolutionaries of Russia were eager to establish relations with China. They did so at three levels—with the government in Beijing, with the nascent Chinese Communist Party (CPC), and with the Guomindang (GMD), the revolutionary movement from Chinese national independence, state unity, and constitutional republicanism based in Guangzhou (Canton) and led by Dr. Sun Yat-sen.

The NKID made its first serious efforts to establish diplomatic relations with the Chinese government in Beijing in September 1920, as part of its diplomatic campaign to normalize relations with the states of Europe and Asia.[58] Both the incentives and the obstacles to regularizing relations between Russia and China were significant. The two countries shared a long border. The Russian-owned Chinese Eastern Railway (CER), which joined the Russian Maritime Provinces with central Siberia, traveled through northern Mongolia, making that area one of special interest to Moscow. Outer Mongolia, considered by Beijing to be Chinese territory, was occupied by the Red Army and governed by an autonomous and pro-Soviet Mongolian People's Republic. To consider these matters and to open negotiations toward a Sino-Soviet treaty of mutual recognition, Moscow dispatched a succession of diplomatic delegations. However, no significant progress was made until May 1924, when the Chinese government followed the lead taken by Great Britain, Italy, and much of the rest of the world and granted diplomatic recognition to the USSR. The Sino-Soviet treaty concluded at that time provided for mutual de jure recognition and special Russian privileges in China. The status of the Mongolian People's Republic was regularized as "an integral part of the Republic of China." The Soviet Union retained control of the Chinese Eastern Railway, but provision was made for China to repurchase it at a future date. The NKID took over the Russian embassy in Beijing, which until that time had been occupied by holdover representatives from the tsarist regime.

Credit for this success went to Lev Karakhan, who, after months of skillful diplomacy and an adept public relations campaign, concluded a settlement with the Chinese minister for foreign affairs and acting prime minister, V. K. Wellington Koo. Karakhan, the Soviet *polpred* in Beijing until 1926, was thirty-four years old at the time, a veteran revolutionary, and a former Russian and then Soviet deputy commissar of foreign affairs. Since the end of the Civil War he had played a prominent role in shaping Soviet policy in East Asia, and he was one of the strongest voices among the Bolsheviks in favor of turning the world revolutionary process eastward. Shortly before departing for Beijing in June 1923, he stated to Chicherin: "The arena of the internationalist imperialist struggle is moving from Europe, from the Atlantic, to the Pacific, and China is emerging as its focal point. The imperialist powers dread a unified, strong and independent China. Only the Soviet Union is ready to support China in her struggle for total independence."[59]

Meanwhile, the Communist International was instrumental in the formation of the Chinese Communist Party. In April 1920, even before the Second Comintern Congress, Grigori Voitinskii, a twenty-eight-year-old Civil War veteran and subsequently chief of the Comintern's Far Eastern Secretariat (1921–24), was dispatched to China along with a small number of comrades. There he worked among the radicalized students and aspiring Marxists of Shanghai, Beijing, Jinan, and Wuhan, spending the spring and summer informing them about the Bolshevik Revolution, conditions in Russia, and the revolutionary program of the Comintern. In each city he assisted in establishing party cells and in training cadres in party work. Marxism did not come to China from Russia; it had arrived via Japan, and Voitinskii did not create the CPC. The party was the result of multiple initiatives taken by Chinese revolutionary intellectuals both in China and in Europe.[60] However, as recent research indicates, Voitinskii was much more than a catalyst or a guide.[61] His ability to interpret the October Revolution in Chinese terms transformed radicals into Communists, and his considerable organizational skills and efforts started them on the road to forming a party on the model of the RCP(B).

The tactics of the "united anti-imperialist front"—as advanced by Lenin at the Second CI Congress in 1920 and worked out in the ECCI the following year—mandated that the Chinese Communist Party ally itself with the party of national independence and unity, the Guomindang, while keeping its organization separate and intact. This two-party alliance, which was expected to give CPC organizers access to the proletariat of south China, was rejected by Sun Yat-sen, however. In turn, the ECCI adopted what was called the "bloc within" strategy; members of the CPC were instructed to enlist as individual members in the GMD and to obey its rules. The chief Comintern representative in China personally accompanied Chen Duxiu, CPC party founder and its secretary general (1921–27), and other members of the party's Central Committee to be sworn into the GMD in a special ceremony presided over by Sun Yat-sen.[62]

That representative was H. Maring (Hendricus "Hank" Sneevliet), who devised the "bloc within" strategy. Maring was a Dutch citizen and a founding member of the Communist Party of Indonesia (1920). He attended the Second CI Congress, served as secretary of the Commission on the National and Colonial Question, and supported Lenin's position in opposition to that of M. N. Roy. Following the congress, he was dispatched to China as the Comintern delegate to the CPC. By July 1922, Maring had convinced the Presidium of the ECCI (including Zinoviev, Bukharin, Radek, Béla Kun, and Boris Souvarine) that the best revolutionary nationalist ally for the CPC was the GMD and that "bloc within" was the strategy to adopt. An ECCI missive, signed by Voitinskii (as chief of the Far Eastern Bureau of the Comintern at Irkutsk), instructed the CPC to work closely with Maring, who personally carried the instruction back to China along with a certificate signed by Radek providing him with cover as the East Asian correspondent for the *Communist International* and the *International Press Correspondence.*[63] To further strengthen Maring's position, the "bloc within" strategy was made public and official in two directives from the ECCI to the CPC in January and May 1923. These stated that the first item on the revolutionary agenda in China was a nationalist revolution against the imperialist powers and their internal "feudal" agents (principally the warlords), that the GMD was the only "serious nationalist-revolutionary group in China," and that the membership of the CPC was to work within the GMD and reform it for the purposes of proletarian revolution and agrarian revolt.[64]

The "bloc within" strategy was to prove highly controversial and a source of deep disagreement within both the CPC and the Communist International. The Third Congress of the CPC adopted it in June 1923 by a margin of only 21 to 16. It was widely unpopular, could be implemented only very slowly, and inspired continuing debate. Beginning in mid-1924, one element of the party represented by Chen Duxiu and Mao Zedong repeatedly and unsuccessfully petitioned the Comintern to approve a break with the GMD.[65] In opposition, Voitinskii, speaking for the ECCI, per-

sistently insisted that the "bloc within" be sustained. The strategy remained the rule of the CPC-GMD alliance until 1927, when the alliance
came to a violent end, and the "bloc within" strategy became the major
issue in the struggle between the United Opposition of Trotsky, Zinoviev,
and Radek on the one hand and the forces of Bukharin and Stalin on the
other.

The third Soviet presence in China was the money, the military training,
the advice, and the weapons the Russians provided to the nationalist movement—the Guomindang—based in Guangzhou. Sun Yat-sen, its founder
and leader, was one of the first revolutionaries in Asia to be attracted to the
Russian Revolution. As early as February 1918 he had sent a telegram of
congratulations to Lenin hailing the success of the Bolshevik Revolution
and urging him to continue the struggle against imperialism. He made
contact with the Comintern in 1920 and consulted with CI representatives—Voitinskii in autumn 1920, Maring in August–September 1921, and
S. A. Dalin in April–June 1922—during their missions to China. Sun's
representative to the Congress of the Working Peoples of the East, which
met in Moscow in January–February 1922, consulted with Chicherin and
Karakhan, two of the leading figures in the NKID most in favor of giving
Soviet foreign relations an Asian emphasis, and negotiated what was
probably an oral agreement granting the GMD de facto recognition by the
Comintern.[66]

There were nevertheless major impediments to Comintern-Guomin-
dang cooperation. Sun Yat-sen was wary of "peaceful coexistence," suspecting that it implied a retreat from the anti-imperialism which he believed united the Russian and Chinese revolutions. Chicherin reassured
him however: "Regardless of the future development of our political positions in Europe and elsewhere, our government will never abandon the
road of the most sincere, cordial, and faithful friendship and cooperation
with the Chinese people."[67] Moreover, Soviet policy toward the government of China posed difficulties. Moscow regarded the government in
Beijing as the official central state authority in China, and the NKID
persistently strove to conclude a treaty of mutual recognition with it. Sun
Yat-sen tried to derail these negotiations by inviting Karakhan to Guangzhou for talks. When his efforts failed, and the Moscow-Beijing treaty was
signed, a majority of the GMD membership reacted with hostility, and Sun
Yat-sen found it necessary to take serious steps to quell anti-Soviet opinion
in his movement. He dismissed one journal editor who published an article
critical of the treaty and he personally orchestrated a favorable official
response to the agreement: "Our party thinks that the Chinese people

should express its deepest gratitude to Russia for the Russian-Chinese treaty."[68]

Preliminary steps toward Comintern assistance to the Chinese Nationalist movement came at about the time that the ECCI publicly instructed the CPC membership to join the GMD. Ioffe, who was in Beijing attempting to negotiate a recognition agreement with the Chinese government, found his efforts obstructed by differences over the Russian presence in Manchuria and the future of Outer Mongolia. In January 1923 he traveled to Shanghai, where he held a series of meetings with Sun Yat-sen.[69] He found Dr. Sun eager for foreign assistance but disillusioned with the prospect of obtaining it from Europe or America. The two of them agreed that the purpose of the GMD was the independence and unity of China, and that neither Communism nor Soviet institutions should or could be introduced there. Sun Yat-sen informed Ioffe that he intended to reorganize the Guomindang, reform its army, and launch a military expedition against the Beijing regime.[70] Ioffe relayed his request for financial assistance and for military and political advisers to Moscow. After considerable debate in both the Politburo and the ECCI, the collective leadership (Lenin no longer participated in foreign-policy decision making) decided to aid the GMD, offering 2 million gold rubles, a limited number of weapons, and assistance in creating a training school at which the officer corps of a Chinese army of nationalist revolution would receive both military and political education.

On 21 June 1923—two weeks after the Soviet government had given way on the "Curzon ultimatum" and formally renounced support for revolution in Persia, Afghanistan, and India—five Russian army officers arrived in China. They were the first members of what would eventually become a Soviet/Comintern mission of more than 250 military and political advisers, many of them veterans of the Civil War and graduates of the Frunze Military Academy.[71] In south China the mission was led initially by General P. A. Pavlov and subsequently by General Vasilii Bliukher (code-named "Galen" in China), the former minister of war, military commander, and head of the Revolutionary Military Council of the Far Eastern Republic, who served through 1927.[72] The first significant efforts of the south China mission were directed at establishing and staffing a military academy at Whampoa (an island south of Guangzhou) and channeling Soviet financial support to it. (During its first year of operation, the USSR paid the entire costs of the academy.) Beginning in the spring of 1924, the officer corps of the National Revolutionary Army (NRA), the military wing of the Guomindang, was organized, trained, equipped, and politicized at Whampoa. The Political Training Department, headed intermittently between

1924 and 1926 by CPC organizer Zhou Enlei, directed the work of GMD party representatives who were appointed to each of the larger units of the army. By March 1926 there were 867 political workers in the NRA, an estimated 75 percent of whom were Communists or members of the left wing of the GMD. Their task was to identify the Communism of Lenin with the nationalism and republicanism of Sun Yat-sen. To that end, the walls of the academy were adorned with the slogans "Down with Feudalism!" "Let us defend the Three Principles!" and "The People's Welfare Means Communism!"[73]

The political reorganization of the Guomindang party was the assignment and the achievement of Mikhail Borodin (born Mikhail Markovich Grusenberg).[74] Borodin was a veteran revolutionary who had done underground work for the Communist International in Spain, Mexico (in collaboration with M. N. Roy), and the United States. His most recent mission before going to China had been in England, where as "George Brown" he guided the reorganization of the Communist Party of Great Britain. He arrived in Guangzhou in October 1923, just prior to the abortive Communist revolution in Germany. There he became, arguably, the most influential foreign adviser of all time.

When Borodin arrived, the Guomindang had no coherent organization, no clear revolutionary strategy, little popular support, and only a few thousand party members, very few of whom supported Sun Yat-sen's collaboration with Communism.[75] Throughout his stay in China, which lasted until 1927, Borodin worked without adequate information regarding the political situation within the GMD, without much opportunity for contact with the Chinese people, and without reliable communications with Moscow.[76] However, during his first seven weeks in Guangzhou, Borodin and Sun Yat-sen met regularly and frequently and the two of them reorganized the Guomindang along Leninist lines. Borodin personally drafted a new constitution for the GMD and modeled its organization on that of the RCP(B). At the First Party Congress in November, he saw to it that the resolution of the ECCI Presidium entitled "On the National Liberation Movement in China and the Guomindang Party" was incorporated in the party's manifesto. Communists were accepted as individual members of the Guomindang and three of them were elected to its Central Executive Committee. In 1923–24, Soviet advisers even arranged unofficial discussions between Dr. Sun and representatives of the Mongolian People's Revolutionary Party, talks that laid the basis for subsequent cooperation between Chinese and Mongolian revolutionaries during the Nationalist Revolution.[77]

Despite the introduction of Soviet military and political advisers into the

Chinese Nationalist movement in 1923 and the incipient Leninization of both the CPC and GMD that same year, China played no more than a minor role in the grand strategy of revolution formulated within the Communist International at this time.[78] The Comintern-sponsored Congress of the Working Peoples of the East in January–February 1922 did not signal a major revolutionary initiative in East Asia. When the tactics of the "united anti-imperialist front" were initially developed in the ECCI, China was not discussed. Even in 1923–24, Chinese affairs received only limited coverage in *Inprecor* and the *Communist International.*[79] And when the strategic problems of global revolution were debated at the Fifth Comintern Congress in June–July 1924, the "national question" (the failure of the October 1923 uprising in Germany) and the "Russian question" (the Opposition within the Russian Communist Party) all but pushed the "colonial question" (revolution in Asia) out of the discussion.[80] China was comparatively absent from the formulation of the theory and strategy of global revolution until the spring of 1925, with the beginnings of the Chinese Nationalist Revolution, and only in the summer of 1926 did the Politburo and the ECCI decide to support a revolutionary offensive in China. Then the Chinese situation came to occupy *the* place of prominence within the Comintern's strategic conception of world revolution, and China policy became a major factor in Soviet foreign relations. These matters are discussed in Chapter 8. Meanwhile, as will be seen next, the challenges of capitalist stabilization in Europe and America compelled the Soviet party/state elite to undertake an extensive reappraisal of the future of socialism in Russia, the place of the USSR in the world economy, and the direction of Soviet foreign policy.

6 The Challenges of Capitalist Stabilization

Soviet Security and the German Revolution

Of all the countries with which the USSR had revolutionary and diplomatic relations during the 1920s, it was in Germany that the clumsy dialectic of "peaceful coexistence" and "world revolution" appeared most prominently. In the thirty months following the Genoa Conference, Soviet-German relations were infused with the "spirit of Rapallo," a "community of fate" the two countries shared as states excluded from the European order created by the victors of the World War. Relations between Berlin and Moscow—political, economic, and military—were closer during this period than at any time in Soviet history.[1] They were nurtured by Count Ulrich von Brockdorff-Rantzau, formerly German foreign minister, who was dispatched to Moscow as ambassador from Berlin (1922–28) and who quickly developed a close working relationship with Chicherin.[2] Brockdorff was obsessed with the thought that politicians in Berlin might make the mistake of aligning Germany with England or commit some other diplomatic gaffe that would push the USSR into alliance with France. In his dispatches to Berlin, he continually and demonstratively insisted that nothing be done that might impair Germany's "special relationship" with the Soviet Union. However, because of the ideological differences separating the elites of the two countries, he did not expect German-Soviet relations to develop beyond a mutual hostility toward the postwar settlement. These relations were, he wrote to President Hindenburg in July 1926, "a marriage by force"; "a marriage by love was out of the question."[3]

Nikolai Krestinskii, the Soviet *polpred* in Germany, was a lawyer by training, a former member of the party's Central Committee and Politburo, and people's commissar for finance (1918–22). Before the revolution he had been both legal adviser to the Bolshevik faction in the Duma and a staff member of *Pravda*. His family was close to Lenin; his wife was the first doctor to examine and treat the leader in the Kremlin after the attempt on his life in 1918. Krestinskii was fluent in Latin as well as in modern European languages, and his memory was legendary. When Lenin failed to recall important information, he would say "you'd better ask Krestinskii." A man of strong convictions and exceptional courage, Krestinskii was the only defendant at the trial of the "right-Trotskyist bloc" in 1937 publicly to plead not guilty. He refused to state that he had been a spy and maintained that he always was and remained a Communist. The trial was disrupted for one day while Krestinskii was tortured severely; at the next session he nodded his assent to the guilty charge.[4] It was political, legal, and personal credentials such as these that Krestinskii brought to Germany in 1922. He was an appropriate choice because within the NKID, ties to Germany were considered vital, and Berlin was considered the most important post in the Soviet diplomatic service.

It was the post-Versailles geopolitical situation that made relations with Berlin crucial. Germany was situated in the center of Europe, separating Russia from the powers of Western Europe, juxtaposed to Poland, France's chief ally in Eastern Europe, and adjacent to the newly independent Baltic states bordering Russia to the northwest. For this reason it would have been difficult for the Allies to launch a second military intervention, or even to threaten military action against the Soviet Union, without German cooperation. Diplomatically, too, decisions made in Berlin determined what pressure the former Allied powers could apply to Moscow. To be sure, the Treaty of Rapallo ensured that no full capitalist coalition based on denying diplomatic recognition to the Soviet regime until the debts of the Russian past were acknowledged could be formed; nevertheless, Soviet diplomatic isolation diminished or increased as Berlin's relations with the victors of the World War fluctuated between antagonism and partial integration. Militarily, diplomatically, and commercially, also, German foreign policy determined whether the imperialist powers could form a constellation of anti-Soviet states in Europe—what the Bolsheviks called "capitalist encirclement."

At times, Soviet intentions toward Weimar Germany have been described as ideologically driven and depicted as an effort to isolate Germany from the assistance of Europe and America, thereby leaving it vulnerable to economic dislocation and revolutionary upheaval. At other times, Soviet-German relations have been described in the terminology of political realism, as based on a community of interest between those against whom the World War peace settlement was directed. In both explanations, Mos-

3. European USSR in 1923

cow's relations with Berlin after 1922 are represented as an effort to separate Germany from Western Europe and to form an exclusive Russo-German partnership. An alternative to both these explanations not only denies that the central intention of Russia's German policy in the 1920s was to preserve an exclusive relationship; it also rejects the notion that favorable relations with Germany were the primary goal of early Soviet diplomacy. It asserts instead that Soviet relations with Germany were regarded as a bridge to Europe.[5] Their primary purpose was to facilitate agreements with the other states and to gain entry into the association of world powers by serving as a model for relations with other capitalist states. Rather than being aimed at forming an exclusive relationship with Germany, Soviet policy at the time of the Genoa Conference was directed at forming a British-German-Soviet combination. In 1923 and again in 1927, it was aimed at making a German-French-Soviet combination, and then in 1928 at a German-American-Soviet understanding, and finally in 1931 at a five-power pact.

Such was the maximum goal of relations with Germany; the minimum goal was to prevent Germany from being absorbed into a coalition of European powers, one from which the USSR was excluded. Prior to the 1925 Locarno rapprochement between Germany and France and Britain, the minimal objective was a neutral Germany balanced between Russia and the West—if possible, with a tilt toward Moscow. After Locarno it was neutrality and balance—with a tilt toward the West, if necessary. To these ends the Russians employed two strategies. In Berlin, Soviet representatives promoted enmity toward the former entente by reminding the Germans of their defeat and by depicting France as an aggressive power capable of mobilizing Poland and its other client states in East-Central Europe against the USSR. In Paris and London, meanwhile, Soviet diplomats warned of the dangers of German militarism and revisionism.

The Soviet-German Rapallo relationship operated to greatest effect during the Ruhr crisis of 1923. When French and Belgian troops and engineers occupied the Ruhr district of Germany in January in an effort to enforce the reparations provisions of the Treaty of Versailles,[6] the NKID feared for German independence. Were France to gain strategic control of western Germany, Chicherin believed, the geopolitical conditions for a second war of intervention would be established. Moscow responded by warning Poland against using the Ruhr occupation as an opportunity to attack Germany from the east, and the NKID undertook a diplomatic offensive in Latvia, Lithuania, and Poland aimed at guaranteeing nonintervention in German affairs and at maintaining freedom of transit between the USSR and Central Europe.[7]

At the same time, the collective leadership decided that the crisis to which the Ruhr occupation had brought the German economy and the Weimar political system meant that the day of proletarian revolution in Germany was imminent. Meeting on 23 August, the Politburo decided to take the measures necessary to prepare for that event and to supervise it when it occurred.[8] With Lenin incapacitated, the collective leadership was led to a policy of insurrectionary initiative by the enthusiasm of Trotsky, a man with little actual experience in German affairs but with a strong theoretical sense of the interconnection between the Russian and German situations. Zinoviev supported the initiative, but apparently did so with more prudence than Trotsky showed, forecasting that the outbreak of revolution in Germany was a matter of months rather than of weeks. More cautiously, Stalin did not think that a German revolution would occur in 1923, and he doubted whether one could take place by the spring of 1924.

The opinion of Karl Radek played a key role. Although he did not sit on the Politburo, he attended the meeting as the German affairs expert among the Bolsheviks and the Comintern's chief tactician. He had surveyed the German situation firsthand the previous May, and he concluded that the preconditions for proletarian revolution—a massive German Communist Party (KPD) with mass support—did not yet exist. His solution to this problem, which he had proposed at the Third ECCI Plenum in June (with the support of Zinoviev), was a new strategy—a direct appeal to those elements of the lower-middle class that had been drawn to nationalist and fascist politics out of a sense of social despair and national humiliation.[9] It did not work; Communist speakers before nationalist audiences failed to attract many supporters. Radek therefore urged the KPD leadership to continue the "united front" strategy and warned them against premature insurrectionary action. However when asked to report on the German situation at the 23 August Politburo meeting, he reportedly gave an optimistic assessment. Perhaps he sensed the mood of Trotsky and Zinoviev, deferred to them, and gave a report that expressed their beliefs more than his own. A decision to instigate a revolution in Germany resulted.

By the end of September, plans formulated in the Politburo and the ECCI were put in place. The resistance of the cautious Heinrich Brandler, who was chairman of the KPD Central Committee (1921–23) and who complained that he was not "a German Lenin," was worn down. In a series of nighttime meetings in Moscow he succumbed to the enthusiasm of the experienced revolutionaries of Russia and to the criticism of the Left Opposition within the KPD Central Committee led by Ruth Fischer and Arkadi Maslow. According to the plans formulated in Moscow, the German Communist Party, led by Brandler, would form a coalition with the Social Democratic Party (SPD) and enter the government of Saxony. That government would, under the terms of a previous agreement between the two parties, organize the workers of Saxony into proletarian defense units designed to protect the state against fascist attack by arming what were presumed to be 50,000 to 60,000 workers eager for proletarian revolution.

Accordingly, a secret and illegal infrastructure was constructed. The proletarian defense units were formed under the supervision of József Unszlicht, deputy chairman of the GPU and a member of the Revolutionary Military Commission. Russian money and advisers were channeled through the diplomatic mission in Berlin. Weapons were shipped by cargo ship from Petrograd to Hamburg, where they were unloaded by Communist longshoremen and stored on wharves under their control. Radek was appointed head of a commission of four and sent to Germany to supervise the revolution. Larissa Reisner accompanied him and acted as courier and messenger between the Comintern delegation in Dresden and the KPD leadership in Berlin. Trotsky wanted to set a specific date for the uprising, 9 November, the anniversary of the revolution in Russia. Less commemoratively, the Politburo scheduled it for sometime during the six-week period of October through early November. Zinoviev activated the project in a telegram sent to the KPD Central Committee on 1 October.

From a historical perspective, it is evident that the Politburo majority that decided on a German insurrection in 1923, and the ECCI that engineered it, did so in an exercise of wishful thinking. Seduced by the prospect of "a German October," they mistook the Germany of 1923 for the Russia of 1917, and grasped at what looked to them like an opportunity to revive the momentum of proletarian revolution in Europe.[10] Not surprisingly, the revolution aborted. Before the German Communists could act, the commander of the local Reichswehr ordered the dissolution of the proletarian defense units, took control of the Saxon police, and moved army units into Dresden. Without consulting Radek, the KPD leadership called off the mass uprising in Saxony. It was unable, however, to prevent the party in Hamburg from acting. An uprising there was crushed by the police. In Moscow, Kuusinen, Piatnitskii, and Manuilskii sat up all night smoking and drinking coffee while they waited in vain for a telegram from Germany bringing news of the success of the insurrection.[11]

The failure of the "German October" was an event of importance in the seventy-four-year history of Soviet foreign relations. Six years after the revolution in Russia, it made evident, even to the most optimistic of Bolsheviks, that the prospects for successful proletarian insurrection in Europe were highly unfavorable—even in an industrialized capitalist state, and even in conditions of acute social and political crisis. The "stillborn revolution" in Germany confirmed the defensive stance for revolutionary strategy in Europe that had been adopted in 1920–21. Although revolution would be exported to the areas of East-Central Europe where it could be protected by Soviet armed forces in the years 1944–1948, the "German October" proved to be the last armed insurrection against any of the imperialist regimes. Never again would the leaders of the USSR risk their participation in the association of world powers by committing weapons and advisers to the overthrow of one of the major capitalist states.[12]

The Dawes Plan and the "Zinoviev Letter"

By early 1924, Soviet diplomacy appeared extremely successful. The policies of "peaceful coexistence," which were confirmed by the failure of the "German October," were reinforced further when the first of the former Allied powers granted diplomatic recognition to the USSR the following February and when the German government used diplomatic channels to become the first major capitalist power to issue a formal apology to the young Soviet state in May.[13] In Britain the Baldwin-Curzon-Churchill government met defeat in the general election, and England's first Labour government, led by Ramsay MacDonald, granted Moscow formal diplomatic recognition almost immediately upon coming to office.[14] Italy quickly followed; Mussolini had gone on record in November 1923 as favoring recognition without any counterdemand for debt payment.[15] Much of the rest of Europe followed in what E. H. Carr called "the year of recognitions,"[16] and in 1925, China, Japan, and several Latin American states acted also. Spain and the United States recognized the USSR in 1933, the states of the Balkan region in 1934, and Belgium in 1935.

The Labour Party before coming to office had been committed to recognition, but not to unconditional recognition. That was determined in negotiations between MacDonald and the most effective Soviet diplomat of the 1920s, Christian Rakovskii.[17] Prior to becoming diplomatic representative in London in 1923, Rakovskii had served as chairman of the Council of People's Commissars of the Ukraine, where he was a member of the party's Central Committee and of its Politburo. He was also a member of the Central Committee of the Russian Communist Party, a cofounder of the Communist International, and a delegate to the Second and Third Comintern congresses. The son of a prominent Bulgarian intellectual, Rakovskii had attended medical school in Geneva, where he became friends with the Plekhanov-Zasulich group of Russian Social Democrats even before Lenin did and also developed extensive connections among European socialists, including Friedrich Engels, Jean Jaurès, Karl Kautsky, and August Bebel. In manner and experience the most European of the Bolsheviks, Rakovskii spoke a dozen languages and became a prominent figure in Parisian leftist intellectual and artistic circles when he subsequently served as *polpred* in France from 1925 to 1927.

In France, pressure to recognize the USSR came from business groups that wanted access to the Russian market.[18] It was resisted by the strongly anti-Bolshevik president of the Republic, Alexandre Millerand, and by Premier Poincaré, who, while favoring trade with Russia, opposed recognition without full debt settlement. In May–June 1924 the *Cartel des gauches* defeated the *Bloc nationale* in general elections; the Poincaré government resigned, and Millerand was subsequently forced out of office. Edouard Herriot formed a government based on a Radical and Socialist coalition in the Chamber of Deputies in which he served as premier and foreign minister. Almost immediately he came under pressure from two conflicting sources.[19] On one side stood the representatives of the holders of the Russian debt and those whose property had been nationalized in the revolution, who met throughout the summer at the Quai d'Orsay to coordinate their claims against the Soviet government. On the other side stood a group of influential Radical and Socialist deputies and senators led by Anatole de Monzie, Henry de Jouvenel, and Louis Loucheur—politicians who were closely connected to business interests and who believed strongly that economic relations with the USSR could be the solution to France's pressing economic and financial problems. Herriot, who personally favored recognition, decided that the regulation of France's relations with Germany must take precedence over relations with Russia. He adopted this stance in a telegram to Chicherin in mid-July, and not until late October did his government recognize the USSR.

Paris and Moscow then exchanged diplomatic representation immediately. Krasin, the commissar for foreign trade, was dispatched to Paris, and Jean Herbette, an important Parisian journalist and an enthusiastic advocate of Franco-Russian friendship, went to Moscow, where he shook the hand of every member of the honor guard that attended his arrival, greeting each with "Bonjour, comrade!"[20] The British, however, postponed the exchange of ambassadors until subsequent agreements were reached, and in London and Moscow the governments of Russia and Britain were represented at the level of chargés d'affaires. Both the French and the British recognitions were de jure, and neither depended on prior settlement of Russian debts. Diplomatic recognition by the powers of European capitalism constituted a big step toward Russia's reentry into the association of major powers on Soviet terms. A wave of unmitigated optimism swept over the collective leadership. As early as June 1924, Stalin celebrated the international success of the USSR: "Instead of isolation of the Soviet Union, the result has been the isolation of the isolators, the resignations of Poincaré and Curzon."[21]

Rakovskii was chief Soviet negotiator at the Anglo-Soviet Conference that followed recognition and that began in April. By August the conference had produced a treaty composed of two documents.[22] One was a trade agreement extending the one concluded in 1921. The other established the basis on which negotiations on debts and loans, the most thorny issues in

Anglo-Soviet relations, were to be continued. The Soviet government agreed to pay prewar tsarist debts that had been contracted in foreign currencies and that were in the hands of British citizens prior to March 1921, and also to compensate British property owners for losses resulting from revolutionary nationalization. Specific claims would be negotiated between English bondholders and proprietors and the Soviet government. If these negotiations succeeded, the British government would then guarantee a loan to the USSR that would be floated by London banks.

Although MacDonald held the offices of both foreign secretary and prime minister, he took little responsibility for the negotiations and gave to them only intermittent and halfhearted support. Labour's Russia policy was conducted by Arthur Ponsonby, parliamentary under-secretary for foreign affairs, who strongly advocated the integration of the USSR into Europe on a basis of equality.[23] Ponsonby distrusted the Foreign Office, where opponents of expanded relations with Soviet Russia were strong, and he maintained close connections with E. D. Morel and the Union for Democratic Control, which spoke for those trade unionists and radical Labour backbenchers most committed to favorable relations with the USSR. Progress toward the treaty came largely as a result of the personal diplomacy conducted between the two chief negotiators, Ponsonby and Rakovskii, and when their negotiations came to the verge of breakdown, a group of radical backbenchers led by Morel and George Lansbury intervened to rescue them.

When the Anglo-Soviet Draft Treaty was agreed upon in principle, *Izvestiia* published a front-page article praising Rakovskii's qualities as a diplomat. Kamenev, a member of the ruling triumvirate (along with Stalin and Zinoviev), characterized the treaty as "a cornerstone in the development of the Soviet Union." Chicherin hailed it as a document of "tremendous" significance. "For the first time," he stated, "we have signed a final peace treaty regulating our relations with the most powerful state among the Great Powers." The agreement signified, he thought, "international recognition of the October Revolution as the basis of the Soviet state." Looking toward the future, Chicherin foresaw the "entry of the USSR and England upon an era of friendly relations" and what he subsequently termed "a general pacification in world relationships."[24]

Chicherin's expectations went unfulfilled. In late August–September 1924, Soviet foreign relations suffered two historic reversals. The first was the inception of a German rapprochement with the victors of the World War. The adoption of the Dawes Plan in August at a conference in London provisionally settled the issue of German reparations, liquidated the Ruhr occupation, and opened the door to an influx of foreign lending that tied the growth of the German economy to Anglo-American capital.[25] The Dawes Plan was one of a series of agreements by which Germany and the former Allies ended the victor-vanquished antagonisms of the immediate postwar period and reestablished their relations on the basis of mutual compromise and relative goodwill. Another step in rapprochement was taken at the September 1924 meeting of the League of Nations Assembly, at which MacDonald, without prior consultation with his government, and to the surprise of nearly everyone, dramatically proposed that Germany be invited to join the League. Herriot consented, and in December the German government committed itself in principle to joining. It did so without coordinating its move with the other prewar great power that had been excluded since the League's inception in 1919—its Rapallo partner, Soviet Russia.[26] As Chicherin viewed this rapprochement, Germany achieved a degree of internal economic and political stability, but did so at the cost of its economic and diplomatic independence.[27]

The second reversal resulted from what Chicherin called "the English crisis." After ten months in office, the first Labour government fell apart in October 1924 and then suffered a severe defeat in the elections that followed. In this shift in British politics, the rapprochement with the USSR was the chief issue. Lloyd George, who had concluded the first commercial agreement with Soviet Russia in 1921 and who had synthesized the Genoa scheme to reintegrate Russia into the community of great powers, saw in parliamentary ratification of the Anglo-Soviet Draft Treaty an issue by which Labour could be defeated and the Liberal Party called upon to form a government. Faced with this Liberal defection from the coalition on which his government was based, MacDonald responded by committing it more fully to ratification of the treaty. The government would have been defeated over this issue had not MacDonald chosen to call for a vote of confidence over "the Campbell affair."[28]

In the electoral campaign that followed, the détente with the USSR, the ratification of the Draft Treaty, the alleged subservience of the Labour Party leadership to left-wing, pro-Soviet backbenchers within the party, the charge that the Labour government was soft on Communism, a purported campaign of sedition conducted in Britain by the CPGB, and the supposed support given to it by the Comintern in Moscow were all focused into a full-scale Red Scare by the "Zinoviev letter." The latter was a document purportedly sent by Zinoviev, as president of the Presidium of the ECCI, to the Central Committee of the British Communist Party in London. The letter contained three statements. First, it was essential for the Labour Party, and for the British proletariat in general, to undertake a serious effort in favor of ratification of the Anglo-Soviet Draft Treaty and to counteract those reactionary elements of the British bourgeoisie who opposed settlement of the differences between the two countries. Second, a settlement would "assist in the revolutionizing of the international and British proletariat" and in extending and developing "the ideas of Leninism in England and the Colonies." Third, the CPGB was to establish cells in all units of the British army, in munitions factories, and in arms depots, which would form the nucleus of a British Red Army in time of civil strife. The letter was published in the anti-Communist *Daily Mail* four days before the parliamentary election, and the headlines above it read: "Civil War Plot by Socialists, Moscow Order to Our Reds, Great Plot Disclosed Yesterday." The "Zinoviev letter" alone did not decide the outcome of the election, but it did ensure that the victory of the Conservative Party, which had consistently taken an anti-Soviet stand, would be an overwhelming one.[29]

The authenticity of the "Zinoviev letter" was debated from the moment it appeared in print. Over the years, historical scholarship has put certain facts beyond dispute. As president of the ECCI, Zinoviev did send messages to foreign Communist parties instructing them in matters of organization and strategy, and, in the case of the German party, authorizing it to launch a proletarian insurrection. Since 1920, British intelligence had come into possession of genuine ECCI and NKID correspondence, mainly through intercepts. The Labour government, like the governments that preceded it, sanctioned these intercepts and accepted the authenticity of the intelligence gained thereby. The "Zinoviev letter," however, was not an intercept but one of three similar documents that had come to the attention of Mac-Donald and the Foreign Office via the Special Branch and the Home Office since April. Nevertheless, Scotland Yard, the Foreign Office, and the Secret Service, organizations that had considerable experience dealing with forgeries, considered all three documents authentic. MacDonald accepted the authenticity of the first two letters, dated 17 March and 7 April; not until the third letter, dated 15 September, appeared in October, however, did he authorize lodging a protest in Moscow. All this lends some credence to the argument that the document might have been genuine.[30]

On the other hand, scholarly examination of the style and content of the letter reveals a pattern of forgery rather than one of authenticity. The language of the three letters, which are similar in style and content, does not consistently resemble that of other Comintern documents. The suggestion that the ratification of the Anglo-Soviet Draft Treaty would help revolutionize the British working class and lead to proletarian insurrection in England is not to be found in any other known Comintern or CPGB document. The actual instructions of the ECCI to the CPGB for the October election are in line with the doctrines expressed in published Comintern resolutions during the same period, and are not consistent with the "Zinoviev letter." These instructions did not call for subversion of the military and preparation for insurrection, but rather for the CPGB to work to "return a Labour majority in the election as a challenge to the capitalist class."[31] Each of the three intercepted letters reads as if it had been deliberately designed to discredit the Labour government and its foreign policy by suggesting that the government was being duped by the Soviet delegation in London, which was conducting propaganda and subversive activities while negotiating the treaty.

MacDonald's Foreign Office dispatched a note of protest to the Soviet government on 24 October and condemned the "Zinoviev letter" as outside interference in British internal affairs. Rakovskii replied on his own the next day dismissing the letter as a forgery. The NKID Collegium responded on 27 October with a note demanding an apology and the punishment of those involved in the forgery. The Foreign Office rejected it.[32] The full extent of the damage done to Anglo-Soviet relations became evident on 21 November 1924 when Austen Chamberlain, foreign secretary in the new Conservative cabinet (1924–29), inaugurated the government's relations with the USSR with two notes to Moscow. One stated that the government would not present the Anglo-Soviet Draft Treaty to Parliament for ratification; the other asserted the authenticity of the "Zinoviev letter."[33] Then in December, on his first trip out of the country as foreign secretary, Chamberlain visited Paris, where he met with Herriot and officials of the Quai d'Orsay. There they agreed that London and Paris would coordinate their policies toward Russia. They would collaborate against the Comintern by exchanging information regarding the activities of its agents, and they would consult each other prior to any further debt/loan transactions with the USSR.[34] Before long, the newly opened, postrecognition negotiations between Paris and Moscow became deadlocked over such issues as the repayment of private debts and relaxation of the trade monopoly. Discussions soon came to a halt.

Chicherin responded vigorously. With the publication of the "Zinoviev letter," he went to Comintern headquarters, where he spoke with Piatnitskii and Kuusinen and raged about the damage done to Soviet diplomacy.[35] No longer did he speak of the "entry of the USSR and England upon an era of friendly relations," and he referred to the "general pacification in world relationships" as a thing of the past. Instead, he suggested to the Central Committee on 18 October that the "Zinoviev letter" incident "may be the first of a series of crises on a world scale and the beginning of new trials for our Republic." Evidence existed, he added, of a "united front of bourgeois governments against the USSR, largely resuscitated as a result of the intensification of imperialist and reactionary tendencies."[36]

Had an anti-Soviet coalition come into existence and, if so, was it a mutable, transient, and tactical diplomatic alignment, or was it the embryo of a permanent offensive alliance against the USSR? These questions troubled both the NKID and the party leadership in October–November 1924. And both continued to ponder them for the next twenty-four months—the period during which London and Paris settled with Berlin and Washington the issues of war debts and reparations, of security and disarmament, and of international trade, currency exchange, and industrial relations.[37] Did this comprehensive and complex resettlement of postwar international relations, which party and Comintern resolutions called "international capitalist stabilization," include an anti-Soviet front directed from London? Chicherin's assessment was consistently tentative and subtle. There were opposing currents in the European situation, he thought; the dominant characteristic of international relations was their fluidity, fluctuation, and a lack of definition and clarity. "The present moment," he reported to the Third Congress of Soviets in May 1925, "is distinguished by the extraordinary abundance of obscure and inconclusive indications in world affairs and in particular in the system of relations with us." There was "a wealth of indications" in the English and world press, he stated, that "English influence is playing a part in creating an atmosphere of general hostility towards us, in which we now have to work." However, he was extremely cautious about directly accusing Chamberlain, or the Foreign Office, or even the Conservative government specifically of any overt anti-Soviet action.[38] He professed not to know with certainty the direction in which international relations were moving or whether an anti-Soviet alliance was being formed in London. The tentativeness of Chicherin's estimate of the international situation contrasted strongly with the one made by the post-Lenin leadership emerging within the RCP(B). Among them were those certain to the point of dogmatism in their definition of the current international situation and of the direction relations between the USSR and the major capitalist powers were taking.

The Foreign Relations of "Socialism in One Country"

The doctrine of "socialism in one country" had as its central proposition that it was possible to construct socialism in the Soviet Union alone—in the absence of proletarian revolution in Europe, and out of the social circumstances and economic resources present in the USSR. Russia had, after all, achieved and consolidated proletarian power without the assistance of revolution in Europe. A secondary proposition was that, although socialism could be constructed in the USSR independently, there would be no "complete victory" for socialism, and no guaranteed security for the revolution in Russia, until the threat of imperialist interference and intervention was banished by proletarian revolution in several European countries. "Socialism in one country" formally deprioritized international revolution on the agenda of Soviet politics and asserted the primacy of the task of internal development. Revolutionary internationalism was not ideologically renounced, however; it remained an integral feature of the Bolshevik theory of global history.

"Socialism in one country" was implicit in elements of Bukharin's thought as early as November 1923, at the time of the failure of "the German October." Stalin first enunciated the idea formally in December 1924. Bukharin began to address the question publicly and explicitly in April 1925. The resolutions of the Fourteenth Party Congress the following December adopted the doctrine as the central principle of socialist construction. In general, it was Bukharin who worked "socialism in one country" into a proto-program for the socialization and industrialization of Soviet Russia, and who developed the theoretical basis for it. Stalin popularized the idea by proclaiming it in his speeches and writings during the two years extending from late 1924 to late 1926. He thereby gained the political benefit that accrued from the acceptance of the doctrine among the party rank and file.[39]

"Socialism in one country" was a significant ideological innovation. Before the years 1924–1926 the transition from capitalism to socialism had been linked in Marxism-Leninism to transnational proletarian revolution. Socialism would emerge throughout Europe as the result of a single process during one historical period lasting, the Bolsheviks thought, at first weeks, then months, and then perhaps years. This was Lenin's original vision of "world revolution," and it was this conception of Lenin's, rather than the "permanent revolution" of Trotsky, against which Stalin was really polemicizing between 1924 and 1926, although for obvious political reasons he could not and did not say so.[40] By contrast, "socialism in one country" formulated in ideological terms the proposition that socialism could be achieved independently in separate nations at different times, that Soviet Russia would survive into the indefinite future in a world composed of nations as well as of classes, and that its "complete victory" would be guaranteed when revolution in one or more of the imperialist powers rendered impossible outside capitalist interference with socialist construction in Russia. Thus, in the doctrine of "socialism in one country," the achievement of socialism became a national occurrence, its survival and ultimate triumph a matter of international relations. It has been aptly termed "a theory of international relations *par excellence*."[41]

Indeed, declaration of the doctrine was accompanied by a thorough consideration of the matrix of foreign relations in which the USSR was set in the mid-1920s. Stalin and Bukharin were impressed by the twin reversals of late 1924: on the one hand, the "Zinoviev letter," the fall of the Labour government, and the rejection of the Anglo-Soviet Draft Treaty; on the other, the Dawes Plan, the intervention of American capital in Europe, and Germany's attraction to what Stalin now consistently called "the capitalist camp."[42] In these events they saw a decisive turning point in the international situation, one that would influence an entire phase of historical development. Bukharin first proclaimed—in June 1924 at the time the Dawes Plan was formulated—that a new stabilization period in the history of capitalism was beginning, a notion he then vigorously defended in theoretical debates.[43] Stalin meanwhile explained the international situation to the party membership in a series of articles, interviews, speeches, and reports beginning in September 1924 and culminating in December 1925 with his presentation of the Political Report of the Central Committee to the Fourteenth Party Congress.[44]

The Stalin-Bukharin conception of world politics began with the proposition that "world revolution" was not an event but a lengthy process. The "epoch of world revolution," which had begun with the struggle of the proletariat in Russia in 1905, comprised "a whole strategic period, which will last for a number of years, perhaps even a number of decades." As did Lenin, Stalin and Bukharin regarded the state of equilibrium that resulted from the ebb of the revolutionary tide and from the stabilization of capitalism as the characteristic feature of the international situation. They then expanded and extended the notion: The imperialist system had "succeeded in extricating itself from the quagmire of the postwar crisis" and achieved a "partial" and "temporary" stabilization. The Soviet system had also stabilized. The Russian economy was growing; socialism was under construction; the exploited of Europe and the oppressed of Asia were rallying around the USSR. "A certain temporary equilibrium between these two stabilizations" resulted. Although the duration of this equilibrium could not be predicted, "there is no doubt," Stalin stated, "it will be a long one." In 1918, Lenin had thought the end of the war with Germany would be followed by a short "peace break"; after the Civil War he predicted a lengthier truce; in 1924–25, Stalin announced what he called "a whole period of respite." What had begun in 1920–21 as a tenuous breathing space, Stalin told the Fourteenth Party Congress, "has turned into a whole period of so-called peaceful coexistence of the USSR with the capitalist states."[45]

The data informing the Stalin-Bukharin analysis of capitalist stabilization and international equilibrium came from the events of global politics: With the failure of the revolution in Germany in November 1923, "the period of revolutionary upsurge has come to an end." There existed now "a new situation" in which the Communist parties would have to find their bearings again.[46] The stabilization of capitalism, although it remained temporary and partial, was now definite in a way it had not been in 1921. In Europe, the postwar inflation had ended; currencies were stabilized; agricultural output and industrial production were increasing; international trade was expanding; both production and commerce were approaching prewar levels. This financial-economic stabilization had been achieved "mainly with the aid of American capital, and at the price of the financial subordination of Western Europe to America."[47] Most important, Germany—once the locus of revolutionary upsurge in Europe—had been "Dawesified" into an appendage of Anglo-American capital. With the Dawes Plan, the British, the Americans, and the French had struck a deal regarding "the scale on which [Germany] was to be robbed," and the United States had come to the verge of financial hegemony in the capitalist world.[48] While capitalism was stabilized on these conditions, there were others in addition. The British, the Americans, and the Japanese had struck a "deal" over China (the Washington treaties of 1922), and the imperialist powers had made arrangements among themselves promising mutual respect for each other's colonial possessions. And there was one more. "The stabilization of capitalism," Stalin forecast in May 1925, "may find expression in an attempt on the part of the imperialist groups of the advanced countries to strike a deal concerning the formation of a united front against the Soviet Union."[49]

Capitalism had stabilized for the present, but, according to the dialectic Stalin elucidated in 1925, "the process of capitalism's 'recovery' contain[ed] within itself the germs of its inherent weakness and disintegration."[50] Stabilization had not settled the issues over which the World War had been fought. The imperialist powers still struggled with each other for markets. Anti-imperialist national liberation movements were "growing step by step" and "beginning in some places to assume the form of open war against imperialism (Morocco, Syria, China)."[51] And while "the capitalist world [was] being corroded by a whole series of internal contradictions, . . . the world of socialism [was] becoming more and more closely welded, more united." Industry had revived and would continue to develop, giving the proletariat of the USSR "a new way of life" and leading the workers of Europe to demand workers' states of their own. At the same time, the working class of Europe had come to regard the Soviet state "as its own child," Stalin stated, and "having adopted our state . . . is ready to defend it and fight for it" "against imperialism and its interventionist machinations."[52]

In predicting the eventual demise of capitalism, the Stalin-Bukharin duumvirate counted heavily on the Dawes reparation agreement of 1924 proving incapable of stabilizing the Weimar Republic. Their prognostication was that German workers would be required to bear the costs of reparation payments to France, Britain, and Belgium in addition to the surplus extracted by the German bourgeoisie, and would impose on them a "double yoke" of exploitation. "To think that . . . the German proletariat will consent to bear this double yoke without making repeated serious attempts at a revolutionary upheaval means believing in miracles." "The Dawes Plan must inevitably lead to a revolution in Germany." Correspondingly, the governments of Britain, France, and Italy had to increase the burden of taxation on their populations to make war debt payments to the United States, meaning that "the material conditions of the working people in Europe . . . will certainly deteriorate and the working class will inevitably become revolutionized."[53]

The developing international conflict was disguised, Stalin claimed, by a facade of "false and mendacious bourgeois-democratic pacifism." When the London Conference adopted the Dawes Plan in July–August 1924, MacDonald and Herriot had indeed emphasized the peaceful collaboration of Britain and France, reconciliation with Germany, and normalization of relations with the USSR. Stalin maintained that such statements camouflaged not only the contradictions among the victors of the World War but also "the intense antagonism between Germany and the entente" and "the deadly enmity of the bourgeois states" toward the Soviet Union.[54] When the Locarno agreements were concluded in October 1925—accompanied by further rhetoric lauding a new spirit of international cooperation and peace—they confirmed in Stalin's mind the view that international relations were recapitulating those of the pre-1914 era. Like the treaties, agreements, and conferences that preceded the World War, Locarno was "an example of the matchless hypocrisy of bourgeois diplomacy, when by shouting and singing about peace they try to cover up preparations for a new war." "If the Dawes Plan is fraught with a revolution in Germany," Stalin told the Fourteenth Party Congress, "Locarno is fraught with a new war in Europe."[55]

Such was the concept of international relations generated by the Stalin-Bukharin duumvirate for the collective leadership and adopted by the Fourteenth Party Congress in December 1925. What was its significance for the development of Soviet foreign relations? The adoption of the Dawes Plan and the signing of the Locarno Treaties called into question the fundamental precepts of post-revolution Leninist foreign relations as they had been formulated in 1920–21: that the German problem was insoluble, that the postwar crisis would bring proletarian insurrection to Europe despite the setbacks of 1919, and, most important of all, that the inevitability of interimperialist conflict could be counted on to make the Soviet Union secure from the danger of a united anti-Soviet coalition. The developing reconciliation between Germany and the former Allies and the increasing stabilization of international relations in the West made imperative a comprehensive and agonizing reappraisal of Soviet security policy in the light of new realities seven years after the October Revolution. Seemingly no such reappraisal took place either in the ECCI or the NKID, or in the Politburo, despite a few inconclusive efforts in this direction.[56] Instead, the party reaffirmed Lenin's notion that the antagonisms among the imperialist powers could be depended on to benefit Soviet security. That reaffirmation was strongly influenced by the position Stalin had articulated to the Moscow party organization the previous January. "The struggle, conflicts, and wars between our enemies," were among what Stalin called the three available "allies of Soviet power," the other two being the proletariat of the advanced capitalist societies and the oppressed colonial peoples.[57] Here was a statement remarkable in two respects. Stalin not only reaffirmed Lenin's belief that interimperialist conflict would protect the USSR but he also formally raised relations among nations to the level of class relations in deciding the eventual outcome of the contest between socialism and capitalism.

From the principle that Soviet security could depend on intercapitalist conflict, the collective leadership derived an optimistic prognostication for the future of the one country in which socialism was being constructed. To wit, it was within the capability of foreign policy to extend the prolonged respite from imperialist war by centering foreign relations on "the struggle for peace." Both by means of diplomacy and through the activities of foreign Communist parties, they could moderate the war-prone tendencies of the imperialist powers and extend the conditions of "peaceful coexistence." Such a prolonged respite constituted an opportunity for constructing an independent industrial economy in the homeland of socialism. This prognostication was resolved by the delegates to the Fourteenth Party Congress. However, the doctrine of the inevitable resumption of imperialist warfare was not forgotten. The potential threat it posed to the USSR, the resolution continued, made imperative the creation of a modern defense establishment.[58]

In promoting this defense establishment, Stalin personally played a particularly important role. Although he informed the Party Congress in December that the international situation was at a point of stable equilibrium that would last for years, Stalin had told a closed session of the Central Committee the previous January that "a radical change in the international situation has begun lately." In fact, on at least three separate occasions during the relatively tranquil year of 1925, he stated that current international relations resembled those which had existed during the prelude to the outbreak of the great imperialist war in 1914.[59] There was another crisis in Morocco, and the powers of Europe were again contesting among themselves for control of North Africa and the Balkans. A renewed postwar arms race was under way. The French were building a large air force, and the British, Americans, and Japanese were competing over naval power. "The conflict of interests among the victor countries is growing and becoming more intense," he stated; "collision among them is becoming inevitable, and in anticipation of a new war, they are arming with might and main." Coming to a conclusion that differed strikingly from the line adopted by the party as a whole—"a whole period of peaceful coexistence" based on prolonged capitalist stabilization—Stalin maintained that a new war was inevitable within a few years and that the USSR must prepare for it by building up its armed forces.

Thus, as Stalin emerged as a member of the duumvirate that directed the collective leadership and as spokesman for the party's conception of foreign relations, he brought with him a distinctive set of opinions about international relations in the mid-1920s. The stabilization of capitalism, he thought, was "ridiculously unstable" and a second imperialist war was both inevitable and imminent, "not tomorrow or the day after, of course, but in a few years time." The approach of war would "intensify the internal revolutionary crisis both in the East and the West," bringing revolution to Germany and uprisings to the colonies of the European powers. That revolutionary surge, Stalin's scenario continued, was "bound to turn the ruling strata of the Great Powers against us." Threatened with global revolution, they would attack at its source. "The danger of intervention," Stalin concluded as early as January 1925, "is again becoming real."[60]

During 1925, Stalin's version of the international situation made significant inroads among the Soviet party/state elite. In May the resolutions of the Third Soviet Congress stated: "The capitalist states are making preparations for new conflicts and new wars," preparations that are accompanied by "a hostile encirclement of our Union which takes the form of an entire system of military conferences, agreements, and support for the measures taken by different governments against the USSR, and also of campaigns based on forgeries and lies." The delegates to the Fourteenth Party Congress in December, selected by Stalin (except for those from the Leningrad Soviet controlled by Zinoviev), partially incorporated Stalin's foreign relations concept in the resolutions they adopted. Those resolutions assailed the "blocs of capitalist states under Anglo-American hegemony [that are] accompanied by the frenzied growth of armaments and therefore fraught with the danger of new wars, including the danger of intervention." The resolutions of both May and December stressed the need for the USSR "to guard its frontiers from possible attack," to strengthen the country's defense capabilities, and "to intensify the power of the Red Army and the Red Navy and the Air Force."[61]

The USSR and the World Economy: Isolation or Integration?

During much the same period that the doctrine of "socialism in one country" was being introduced and adopted, what has been called "the industrialization debate" was also going on among the party/state elite. Contrary to what has at times been assumed, the context of this debate was not a turn away from the international scene and toward the tasks of internal development as part of an ideological assimilation of the disappointing results of the revolution export project of the years 1917–1923. In actuality, the debate over industrialization was closely linked to considerations of foreign relations and, in particular, to a foreboding conception of world politics: The world was divided into two camps, a "capitalist camp" headed by the Anglo-Americans, and the camp of the Soviet Union. As both camps stabilized, the contradictions between them became stronger. New wars loomed, both interimperialist and interventionist, and, as a prelude to such wars, capitalist Europe would impose diplomatic isolation and economic blockade on the USSR. It was on the basis of this scenario that the collective leadership of the party concluded that the Soviet Union must achieve economic independence from the capitalist states.

Bukharin was convinced that the capital required for the economic development and socialist construction of the USSR would not come from Europe. The abortive "German October" insurrection made clear that a Communist Germany was not about to become Soviet Russia's economic provider. And neither the Genoa Conference of 1922 nor the Anglo-Soviet Conference of 1924 had resolved the issue of Russian debts or unleashed large-scale, long-term development loans from European banks. Initially, Bukharin believed that the grain surplus held by prospering farmers might be sold abroad to finance imports of industrial equipment. However, the difficulties encountered by the government in procuring that surplus from the harvest of 1925 convinced him that the economy could not be dependent on an international market controlled by the bourgeoisie. He concluded that the capital for economic development could be amassed only from the increasing profitability of state industry, from a progressive income tax on entrepreneurs prospering under NEP, and by mobilizing the voluntary savings deposits of the peasantry. None of these sources would

provide vast sums very soon, however, and Bukharin's program for socialization included no clear solution to the problem of capital accumulation
for industrialization. Apparently it was not a critical issue for him. Vast
amounts of capital were unnecessary, he thought, because existing industrial machinery could be used more intensively, and socialism could develop in the USSR without vast new investment—slowly, gradually, and
"at a snail's pace," as he stated in December 1925.[62] Bukharin's contribution
to the industrialization debate was, therefore, to recast the New Economic
Policy, which Lenin had introduced in order that the Russian economy
could be partially integrated into that of the capitalist world system, and
identify it with building socialism in isolation under conditions of slow,
autarkic economic development.

Stalin seems to have given little thought to how industrialization would
be financed when he first proclaimed that socialism could be constructed in
Russia separately in 1924–25. Apparently he believed that funds for capital
investment could simply be borrowed from the state treasury. Of greatest
importance, he thought, was the international political situation. Ties to
world capitalism, that is, economic dependence on Europe, led "to a whole
series of new dangers," as it was expressed in the phrase incorporated in the
resolutions of the Fourteenth Party Congress, or, as Stalin himself stated it,
the USSR would be "vulnerable to blows from the side of our enemies."[63]
The immediate challenge, he thought, was the Dawes Plan. Western observers from John Maynard Keynes to Stanley Baldwin were suggesting
publicly that the best solution to the problem of postwar international
indebtedness would be for Germany to create the favorable balance of
payments necessary to fund reparations to France and Britain by selling
manufactured goods to the USSR in exchange for agricultural commodities
and raw materials. Stalin objected to such proposals. They were intended,
he maintained, to "squeeze money out of the Russian market for the
benefit of Europe." "We have no desire," he added, "to be converted into an
agrarian country for the benefit of any other country whatsoever, including Germany."[64]

Stalin's own distinctive program for the industrialization of the USSR
aimed directly at economic independence, which to him meant that Russia
would produce the means of production rather than acquiring them from
abroad. The Soviet Union must be converted, he stated, "from a country
which imports machines and equipment into a country which produces
machines and equipment. . . . In this manner the USSR . . . will become a
self-sufficient economic unit building socialism."[65] This policy position
contrasted sharply with the integrationist consensus that had formed in
1920–21, and it constituted a sharp break from the intentions that had

guided economic development and foreign policy since then. Moreover, it is significant that, in Stalin's concept of economic development, independence was the goal of industrialization, but not only the goal. Industrialization was not merely the way for the USSR to become independent of capitalism; the USSR had to be independent in order to industrialize. The central premise of Stalin's economics as of 1925 was that both the capital and the technology for industrialization could, should, and would come from Russia's own resources. Otherwise, the capitalist states could stifle or interrupt Soviet industrialization by imposing economic blockades. In this manner, autarky was the means as well as the end of Soviet economic development for Stalin.

The alternative to the autarkical development strategies of Bukharin and Stalin was formulated by Trotsky, who of all the leading Bolsheviks, Richard B. Day has argued, examined the difficult and complex issues of industrialization most realistically.[66] After his dismissal from the office of commissar for military and naval affairs in January 1925, Trotsky served on the Supreme Council of National Economy (Vesenkha) and as chairman of the Principal Concessions Committee, posts at which he experienced firsthand the many problems involved in planning and managing the weak and undeveloped industrial sector of the Soviet economy. During the most intense period of the industrialization debate, Trotsky identified low labor productivity—rather than the threat of dependence on the capitalist camp— as the most critical problem for Russian economic development. And the solution, he decided, was to encourage foreign trade and capital imports, to transfer the advanced technology of America and Europe to the USSR, and to achieve thereby a rapid tempo of industrialization and a high level of productivity. Industrialization "at a snail's pace," he thought, simply perpetuated the misery of the masses. Development based on Russia's indigenous engineering and metallurgy would merely bind the USSR to a primitive technology, require an industrialization period of ten to twenty years, and result in low-quality products. Importing the most sophisticated and expensive technology, by contrast, would catapult the USSR into the industrial future and allow it to create the objective basis for true economic independence from capitalism. For these reasons, Trotsky argued, the Soviet Union could not isolate itself from the global economy. Industrialization required, he concluded, not a reduction but an increase in relations with the outside world and, likewise, a temporary increase in dependence on the world market.

Accordingly, Trotsky was in 1925–26 the leading exponent among the party leadership of economic integration into the world economy and political accommodation with Europe and America. Russia, he maintained, lacked not only advanced technology but also capital; it needed foreign concessions to develop Russia's natural resources and foreign credits to purchase machinery. He announced this in a *Pravda* article in June 1925, and in August he told the British representative in Moscow of the horrible state of Soviet technology, stressed the crucial importance of a machine-building industry, and informed him that unless the British stopped insisting on cash-and-carry and granted the USSR credits, they would lose out in machine sales to the United States.[67] Trotsky did not hesitate to follow the logic of his development strategy and economic foreign policy to their diplomatic consequences. He supported the debt/loan negotiations that opened with France in February 1926, seeing in them prospects for foreign credits three times the size of what Vesenkha expected to be able to invest in industry in 1925–26, and he urged noninterference in the British General Strike the following May in order not to jeopardize the prospects for loans from Britain and other European states.[68]

The crucial issues of socialist construction and economic development were the material of the Fourteenth Party Congress in December 1925. There the Central Committee committed the party to building socialism separately and to transforming the USSR into a self-sufficient industrial nation. Important issues were left undecided, however. At what tempo would socialism be constructed? With what technology would the USSR be industrialized? How would industrialization be capitalized? The reason for such irresolution was intraparty politics. The commitment of Stalin and Bukharin to "socialism in one country," transcribed as "autarkical economic development," bound them in theory to industrializing the USSR with indigenous technology and capital. To deny this would have constituted a victory for Trotsky. On the other hand, to call for industrialization and to prioritize production of the means of production, and to do so without designating the sources of investment capital and assuming that it could come from the state treasury, that is, from deficit spending, ran the risk of ruinous inflation.

Unless capital was supplied by foreign loans, the only available policy alternative was the one espoused by the leading party economist, Evgenii Preobrazhenskii. He advocated immediate and rapid industrialization, with priority given to large-scale heavy industry, and with investment capital mobilized by transferring to state industry what could be accumulated internally within the private sector, especially in agriculture. At the center of his strategy for industrialization was the expropriation of agrarian surpluses, which he termed "primitive socialist accumulation."[69] Preobrazhenskii's proposal represented a direct challenge to the *smychka*, the worker-peasant alliance on which NEP was based, and to Bukharin's gradualist, voluntarist, and harmonious concept of how "socialism in one country" would be constructed. Bukharin in turn ridiculed Preobrazhenskii's strategy as "super-industrialization," industrialization at any cost, and he included in his condemnation Trotsky, who shared Preobrazhenskii's preference for rapid industrial growth but did not identify himself with the notion of peasant expropriation.[70] Stalin simply ignored the problem of industrial investment, probably to avoid possible dispute with his ally Bukharin.

"The stabilization of capitalism" was no mere Comintern catchphrase. It integrated ideologically the concepts of socialist construction, economic development, and foreign relations adopted in the period 1924–1926. It also had a basis in international reality. Starting in late 1924, following within months of the breakthrough to diplomatic recognition that had begun the previous February, Soviet foreign relations sustained serious reversals. The Germans engineered a rapprochement with Britain and France that undermined the "specialness" of the Soviet-German relationship symbolized by the Treaty of Rapallo. That rapprochement posed a possible threat to Soviet security, in the estimate made by the NKID, unless Berlin gave the proper guarantees to Moscow. Moreover, the Conservative government in England renounced the Anglo-Soviet Draft Treaty negotiated by their Labour predecessors and subsequently refused to discuss measures to improve or even to repair relations with Moscow. And as part of the reestablished Anglo-French Entente of 1924, the British Foreign Office and the French Foreign Ministry agreed to coordinate their policies toward the USSR. Finally, all three powers—Germany, Britain, and France—in effect put relations with the USSR on hold in 1925 while they resolved their differences and subjoined treaties regulating war debts, trade, and security to the Dawes Plan. Chapter 7 considers how these reversals were managed by those who conceived and conducted the foreign relations of the USSR.

7 Narkomindel and the Diplomacy of European Security

Offering an Alliance to Germany

On what could Soviet security depend at a time when international capitalism was stabilized and when the march of proletarian revolution had come to a halt in Europe? If the USSR was to provide for its own security, as well as its own economic development, what resources were available?

The army of 5.3 million men that had fought and won the Civil War was demobilized beginning in 1922; by December 1924 its size had been set at 562,000 troops, and a series of reforms had been proposed to reorganize it on a permanent peacetime basis. The central purpose of these reforms, which were formulated by a special military commission headed by Mikhail Frunze and composed largely of veteran Civil War commanders, was to resolve the problems of organization and supply that had plagued the Soviet effort during the Civil War and to establish the basis for a modern army that could contend with those of the nations of Europe.[1] The army the commission refounded was headed by a Red Army Staff designed to become the "military brain" of the Soviet state and was composed of both regular army divisions made up of men serving two-year terms of duty, who were kept combat-ready, and an army three times larger made up of less well-equipped, less highly trained, and less costly territorial militia divisions. The conscripts enrolled in the latter served three months of active duty and then five years in a reserve mobilized for exercises one month each year. This "mixed system" of military organization, which was abandoned only in 1935, was designed to enable the Red Army Staff to mobilize the extensive manpower resources both of Russia and the entire USSR, while limiting military expenditures at a time when reconstruction of the civilian economy was the national priority. However, the "Frunze reforms" did not immediately resolve Russia's military predicament; the problems of technological inferiority, inadequate training, and inefficient supply persisted. Nor did the reforms create an army capable of launching a strategic offensive against a well-equipped foreign enemy or conducting bold operations in support of revolutionary movements beyond the borders of the USSR.

Soviet military doctrine in the 1920s was debated between those military intellectuals who "wanted to take the combat realities of World War I and the Civil War and codify them into military doctrine" and those who "sought to envision a future 'class war' that negated the more mundane concerns of the military art."[2] Among those at the Military Academy and on the General Staff of the Red Army who took seriously the study of strategy and tactics, the relative merit of war of attrition and war of annihilation were considered. From the studies of the latter emerged a distinctively Soviet contribution to military science, the concept of the "operational art" of conducting successive operations combining breakthrough and deep pursuit and aimed at the total destruction of the forces of the enemy. What united the advocates of both annihilation and attrition, however, was the assumption that the future war would be fought against a coalition of East European successor states made up wholly or in part of the former Tsarist Empire and sponsored by one or more of the great capitalist powers. The most plausible scenario for a Soviet national security emergency between 1921 and 1933 began with an alliance of Poland, Romania, and the Baltic states, perhaps joined by Finland, and supported by France and/or England. For this reason, Soviet security depended on knowing what encouragement London and Paris might give to an anti-Soviet coalition of East-Central European states, and what Germany would do in the event of a crisis in the region. The answers to these questions were by no means obvious at a time when the Dawes détente attracted Germany westward and when a peace settlement with England had been aborted by the electoral victory of the Conservatives. Dealing with this situation became the first task of Soviet diplomacy during the years of "socialism in one country." How it did so forms the subject matter of this chapter.

With Germany the NKID made use of two strategies in 1923–25. One was intended to keep Germany out of any possible anti-Soviet coalition by concluding a well-defined and well-publicized political treaty with Berlin and thereby fortifying the Rapallo "special relationship." The other was intended to encourage a German rapprochement with France as a way of limiting British influence in Berlin and Britain's position on the Continent in general. It was in execution of this latter strategy that the NKID attempted to mediate the Ruhr conflict. In his conversations with German diplomats and politicians during the summer of 1923, Chicherin gave strong support to the idea of collaboration between French and German industry as a way of ending the long postwar struggle between the two nations. He rationalized his support for the advance of capitalism in Europe in Marxist terms: Only when the bourgeoisie had accomplished its historic task, he told them, would it give way to the proletariat.[3] Nevertheless, it is hard not to see the contradictions within the dual policy operating in fully developed form in the summer of 1923. The NKID worked to stabilize capitalism in Germany while the Politburo made preparations to overthrow it.

A stabilized Germany in rapprochement with France could serve more effectively as Soviet Russia's bridge to Europe. And to this end, Chicherin welcomed the Western European détente that developed in late 1923 and early 1924 with the liquidation of the Ruhr invasion and the settlement of the reparations problem. He calculated that the Soviet-German Rapallo relationship combined with the German rapprochement with France could be fashioned into a "continental bloc" that would constitute a counter-British coalition of European states. This alignment would also reinsure Moscow's relationship with Berlin as Germany turned westward and possibly reduce the likelihood that France would support Poland against the USSR, either militarily or diplomatically. Occasionally, over the next two years, Chicherin, Rakovskii, and Litvinov pushed the "continental bloc" idea in Paris and in Berlin. They met with no success; neither France nor Germany was available for a counter-British coalition.

To the contrary, the German government committed itself in principle to joining the League of Nations in December 1924, and the German Foreign Ministry in January–February 1925 proposed to London and Paris what came to be called the Treaties of Locarno. These treaties were concluded the following October at a celebratory and celebrated conference in Switzerland, and they were formally signed in London in December. The Locarno Treaties included a multilateral regional security agreement comprising both a nonaggression pact and a treaty of mutual guarantee. Germany, France, and Belgium promised not to attack, invade, or conduct warfare against each other and to respect the demilitarized status of the Rhineland. Britain and Italy agreed to render military assistance to any one of the three powers in the event that it became the victim of aggression and to keep the Rhineland demilitarized. As similar guarantees were not issued in Eastern Europe, the security of France's allies there, Poland and Czechoslovakia, accordingly suffered by neglect. In the years that followed, Gustav Stresemann, the German foreign minister (1923–29), and his British and French counterparts, Austen Chamberlain (1924–29) and Aristide

Briand (1925–32), held regular summit conferences as they attended meetings of the League of Nations Council or Assembly in Geneva four times each year. In these meetings Stresemann aimed at realizing what he maintained constituted the political consequences of Germany's promise of nonaggression and international good citizenship, that is, a negotiated revision of the Treaty of Versailles, including further reductions of Germany's reparations obligations, a quick end to the Franco-British-Belgian military occupation of the German Rhineland, a lenient settlement of the matter of German disarmament, and the return of territories ceded to Poland after the World War. The success of his policy depended on the willingness of Britain to mediate Germany's relations with France and to bring Paris around to accepting German recovery.[4] Developments in Russia rarely entered into their discussions. They made no effort to turn their post-Locarno cooperation into an anti-Soviet coalition, but neither did they consider involving the USSR in their deliberations.

Largely uninformed about the content of the negotiations between Berlin, London, and Paris, the NKID became concerned that Germany was being drawn into an English-led, anti-Soviet coalition. From late 1924 until mid-1926, it repeatedly presented the same argument both in discussions with German diplomats and in public statements: A Germany that joined the League of Nations would become subject to the decisions of a British-dominated League majority and no longer able to pursue an independent policy toward the USSR. By concluding a security pact with Britain and France—a pact Chicherin believed had been instigated by England—Germany would become the tool of British efforts to undermine the military and political power of France on the Continent, to attain predominance in Europe, and to lead Europe to a confrontation with the USSR—one that would be surely diplomatic and economic, and potentially military. Thus the German rapprochement with France and Britain appeared to be a direct challenge to Soviet security.

How might this come about? As viewed from Moscow, it would happen as a Russo-Polish border dispute escalated into a threatening international crisis.[5] The League of Nations Council would declare the USSR the aggressor and call upon its members to impose economic and even military sanctions. At this point, German League membership would have direct implications for Soviet security. If Germany were not a League member, Berlin could remain neutral, abstain from action, and continue commercial relations with the Soviet Union. Most significantly, Berlin would not be called upon to allow France and other League members to transport their troops across German territory to the aid of Poland. During the Soviet-Polish War of 1920, German neutrality had provided an element of protection for Soviet Russia, and the capability to transfer troops and supplies from Western Europe via Germany remained crucial to the success of any second Allied intervention. If, however, Germany joined the League and took on the obligations of the League Covenant, the power to decide whether Germany would be neutral or engaged would be taken over by the member states of the League Council. Germany would be transformed from a protective shield against a hostile coalition to a vital element in a League-gathered, anti-Soviet Europe. And this would occur despite any intention Berlin might have of preserving its ties to Moscow. Objective circumstances, the logic of the League and Locarno, would compel it. When Chicherin stated, as he did repeatedly in 1925, that Germany's policy of understanding with Britain and France was incompatible with the Rapallo relationship with the USSR, he had in mind a scenario such as this.

The NKID's initial response to MacDonald's proposal that Germany join the League of Nations was to propose an agreement between Berlin and Moscow by which neither party would enter the League without the agreement of the other. When Stresemann rejected this, Chicherin proposed to Brockdorff-Rantzau that Germany join in a Franco-Soviet alignment against England, the "continental bloc"; the German ambassador rejected this proposal out of hand. The NKID then responded with what has been called its "December initiative." In a series of conversations with Brockdorff-Rantzau, beginning in December 1924 and continuing until early March 1925, Chicherin proposed and elaborated on what amounted to a Soviet-German alliance, a comprehensive political agreement that would extend far beyond the relationship defined in Rapallo and that would be embodied in a formal treaty.[6] Both countries would refrain from military, political, or economic coalitions directed at the other; they would coordinate their policies toward the League of Nations; neither would guarantee or recognize the present borders of Poland. These proposals were obviously aimed at preventing any reinforcement of the League of Nations, at keeping Germany diplomatically, militarily, and economically neutral in any future conflict, and at not releasing Poland from the pressures of joint Soviet-German hostility. The treaty offer was serious, made with the approval of the Politburo, and had the support of the collective leadership as a whole.[7]

West German historians, writing during the years 1955–1965, and attempting to discern the goals of Chicherin's German policy from the papers of Gustav Stresemann and from the records of the German Foreign Ministry, concluded that Chicherin's objectives were to prevent Germany from joining the League of Nations and from concluding the Locarno agreements, and to draw Berlin into an offensive alliance, the objective of which was to partition Poland—a suggestion to which German diplomats reacted with great reservation.[8] The research of the 1970s, however, suggests that Chicherin was too cautious to propose a military alliance—although Rykov, chairman of the Council of People's Commissars and a member of the Politburo, urged one on Brockdorff-Rantzau in February[9]—and that he was too realistic to expect Germany to break off negotiations aimed at concluding a Western European security pact and at joining the League of Nations once Berlin had become committed to both.

Did Chicherin want the USSR and Germany to divide Poland via some sort of proto-Molotov-Ribbentrop pact? The idea of an agreement directed specifically against Poland was first broached in December 1924 by Soviet diplomat Victor Kopp, who suggested somewhat vaguely to Brockdorff-Rantzau that Berlin and Moscow together could exert pressure on Poland, provided that in joining the League of Nations Germany did not guarantee Poland's territorial status quo. The German Foreign Ministry may have calculated that a trial balloon such as this must have had the considered consent of the NKID Collegium, of which Kopp was a member, and it jumped at the prospect of a joint anti-Polish policy. Ago von Maltzan, state secretary at the German Foreign Ministry—seemingly with the knowledge of both Carl von Schubert, his soon-to-be successor, and Stresemann—authorized Brockdorff-Rantzau to tell Chicherin that the solution to the Polish question for both Germany and the USSR lay in "forcing Poland back to its ethnographic borders." In this way, Berlin extended Moscow's proposal considerably, made it more precise, gave it a clearly military purport, and put it at the center of the negotiations. Chicherin, however, repudiated Kopp's suggestion during his famous Christmas Eve discussion with Brockdorff-Rantzau, and in subsequent conversations he showed no interest in an aggressive military alliance against Poland or in putting the Polish question at the center of the discussions with Berlin.[10] The explanation? The objective of the NKID in the period 1924–1926 was not to partition Poland but to make the frontiers of the USSR secure from an attack launched from Poland. This security was to be attained by coming to an agreement with Warsaw—but only after having first done so with Germany. In the meantime, Narkomindel's objective was to keep Poland in an unsecured situation between Germany and the Soviet Union and therefore unable to concentrate its forces against the USSR.

The key to the NKID's German policy is to be found, I think, in Chicherin's repeated statements that the Treaty of Rapallo must remain the basis of Soviet-German relations. On this he insisted because the Rapallo relationship served two essential functions in Soviet foreign relations: It constituted the main component of the Soviet Union's security system and it was at the same time the USSR's bridge to Europe. Chicherin aimed to preserve both functions of Rapallo. His effort to maintain the German bridge is evident in his proposal that Berlin and Moscow coordinate their policies toward the League of Nations.[11] His endeavor to prevent Soviet security from being undermined—his central concern in 1925—is revealed, first, in the treaty he proposed to Germany and, second, in his demand that Berlin give binding guarantees that Germany would not participate in League sanctions against the USSR and that it would not guarantee the German-Polish border. Rapallo was to be reaffirmed and sustained as the basis of Soviet-German relations and not altered by Germany's détente with the Western powers. To ensure this, Chicherin demanded that the new Soviet-German neutrality treaty be concluded simultaneously with, or preferably before, the Locarno Treaties and Germany's entrance into the League of Nations. In Chicherin's foreign policy conception, it would form the basis for German agreements with France and Britain and not be merely an amendment to them.

The issue that Chicherin and the NKID strove to place at the center of the discussions with Berlin was not the partition of Poland but the larger question—the orientation of German foreign policy and the effect a German rapprochement with France and Britain would have on it. Brockdorff-Rantzau regarded such discussions as an opening for his personal grand strategy of building a Soviet-German political agreement that could be utilized to compel the French to revise the settlement of 1919. The Wilhelmstrasse, on the other hand, was exceedingly hesitant about such discussions and adopted a strategy of procrastination. By using a series of pretexts—first a cabinet crisis, then the ill health of President Friedrich Ebert (1919–25), then Ebert's death and the election of his successor, Paul von Hindenburg (1925–34)—Schubert and Stresemann delayed any serious discussion of Chicherin's treaty proposal until June. None of this, however, prevented the Wilhelmstrasse from dispatching a lengthy and complicated note to Geneva expressing Germany's willingness to enter the League of Nations (December 12), from preparing a proposal for what were to become the Locarno Treaties, and from dispatching and explaining it to London (January 20) and Paris (February 9). Meanwhile, none of these steps were explained to the German embassy in Moscow until March 19, or to the NKID officially until Brockdorff-Rantzau's talks with Litvinov and Chicherin on 7–8 April. From this, the priorities of German foreign relations are unmistakable—first a security settlement with the Western entente, then, eventually, a new treaty arrangement with the USSR.[12]

Ebert, Stresemann, Schubert, and Erich Wallroth, director of the Eastern Department at the Wilhelmstrasse, all agreed that the security initiative with France and Britain had priority over any neutrality agreement with the USSR. When it came to the question of the basic orientation of German foreign policy, they were all "Westerners." Even Maltzan, who had managed the Rapallo negotiations three years earlier, urged—in his last action before departing for his new post as ambassador to Washington— that great caution be exercised in negotiations with the Russians. Chicherin's proposals were too extensive, he warned, and it could not be assumed that the Russians would honor any treaty concluded with Germany, or, if they did, that they would keep it secret. Consequently, the Wilhelmstrasse declined to conclude any agreement with the USSR before the success of the negotiations with the Entente powers was assured. As Stresemann told Krestinskii: "I may not conclude a secret treaty with Russia so long as our political situation is not clear in the other direction; for if I am asked whether we have a secret treaty with Russia, I must be able to answer no."[13]

Risks accompanied this strategy and the Wilhelmstrasse took them into account. If the negotiations with London and Paris failed, the Russians would be in a position to exploit Berlin's diplomatic defeat and isolation and "kick Germany around," as one German diplomat put it. If, on the other hand, they succeeded, Moscow could claim that Germany's ties to London and Paris made any agreement with the USSR valueless. In either case, the Rapallo relationship initiated in 1922 would suffer heavy damage. Moreover, clear tactical reasons compelled negotiating with the USSR. Discussions with Moscow might be used as leverage with Paris and London, as a way of advancing the progress of the security pact negotiations that lagged through the spring and summer of 1925.[14] Nevertheless, the Germans declined to open negotiations with Russia. German-Soviet negotiations could precipitate, Schubert said, another Rapallo incident, "ein neuer Rapallo-Fall."[15]

With the future of Soviet relations with Europe at stake, the NKID resumed the offensive, complaining that Germany was conducting negotiations with Britain and France that would lead to a written treaty while making only verbal assurances to the USSR and postponing any serious negotiations that would lead to the binding bilateral obligations Moscow desired. On 3 July the NKID sent to the German Foreign Ministry the draft text of a treaty by the terms of which both parties would promise "not to resort to direct attacks or any other unfriendly actions against each other and not to enter into political or economic blocs, treaties, or agreements or combinations with other powers against the other contracting party . . . [and] henceforth to coordinate their actions in the question of membership of the League of Nations or sending observers to the League." To ascertain the reaction of the Wilhelmstrasse, Litvinov eventually traveled to Berlin and spoke with Stresemann on 8 April, and then conferred with Brockdorff-Rantzau in Moscow.[16] During the period from April to July, however, the German Foreign Ministry offered only lengthy explanations of German *Westpolitik*, verbal assurances, indications in principle, vaguely worded formulas, and postponement. Europe's security was being discussed and resolved, Rakovskii stated in July, "as if the Soviet Union did not exist."[17]

Overtures to Poland and France

The problem facing the NKID in 1925 was that of persuading Berlin of the need for a comprehensive political agreement with Moscow at a time when the benefits of cooperation with the United States, Great Britain, and France looked so promising. Chicherin's strategy for doing so did not include threats to sever relations with Berlin. He did, however, state that if Germany did not negotiate a political agreement, Moscow could no longer cooperate on a common policy toward Poland. Brockdorff-Rantzau interpreted such statements as efforts at "extortion." Moscow held Germany hostage, he maintained, and could deal with Berlin as ruthlessly as it pleased. Germany could not respond by breaking off relations, he argued, because the Russians would then reveal to the world the full extent of the secret military collaboration between the two countries. Were fears such as these well founded? Soviet diplomats did indeed remind the Wilhelmstrasse that they possessed information that would compromise, and perhaps even nullify, Germany's rapprochement with London and Paris— regarding both the secret military cooperation and the German offer to collaborate in "forcing back Poland to its ethnographic borders." These reminders were issued on crucial occasions, first in early June 1925, after Berlin had delayed responding to Chicherin's December initiative for five months, and again in October, on the eve of Stresemann's departure for Locarno.[18]

Chicherin's warning that Moscow might no longer cooperate with Germany on a common Polish policy gained some substance with the initiation of Soviet overtures to Warsaw.[19] These overtures were, however, more than simple efforts to demonstrate to Berlin the dangers of jeopardizing the Rapallo relationship; a settlement with Poland was the key to Russia's Eastern European security policy. As Chicherin informed the Fourteenth Party Congress in December 1925, the importance of Poland was

> that it is the only large state bordering on us in such a way that no military attack on us may be possible without Poland's participation.

This crucial strategic significance of Poland in case of any collisions in the West serves as the major stimulus to us for development of consistently friendly relations with Poland. It is so important that we are even willing to make concessions to the Polish positions on several touchy issues.[20]

The intrinsic strategic importance of an agreement with Poland did not prevent the NKID from making its overtures to Warsaw known to Berlin at particularly crucial stages in the development of the German rapprochement with France and Britain. Chicherin's first public announcement that prospects were favorable for improved relations between Poland and the USSR came in May 1925, at a time when German policy making was vulnerable, Berlin having waited almost four months for an official reply from Paris regarding the security treaty it had proposed in early February. "Our object," Chicherin told the Third Soviet Congress, "is to conclude a lasting agreement with Poland."[21] In early June an NKID memorandum addressed to the Wilhelmstrasse threatened to "look for other roads" in order to guarantee the security of the USSR. Then, in an emotional exchange with Stresemann on 13 June, Litvinov stated explicitly that the Western Europe security pact could leave Poland feeling vulnerable, that Warsaw could react by seeking support from the USSR, and that France too might pursue rapprochement with Moscow. Three days later, Rykov told Schubert that if Germany joined an anti-Soviet front, Russia could develop a rapprochement with both Poland and France. Statements such as these were not mere bluffs. In April, Chicherin had informed Herbette that the USSR was willing to conclude a nonaggression treaty with Poland, and he proposed that it be guaranteed by France, that Paris assure Moscow that Poland would not attack the USSR. All these efforts culminated when the Council of People's Commissars authorized Chicherin to visit Warsaw while en route to Berlin in late September just weeks prior to the Western European security conference at Locarno.[22] He remained in the Polish capital three days, proposed a commercial treaty, and spoke publicly of "an enduring rapprochement between our two countries."[23]

The prospects for a formal Soviet-Polish treaty agreement depended to a significant extent on the policy adopted in Paris. A Franco-Russian rapprochement might lead to improved Soviet relations with Poland—and serve other geopolitical functions as well. Potentially, Germany could be hindered from aligning itself too closely with the Anglo-Americans by the threat of a new Franco-Russian encirclement in response. At the same time, the attraction of relations with Russia might possibly prevent Paris from joining Britain in an anti-Soviet coalition.[24] Such were the possibilities present in the situation when Paris granted the USSR de jure recognition in October 1924 just a few days after the publication of the "Zinoviev letter."

In July 1924 Rakovskii, who as Soviet *polpred* in London at the time negotiated the recognition agreement with France, had announced publicly that French recognition of the USSR was not simply a matter of debts and private property rights; French security was at stake. With the Ruhr occupation ending, France needed protection against "the eventuality of a military danger from German nationalism," security that France would find, he added, only in the Soviet Union.[25] And the following December, when Chicherin first proposed a Soviet-German neutrality treaty to Brockdorff-Rantzau, he put the Franco-Soviet alliance on the table as a bargaining chip: "We won't do anything with Herbette if you don't do anything with Chamberlain."[26] Such statements raised questions that are both intriguing and momentous. Of what value was Chicherin's bargaining chip? How substantial was Rakovskii's threat? Would Paris be sufficiently eager for an agreement with the USSR aimed at containing Germany to write down the debts of the Russian past, grant Moscow long-term credits, and join in a Paris-Warsaw-Moscow axis in opposition to Berlin? Here was the material of which Brockdorff-Rantzau's nightmares were made. Schubert and Stresemann were likewise concerned that a Franco-Soviet rapprochement might be directed against Germany, although Maltzan was not. And at least one historian has maintained that because the French were, by the mid-1920s, much more concerned about the threat to the security of Eastern Europe posed by the Germans than that posed by the USSR, the Franco-Soviet Nonaggression Pact of 1932 and the alliance of 1935 were implicit in the diplomatic logic of 1925–26.[27] In actuality, what were the political prospects for a new Franco-Russian alliance?

After recognizing the Soviet regime, Paris too put relations with Moscow on hold. Herriot told the American ambassador that he did not want to repeat MacDonald's error of rushing into debt-loan-trade talks with the Soviets, an attitude that earned him Chicherin's scorn.[28] And when Herriot left office in April 1925, both Briand, his successor as foreign minister, and Philippe Berthelot, the secretary-general at the Quai d'Orsay, deliberately withheld support from a Franco-Soviet rapprochement so long as relations with Germany were undefined and the security of Western Europe remained unsettled. A committee of French and Soviet experts meeting in Paris from April to September 1925 failed to find a basis for determining the Russian debt, and not until after the Locarno Conference, and more than a year after recognition, was the NKID able to undertake an intensive effort to improve relations with France. Chicherin arrived in Paris on 11 December, and there he and Rakovskii, now *polpred* in Paris, had a ten-day series of receptions, luncheons, and meetings with Briand and Berthelot. The two sides agreed on the agenda for a Franco-Soviet conference—war debts, loans, a trade agreement, and political relations. Briand was cordial and promised that France would never allow itself to be used as a "battering ram" against the Soviet Union.[29] And at the end of the meetings, Chicherin and Rakovskii made a series of optimistic statements to the press regarding what Chicherin, mimicking the rhetoric of Locarno, called "the new spirit" and the "mutual confidence" that had come to prevail between the two countries.[30]

In its effort to maneuver Paris into an agreement, Narkomindel did not fail to refer publicly to the threat German revisionism posed to the security of Eastern Europe. In a statement published in both *Izvestiia* and *Le Temps* in mid-January 1926, Rakovskii warned that France's ally Poland could benefit from some additional guarantees of security (presumably from Moscow and Paris) now that Locarno had given Germany "a certain liberty of action in the East."[31] In Chicherin's policy conception, however, a prospective Franco-Soviet rapprochement was always more a part of an effort to prevent the British from consolidating the continental powers than it was an attempt to warn the Germans against jeopardizing their special relationship with the USSR. In the end, the NKID was unable to engineer a Franco-Soviet security agreement of any kind. While Herbette enthusiastically received its repeated proposals for a Soviet-German-French "continental bloc," Briand and Berthelot rejected them outright.[32] This was just as well, for what Soviet national security interests required in 1925 was not a "continental bloc" but rather a relationship with France close enough to compensate for the deterioration of relations with England and for the loss of the exclusivity of the "community of fate" relationship with Germany.

This sort of rapprochement was not forthcoming either, although a full-scale Franco-Soviet debt settlement conference opened with great fanfare in February 1926.[33] Rakovskii led a delegation of some twenty members that included Preobrazhenskii, Politburo member Mikhail Tomskii, and Central Committee member Georgi Piatakov, indicating the importance the collective leadership attached to a treaty with France. Both sides expected the recently signed Locarno agreements to make the other party amenable. Rakovskii saw in Locarno the formation of a London-Berlin axis that isolated France, and against which Paris needed the reassurance of an agreement with the USSR. *Le Temps* (22 December), on the other hand, wrote that Russia's post-Locarno isolation would allow Paris to impose the terms of settlement on Moscow. As expected, the highest barrier to agreement proved to be the debt-loan nexus. The Soviets insisted, as they had at Genoa in 1922 and in London in 1924, that they could conclude no agreement to pay the debts of Russia's past unless they were granted loans or credits. A typical loan scheme—this one proposed by Trotsky—called for a loan yielding 11 percent, with 7 percent to be treated as interest and 4 percent as payment on the tsarist debt. The French government, however, could neither offer credits from its own treasury nor guarantee loans from French banks. The insolvency of the French treasury and the depreciation of the franc, which reached its greatest postwar extent during the first six months of 1926, made loans and/or guarantees impossible. The French delegation made this point repeatedly and added that the small investors of France—whom the leader of the French delegation, Senator Anatole de Monzie, called "the innocent crowd of little people"[34]—had trusted Russia once and been burned. Instead, they suggested a Genoa-type consortium of international capital. The delegation's adherence to these negotiating principles was strengthened by the opposition of organizations representing bondholders and property owners to any write-off of their claims. Government circles in Paris expressed little optimism regarding a settlement. Edouard Daladier, a Radical-Socialist deputy and an expert on Russian affairs, predicted even before the conference began that "the delegates will go on talking indefinitely and will achieve nothing."[35]

As he had in London in 1924, Rakovskii attempted to break the deadlock by means of personal diplomacy. He had direct access to French politicians, and, above all, he and de Monzie, who presided over the conference, had been friends for twenty-five years. With the consent of the NKID in Moscow, Rakovskii promoted the idea of a practical or pragmatic settlement—one that avoided discussion of the theoretical legal obligations of the Soviet government, limited discussion to redemption of prewar tsarist bonds, and excluded from indemnification the former owners of property nationalized by the revolution. He also made use of the security issue, believing that the political benefits the USSR could offer France would draw the French government into an otherwise diminished financial agreement. His trump card, he thought, was an offer of a Franco-Soviet treaty in which Moscow would make concessions on specific issues going back to the Civil War, including return of the fleet of the counterrevolutionary commander General Wrangel, seized by the Soviets. Berthelot and Briand were not drawn in, however, and insisted that an agreement on debts be concluded prior to any "political" discussions.

Rakovskii and de Monzie actually agreed on a plan. War debts would be written off. On the prewar tsarist debt, the USSR would pay 62 annuities of 60 million gold francs each. A partial moratorium would be imposed, and full payments would begin only during the third year. The French would advance credits of 225 million francs to the USSR. To guarantee repayment, the USSR would grant French lenders concessions to Soviet oil fields, and the interest and the principal on Russian obligations would be deducted from the oil deliveries. As was the case at Genoa and London, it proved easier to draft "a most feasible solution" to the debt-loan problem than to get one accepted by the respective parties involved, both governmental and private. Rakovskii and de Monzie designed their narrow settlement to favor small bondholders. It had less appeal to large bondholders, who could afford to wait. The industrial and commercial firms whose property had been nationalized in the revolution were left out of the proposed settlement. Rakovskii had little success in interesting French manufacturers in the prospects of the Soviet market. French big business had little incentive to support the agreement.

On 15–16 June 1926, Briand and Finance Minister Joseph Caillaux gave tentative approval to the scheme, however, which was composed in the form of a draft treaty. Whether their government or any French government could have survived a Chamber of Deputies vote of confidence on the proposed settlement is doubtful. And any opportunity that may have existed for a narrow settlement and for a successful conclusion to the Franco-Soviet Conference evaporated with the return of Poincaré to office both as premier and as finance minister in July. *Izvestiia* (19 July) predicted that Poincaré, fearing a post-Locarno Europe dominated by England and Germany, and hesitant about any possible entente with Germany, would look instead to an agreement with the Soviet Union to add weight to France's position in Europe. He did not. In fact, he took an even harder line on Russian debts than informed public opinion expected by insisting on compensation to the former owners of nationalized property, requiring payment of war debts as well as prewar debts (a claim France had in practice renounced at the time of the Genoa Conference, and that had been omitted from the de Monzie-Rakovskii proposal), and refusing either to grant government credits to the USSR or to guarantee private credits. Any one of these requirements would have made the settlement unacceptable to the USSR. Together they made further progress toward agreement impossible.

During the era of "socialism in one country," traditional diplomacy and conventional power politics constituted the means by which the USSR confronted the reversals that the resolutions of the RCP(B) and the Comintern termed "the international stabilization of capitalism." In employing these means the NKID Collegium participated in European power politics with exceptional skill and ruthlessness. Russian diplomats offered to Berlin a far-reaching Soviet-German alliance and repeatedly proposed a "continental bloc" to be composed of the USSR, Germany, and France. They threatened indirectly to reveal the secret Russo-German military collaboration as well as Berlin's interest in "pushing Poland back to its ethnographical borders." They made demonstrative public pronouncements about forming a Franco-Soviet alliance and concluding a rapprochement with Poland that would leave Germany powerless to revise the territorial provisions of the peace settlement in Eastern Europe. Thereby they aimed not to isolate Germany from the Western entente in an exclusive relationship with the USSR but rather to use relations with Berlin to prevent Soviet isolation and to regain a place in the councils of the great powers comparable to what the Russian Empire had held prior to the Bolshevik Revolution.

Serious misconceptions shaped the NKID's conduct of power politics with the states of Europe, misconceptions that did not help to extricate the Soviet Union from the international plight in which it found itself. Narkomindel's efforts to keep France out of the Anglo-American camp were based on an overestimation of the magnitude of the contradictions within the Anglo-French Entente. The Soviets calculated that Paris would resent the role of "supreme arbiter" that they thought Britain was assuming in European diplomacy in 1924–25, and that a rapprochement between Paris and Moscow might be built out of this resentment. They based this supposed resentment on an estimate of Anglo-French relations dating back to the antagonism within the Entente at the time of the Ruhr crisis in 1923. But that antagonism did not persist. First MacDonald and then Chamberlain reconciled with Herriot the foreign policies of Britain and France and reformed the Entente into something that was more cordial than it would be at any time between the two world wars.[36] Similarly, Narkomindel's efforts to separate Berlin from London were also misconceived. They were based on an overestimation of the willingness of the German Foreign Ministry to join in an anti-British "continental bloc" or even to appear to be colluding with the Russians at a time when Berlin needed London to intercede with Paris in favor of a negotiated revision of the Versailles peace.

Moscow's view of the sources and direction of British foreign policy itself was also subject to considerable distortion. Beginning in the spring of 1925, the nationalist and anticolonial revolutionary movement in China escalated into a series of strikes and demonstrations against foreign interests there—the May 30th movement. The geopolitics of revolution and counterrevolution suggested that Great Britain would respond to this challenge to the British Empire in Asia with a counterthreat to the Soviet Union launched from Europe. Chicherin realized that any improvements in economic and diplomatic relations with the capitalist states were held hostage to Soviet "good behavior" in Asia. The party leadership meanwhile came to regard the agreements and institutions of international stabilization—the Dawes Plan, the Locarno Treaties, the League of Nations Council—as British-controlled weapons pointed at the USSR. However, no full consensus developed in Moscow after 1924 regarding just what level of hostility the British were directing, or would or could direct, toward them. Nor was there agreement among the policy-making elite in London regarding exactly how dangerous the USSR was to the British Empire, or just what British policy toward Soviet Russia should be.

Great Britain and the Policy of Disregard

When in early 1925 the War Office in London undertook a review of possible threats to the security of the British Empire, it decided that the most serious danger confronting the Empire was posed by the Soviet Union. Soviet forces, it warned, were positioned along the southern rim of the USSR along the frontiers with Persia, Afghanistan, and China, and an incursion into Afghanistan would put the security of India at risk—a serious matter because India was the largest strategic liability in the British Empire, and the Afghan frontier was the weak point in India's defenses.[37] The Foreign Office, however, doubted whether the Red Army was capable of offensive military operations, and Austen Chamberlain regarded a Russian threat to India to be at most one possible danger to the Empire at some point in the future. To make military preparations for a war against Russia in Asia, he warned, would only magnify Soviet fears of encirclement and lead to further threats against Britain.[38]

Chamberlain's central purpose was to reorganize Europe into a new concert of powers in which Britain would hold the balance and over which London could preside from what he called "a semi-detached position." The prime prerequisite to this new concert, he thought, was reconciliation between France and Germany. One day Russia would reemerge as a major power, but Chamberlain did not think that day would come very soon. When it did come, however, he wanted Germany to have been already linked to the West and precluded from joining the USSR in an anti-Entente, anti-Versailles alliance. Chamberlain intended the containment of Soviet power to be a consequence of his reorganization of Europe, but it was not the immediate objective at which his policy was aimed. In his conception of European international relations, the Russian problem would be solved by the reconciliation of Germany, which was in turn based on maintaining the British Entente with France.[39]

Chamberlain believed that the "great mass of information" assembled by British intelligence regarding Soviet/Comintern subversion in the British Empire justified severing diplomatic relations.[40] However, he opposed a break with the USSR, largely because it would disrupt the project on which he was most intent—the pacification of European international relations. Instead, on the advice of the Foreign Office, he recommended to the new Conservative Cabinet a policy of ignoring the Soviet Union as much as possible and for as long as possible. It was July 1925, seven months after coming to office, before the Cabinet thoroughly examined the general policy to be followed in relations with the USSR, and then it adopted a policy Chamberlain characterized as treating the Russians "as though they didn't exist" and keeping formal relations "as distant as possible." Toward the USSR the Conservative government adopted what has been aptly termed "a policy of disregard."[41] This was not the policy of Lloyd George, who tried to tame the Bolsheviks with trade. Nor was it the policy of Curzon, who sought to menace them into timidity. Nor was it the policy of the die-hard intransigents within the Conservative Party leadership, who wanted to break off relations entirely. Rather, it was a policy that put Moscow in a holding pattern in November 1924 and kept it there while Britain arranged the security of Europe with Germany, France, Belgium, and Italy. It coincided with Berlin's strategy of procrastination and with the similar policy adopted by Herriot and Briand in Paris, both of which also left the NKID waiting, thereby nourishing Moscow's fears of isolation.

Through diplomatic channels and in the press, the Soviet government made clear to London that it wished to resume negotiations along the lines of the Anglo-Soviet Draft Treaty negotiated by the Labour government in the summer of 1924 and that it wanted to apply for credits from London banks.[42] Chamberlain, however, refused either to recommend the treaty to Parliament or to renegotiate it, and he urged Churchill, now chancellor of the exchequer (1924–29), to advise the banks of the City to refuse credits to the USSR. In response to NKID efforts to initiate negotiations, Chamberlain made unspecified allegations of Soviet subversion against British interests in Asia (conducted, he charged, by Soviet diplomatic and trade representatives), demanded that the Soviet government take responsibility for the Comintern's statements and actions, and stated that only a change in Soviet policy regarding debts and propaganda would clear the way for improved relations.[43] Soviet representatives in London complained that they were "kept at a distance and practically ignored by the British government."[44]

Meanwhile, Sir William Joynson-Hicks, the home secretary (1924–29), conducted a campaign, both within the government and with the British public, calling for an end to relations with the USSR. Launched in May 1925, his campaign was soon joined by Lord Birkenhead, secretary of state for India (1924–28), who called the Soviet government "a band of murderers and robbers" and who warned publicly that England would not always stand by helplessly while the USSR worked to destroy the British Empire. Chicherin in return called Birkenhead's statement "aggressive in the extreme, and [amounting] to a demand for the most hostile measures against us, beyond which there is only war." Chicherin's charge was supplemented in the Soviet press by descriptions of British intrigues aimed at organizing an anti-Soviet bloc. Joynson-Hicks, Birkenhead, and Churchill were the leading figures among the diehards, those within the Conservative Party who called for an end to relations with the USSR and for the adoption of an aggressive anti-Communist policy at home and abroad. Churchill, who referred to the Soviet government "as the dark conspirators of the Moscow Kremlin," promoted the idea of a worldwide diplomatic front against the USSR. That front could be formed in East Asia, he suggested, by a revival of the Anglo-Japanese alliance and through further economic penetration of China, and in Europe it could be achieved by "giving effect" to the Locarno Treaties.[45] It was Churchill's policy position that came closest to what was represented in CPSU and ECCI resolutions as the primary objective of British foreign policy—to construct a hostile encirclement of the USSR.

Robert Hodgson, the British representative in Moscow, was a voice of moderation and conciliation. He criticized the government's policy of disregard; he made unauthorized attempts to improve relations with the Soviet government; he supported resumed negotiations along the lines of the Anglo-Soviet Draft Treaty; he advocated increased trade with the Soviet Union; he recommended that export credits be extended. Hodgson's efforts came very near to success in the late winter and spring of 1926, when for both economic and geopolitical reasons Chamberlain gave serious consideration to his recommendations. British industry was pressing the Foreign Office to open the Russian market to English goods; the Franco-Soviet debt-loan-trade negotiations in Paris seemed on the verge of success; and in Berlin, Germany concluded a political treaty with Moscow. In this situation, Chamberlain instructed the Foreign Office staff to prepare the materials necessary for reopening negotiations with Moscow.

These preparations were interrupted by Soviet involvement in the General Strike in Britain in May. The Red International of Trade Unions (Profintern) attempted to transfer strike funds collected by the All-Union Central Council of Trade Unions to British strikers, and when the Trades Union Congress (TUC) rejected them, the funds were offered directly to striking British miners. Although Profintern made no effort to advise the miners in the practical matters of organizing their strike, the die-hard campaign against the "Red Menace" intensified and the prospective revision of Britain's Soviet policy was aborted. The best opportunity to achieve export credits and ambassadorial-level diplomatic relations with Britain that occurred during the era of "temporary capitalist stabilization" was thus spoiled, after which Anglo-Soviet relations deteriorated steadily.[46] By December 1926, John D. Gregory, the expert on Soviet affairs at the Foreign Office, had come to see the merits of a quick and decisive break in relations, a sort of diplomatic surprise attack. An action such as this, one of "sudden and unexpected violence," he stated, would "cause a panic in the Bolshevik camp."[47]

During the months following the General Strike, Chamberlain, with the support of Prime Minister Stanley Baldwin, fought a rearguard action against a mounting die-hard campaign to sever relations with Moscow. Although he argued that a break in relations would deprive British industry of Soviet orders for machinery, reasons of geopolitics and considerations of high policy were most central to his position. An overt display of British hostility toward the USSR would, Chamberlain maintained, evoke pro-Soviet sentiment in China and undermine the position of Britain there as well as that of the other China powers. In Europe, he thought, a break with the USSR would complicate Stresemann's efforts to balance Germany between Russia and the West. Because Germany played a key role in his vision of a pacified Europe, Chamberlain accepted Stresemann's efforts at diplomatic balance as necessary to German foreign policy. In the words of his accustomed metaphor, Chamberlain did not want to drive either China or Germany "into the arms of the Russians." Nevertheless, this consideration was not a sufficient reason for him to recommend improved relations with the USSR to the Cabinet. When Stresemann tried to promote diplomatic reconciliation between London and Moscow—in order to avoid the dilemma of having to opt either for the Soviet Union or for the Western entente in the event of crisis—Chamberlain and the Foreign Office made no response. On the other hand, Chamberlain did not urge the other Locarno powers to follow the British lead into policies of disregard. He welcomed improved relations among France, Germany, and Russia, he stated, because he believed that any rapprochement between Russia and the other powers of Europe could only contribute to European pacification.[48] Chamberlain thereby assiduously avoided any appearance of initiating an anti-Soviet coalition.

Thus, the policy of disregard was one that neither broke off relations with Moscow nor negotiated a debt settlement and guaranteed loans. The policy was inherently unstable largely because Chamberlain shared a common set of beliefs with his chief critics, the diehards. Together they paid disproportionate attention to the revolutionary statements issuing from the Comintern and were impressed by the evidence of propaganda and subversion reported by British intelligence and security services. Both exaggerated the ideological motivations behind Soviet policy and were deeply suspicious of the NKID's campaign for normal relations. They ignored the pragmatic purposes behind Soviet policy—the real need for a period of peace in which to construct socialism and the equally real need for foreign credits with which to finance trade and promote economic development. Both made "honoring debts" and "ending propaganda" the center of British policy toward the Soviet Union. From the time the Conservatives entered office in November 1924, Chamberlain and the diehards regarded the USSR from a common policy perspective. Eventually, in May 1927, Chamberlain would yield to their determination, and to the advice of the Foreign Office, and suspend diplomatic and commercial relations with Moscow.

Until that time the "dual policy" characterized Soviet relations with Britain. That policy was conducted through a "united front" alliance of the Soviet and the British trade union movements as well as through the newly established but faltering diplomatic channels. That "united front" was embodied in the Anglo-Russian Joint Advisory Council (ARJAC), formed in April 1925 and presided over by Mikhail Tomskii, president of the Soviet Central Council of Trade Unions and a member of the Politburo.[49] Trotsky, Zinoviev, Bukharin, and Stalin all supported the "united front" with the TUC as the means of creating a mass revolutionary movement in England. There was a diversity of opinion among them, however, about the ultimate direction in which the "united front" would take that movement.

That disagreement was latent in the contrasting attitudes adopted by Stalin and Trotsky in the spring of 1926. Stalin viewed "united fronts" as a means of organizing the working class of England and of other European states against "new imperialist wars" in general and against wars of intervention against the USSR in particular. They were a deterrent against aggression. If attacked, he stated, "we shall take all measures to unleash the revolutionary lion in every country on earth. The leaders of the capitalist countries must realize that we have some experience in such matters."[50] Trotsky, on the other hand, saw the "united front" in Britain in terms of class rather than of national relations. In *Where is Britain Going?* (1926) he cautioned that the alliance with the TUC could strengthen the collaborationist right and center leadership of the British labor movement, hamper the development of the British Communist Party, and leave the working class unprepared for what he saw as the developing social crisis and class conflict there.[51]

The General Strike in May brought this divergence among the Bolshe-viks into the open. Although Zinoviev had stated, in his report to the Sixth ECCI Plenum in February 1926, that Britain had replaced Germany as the most likely candidate for proletarian revolution in Europe,[52] no one among the CPSU leadership was prepared for the General Strike. This may explain in part why their reaction to it was so counterproductive. Profintern support for British strikers destroyed the Soviet's best opportunity to improve relations with the second Baldwin government, and it gave new inspiration to the campaign of the diehards without ensuring the victory of the strikers. Trotsky, who had allied himself with Zinoviev and Kamenev in a "new" or "united" Opposition at the time of the Central Committee meeting in April, attacked the Stalin-Bukharin leadership for transforming the "united front" into an alliance with trade union bureaucrats for the purpose of getting the CPGB to fulfill the diplomatic interests of the Soviet state.[53]

Stalin responded in a series of statements made at sessions of the Politburo, the Central Committee, and the ECCI during the period from June to December. He anticipated many of Trotsky's criticisms and justified the purposes of the "united front" completely in terms of interstate rela-tions. In summary, he stated that, at a time when capitalism was in a phase of "temporary stabilization," when socialism was under construction in one country, and when the USSR was economically and militarily vulner-able, both the national security and the economic development of Russia depended ultimately on the united efforts of the working class in Britain and elsewhere to oppose anti-Soviet tendencies within their countries. The task of the ARJAC, he stated in June, was "to organize a broad movement of the working class against new imperialist wars in general, and against intervention in our country by (especially) the most powerful of the European imperialist powers, by Britain in particular."[54] In effect, mobi-lizing the proletariat of England was supposed to do what the Red Army and the NKID together were not capable of—counteracting the growing hostility of the diehards and preventing the most powerful imperialist nation of Europe from intervening in either the Russian or the Chinese revolutions.

Locarno, the Party, and the NKID

We have seen that when the governments of Europe first granted diplo-matic recognition to the Soviet Union in 1924, the Politburo and the NKID Collegium together celebrated the successes of Soviet foreign relations. Party leaders and diplomats were in substantial agreement as to their analysis of both the international situation and the direction they expected foreign relations to take. However, between the publication of the "Zinoviev letter" in the autumn of 1924 and the break in relations with England in the spring of 1927 that consensus broke down. A divergence emerged between the stated position taken by the party leadership and that taken by Narkomindel.

In its estimate of the situation, the NKID was cautious and tentative. Chicherin maintained that world politics were in flux, that the direction of international relations was indeterminate, and that the situation seemed to be both improving and worsening for the USSR. He and Litvinov did not directly accuse Chamberlain, the British Foreign Office, or the Baldwin government of pursuing a policy aimed at encircling the USSR with a hostile coalition of capitalist states, although the NKID did protest in London the anti-Soviet statements made by individual members of the British government. This suggests that Narkomindel intended to conduct a flexible and nuanced foreign policy, one aimed not only at maintaining Moscow's ties to Berlin and settling outstanding differences with France, but also at reopening debt/loan negotiations with England.

This policy position contrasted sharply with the view agreed to by the majority leadership of the Central Committee. To them the events of 1924 represented a decisive turning point in international history, one that would influence an entire phase in the development of Soviet society and foreign relations. The stabilization of both capitalism and Communism would provide a prolonged period of respite from capitalist attack, one that would last for years, even decades, and that would allow the USSR to industrialize, construct socialism, and consolidate its alliances with the exploited workers of Europe and the oppressed peoples of Asia. Eventually capitalist stabilization would be undermined by armed uprisings within the colonies of the imperialist powers and by the resistance of the German proletariat to the burdens of paying reparations.

By contrast, Stalin's own personal conception of the future direction of international politics denied that a protracted respite existed. In the events leading from the publication of the "Zinoviev letter" to the signing of the Treaties of Locarno a year later, he envisioned the approach of a second imperialist war that would begin "in a few years time." From the conferences, treaties, and anti-Soviet campaigns of 1925 he concluded that the imperialist powers were arming themselves, encircling the USSR, and preparing for military conflict. In all probability, this conflict would be preceded, he thought, by a preemptive strike against the USSR, a second war of imperialist intervention launched by the threatened ruling strata of the major powers to prevent the homeland of socialism from benefiting from the struggle among them.

Regarding the Locarno Treaties, there was considerable unanimity among the party leadership. Spokesmen from Bukharin to Zinoviev denounced them as a set of agreements that would complete the domination of the Continent by Anglo-American capital, consolidate and stabilize bourgeois control over Europe, and form the nucleus of a British-led coalition of powers hostile to the USSR.[55] In December 1925, the month the treaties were signed in London, the Stalin- and Bukharin-dominated Fourteenth Party Congress resolved that "the relative stabilization and the so-called pacification of Europe under the hegemony of Anglo-American capital has led to a whole system of economic and political blocs, the most recent of which was the Locarno Conference, and the so-called 'guarantee pacts' which were directed at the USSR."[56] In this response to the Locarno Treaties, Leninist ideology functioned obviously and significantly: Because of the presumed unremitting hostility of the international bourgeoisie toward proletarian power, Chamberlain's policy of disregard, Stresemann's policy of postponement, and the similar policy adopted by Herriot could not be passive. They had to be active ingredients in the formation of a hostile anti-Soviet coalition.

In turn, the allegation that the Treaties of Locarno formed the basis for a British-led capitalist coalition directed against the USSR functioned unmistakably in intracommunist relations. The emergence of a tangible foreign threat to the security of the socialist homeland was a means of committing foreign Communists to the defense of the USSR, thereby integrating the sections of the Comintern behind the purposes of the CPSU. As such, that threat functioned as an instrument of "bolshevization." By characterizing Locarno as a threat to the Soviet Union, the party's leaders suited their analysis of the European diplomatic situation both to their concern for Soviet security and to their increasing control over relations among the parties of the international Communist movement.

In reality, Locarno did *not* represent a direct threat to the USSR—largely because Chicherin was able to prevent German affiliation with the Western European security project and with the League of Nations from endangering Soviet security. In face-to-face negotiations with Stresemann in Berlin on the eve of the Locarno Conference, he reduced Soviet policy concerns to two fundamental elements and presented them to the German foreign minister. One was that Germany not participate in League sanctions against the USSR; the other was that Berlin not guarantee the borders of Poland. In that neither of these were in the interests of Germany, Stresemann gave to Chicherin binding commitments on both counts. Then at the conference in Locarno, the German delegation was able both to gain exemption from League sanctions and to avoid endorsing Poland's frontiers.[57]

Significantly, it was conventional diplomacy conducted by the NKID, more than anything else, including international proletarian solidarity, that provided security for the USSR eight years after the October Revolution.

Not surprisingly, the NKID adopted a less strident attitude toward the Locarno agreements than did Stalin in his Political Report of the Central Committee to the Fourteenth Party Congress. In Chicherin's report to that same congress—which was then kept secret and not published until 1991— he surveyed what he called "the landscape after Locarno." While disparaging what he called the "phony noise of Locarno" and the "constant pacifist phraseology" surrounding the treaty, Chicherin concluded that, so far as the interests and security of the USSR were concerned, there were "no reasons for panic." With the exception of England, the major nations of the world from France to Japan have "finally become convinced of the stability of Soviet power." Earlier, a series of events from the Kronshtadt rebellion in 1921 to the death of Lenin in 1924 had led them to hope for its collapse, but that had changed. "The opinion that Soviet power is here to stay, and that there will be no other Russia to deal with, is becoming almost universal." Convinced of the value of Soviet natural resources, the importance of the Russian market, and the influence of the USSR in world politics, the governments of France, Germany, Poland, and perhaps Italy would soon be conducting negotiations with the Soviet Union. (With England, he admitted, there was at "this moment no hope of making a deal, . . . and we must abandon any thought of entering talks with her.") The NKID was engaged, Chicherin explained further, in a "program of reaching separate bilateral agreements with separate states," a diplomatic system for Europe that it offered in opposition "to the hypocritical system of Locarno."[58]

Regarding the purposes of British foreign policy, Chicherin's views differed sharply from those of Stalin. "I must tell you," he stated bluntly to the party congress, "that my conclusion is that the English leadership is not considering a military intervention. There may be occasionally some chit-chat about this, but that is superficial, not serious." Nor did the English government expect "to see Soviet power toppled," he added. Rather, their goal was to alter Soviet foreign relations, to "soften us, to make us repay the debts and to give up our policy in the East." The apparent means by which they were attempting to do this was economic pressure. By cutting the USSR off from foreign credits and by impeding Russia's foreign trade, London was trying to "exploit the discontent of peasants inside the Soviet Union" and to accentuate the social crisis within the USSR.[59] Chicherin's bluntness reveals his confidence and his political realism at a time when the intraparty discussion of foreign relations was becoming both doctrinaire and contentious.

Thus, by the end of 1925, three not completely compatible concepts of world politics had been formulated in Moscow. Each differed from the others in its analysis of the international situation, in its predictions for the future, and in its prescription for Soviet foreign relations. The years 1924–1926, usually viewed in terms of the struggle among the party leadership over the issues of "socialism in one country" versus "permanent revolution" and over isolationist versus integrationist strategies of economic development, were also the years when the future of Soviet foreign policy was at stake.

8 Russia, Europe, and Asia after Locarno

Southwest Asia and the Soviet Security System

The Treaties of Locarno were of historic significance in that they incorporated the two most significant developments of post–World War international relations—the reconstruction of the Entente between France and England and the rapprochement between Germany and the victors of the war—and ratified a third—the influx of American capital. The rapprochement between Germany and the West provided material for apprehension in Moscow, although opinion differed regarding whether it posed an immediate threat to the USSR. The Anglo-French Entente, however, caused fear in Ankara and Tehran. The postwar colonial rivalry between Britain and France had created diplomatic space in which the governments of Turkey and Persia could maneuver; as a result, the two states had become increasingly independent of European control and influence, as had Afghanistan. A reconstituted Anglo-French Entente threatened that independence. What if the agreements London and Paris had made regarding reparations and security were extended to their colonial affairs? Reconstruction of the Franco-British colonial entente concluded in 1904 could lift from British colonialism the restrictions imposed by European high politics and unleash a newly confident imperialism in Asia.

By suggesting the possibility of a linkage between the security of Europe and Asia, the Locarno agreements constituted an important factor in the way international relations were regarded both in southwest Asia and in Russia. A settlement on the Rhine potentially endangered the modernizing nationalism of Kemal Pasha and Reza Shah. And to the collective leadership in Moscow, Locarno looked not only like an anti-Soviet front of European states but also like an agreement that could potentially transform the alignment of global politics. If the Western

European security pact were succeeded by "Locarnos" among the states on the frontiers of the USSR—in Eastern Europe, southwest Asia, and East Asia—then "hostile capitalist encirclement" would become a substantial reality.

The first line of defense against this possibility was encouragement for nationalist, anti-imperialist movements in Asia. The CPSU and the NKID agreed on this. As Chicherin explained the situation to the Fourteenth Party Congress, support for the nationalist regimes in Turkey, Persia, Afghanistan, and China was necessary for what he called "elementary security reasons." Leaving aside "general ideological perspectives" and "the ultimate goals of our policy," "the narrowly national-interest outlook" required close collaboration with these regimes.[1] At the same time, he took a clear stand in favor of an Eastern orientation for Soviet foreign policy. In what may have reflected the outcome of a debate within the NKID Collegium, he definitely rejected the possibility of abandoning support for Asian nationalism for the sake of closer relations with Europe and America. "Any speculation that through some changes in our Eastern policy we may gain any advantages in the West is nothing else than empty chat, based on the ignorance of history and our true position both in the West and in the East." "Indeed exactly at the present moment when our relations in the East turn out to be the main obstacle for final normalization in the West, we must unambiguously postulate the unquestionable importance of our present Eastern policy."[2]

To prevent the formation of hostile coalitions on the frontiers of the USSR either in Asia or in Europe, the NKID undertook a major diplomatic offensive in both regions. Its purposes were to prevent states on the borders of the USSR from being incorporated into what were viewed as diplomatic, economic, or military coalitions inspired by Locarno and led by Great Britain, and to prevent these states from being drawn into League-organized sanctions directed against the USSR. To these ends, the USSR concluded a series of bilateral treaties and trade agreements both with the states of southwest Asia and with those of the Baltic region. The first was a treaty concluded with Turkey in December 1925. Similar compacts followed with the two other states on the southern rim of the USSR, Afghanistan (August 1926) and Persia (October 1927).[3] The three treaties were then augmented by agreements concluded among the three states with the encouragement and sponsorship of the USSR—a Turco-Persian treaty in April 1926, a Perso-Afghan treaty in November 1927, and a Turco-Afghan treaty in May 1928. With the states on its northwest frontier, the USSR concluded treaties with Lithuania (September 1926), Latvia (July 1927), and Estonia (August 1927). Each of the treaties signed by Moscow contained similar provisions for mutual nonaggression and for neutrality in the event of war with a third power. Each party pledged moreover not to participate in commercial, financial, or military coalitions hostile to the other, to interfere in the internal affairs of the other, or to engage in hostile propaganda.

Construction of this elaborate and complex set of agreements was a remarkable diplomatic achievement. With these treaties the NKID precluded the formation of hostile economic blocs, neutralized adjacent states in the event of a second armed intervention, claimed a series of diplomatic victories in the aftermath of the Locarno "defeat," and helped stabilize the international status quo in the two regions. Narkomindel publicly represented them as an alternative security system, one incorporating bilateral agreements between nations rather than collective arrangements, sanctions, and other compulsory measures under the auspices of the League of Nations. *Izvestiia* proclaimed the treaties as "a new political system in international relations," "unprecedented in history," and the basis on which "true coexistence between this state and the [capitalist] world can be attained."[4] Rakovskii labeled the first of them, the treaty with Turkey, "our reply to Locarno." Chicherin explained it to the Central Committee as a document that should "serve as a model of the kind of agreements that we are ready to conclude with any country," and he announced that the Soviet government was prepared to conclude similar bilateral treaties with other states—including England. Such agreements represented "true pacifism," he stated, "in place of the phony noise of Locarno and Chamberlain's policy." These treaties, "and not the machinations of the League of Nations or pacts like Locarno," Litvinov added, "will really help to avert war."[5]

Significantly, two terms were missing from the rhetoric surrounding this succession of treaties. The spokesmen for Soviet foreign policy made no mention of forming a "united anti-imperialist front" in southwest Asia, such as had existed from 1921 to 1923, and they undertook no discussion of the prospects for socialist revolution there.[6] Indeed, the bilateral treaties marked another giant step in the historic compromise made by the initiators of global proletarian revolution with the forces of authoritarian and anticommunist modernization. At the very time the treaty with Turkey was under negotiation in 1925, the Turkish government made membership in the Communist Party of Turkey a criminal offense, arresting eighteen leading party officials and sentencing them to prison for a total of 177 years. The Soviet government ignored these actions; the NKID issued no protest; the publications of the Communist International greeted the proclamation with silence and continued to praise the government of Turkey for its progressive social legislation.[7]

In like manner, Soviet foreign policy objectives in the Arabian peninsula were derived from classical balance of power principles, and the methods their diplomats used there were uninformed by a theory of class relations. Chicherin took a keen interest in Arab affairs. As part of a counter-British policy in Arabia, he envisaged coordinating diplomacy in the area, at least tacitly, with the efforts of France, Italy, and the United States, as well as cooperating closely with Turkey in the region. He even considered sponsoring a Turkish-Arab rapprochement, after centuries of hostility. At the same time, he was intent on honoring the antipropaganda commitments his government had made to London at the time of the trade agreement of 1921 and the "Curzon ultimatum" in 1923 and instructed the Soviet representative in Hejaz to keep all his contacts "such as to preclude being seen as elements of anti-British agitation." In its relations with Arab leaders, Narkomindel aimed to strengthen their independence against British influence, to establish normal relations with them, and, above all, to foster Arab nationalism and unity. "In a nut shell, what we are after on the Arab issue," Chicherin wrote, "is to see all the Arab lands united into one state unity."[8]

Initially, conducting this policy entailed exchanging representatives (from August to October 1924) with Husein ibn-Ali, sharif of Mecca, king of the Hejaz, and leader of the Hashemite clan of the Kureish tribe to which the Prophet himself had belonged. Husein refused to recognize the Paris peace settlement and the League of Nations mandate system, and he supported the Arab cause in Palestine. Chicherin saw in him a source of trouble for the British. Soon, however, he identified the "vigorous, warlike, and powerful" (in Chicherin's words) Abdul-Aziz ibn-Saud, the leader of the Wahhabis of Nejd, as the "champion of Arab unification," a potential "prominent leader of the East," and a probable Soviet ally.[9] Because London had cut off the subsidy it had granted ibn-Saud during the World War as an anti-Turkish leader, Chicherin regarded him as available for alignment with Moscow. "We are sure," he told Philippe Berthelot during the Lausanne Conference, that a new Saudi-led Arabia "will eventually become our friend."[10]

Soviet diplomacy was conducted accordingly. In the war between Husein and ibn-Saud that began in the spring of 1921, the Saudi forces stood accused in the international community of damaging holy shrines as they captured first Mecca (October 1924) and then Medina (December 1925) from Husein and his son Ali. Chicherin instructed the Soviet representative in Tehran to undertake a defense of the Wahhabis against the charges. And when ibn-Saud took Jidda and proclaimed himself "King of Hejaz and Sultan of Nejd and adjacent territories" in January 1926, the NKID recognized the Saudi state almost immediately, thus making the USSR the first country to do so. The following June at the Islamic Congress in Mecca, the representative of the Muslims of the USSR cast his ballot for the election of ibn-Saud as chairman of the congress—a position of importance if the Saudis were to be recognized as keepers of the holy places.[11]

For the Saudis, the USSR represented a way out of diplomatic isolation (Great Britain recognized Saudi sovereignty and independence only in May 1927) and toward recognition in the Arab world. For the USSR, Hejaz was a place from which to frustrate British predominance in southwest Asia as well as a channel for Soviet intelligence and influence over Islam. "Getting to Mecca is of crucial importance to us," Chicherin had written in 1924.[12] And it was so that they could travel to Mecca that the NKID appointed Muslims as counsels-general at Jidda—K. A. Khakimov (1924–26) and N. T. Tiuriakulov (1926–36). Because the *hajj*, the annual pilgrimage to Mecca, brought together Islamic leaders from Egypt to India, Mecca constituted, in the opinion of the NKID, an ideal listening post and contact point in their relations with diverse political movements among Muslim peoples. (Tiuryakulov actually performed the *hajj* and was greeted in Mecca as a pilgrim by ibn-Saud.)[13] Much to the consternation of the NKID, the OGPU (the Soviet state security service) obstructed the pilgrimage movement in the USSR. By contrast, Narkomindel recommended to the Politburo in February 1926 that "persons of influence in Muslim quarters who could promote our policy there" should be sent on the *hajj* "under the guise of ordinary pilgrims." "The best policy," the recommendation continued, "would be to bring the Muslim masses' spontaneous drive for the Hajj under our own control" and to provide the pilgrims with direct passage to the Red Sea on Sovtorgflot ships.[14]

By the end of 1926, the NKID Collegium had great expectations for its Saudi policy.[15] It hoped to strengthen the new king's position in southwest Asia, to use Russian good offices to improve his relations with Persia and Turkey, to prevent him from joining the League of Nations, to conclude a treaty of friendship with him, and to upgrade relations to the ambassadorial level. Ibn-Saud's son, Prince Faisal, made plans to visit Paris and Moscow, and it appeared as if another authoritarian modernizer in Islamic Asia, independent of the control and influence of Great Britain and with ties to the USSR, would emerge in southwest Asia. However, the friendship treaty was never signed, probably because ibn-Saud's Arabia was still formally under a British protectorate and was therefore vulnerable to any potential exertion of British power. The state visit was cancelled.[16]

Thus the Saudi kingdom did not become part of the Soviet post-Locarno security system. Nor did it become an important market for Soviet goods. The largest single export to the Arab world—prior to the discovery of

petroleum reserves on the Arabian peninsula—was gasoline/kerosene re-
fined at Baku and shipped to Arabia via Batum. The deliveries agreed to in
August 1930 did not arrive on schedule, however, and all modern services
in the kingdom, from mail delivery to health care, came to a standstill.[17]
Although Soviet-Saudi relations were upgraded to the ambassadorial level
in 1929 and the state visit of Prince Faisal finally took place in 1932, the
diplomatic mission in Jidda was closed in 1936 and never reopened. Ultimately, reactionary fears of social and political change precluded a rapprochement between the Saudi ruling family and those who had made the
October Revolution.

In the aftermath of Locarno, the NKID directed its most all-out diplomatic effort in southwest Asia at Persia. On 16 October 1925, the day the
Treaties of Locarno were initialed in Switzerland, Reza Shah announced
that he would visit Berlin as well as Moscow during his imminent trip to
Europe. When Soviet diplomats combined this statement with evidence of
conciliatory steps taken by the British government toward Tehran, they
became alarmed at the prospect that the Locarno of Europe was about to
spread to southwest Asia. On both continents, apparently, the British were
initiating coalitions with possible anti-Soviet purposes. "Hostile encirclement" loomed. The response of the NKID was to instruct Konstantin
Yurenev, the veteran diplomat and *polpred* in Tehran (1927–33), to press
for a treaty of neutrality and a new trade agreement. The arm-twisting,
aimed at keeping Persia away from the Locarno powers, was intense.[18] On
the day the shah announced his visit to Berlin, the Soviet government
declared that it would temporarily suspend aid to Persia, and soon thereafter the USSR suddenly imposed a total embargo on Persian imports.

The trade embargo had disastrous consequences for Persian agriculture
because the northern provinces of Persia were cut off from the rest of the
country by poor communications and transportation and depended heavily
on markets in the USSR. However, the most significant and effective
pressure Moscow could exert on Tehran was manipulating the ethnic
situation in northwest Persia. Political-geographical conditions along the
Perso-Turkish frontier were not well defined, and the two countries disputed the location of their common border. The area was populated by
Kurdish tribes that moved readily from one location to another. They
resisted rule from Tehran, and that resistance was penetrated by the
OGPU. Soon after Reza Shah announced his decision to visit Berlin,
Chicherin began to issue hints that the USSR favored Turkey in its border
dispute with Persia. And until a Soviet-Persian treaty was concluded two
years later (October 1927), OGPU activity among the Kurds—conducted
by a network of Soviet agents, mostly ethnic Armenians from Persia—con-

tinued and increased. It was centered at Saujbulagh and directed by the OGPU representative in Tabrīz.[19] At one point, formation of a Soviet Kurdish Republic was even considered at the upper levels of decision making in Moscow as a way of winning the sympathies of the Kurds of Persia, Turkey, and Iraq for the Soviet cause. The NKID defeated this scheme, however, by pointing out the damage it would cause to relations with both Turkey and Persia.[20]

In early 1926 the NKID shifted gears and introduced a policy of conciliation toward Tehran in an effort to attract Persia into its counter-Locarno treaty system. Moscow renewed offers of economic and military assistance and declared the USSR neutral in the Turco-Persian border dispute. The NKID sponsored the negotiations that led to the Turco-Persian neutrality treaty in April, from which a settlement of the border issue was expected to result. However, negotiations on the Soviet-Persian treaty were protracted by pressure on Tehran from London and by the opposition of nationalist-minded parliamentary leaders led by the future prime minister and martyr to Iranian nationalism, Dr. Mohammed Mossadegh. In the end, negotiations were accelerated by Persian resentment of London's support for the claims of the Kingdom of the Hejaz to the Bahrein Islands and by Moscow's isolation anxieties resulting from the war scare of the summer of 1927.

Consequently, Moscow and Tehran concluded six agreements, including a bilateral treaty of neutrality and nonaggression and a commercial agreement in October 1927.[21] Together with the Perso-Afghan treaty concluded in November, they completed the construction of a security zone of international stability along the southern rim of the USSR. The particular agreements signed with Tehran offered more advantages to Russia than they did to Persia. Tehran agreed not to join anti-Soviet coalitions of any kind, and a British presence in the country was all but excluded. Articles V and VI of the 1921 treaty, allowing the USSR to send troops to Persia in peacetime, were confirmed. Anti-Soviet émigré organizations in Persia were dissolved and their headquarters closed. The USSR retained partial control over the sturgeon fisheries of the southern Caspian Sea, but the port of Enzeli, which Soviet forces had continued to occupy and which was the symbol of Soviet penetration of Persia, was returned and its name changed to Pahlavi.[22]

Weimar Germany and Soviet Russia

The Treaty of Berlin—the German-Soviet Neutrality and Nonaggression Pact of April 1926—was the second treaty in the Soviet post-Locarno, counter-League security system to be signed, following the treaty with Turkey and preceding those with Afghanistan and Lithuania.[23] A European policy based on close ties to Germany and favorable relations with Turkey in the Middle East (along with détente with Japan in East Asia) were in Chicherin's eyes the crucial and indispensable elements of Soviet diplomacy, and had been so since 1921–22. In the context of the four-year-long Rapallo relationship, the Berlin Treaty had special meaning both in Moscow and in Berlin. Neither Soviet Russia nor Weimar Germany could have afforded *not* to conclude a formal agreement after Locarno. Failure to do so would have seemed an indication of serious discord between the two countries, the equivalent of a break in relations, something both Berlin and Moscow had a common interest in avoiding. However, different sets of considerations motivated Moscow and Berlin.

On the Wilhelmstrasse, Carl von Schubert feared that if Germany did not conclude an agreement with the USSR, the danger of a Franco-Soviet rapprochement would be heightened, the German economy would be disadvantaged by a decline in trade with Russia, and the domestic opponents of the Locarno rapprochement between Germany and the Western powers would be strengthened. Obversely, a treaty with Russia would enhance Berlin's position in international politics in that it would be associated with a USSR that was evolving toward increasing stability and prosperity under the conditions of NEP. And a neutrality agreement with the Soviet Union, when added to Germany's exemption from participation in League sanctions against the USSR, would strengthen German security. Germany would not become the battlefield of a war between Russia and the powers of Western Europe. Most of all, a German-Russian treaty would make clear to Warsaw that Germany would give Poland no assistance, either direct or indirect, in the event of a Polish conflict with the Soviet Union. In particular, no French military assistance would cross German territory. The time at which the Berlin Treaty was concluded was the period of greatest optimism for Weimar Germany's revisionist ambitions toward Poland. By keeping Poland militarily vulnerable, the Wilhelmstrasse calculated, Warsaw would be required to spend excessively on armaments. Polish public finances would be destabilized. A bailout by foreign capital would then become necessary. For its part in that rescue operation, Berlin would demand the return of the Polish Corridor and Upper Silesia.[24] The effect of the Berlin Treaty was to keep the issue of Poland's frontiers unsettled pending an international renegotiation of the borders of Eastern Europe.

In the explanation of Germany's Russian policy that Stresemann offered to the foreign ministries of Europe, he argued that Communism was not going to collapse in Russia and that the Berlin Treaty constituted the least costly way of reintegrating Russia into world politics. To that end the treaty was not incompatible with Locarno, he maintained; it actually effected "the completion of Locarno" by easing Russian fears about it and by promoting European-wide international reconciliation. The British bought Stresemann's line. Chamberlain described the treaty to the Cabinet as "innocuous" and "in conformity with the Locarno model." Lord D'Abernon, the British ambassador in Berlin (1920–26), called Stresemann's policy a bridge from Russia to Europe, and Chamberlain agreed. Germany could serve, he stated, as "the natural link between Russia and Europe," a connection that could "gradually give to Russian policy a western orientation, which would be the basis of cooperation between Russia and the other European powers." The best response to the Berlin Treaty, he thought, would be to demonstrate further to the Germans the advantages of cooperation with the West. To oppose the treaty would only "drive Germany further into the arms of Moscow."[25] In Warsaw and Prague, the foreign ministers of France's Eastern allies were alarmed by the treaty, and they were prepared to demand an explanation from Berlin. The worst thing to do, stated Edvard Beneš, the Czech foreign minister, would be to act as "if nothing happened." However, the British Foreign Office restrained them. In Paris, Briand seemed to regard the treaty as primarily a British concern and fell in readily behind London's policy.[26] The relatively calm response of London and Paris, when compared with their reaction to the Rapallo Treaty four years earlier, demonstrated the extent to which Stresemann succeeded in integrating Germany's relations with Russia and its rapprochement with France, Britain, and the United States into a coherent policy that was understood and accepted in Europe and America.

Was the German-Soviet neutrality treaty consistent with the Treaties of Locarno? That depended on what "Locarno" meant, Litvinov cleverly pointed out when he reported the agreement to the Central Committee. If the Locarno agreements were pacific and integrative in intent, the Berlin Treaty was consistent with them, and the supporters of Locarno should welcome it. If, on the other hand, the Locarno powers aimed at forming an anti-Soviet coalition, then "we must admit that the [Berlin Treaty] does contradict the spirit of Locarno, and we can only rejoice that we have succeeded to some extent in depriving Locarno of its anti-Soviet sting." Regarding the significance of the treaties of Berlin, Locarno, and Rapallo for Soviet-German relations, Litvinov maintained that the Treaty of Berlin meant not only a resumption of the Rapallo relationship after the interruption of Locarno, but also "an amplification of the Rapallo Treaty." Radek stated most directly what the Berlin Treaty meant to Moscow. It guaranteed that Germany would not be recruited into an anti-Soviet bloc—a pledge "taken openly before the whole world," he wrote, not to become "a weapon in the war against the Soviet Union."[27]

The Treaty of Berlin was neither a "high water mark" in Weimar-Soviet relations nor a major step in a long decline in German-Russian friendship since 1922.[28] Analyzed in terms of realpolitik, the Treaty of Berlin controlled the damage that might otherwise have been done to the security interests of the USSR by the German rapprochement with the victors of the World War. How did it do so? In effect, Germany obtained at Locarno unrestricted freedom from participation in sanctions against the Soviet Union, both direct and indirect, military and economic. This did not, however, satisfy the requirements of Soviet security as the NKID defined them. The problem with the agreements concluded at Locarno was that they justified Germany's exemption from imposing sanctions in terms of Germany's disarmed status under the Treaty of Versailles, and that they were agreements to which the USSR was not a party. From the perspective of the NKID, the British were fully capable of allowing the Germans to rearm, thereby enabling Germany to participate in sanctions. Chicherin and Litvinov insisted that Soviet security could not be left simply to declarations exchanged between the Western powers and Germany. Nor were they content with the vague statements embodied in the long, loosely worded preambles and protocols the Wilhelmstrasse had been proposing to the USSR ever since negotiations had begun in earnest in June 1925. They insisted that Berlin undertake binding commitments to the Soviet Union, and that these commitments be expressed in the form of a short, precise, unequivocal, formal, and published treaty. The Treaty of Berlin did all this.[29]

It also defined Germany's place in Soviet foreign relations more definitely than had been done at Rapallo. Despite the anti-Versailles statements that appeared in the theses adopted by congresses of the Comintern, Soviet diplomacy had shown little interest during the years since 1922 in collaborating with Weimar Germany for the purpose of overthrowing the World War peace settlement. "Forcing Poland back to its ethnographical borders" was a phrase employed by the NKID to manipulate Berlin tactically; it was not an element of a grand design for rearranging the frontiers of East-Central Europe. Moreover, Soviet Russia's German policy was aimed not at isolating Germany in an exclusive relationship with Moscow but at improving relations with the other capitalist powers. In this context, the purpose of the Berlin Treaty was to preserve, repair, and buttress "the German bridge" to Europe. As Krestinskii reported back to Moscow, continued close Soviet-German relations would be useful in negotiations with third parties. This was particularly important in April 1926, when Narko-mindel was making its most serious effort to resume treaty negotiations in London.[30] The Treaty of Berlin, like the treaty with Turkey, was regarded as a model for similar agreements with other European states, including England and even Poland.

In 1926 a treaty with Poland was both an objective of Soviet security policy and a lever to be used on Germany in the negotiations that led to the Berlin Treaty. On the one hand, Litvinov told Brockdorff-Rantzau that the less forthcoming Berlin was in its promises of neutrality to the USSR, the more Moscow would need to consider bringing third powers into its security system.[31] On the other hand, Poland's strategic location made it vital to Soviet security. Without Polish participation, no significant military offensive could be conducted against the USSR. If Germany was the corridor for an attack on the Soviet Union, Poland was the door. To obviate such participation, the NKID had in mind a three- to five-year Soviet-Polish nonaggression pact, and to obtain such an agreement, Chicherin informed Brockdorff-Rantzau, the Soviet government was prepared to reconfirm the results of the Russo-Polish War of 1920 as set down in the Treaty of Riga, to guarantee Poland's eastern frontier, and to write off large tracts of Byelorussian and Ruthenian territory—but not to guarantee Poland's border with Germany. It was imperative, he stated, to "create settled conditions along the western border [of the USSR] and above all prevent England from using Poland as a battering-ram against the Soviet Union."[32]

The Wilhelmstrasse objected to any arrangement that would satisfy or partially satisfy Poland's security requirements—whether by way of a guarantee treaty, a nonaggression pact, or even a treaty of arbitration and conciliation. Stresemann and Schubert informed the NKID during the Berlin Treaty negotiations that any such agreement would damage German-Russian trade relations and would be incompatible with the Soviet-German treaty under discussion.[33] In response, Litvinov and Krestinskii assured the Wilhelmstrasse verbally that the USSR would not join in an Eastern Locarno with Poland and the Baltic states and that it would not guarantee Poland's border with Germany. However, Moscow's distinction between Poland's eastern and western frontiers did not bridge the fundamental divergence between Russian and German policies in Eastern Europe, a divergence that rendered relations between Moscow and Berlin inherently unstable, despite the Berlin Treaty and Litvinov's periodic ceremonial reaffirmations of the Rapallo relationship thereafter.[34]

Soviet efforts to negotiate a treaty with Poland extended this instability. Following the signing of the Berlin Treaty, Litvinov informed the Central Committee that the USSR attached "the greatest importance" to a "lasting agreement" with Poland.[35] And in August 1926 the NKID publicly offered to Poland a treaty of nonaggression and neutrality.[36] Warsaw rejected the idea of a bilateral pact and insisted instead on a multilateral guarantee extending to the Baltic states as well—in other words, an Eastern Locarno.[37] Moscow interpreted this as an indication of Poland's ambition to lead a coalition of Baltic states against the USSR. The NKID frustrated the Baltic bloc project by concluding a nonaggression and neutrality pact with Lithuania in September,[38] but discussions with Warsaw were inconclusive, and Polish-Soviet relations remained unsettled, leaving an extensive gap in the Soviet security system.

Nationalist Revolution in China

In May 1925 students from eight colleges in the Shanghai area gathered in the city's International Settlement to demonstrate against the system of unequal treaties by which the imperialist powers held their privileges in China and to protest warlord rule throughout the country. A citywide general strike, assisted by funds from Soviet trade unions, followed. Similar antiforeign demonstrations, strikes, and boycotts occurred in more than twenty cities, including Beijing and Wuhan. The May 30th movement, as it was called, set off a massive strike and boycott in Guangzhou (Canton) and Hong Kong, which lasted sixteen months, and led to two years of urban demonstrations, rural rebellions, and military conflict. Together these events comprise the Nationalist Revolution in China.[39]

The ECCI quickly recognized the May 30th movement as an event of historic significance. It signaled what Zinoviev called the beginning of "a new epoch of wars and revolutions."

> The events in China [he stated] will doubtless have a tremendous revolutionizing significance for the other colonies and the countries dependent on imperialist England. Just as in its day the Russian revolution of 1905 had the greatest revolutionizing influence in Turkey, Persia, and China, the present great movement in China will, without doubt, have a tremendous influence on Indo-China, India, etc. The enormous contingents of oppressed humanity who live in the East, numbering hundreds of millions, will greedily seize on every item of news from revolutionary China and will concentrate their thoughts on how they themselves can organize and revolt against the oppressors, the imperialists. . . . China has revolted today: tomorrow Indo-China and India will rise.[40]

The ECCI Presidium assisted the May 30th movement by organizing a "Hands Off China" campaign among the parties of the International, a campaign aimed at snarling possible antirevolutionary intervention by the

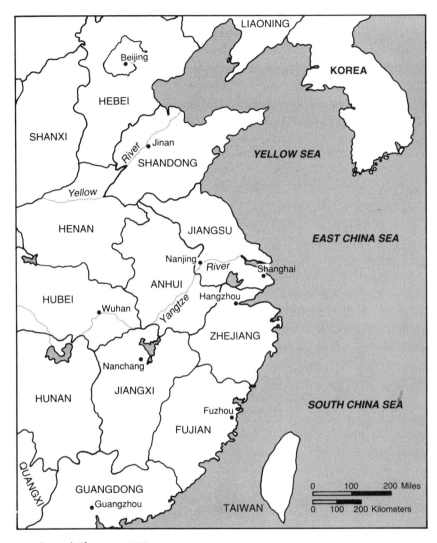

4. Coastal China in 1925

China powers—Britain, Japan, France, Italy, and the United States.[41] In addition, Chinese students, selected by the Control Committee of the Chinese Communist Party, were trained as Russian-speaking military officers and political workers at the Comintern-sponsored Communist University of the Working People of the East (KUTV) in Moscow. The first thirty of them arrived at the highly secret training center in the autumn of 1925; during the next two years over a thousand cadets would be trained. At the same time, Russian and other Soviet citizens were given training in

Chinese and other Asian languages by approximately 100 instructors of the university's Department of Asian Languages.[42] Thus, Soviet/Comintern involvement in the Chinese Nationalist Revolution was significant. Most important, Soviet military advisers in south China participated directly in planning and carrying out the Northern Expedition, the military campaign that extended the revolution from Guangdong Province into the Yangtze River basin of coastal central China in 1926–27. By the summer of 1925, Bliukher and his staff, working with GMD political and military authorities, had drawn up what he called "The Great Guomindang Military Plan,"[43] formally recommended the plan to Moscow, and urged financial assistance for it.[44]

To determine the value of Bliukher's plan, the Central Committee in Moscow appointed a secret commission to conduct an on-site inquiry in China in February-March 1926. The commission was headed by Andrei Bubnov, an early Bolshevik who had been a prominent Red Army staff officer during the Civil War and who directed the army's Central Political Administration and was a member of the Revolutionary Military Council. Its tasks were to study the work of the Soviet military missions in China, to assess the prospects of the Nationalist Revolution, and to make policy recommendations to the Central Committee. After hearing from an extensive list of Soviet representatives in both north and south China, including Borodin and Karakhan, the commission put the most optimistic possible interpretation on the information and opinion it had gathered[45] and recommended to the Central Committee that the requests of the GMD for military aid be met and that preparations be made for a military campaign to take place within six months.

In this way military advisers from the Red Army, political advisers from the Comintern, and cadres of the Chinese Communist Party were all committed to a massive revolutionary offensive. Never before or afterward did the leadership of the USSR risk assets on this scale in a revolutionary initiative extending beyond the protective umbrella that the forces of the Red Army could provide. Their decision to do so directly influenced the course of the Nationalist Revolution in China, the development of the Chinese Communist Party, the future of the international Communist movement, and the direction of Soviet high politics. How and why a decision of this historical magnitude was taken is one of the great "blank spots" of Soviet history.

What historical scholarship knows from evidence is that a Politburo special committee convened in February 1926 to review policy in East Asia did *not* recommend sponsoring a revolutionary military offensive in China. Chaired by Trotsky, the committee had as members—in addition to

Chicherin—Kliment Voroshilov, the chairman of the Revolutionary Military Council who would soon become people's commissar for military and naval affairs (1925–40), and Feliks Dzerzhinskii, head of the Cheka/GPU/ OGPU (1917–26) and chairman of the Supreme Council of the National Economy (1924–26). The committee issued a report on March 25 entitled "Problems of Our Policy with Respect to China and Japan."[46] The analysis in the report was based on the axiom that the international situation had become more difficult and dangerous for the USSR, and for all opponents of imperialism, since the onset of capitalist stabilization. The immediate threat confronting them was the possible extension of Locarno (as they saw it) to Asia in the form of a British-led coalition of capitalist states directed against the Chinese Revolution. As a way of precluding an Asian Locarno, the report recommended a complex scheme of interrelated diplomacy and propaganda. The diplomatic task was to drive a wedge between the two primary imperialist powers in East Asia, Britain and Japan, and to prevent a renewed Anglo-Japanese alliance. That wedge would be formed by a tripartite pact among the USSR, China, and Japan. Tokyo would be attracted to this agreement by means of concessions in Manchuria that the Chinese government in Beijing would make to Japan. The Chinese government in turn would be persuaded to offer concessions to Japan because the CPC and the GMD would mobilize the articulate Chinese public in favor of such a policy through a propaganda campaign conducted in new journals of opinion, to be founded presumably with Comintern funds. The CPC and the GMD would be persuaded to mount this campaign by the argument that a Soviet-Chinese-Japanese diplomatic alignment would prolong the respite from imperialist intervention—something that was in the interests of both the Chinese and Russian revolutions.

Significantly, when the Politburo adopted the resolutions of the East Asian policy committee in early April, a statement submitted by Stalin was appended to them: "The Government at Guangzhou should in the present period decisively reject the thought of military operations of an offensive character, and generally any such actions as may provoke the imperialists to embark on military intervention." So, two months before it began, the collective leadership of the CPSU seems to have agreed to oppose a Northern Expedition. They envisaged instead a clearly defensive strategy, one that would utilize both propaganda and diplomacy to protect the revolution in China and, indirectly, the Russian Revolution as well. How then is the involvement of the Red Army and the Comintern in the Northern Expedition to be explained?

When Sun Yat-sen died in March 1925, he left behind two potential successors. One was Wang Jingwei, one of Sun's earliest followers and a revolutionary hero. The other was Chiang Kai-shek, the pragmatic and nationalist-minded chief of staff of the National Revolutionary Army (NRA). Archival research indicates that Chiang always regarded the GMD's ties to the USSR as purely tactical. He was sharply critical of Sun Yat-sen's political rapprochement with Soviet Russia, although he was quite willing to accept military assistance in the struggle against the clique of warlords who supported the Beijing government.[47] Moreover, he resented members of the Soviet military mission in south China for their domineering attitudes, for their participation in what Chiang regarded as political matters, and for their control over the distribution of weapons and funds sent from the USSR. He suspected that one of them, Nikolai Kuibyshev, was conspiring with Wang Jingwei to abduct him and send him off to Russia. (Kuibyshev seems to have aroused Chiang's suspicions by dealing with Wang on military matters rather than with Chiang, who, he thought, was misappropriating funds.) On 20 March, at a time when both Borodin and Bliukher were absent from Guangzhou, Chiang launched a successful coup d'état, the results of which were manifold and far-reaching.[48] He removed Soviet advisers from politically significant positions within the NRA and deported those whom he found most objectionable. Wang went into temporary exile in France. Chiang's power was greatly enhanced. Within three months he was commander in chief of the NRA and had gained control over both the GMD Central Party Headquarters and the military, civil, and financial organs of the Nationalist government. And he saw to it that the position of influence and power held by the CPC as a "bloc within" the Guomindang was sharply curtailed.

The Soviet military and civilian advisers in Guangzhou were not forewarned of Chiang's coup; the CPC leadership was caught unawares; the Politburo and the ECCI Presidium in Moscow were taken by surprise. It took six weeks for them to recover fully and for the situation to be clarified as follows: First, in protracted and intense negotiations with Chiang, Borodin agreed to a sharp curtailment of the influence of the CPC within the councils of both the GMD and the NRA. Among the restrictions imposed on CPC activity, Communists would no longer head any of the bureaus at Guomindang Central Party Headquarters. At the same time, Borodin was able to use Soviet military assistance as a lever with which to limit the influence of the GMD right wing. On the same day that the Russian military mission turned over 8,000 rifles along with ammunition to the NRA, a prominent rightist politician was arrested.

Second, from within the Central Committee of the CPC there was renewed agitation in favor of abandoning the "bloc within" strategy and withdrawing from the Guomindang and forming instead an interparty alliance of the two organizations. This move, its proponents argued, would enable the CPC to conduct an independent policy, to appeal directly to the urban and rural masses, and to arm the peasants of Guangdong—thereby providing the CPC with military forces to protect the party organization. When this proposal was discussed among the highest ranks of the CPSU collective leadership, Trotsky, according to his later statements, formally proposed the action. Zinoviev reportedly associated himself with Trotsky's position, thereby reversing his earlier stand. But apparently neither of them pressed the point and the "bloc within" strategy stood.[49] When the issue was fully resolved at a special Politburo session in May, Voitinskii was dispatched to China with specific instructions to correct the separatist tendency within the CPC.

Third, the leadership of the CPSU and of the Communist International agreed to support the long-anticipated Northern Expedition.[50] Borodin informed Chiang of this sometime in May, and Bliukher and his staff began to work on detailed plans for conducting the campaign. The supply of weapons from Russia, which had begun eighteen months earlier, increased rapidly. Chiang then acted quickly and launched the Northern Expedition on 1 June, apparently before Soviet advisers in Guangzhou and Beijing could agree either among themselves or with the Politburo and ECCI Presidium in Moscow regarding the timing and the objectives of the campaign.

These two decisions—(1) to arm Chiang Kai-shek and to support the Northern Expedition despite the coup d'état of 20 March and Chiang's evident intention to relegate the CPC to a weakened position within the nationalist movement, and (2) to instruct the CPC to remain a "bloc within" the Guomindang—set the China policy of the USSR on a disastrous course. Within little more than a year, the Soviet aid mission would be compelled to flee China as Chiang and the anti-Communist sector of the GMD decimated the CPC, destroyed its mass organizations, and ejected it from the Chinese nationalist movement.

The decision to arm Chiang did contain elements of rationality. Documentation from the Soviet military mission reveals that the advisers in Guangzhou favored continued support for Chiang because they regarded him as an authentic nationalist who would advance the global anti-imperialist struggle, and because they believed that they could exert decisive influence on him and, through him, direct the Chinese nationalist movement. In the aftermath of Chiang's coup, their intention, presumably one shared by Borodin as representative of the Comintern, was to conciliate Chiang by political concessions, to manipulate him through his vanity and lust for power, and to surround him with the political influence of the left wing of the GMD—of which the CPC was a significant component.[51]

For the decision to continue the "bloc within" strategy after Chiang had made evident his hostility to the CPC, Stalin and Bukharin have been blamed. When the disastrous consequences of the April–May 1926 decisions became obvious a year later, their China policy became the primary target of an attack launched by Trotsky, Zinoviev, and the United Opposition.[52] However, the responsibility of Stalin and Bukharin does not date from the decisions of April–May 1926, which were in fact taken by the Politburo and the ECCI Presidium without substantial opposition from Trotsky and Zinoviev. Rather, their responsibility is linked to the fact that the two of them held to this policy, as we shall see, not only through the spectacular military successes of the Northern Expedition in July-October 1926 but also through the equally spectacular defeats inflicted on the CPC in 1927. Why did they do so?

European and American scholarship has relied on two lines of argument.[53] One holds that the internal politics of the CPSU limited the policy alternatives available to Stalin and Bukharin. To wit, the most reasonable policy was to withdraw the CPC from the GMD and allow it to pursue an independent revolutionary strategy. This was the policy consistently advocated by a significant sector of the CPC leadership, including the founder and general secretary of the party, Chen Duxiu. However, this policy choice was politically unacceptable to Stalin and Bukharin because it was appropriated by Trotsky in the March to May 1926 period and then by the United Opposition as a whole from April through July 1927. According to this argument, Stalin was unable to "borrow" policies from his opponents for fear that doing so would disadvantage him in the struggle for leadership among Lenin's successors.

The second line of argument contends that Stalin would not have shifted course even if his policy choice had not been constrained by the leadership struggle. It asserts that the political strategies conceived by Lenin had a powerful and lasting influence on the political behavior of his successors, and on Stalin in particular. Lenin "taught" that the correct strategy for Communist parties in Asian anti-imperialist revolutions was support for the nationalist revolutionaries in "united fronts." From this revolutionary coalition, a "democratic dictatorship of the proletariat and peasantry" would emerge, and the proletariat would gain control of it. The "united front" would then terminate with the disposal of the non-Communist revolutionaries. In Stalin's words, Chiang Kai-shek would be used, "squeezed dry like a lemon, and then flung away."[54] In Stalin's narrow vision and rigid thought, there were no alternatives to these Leninist precepts. Thus, this line of argument emphasizes Stalin's ideological obedience, his lack of political imagination, and the cautiousness of his strategic thinking. To these may be added a corollary developed in pre-1985 Soviet scholarship: During the Chinese Nationalist Revolution, as at other crucial junctures in Soviet foreign relations (most notably in 1941), Stalin engaged in "wishful thinking" that left Soviet foreign policy unable to adjust quickly to rapid changes in the international situation.[55]

However Soviet Russia's involvement in the conquest phase of the Chinese Nationalist Revolution was decided upon, it was initially re-warded. By October 1926, the NRA's expedition into central China was a military success, one in which Soviet military assistance played a signifi-cant role.[56] Bliukher and his staff planned the general strategy, and during the military campaign Chiang made no strategic decisions without consult-ing him. Fifty-eight Soviet military advisers, with a technical staff of eighteen, were attached to specific NRA units. They planned operations, oversaw their execution, and gathered intelligence. Sometimes they led attacks. Soviet pilots acted as scouts, terrorized enemy troops, and dropped bombs on tactical targets. The flow of supplies and equipment from the USSR increased once the Northern Expedition was under way. By August, six Soviet ships traveled regularly from Vladivostok to Guangzhou loaded with oil, large and small arms, and disassembled aircraft. CPC political commissars accompanied the Nationalist armies; Zhou Enlei was attached to the elite First Division of the First National Republican Army. And CPC organizers followed the troops, founding farmers' organizations in the countryside and reorganizing labor unions in the cities.

The ECCI celebrated the victories in China at its Seventh Plenum in De-cember 1926. In the words of the "Resolution on the China Question" adopted there, the Northern Expedition had "effectively wiped out imperi-alist rule from half of China" and brought the Chinese Revolution close to the point at which the proletariat, led by the Chinese Communist Party, could take control of it.[57] The CPC was instructed not only to remain a "bloc within" the GMD, but also to enter the Nationalist government, which, the resolution maintained, contained the nucleus of a revolutionary democratic dictatorship of the proletariat, the peasantry, and the petty bourgeoisie. The primary task of the CPC was specified as leading the GMD and the Nationalist government leftward to a radical agrarian pro-gram in the newly liberated areas, a program that included arming the poor and middle peasantry and confiscating the land holdings of the warlords, the temples, and those gentry who opposed the revolution. The success of the revolution in China depended on this program, the resolution concluded, and only the CPC could initiate it. European and American scholars have condemned these instructions as unimplementable and self-contradictory.[58] In response, the leading official specialist during the Brezhnev era on the Asian policy of the Comintern defended them as reasonable, flexible, and empirically based.[59] Subsequent research in archival Chinese sources has demonstrated that they undermined the efforts of Chen Duxiu to unify the CPC at the very moment he was on the verge of success.[60]

Scholars of all political persuasions have conventionally understood that it was at the Seventh ECCI Plenum that the definitive Stalin-Bukharin China policy was formulated, pronounced, and imposed on the CPC. By this time the leadership of the United Opposition had been removed from all important offices in the government, the party, and the Comintern. In particular, Zinoviev had been removed as president of the ECCI in October and the office then abolished by Comintern resolution. In his place, Bukharin gave the opening address to the Seventh Plenum and reported that, despite capitalist stabilization, the world revolutionary process was moving forward along three paths—in Russia, in England, and in China. Three sessions of the plenum were set aside for discussion of the Chinese question. Stalin, who openly participated in the workings of the CI for the first time, delivered an address to the China commission in which he attempted to set out in theoretical terms the strategies then in operation in China.[61] As conventionally understood, "The Resolution on the China Question" was the result of Stalin's decisive intervention, one that went without challenge from within the plenum.

This long-held belief was modified by research done in Soviet archives during *perestroika*.[62] An investigation of the transcript of the proceedings of the plenum contained in the CPSU Central Archives reveals that considerable and heated debate on the issue of agrarian revolution in China took place. The resolution itself—the immediate authorship of which was previously attributed by some sources to Bubnov, Raskolnikov, and Voitinskii and by others to Pavel Mif, the Comintern expert on East Asian revolutionary movements, or to Bukharin and Roy[63]—was actually formulated through the efforts of members of the CPC delegation to the ECCI Plenum, who were aided by Roy and Raskolnikov, both members of the CI Commission on China, and by William Gallacher, Dmitrii Manuilskii, and Sen Katayama, all members of the ECCI Presidium. Stalin's particular contribution to the deliberations was a proposal to add to the resolution a statement singling out the special role played by military conquest in the successes of the Chinese Revolution. This proposal was sharply criticized, and it was not incorporated in the resolution. Both Stalin and the ECCI were thereby spared additional severe embarrassment when Chiang Kai-shek's allies deployed their armies against the CPC from April to July 1927.

A New Direction for Soviet Foreign Policy?

As "the world revolutionary process" progressed in China during the second half of 1926, no successes of similar magnitude could be credited to Soviet diplomacy in Europe. It was clear that the major capitalist powers would regulate their international relations without Soviet participation; it even seemed that their Dawes-Locarno relationships might well survive what were perceived in CPSU and Comintern resolutions to be their inherent contradictions. In the NKID, Litvinov and Chicherin did gloat considerably when Germany's admission to the League of Nations was delayed in April while a seat on the League Council was arranged for Poland. The anti-Soviet coalition that Chamberlain had tried to construct, they announced, had collapsed from its own internal contradictions. "Instead of the firm international structure in which Germany hoped to find its corner," Chicherin stated, "there is nothing but a heap of ruins."[64] Nevertheless, Stresemann's relations with Chamberlain and Briand survived the League Council crisis, and when Germany did join the League in September, Briand celebrated the event with a speech before the League Assembly proclaiming the rapprochement with Germany as the basis for world peace.

Meanwhile the last best hope for renormalizing relations with the Conservative government in England was lost. Following the aid given to British strikers in May, the demands of the diehards grew louder, and the Foreign Office made clear to the NKID that little could be done to improve Anglo-Soviet relations. In Paris, the return of Poincaré to office in July doomed any hope of a debt/loan agreement with France—to say nothing of a more comprehensive Franco-Soviet rapprochement. The strategy of walking westward over the German bridge, shored up by the Berlin Treaty in April, had produced few results. Rakovskii, who served in the diplomatic front lines as chargé in London and *polpred* in Paris, decided that the USSR was compelled to practice what he called a policy of "super-isolation."[65] The NKID did not adopt this policy, however. To the contrary, Soviet diplomacy constructed a set of bilateral neutrality and nonaggression treaties on the European and Asian frontiers of the USSR. And it undertook other significant initiatives as well, including a foreign trade offensive, a policy of participation in organizations of multilateral international cooperation, and a renewed pursuit of agreements with Europe and America.

These initiatives were a significant departure in Soviet foreign relations. In 1924 it had been assumed that, once normal diplomatic contacts had been established with the major capitalist powers, a breakthrough to debt settlements and long-term credits would follow as a matter of course, and that a far-reaching rapprochement between Russia and Europe and America would result. The policy of 1926 was more complicated. The first step was to contact representatives of European and American business and government and to convince them that the USSR was involved in a process of stable political and economic development. As this was acknowledged, economic relations (trade based on credits as well as on cash payments) would expand. Trade would in turn provide the basis for increasingly friendly political relations, and Soviet isolation would diminish.[66]

In their efforts to convince Europeans and Americans of the political and economic stability of the USSR, Soviet diplomacy had several instruments at its disposal. One was the image of Stalin that European diplomats in Moscow sent back to their governments. This depicted Stalin as the emerging leader of an increasingly stable USSR, as a strong, quiet, moderate, pragmatic politician, in contrast to Trotsky and, even more so, Zinoviev, who were identified in European and American diplomatic circles with policies of revolutionary excess.

A second instrument was participation in the organizations and agreements of multilateral international cooperation. In the aftermath of Locarno, the Soviet government agreed to join in the preparations for the World Disarmament Conference to be held in Geneva under the auspices of the League of Nations.[67] It did so without formally abandoning its objections to the League or its refusal to join the organization in its current form. The reason is patent. The USSR could not afford the intensified isolation that would have resulted from remaining outside the deliberations on disarmament while European security negotiations had concluded successfully at Locarno and Germany joined the League of Nations. However, three sessions of the League's Preparatory Commission on Disarmament were held beginning in May 1926 without the participation of the USSR. The Soviet government refused to send delegates to a conference in Switzerland until the Swiss government expressed its regret over the May 1923 assassination of Waclaw Vorovskii, secretary general to the Soviet delegation at the Lausanne Conference, and made pecuniary compensation to his daughter. International diplomatic pressure on Bern brought a settlement of the question in April 1927, although the USSR and Switzerland did not restore diplomatic relations until 1946.[68] The USSR then participated in the World Economic Conference in Geneva in May and dispatched a Soviet delegation headed by Litvinov to the Preparatory Disarmament Commission the following November. The delegations to both conferences were instructed to take on as one of their primary functions the development of intensive personal contacts with Western governmental, diplomatic, and business representatives and to impress on them the political and economic stability of the Soviet system and the possibilities for mutually beneficial economic exchange. Sokolnikov represented the USSR at the economic conference, where he called for "peaceful coexistence between the two economic systems"—to the applause of the other delegations, "even the English," as one Swiss newspaper observed.[69] His most important work took place outside the conference hall, however, where, according to one observer, the Soviet delegation was "too busy . . . obtaining loans and factory equipment to worry about the progress of world revolution."[70]

The third instrument was expanded trade. To improve commercial, financial, and political relations with the industrialized nations, the Soviets launched a trade offensive in September–October 1926, placing orders for machinery and other producer goods with companies in the United States, Britain, and elsewhere. It was as part of this offensive that Soviet diplomatic and trade representatives undertook the campaign to convince their Western counterparts that the Soviet political system was stable, that the economy was sound, and that the growth of their own economies depended on trade with the USSR. The political purposes of the trade offensive were well defined. In Britain, for example, it was intended to control the damage inflicted on Anglo-Soviet relations by Russian intervention in the General Strike. By convincing trading and banking circles in London of the value of economic relations with the USSR, the Soviets hoped that these circles would in turn influence the Foreign Office and the Cabinet toward a policy more favorable to the Soviet Union.[71] Thus, more extensive economic relations were to provide the basis for improved political relations.

What place did the Rapallo-Berlin relationship with Germany occupy in this new world of gradually improving economic and political relations with Europe and America? Since 1922 the NKID had used relations with Germany both to set the pace of relations with the other European states and as a model for those relations. Relations with Germany had in actuality developed more fully than those with any other country, and in 1926 Germany became the USSR's primary creditor. As a result of the Soviet-German Commercial Treaty of October 1925, the leading German banks granted the USSR a credit of 100 million marks, and in March 1926, as the Berlin Treaty was being concluded, the German Ministry of Economics announced a credit of 300 million marks for the purchase of locomotives, tractors, heavy machinery, and machine tools; 35 percent of the loan was guaranteed against default by the German government, 25 percent by German banks, and 40 percent by manufacturers interested in the market for machinery in Russia. The funds for the loan originated with American lenders, primarily Dillon, Read, and Company, and were transferred through the Reichsbank and administered by the Ministry of Economics.[72] These were short-term, revolving credits; long-term loans were negotiated in 1930–31 by the German ambassador at that time, Herbert von Dirksen.

However, the conditions in which the diplomatic and economic interdependence of the Rapallo relationship had first developed no longer existed. The German rapprochement with Britain and France culminated in September with Germany's entry into the League of Nations and a celebratory speech by Briand. Almost immediately thereafter, he and Stresemann held a private luncheon meeting in the French countryside adjacent to Geneva. The exact content of their discussion was kept secret, but the event was highly publicized, and there was much speculation in the press that all the differences outstanding in German relations with France were about to be negotiated away.[73] At the same time, the economic policy of the USSR was transformed from one designed to promote recovery from the World War and the Civil War to one aimed at the industrialization of the country. The capital and technology requirements of the Soviet economy increased accordingly; German financial institutions were even less capable than they had been previously of fully satisfying those requirements; expanded trade with the United States, Britain, and other countries was necessary. As a consequence of these developments, the value of the Rapallo "special relationship" to German diplomacy and to the Soviet economy declined sharply.

The Wilhelmstrasse welcomed the end of Soviet dependence. So long as Soviet relations with Europe rested almost exclusively on Germany, Berlin ran the risk of becoming deeply entangled in almost any foreign conflict in which the USSR became involved. This complicated Stresemann's strategy of *Westorientierung und Ostpolitik* by posing the possibility that at some point Berlin might have to choose between London and Moscow and side with one against the other. The Foreign Ministry's policy response—the "Schlesinger line"—was devised by Moritz Schlesinger and approved by State Secretary von Schubert in July 1926. The resources of German diplomacy would be deployed when and where necessary in order to restrain the USSR from confrontation with other powers and to foster and strengthen Soviet economic ties with Europe and America. To this end, Germany would sponsor and direct the reintegration of the USSR into the world economy—and reap the diplomatic influence and international status that would come from doing so. In this manner, the Soviet-German relationship became what one historian has called "a potential force for European peace."[74]

One scheme devised on the Wilhelmstrasse, which apparently had the blessing of President Coolidge, was expected to work in this way: Private American loans to the USSR, perhaps guaranteed by the German government, would be used to purchase American cotton and the products of German industry, and the resulting German payments surplus would be allocated to a reduction in Berlin's reparations obligations. Another proposal would have made Germany the head of a German-American-French-Dutch investment group formed to make loans to Russia. Then, the Wilhelmstrasse calculated, as the interests of the other states became merged with those of Germany in an involvement in the Soviet economy, potentially dangerous confrontations between Russia and the West would become less likely. The place of the USSR in the world political economy would be stabilized and enhanced; ties between Moscow and Berlin would become less of a liability to Germany; and the position of Russia's German sponsor in world politics would be accordingly enhanced and strengthened. The danger that the USSR would enter into alignments and alliances unfavorable to Berlin as it emerged from economic and political isolation—perhaps resulting in Germany's own relative isolation—would be obviated by Germany's role as coordinator of the Soviet Union's expanding trade relations.[75]

In December 1926, the Politburo gave its formal approval to the policy aimed at improving relations with the industrialized capitalist states and to the decision to conclude agreements with them. In internal documents this policy may have been called *politika dogovorennost,* "the politics of understanding."[76] Although it was directed at improving relations with the United States, Britain, and France, as well as with Germany, official government statements referred less specifically to "the establishment and reinforcement of friendly relations with foreign states,"[77] thereby making the policy less vulnerable to the accusation that it constituted a rapprochement with the enemy. In a statement issued in Berlin and published in *Izvestiia* on 8 December, Chicherin characterized it as "the gradual improvement and consolidation of our relations with other countries."[78]

Gradualism was the crucial new ingredient in Soviet foreign relations. Adoption of a policy of gradually developing mutual understanding indicated an abandonment of the expectations of 1924 that comprehensive settlements with the world powers would follow rapidly upon the establishment of diplomatic relations. Instead, piecemeal agreements would be concluded with them and relations of confidence would develop gradually as socialism evolved in the USSR. Soviet foreign policy in the post-Locarno era had a common basis with the strategy of internal development adopted during the era of "socialism in one country." Both were premised on the belief that socialism would be constructed peacefully and gradually out of the conditions of NEP.

The adoption of *politika dogovorennost* coincided with a dramatic change in the composition of the policy-deciding bodies of the CPSU. In response to the emerging Stalin-Bukharin alliance and to the doctrines of economic development and foreign relations that the two of them propounded, Trotsky, Zinoviev, and Kamenev formed a United Opposition in April 1926. When they failed to convert the leadership to their position, they suffered the political consequences. In October, Trotsky was expelled from the Central Committee and the Politburo. At the same time, Kamenev lost his candidate membership on the Politburo and was compelled to surrender control of the Moscow party organization, although he remained a member of the Central Committee and was appointed *polpred* to Italy. The other opponent of "socialism in one country," Zinoviev, who had lost his position on the Politburo the previous July, was dropped from the Central Committee along with Trotsky and surrendered control of the Leningrad party organization. He was also relieved of all Comintern duties, including the presidency of the ECCI. At the Seventh Plenum in November-December, Kamenev was dropped as a delegate and addressed the body for the last time. The office of president was abolished, and Bukharin took over leadership of the Communist International.[79] The spokesmen for the majority that emerged on the Central Committee and in the ECCI with the forced retreat of the Opposition were Stalin, Bukharin, and Rykov. And it was they who assumed responsibility in late 1926 for the foreign relations of "socialism in one country," including the politics of understanding.

The latter had strong implications for the Rapallo-based "special relationship" with Germany. As a common approach to all industrialized capitalist countries, the policy of understanding had two corollaries: (1) that Soviet foreign relations would no longer depend primarily on Germany as the USSR's channel to Europe and as the pacesetter and model for relations with other European states; and (2) that favorable relations with the United States, Britain, and France were to be cultivated with less consideration for the relationship with Germany. Thus it represented a crucial turn in Soviet foreign relations, a new policy course. Not wanting to make Russian economic development dependent on German intercession with the other powers, the Soviet government rejected the schemes for German-organized investment consortiums advanced by Berlin.

Moreover, the policy of understanding contained within it the embryo of a still more fundamental shift away from the established precepts of

Bolshevik foreign relations. Downgrading the relationship with Germany and including all capitalist states in a single policy initiative suggested that Soviet diplomacy would depart from the practice of exploiting the contradictions between the victors of the war on the one hand and Germany on the other. This constituted a departure from one of the axioms of Leninist foreign policy—that the antagonisms inherent in the peace settlement could be counted on to advance both Soviet security and "the world revolutionary process." It also directly contradicted the 1925 version of "the catastrophic premise" expressed in the Political Report of the Central Committee to the Fourteenth Party Congress—that the Dawes Plan would bring revolution to Germany, that Locarno would bring war to Europe, and that proletarian revolution would emerge victorious.

There is some basis for hypothesizing that an alternative foreign policy was being advanced in late 1926 and early 1927. At the Seventh ECCI Plenum in November-December, Bukharin suggested that "a new war between the imperialist powers in Europe" would have destructive effects greater than those of 1914–18 for the entire Continent, the USSR, and the international Communist movement. At the same time, he denied the existence of "a real revolutionary situation" in Germany and stated that Germany was the one power in Europe most likely to increase the international tensions that would lead to another world war. It was time, he stated, for both the government of the USSR and the Comintern to abandon their policies of support for the defeated powers and instead to promote a program of security guarantees aimed at achieving a "real world-wide peace."[80] In this call for a reorientation of the foreign relations conducted by the USSR and the ECCI, Bukharin moved Germany conceptually from the ranks of the victims of imperialism to one of its representatives. When he then did so explicitly at the Moscow Party Conference in January, the German Foreign Ministry lodged a protest in Moscow, and Chicherin, in a letter addressed to Stalin and Rykov, sharply criticized Bukharin's statement as damaging to Soviet-German relations.[81]

Thus, in addition to a new course for Soviet diplomacy, rudiments of an alternative set of foreign relations for the ECCI and for the USSR seem to have existed in late 1926. Central to these relations were the questions whether a second imperialist war was the necessary cause of proletarian revolution in Europe and of the final victory of socialism, and whether Soviet security was to be premised on a perpetual antagonism among the capitalist nations. These questions, together with the announced willingness of the government to participate in multilateral international organizations and agreements, formed the basis for a possible whole new direction in Soviet foreign policy. However, this was not the only concept of foreign relations propounded in late 1926; nor was it the dominant one. The official foreign policy concept of the ECCI and of the Central Committee majority differed significantly. The resolutions and theses of both these organizations regarded the revolution in China as the harbinger of "a new era of wars and revolutions" and as the portent of the end of "the temporary stabilization of capitalism." Stalin meanwhile developed his own personal variant of the party line, one that contrasted sharply with Bukharin's. It counted heavily on contradictions among the capitalist states and foresaw a new war "in a few years time." With this, Chicherin disagreed, denying to the Fourteenth Party Congress that war was in sight.

So by late 1926 the intentions of Bolshevik foreign policy had become diverse, complex, and in some cases contradictory. The Communist International was supposed to preserve its identity as the organization of international proletarian revolution while coordinating its stands with the requirements of Soviet national security. The Chinese Communist Party was to remain a vulnerable "bloc within" an increasingly menacing Guomindang, which was in turn advised and armed by Russians. The cause of the nationalist authoritarian modernizers of southwest Asia was to be promoted with the expectation that they would resist imperialist penetration on the southern rim of the USSR, and with the knowledge that they would extinguish domestic Communism. At a time of military unpreparedness and relative diplomatic isolation, the construction of socialism in Russia was to be protected by the protests of working-class organizations in Europe against capitalist intervention. The persistent exclusion of the USSR from the councils of the world powers was to be overcome by demonstrating the economic and political stability of the country and the willingness of the Soviet government to participate in the organizations and agreements of multilateral international cooperation.

Perhaps the most crucial contradiction was the simultaneous hope for improved relations with Great Britain, the United States, and Japan on the one hand and the effort to undermine their position in China on the other. In a search for economic agreements with Europe and America, Soviet foreign policy depended on the stability and prosperity that these countries were achieving within the Locarno security system with its underpinning of American loans. At the same time, the Soviet regime directly and immediately threatened international stability, if no longer in Europe or Islamic Asia then certainly in support of the Nationalist Revolution in China. Chicherin recognized the difficulties that involvement in the "anti-imperialist struggle" in Asia created for the quest for "peaceful coexistence" with the capitalist powers. He had stated them clearly in 1924:

In our world policy there exists an extremely difficult question. There is a difference in attitude on our side to the West and the East. Our goals, both economic and political, are formulated in different ways in the East and West. The West however, watches what we are doing in the East. We can not act in the East without regard for our actions in the West. How can this problem be resolved?[82]

The crisis of 1927 would demonstrate just how critical the problem was and how difficult it was to resolve.

9 The Drive for Industrialization and the War Scare

The Industrialization Drive

As Soviet Russia entered world politics, the leaders of the first socialist republic were confronted not with a single challenge but with three successive ones. The first was posed during the years 1917–1921, when the revolution in Russia was not succeeded by successful proletarian revolutions in Central and Western Europe, thus leaving the USSR in ideological, diplomatic, and economic isolation. The second challenge came in the period 1924–1926, when the capitalist powers of Europe and America stabilized their international relations by a series of agreements that did not include the Soviet Union. The third emerged in 1926.

By the economic year 1926/27, the industrial plant of the USSR was restored to its prewar capacity, and total output had regained and slightly surpassed the level reached in 1913.[1] This recovery was a not unimpressive achievement when the extent of the World War and Civil War damage to the areas of the Russian Empire that became the Soviet Union is taken into account. Nevertheless, the gap in industrial productivity between Russia and the industrialized nations of the world remained as great as or even greater than it had been before 1914. In iron, steel, and petroleum production, the USSR had lost ground relative to Europe and the United States. And while the manufacture of automobiles, trucks, and tractors had led the United States in particular into a new period of economic expansion based on the introduction of new technologies and methods of production, Soviet industry depended almost completely on prerevolutionary plants, machinery, and methods. With the USSR cut off from advanced technology and unable to make substantial new investment, and with a comparatively low level of labor skills available, industrial productivity in the USSR remained one-half of what it was in Britain and only one-seventh that of the United States.

This widening gap in industrial technology and productivity posed a challenge to the collective leadership of the USSR, one that had clear implications for the task of building socialism—and for Soviet security. How long could the first socialist country be safe in a world dominated by capitalist states that were not being transformed by proletarian revolution, that were becoming relatively and absolutely more prosperous and powerful, that were being integrated into a more stable international system, and that, with the exception of Germany, had not concluded the type of political and economic agreements with the USSR that were vital both to its military security and to its economic development?

It was under these conditions that the party/state leadership undertook what historians have called "the industrialization drive of 1926." The resolutions of the Fourteenth Party Congress in December 1925, sometimes called "the congress of industrialization," committed the party to transforming the USSR into a self-sufficient industrial nation. Neither the tempo nor the mode of that transformation was determined, however. The Fifteenth Party Conference in October–November 1926 rejected "snail's pace" industrialization in favor of a faster pace, although it did not establish an exact time frame for the program. Instead, the party, drawing on a formula articulated by Lenin, resolved "to catch up and then to surpass" (*dognat i peregnat*) the level of industrial development of the advanced capitalist countries "in a relatively minimal historical period." The exact meaning of these phrases was not defined, but the broad outlines of industrialization policy had been established by the end of the year. Priority was assigned to the expansion of industry over the development of agriculture, although NEP equilibrium in the agricultural market was to be maintained. And the capital goods industry was to be expanded first, a strategy that was termed "the strengthening of the hegemony of large scale socialist industry over the economy of the country."[2] These principles were in turn premised on a trio of sanguine assumptions: (1) that NEP could be transformed for the purposes of socialist reconstruction; (2) that the USSR could be industrialized by means of "a relatively smooth, crisis-free type of development";[3] and (3) that the process of socialist industrialization would be favored by a prolonged period of peace free from the threat of imperialist war and capitalist intervention. Around these principles and assumptions an approximate consensus formed among the newly emerged majority in the Central Committee—the majority for which Rykov, Stalin, and Bukharin spoke and the one that expelled Trotsky,

Zinoviev, and Kamenev from their positions of power in the party and the Comintern.

Remarkably, just as Trotsky was being removed, important elements of the industrialization strategy he espoused—a quickened tempo, advanced technology, expanded foreign trade—were incorporated in economic policy despite the open commitment of Stalin and Bukharin to "socialism in one country" and to autarkical economic development. On the one hand, non-party economic planners recognized that the industrialization drive, with its high growth targets and technological imperatives, required an increased volume of industrial goods, much of which they projected would come from abroad, and based their plans and projections on expanded imports of industrial raw materials and of semifinished goods and capital equipment and on reduced or excluded importation of finished products, consumer goods, and foodstuffs. On the other hand, technology transfer, expanded foreign trade, and import substitution became the economic policy of the party. A Central Committee resolution in April 1926 stated that the expansion of foreign trade was "an indispensable condition for the industrialization of the country and for the quickening of the tempo of industrial development." The ideological goal of industrialization remained self-sufficiency, but, because development was to be based on advanced technology, the importation of sophisticated machinery from abroad was deemed necessary during the period when industry was being established. The resolution of the Fifteenth Party Conference, the conference of *dognat i peregnat*, was absolutely categorical on this point: "The realization of industrialization at the present stage results in the necessity for a maximum import of machinery, the possibility of expanding which depends on the development of exports and the exclusion from imports of those goods which can be produced within the USSR."[4]

The assumed optimal method for financing these imports was a combination of long-term loans and export of natural resources and agricultural products, particularly grain. This had been the foreign trade model of the tsarist regime prior to 1914; it was the model on which economic planners initially aimed to restore foreign trade under NEP; and it was the basis of the commercial agreements signed with England, Germany, and other states beginning in 1921. Making it operate depended on gaining control over an exportable output (mainly grain), on finding export markets, on purchasing the required imports, and on obtaining favorable terms of trade. These were, however, conditions that did not exist with any consistency in the Russia of the New Economic Policy. To the contrary, foreign trade was trapped in a vicious circle of stagnation. The amount of grain available for export varied widely with the harvest; moreover, peasants would not supply grain to the state for export unless the market was stocked with consumer goods priced at favorable rates of exchange, and consumer goods could not be manufactured in the quantity necessary without the industrial raw materials paid for by exports. Consequently, shortages of both grain exports and of light industrial raw material imports plagued the economy throughout the NEP period. Foreign trade was the "commanding height" of NEP that had recovered least from the devastating effects of war, revolution, and War Communism by 1926.[5]

The best year for foreign trade under NEP was 1923/24. Just two years after the famine, grain exports rose to 2.686 million metric tons, a NEP record. (The 1913 level equalled 10.331 million metric tons.) Volume nearly tripled from the previous year; imports increased by 70 percent; the trade surplus (the largest during the NEP period) amounted to 94 million rubles. Gold, silver, coinage, and foreign exchange could be imported to support Sokolnikov's 1924 effort to end inflation, reform the currency, and reestablish a convertible ruble. A new currency was introduced at the rate of 50 billion old *svoznaks* to one new ruble, and by 1925 a relatively free hard currency exchange existed within the USSR. With stabilization came efforts to strengthen financial links with the world economy. The *chervonets* (a ten-ruble bank note) was promoted abroad and even achieved an unofficial, de facto recognition on European money markets. Some restrictions were lifted on imports and exports, and ambitious foreign trade plans were drawn up for 1924/25 and 1925/26.

All this came to a sudden halt. Owing to a poor harvest, grain exports fell to 606 thousand tons in 1924/25, and they actually ceased altogether between October 1924 and June 1925. Grain had to be imported on an emergency basis, and the country was a net grain importer for the year. The resulting trade deficit was partially covered by the German loan and by the sale of gold abroad. However, the next year there followed what one economic historian has called "the foreign trade debacle of 1925/26."[6] Because of a rapid increase in grain procurement prices in the autumn of 1925 and other problems, the Politburo had to intercede and cut back both export and import quotas. By the end of the economic year, grain exports had reached only 40 percent of the level planned, although total exports actually grew by 21 percent for the year. Imports pushed the trade deficit to 80 million rubles. The prospects for restoring foreign trade to prewar levels and along prewar lines were now considerably dimmer than they had been at the end of 1923/24, and plans for industrialization had to be postponed.

Conditions improved in 1926/27, with 2.256 million metric tons of grain exported and a trade surplus of 66 million rubles. However, that surplus was achieved only by a decisive change in trade policy to one based on the recognition that foreign trade lagged well behind the rest of the economy and the assumption that it could not meet the demands for raw materials and machinery imposed by an accelerated industrialization. The new policy involved cutting back investment plans by 20 percent, imposing strict controls on imports (particularly on foodstuffs and consumer goods), and withdrawing the ruble from the foreign exchange market (permanently, as it turned out). Sokolnikov, who was associated with the Opposition, resigned from the Commissariat for Finance.

European and American scholars have attributed this policy about-face to a combination of bad harvests and faulty macroeconomic management that occurred as officials raised and lowered grain procurement prices in an effort to combat inflation and preserve export profitability, on the one hand, and to encourage sowing and marketing, on the other.[7] *Perestroika* scholarship pointed to structural problems within the NEP economy and to the resumption of inflation, which was attributed to the monopolistic and bureaucratic character of the economy and to the softness of the budgetary constraints on the state-owned trusts.[8] At that time, a leading Soviet expert on the topic challenged the "bad harvest and bad management thesis" by suggesting that the reasons for the 1926 policy turnaround were political rather than economic, and called for further investigation of the question.[9]

Whatever was the source of this shift in economic foreign policy, the plans for 1926/27 had built into them the assumption that exports could not balance out the machinery import requirements of an accelerated industrialization. How did the Stalin-Bukharin-Rykov leadership cope with this? They did so in part by bravely reasserting the doctrine of self-sufficiency as both the end and the means of industrialization. Rykov informed the Central Committee in April 1926 that the goal of industrialization remained freedom from foreign dependency and that the machinery imports required for industrial growth could be financed out of domestic resources (the state budget). Stalin meanwhile disparaged "enslaving" loans and concessions, and in July a *Pravda* editorial criticized foreign concessions as contrary to socialist construction, amounting to "the surrender of our industry to international capital" and to a policy of "Dawesation . . . which is a prologue to the return of capitalism." The industrialization resolution of the Fifteenth Party Conference in October–November repeated what the Fourteenth Party Congress had stressed the year before, that the construction of industry was to be financed out of internal sources. These assumptions were carried over from the "outline sketch" for a five-year plan presented to the first congress of Gosplan, the State Planning Commission, the previous March: "The problem of the accumulation of the resources necessary for the regeneration of our economy on new foundations can be solved quite satisfactorily even without assistance to us from the outside—on the basis of the internal resources of the country alone."[10]

Programmatic statements such as these meshed with the ideological precepts articulated by Bukharin at a time when the debate over industrialization coincided with the polemicized struggle against the Opposition. Industrialization out of indigenous resources was a principle that seemed to follow from the doctrine of "socialism in one country" and to contradict clearly Trotsky's appeal for increasing integration into the world economy and avoidance of autarky. However, because prioritizing heavy industry could not break the vicious circle of stagnation caused by the shortages of grain and goods, any plan to finance the construction of heavy industry out of internal sources presented economic planners with very difficult policy choices. The capital for industrialization from internal sources could be amassed either by means of balanced capital and consumer goods production and the selective importation of consumer goods (the solution recommended by Trotsky in 1925–26) or through a policy of forcible grain requisition and repression of the peasantry (the measures put forth by Preobrazhenskii). Financing industrialization out of the USSR's own resources required either giving up "the hegemony of large scale socialist industry" or undertaking the expropriation of the accumulations of the countryside.

Confronted with this dilemma, Stalin, Bukharin, and Rykov compromised extensively with existing circumstances, became fully pragmatic, and disregarded their doctrinal objections to economic interdependence with the capitalist world. In a 1926 ECCI debate Rykov and Bukharin explained how short-term dependence could lead to independence in the long run, and Stalin added that, while Russia, as the vanguard of proletarian revolution, must avoid becoming "a cog in the international capitalist economy," it was nonsense "to depict a socialist economy as something absolutely self-contained and absolutely independent."[11] By the end of the year, the collective leadership had developed a strong interest in the possibility of foreign credits. Stalin did. Bukharin did too, although he remained the most economically isolationist of the Bolsheviks. Integrationists like Rykov had never wavered from the belief that expanded commercial relations with Europe and America, and even close political ties, were essential to the building of socialism in the USSR—despite the discouragements of Genoa and thereafter. At the Fifteenth Party Conference in November, he put the matter plainly and without ideological trappings: "We must now energetically and without being afraid, as some people are, set out to get more long term credits abroad."[12]

Meeting on 11 December 1926, the Politburo recognized and accepted the integrationist implications of *dognat i peregnat,* applied them to international political relations, and adopted *politika dogovorennost.* This action implemented the principle that the success of the industrialization drive necessitated expanded trade, new foreign credits, and capital imports from countries other than Germany. It reflected, in particular, the position of Stalin, who was at this time eager to conclude economic agreements with capitalist states. Convinced that industrialization and the transition to socialism were "not possible without foreign financial help," he asserted that "to remain dependent on our own resources" would be "to give up the reconstruction of our economic life and also the realization of the economic dictatorship of the proletariat." To obtain foreign assistance he was willing to "concede to the wishes of foreign capital to some extent," by which he meant relaxing the government foreign trade monopoly and the restrictions associated with it. Such temporary concessions to capitalism did not represent a betrayal of the October Revolution, Stalin insisted; they continued Lenin's strategy of "initiating a breathing spell" when a difficult situation demanded it. Chicherin supported Stalin and also urged relaxation of the foreign trade monopoly; however, the position they adopted did not find immediate support in either the Politburo or the Central Committee, and no action was taken on their recommendation.[13]

Stalin is best known as the autocrat who led the USSR through a period of autonomous economic development during the 1930s. In 1926–27, however, his economic strategy was not autarkical, despite the reports he presented to meetings of the Central Committee and to congresses of the CPSU. Nor were his political powers dictatorial. He was, rather, a spokesman for the Central Committee majority and for a nearly unanimous Politburo led by Bukharin, Rykov, Tomskii, and himself. Since 1925, Stalin had developed his own particular variations on "socialism in one country" and "temporary capitalist stabilization," each with its special implications for foreign relations. However, he subordinated his personal views to the consensus on economic development and foreign relations that emerged as the Opposition was expelled. In late 1926 he stood for agreements with capitalist states, a search for foreign investment, and relaxation of the state monopoly on foreign trade.

The economic policy decisions made in 1926 coincided with Moscow's reassessment of the state of the country's military preparedness, and considerations of national security played an important role in the drive for industrialization. The army reformed by the recommendations of the Frunze commission remained poorly equipped. It was armed with antiquated heavy machine guns and with light machine guns of various foreign manufacture and had no tanks other than those captured from the forces of Denikin and Wrangel.[14] Representatives from both the civilian and military sectors of the leadership considered this situation in 1926 and undertook an assessment of the level of Soviet military technology.[15] As part of that assessment, they conducted a full reappraisal of the role played in the development of the country's military technology by the covert collaboration the Soviets had conducted with the German army since the summer of 1923, when the agreement for German participation in Russian arms production had been reached. The central personalities in the reevaluation were Józef Unszlicht, deputy chairman of the Revolutionary Military Council (RMC); Stalin, who represented the Politburo; and *polpred* Krestinskii, who was recalled from Berlin to participate in the discussions. They concluded that, despite the obvious goodwill of the German military—Generals Hans von Seeckt and Otto Hasse—and of Reichswehr Minister Otto Gessler, three years of military cooperation with the Germans "had rendered next to nothing" in the way of weapons production.[16]

To get technology transfer and weapons production on track, it was decided to allocate to military purposes 20 million marks of the 300-million-mark German credit granted in April and to send a top-level military mission to Berlin to conduct discussions. Krestinskii made careful preparations with von Seeckt and Hasse for what they agreed would be seven to ten days of multilevel negotiations.[17] Unszlicht, who was the officer in charge of procuring weaponry for the Red Army and who was fluent in German, headed the mission. He carried with him to Berlin an elaborate and detailed program for joint Soviet-German military collaboration in weapons production.[18]

Following conversations between the Soviet delegation and the Reichswehr, Krestinskii hosted a reception at the Soviet embassy on 30 March. It was attended on the German side by Chancellor Wilhelm Marx, Foreign Minister Stresemann, State Secretary von Schubert, and General von Seeckt. Unszlicht, assisted by Krestinskii, told the Germans of a plan to create a modern weapons industry in the USSR, and the two of them proposed that the Germans support the project with technical assistance, capital, and orders for weaponry. Specifically, they proposed joint production of a wide range of modern war materials, including machine guns and heavy artillery, tanks and engines, poison gas and optical instruments. Krestinskii hoped that discussions of expanded military cooperation with Marx, Stresemann, and Schubert would facilitate the conclusion of the Treaty of Berlin then under way. Indeed, the Soviet initiative constituted a test of the future of the Rapallo relationship. Could military planners count on it to supply the requirements of Soviet military technology development and weapons production?

The Germans reacted to what Krestinskii called "the Unszlicht enterprise" with extreme reserve. As the Foreign Ministry record of the meeting states, "the Russians continually spoke of the armaments question, and we continually spoke of other things." Seeckt remained silent even when Unszlicht and Krestinskii reminded him that the proposal had been discussed previously with the Reichswehr on several occasions and that agreement in principle had been reached.[19] Stresemann and Schubert, as the latter subsequently informed Brockdorff-Rantzau, regarded the Soviet proposal as incompatible with the basic orientation of German foreign policy. They both realized that, whereas London and Paris might excuse pre-1925 German military involvement with Soviet Russia, post-Locarno covert collaboration would be regarded as a betrayal of trust. They were, however, willing to support continued secret military collaboration within what Herbert von Dirksen called "proper limits" because of its military value at a time when legal rearmament was denied Germany, and because they believed that those who made policy in Moscow regarded sustained military cooperation as the "most persuasive evidence of our wish to continue our relationship with them."[20] The Reichswehr Ministry also sought to reduce its commitment, refusing to allocate any of its limited funds to development of the Soviet defense industry. "The German generals," the Soviet record of the 30 March breakfast meeting states, "wish to reduce their role to that of intermediaries between private German firms and Soviet organizations."[21]

The following December the arrangements between the Red Army and the Reichswehr were exposed in the *Manchester Guardian,* and Philip Scheidemann, a Social Democratic deputy then denounced them in the Reichstag. For this reason and those discussed above, the Germans renegotiated their military collaboration with the Russians in response to Unszlicht's initiative. Reichswehr involvement in joint weapons production was wound down; after 1926 it was handled directly between the RMC and private German firms. Military collaboration was placed on a basis that involved no sizable investment of funds by the German government, that carried less political risk than formerly, and that was as legal as possible.[22] The Germans would maintain installations for aviation training and weapons testing at Lipetsk and for tanks at Kazan, with the proviso that no German officers on the active duty list would be sent to them. Research laboratories for the development of chemical warfare were sustained at Soviet insistence, although Gessler opposed the measure. Because the

USSR and Germany might one day be military opponents, he thought, experimentation with poison gas was best done in East Prussia.[23] Soviet specialists would attend the aviation and armor schools (which the NKID referred to as the "German schools"); the two armies would exchange officers at annual maneuvers, where Soviet army officers would now appear in uniform; and Soviet officers would be attached to German military training centers. Thereby, one Soviet official pointed out, they could acquire the knowledge the Germans had gained from the World War regarding both technology and the organization of staff work. Finally, the two armies could jointly discuss operational questions, such as a "possible plan for strategic deployment by the Baltic states and Poland."[24]

This amounted to considerably less than the full-scale joint weapons production that Unszlicht initially had in mind. Krestinskii, nevertheless, appreciated the value of collaboration on this more narrow basis.

> Every comrade, without exception, who has come here [to Germany] for maneuvers or to attend the academies has found the display of the technological innovations of the German Army very useful. . . . What we are offering to the Germans doesn't cost us anything, because they pay for everything, while there is no problem finding in the depths of the USSR secret locations for their schools and other smaller military establishments.[25]

Beyond this level of cooperation, however, the divergent interests of Soviet Russia and Weimar Germany became manifest. As stated in a January 1927 Soviet memorandum, the purpose of military collaboration for the USSR was "to strengthen our defenses with their aid without allowing them to infiltrate our army system."[26] The German side, on the other hand, was interested above all in maintaining absolute secrecy, which meant that the machinery they supplied openly to the USSR was often incomplete and could be installed and utilized only with significant modification. From this the NKID concluded that the Germans had only a secondary interest in military cooperation with Russia; their chief objective was to obtain from the League of Nations Disarmament Conference the right to rearm legally. Nevertheless, "even Stresemann," the memorandum concluded, wanted to maintain "certain illegal opportunities for a rainy day, in case of setbacks, and possibly also as a strong trump card."[27] Out of these considerations, the Soviet diplomatic mission in Berlin supported continued military collaboration, and representatives of the RMC, including Unszlicht himself, continued to urge joint weapons production on the Germans, although "the Unszlicht enterprise," the embassy recognized, had few prospects of success.[28]

The War Scare of 1927

If socialism in the USSR was to develop out of NEP conditions and if industry, both civilian and military, was to be constructed in Russia with imported capital and foreign technology, then an extended period of respite from crises at home and abroad was a political necessity. Such crisis-free conditions were not in the offing, however. Within months of the resolutions "to catch up and surpass" and to seek agreements with the capitalist powers, there occurred what Trotsky called "the worst crisis since the revolution."[29] It originated in Russia's international situation, and it did not subside until it had fully engulfed the economy and polity of the USSR.

The October Revolution could not change geography. Soviet Russia, like tsarist Russia, remained vulnerable to attack from Europe. From the Gulf of Finland to the Black Sea, Russia's frontier on the northwest and the west was 2,000 miles long and without natural barriers on which to anchor defensive preparations.[30] The geographic problem was aggravated by a post-Civil War political situation that confronted the USSR with a chain of potential enemies in East-Central Europe. The key link in that chain was Poland, which had an army of a quarter of a million men, enjoyed favorable relations with Romania to its south, claimed a kind of diplomatic hegemony over the Baltic states to the north, and maintained a close alliance with a major European power, France. This political and geographic problem was in turn mediated by an ideology of inevitable conflict between the forces of imperialism and those of proletarian revolution. The result was a strategic doctrine that divided world politics into two camps, that rejected the possibility of a durable and stable peace between capitalist and socialist states, and that designated the leading imperialist country as the international headquarters at which anti-Soviet coalitions were designed and armed interventions planned.

The possibility of a British-organized capitalist coalition against the USSR had been a feature of Soviet discourse on world politics since late 1924, the time of the "Zinoviev letter" and of what Chicherin called "the English crisis." However, during the summer of 1926 the content of foreign relations pronouncements made in Moscow changed from a generalized fear of diplomatic and economic isolation leading eventually to war to a more concrete and specific fear of imminent military attack.[31] By September, party, government, and Comintern leaders were all denouncing what they saw as a British-led scheme to launch a second war of intervention against the USSR. They were encouraged in this by the increasing volume of anti-Soviet statements by the diehards in London following the General Strike in May and by Pilsudski's seizure of power in Poland the same month—a coup d'état which, it was believed in Moscow, was engineered from London.

As the Polish general who had inflicted a serious defeat on the Red Army in 1920, Józef Pilsudski symbolized in Moscow the threat of counterrevolutionary military intervention, and he was believed to harbor a scheme for an East-Central European federation made up of Poland, Lithuania, and the Ukraine. While Chicherin characterized Pilsudski as "unpredictable" and Litvinov thought him enigmatic, Stalin and Radek, in articles appearing in *Izvestiia* and *Pravda*, charged him with "fascism."[32]

The basic outline of a scenario for an interventionist war became incrementally more detailed during the following months until in the early summer of 1927 the now elaborate script turned into a full-scale war scare crisis. By diplomatic means, it was believed, Britain would form an antiSoviet bloc of European countries. Germany would be won over to the coalition by promises of reparations relief and the return of Danzig and the Polish Corridor. Poland would be compensated with Memel, all or part of the rest of Lithuania, and an international loan. Finland and Romania would be involved as well. Pilsudski would create an incident involving the USSR, France would come to his assistance, and the second imperialist onslaught against the USSR would then begin.

War was not imminent, however. From January to March 1927 both the NKID and the Stalin-Bukharin-Rykov leadership indicated that they did not believe the scenario would be played out soon. Stalin, who was already on record as stating that another military intervention was a remote possibility "at some future date," assured a meeting of Moscow railway workers that "we shall not have war this year, neither in the spring nor in the autumn." Bukharin recited the many indications of British-led encirclement and preparations for a new imperialist war, but added that "we need not be particularly alarmed at all this." Rykov too pointed to "the number of international events of the kind which, in the history of international affairs, have more than once occurred on the eve of armed conflicts," but he concluded that it was impossible to state whether they would result in any military action against the USSR.[33]

The NKID did take precautionary diplomatic measures. Litvinov called on the British representative in Moscow in February to impress upon him the Soviet desire for peace as the necessary condition for the construction of socialism in the USSR.[34] And in March, following a meeting of the Locarno foreign ministers in Geneva, he sought and received assurance from Stresemann that the Locarno powers were not considering any plans to redistribute territory in Eastern Europe or to launch a capitalist crusade against the Soviet Union. From these contacts, the NKID concluded that no immediate danger of war existed, and that none would exist unless and until London was able to include Germany in an anti-Soviet bloc of European powers and gain the collaboration of Poland. This sanguine sense of foreign relations ended in April, however, when a series of incidents led to the war scare of 1927, a crisis that peaked in late May and early June in an atmosphere of acute panic and fear of imminent invasion. These incidents began in China, where the Bukharin-Stalin "bloc within," united front strategy of alliance between the CPC and the Guomindang ended in disaster.

Following the advance of the Nationalist Revolutionary Army into central China between July and December 1926, the Chinese Revolution split into two factions, each with its own territorial base and military forces.[35] The left wing of the Guomindang established itself in Wuhan, where it was advised by Borodin and supported by the Chinese Communist Party. It was intent on curbing the power that Chiang Kai-shek had assumed over the revolutionary movement since his March 1926 coup. Borodin publicly denounced Chiang in January 1927, and in March the Wuhan-dominated Third Plenum of the GMD Central Committee resolved to end Chiang's position of domination over party affairs, to restore civilian control to the GMD, and to elevate Wang Jingwei, Chiang's chief rival, to important positions in both the GMD and the Nationalist government. It also called for a joint GMD-CPC conference to decide on the joint direction of the mass movements of farmers and laborers organized since May 1925 and on Communist participation in the Nationalist government. From such statements it would appear that the alliance of the CPC and the GMD left wing was in control of the Chinese revolution, or at least believed that it was.

The other faction, based in Nanjing, was composed of Chiang himself, most of the Nationalist government, and much of the apparatus of the GMD Central Party Headquarters, both of which had moved there from Guangzhou. The Nanjing group was intent on continuing the Nationalist conquest of China by means of forming alliances with independent warlords, winning foreign acceptance of the Nationalist regime, and dispatching troops to capture Shanghai and the lower Yangtze. (Bliukher and the Soviet military aid mission remained at Chiang's headquarters and planned strategy and operations). The Nanjing faction became increasingly intent on suppressing Communism within the areas of China that they controlled and on expelling Borodin from the country. However, when they telegraphed the Comintern in Moscow asking for Borodin's recall, they received no reply.

The conflict between Nanjing and Wuhan was a conflict between Chiang and Borodin; it was also a political and ideological struggle for control of the Chinese Nationalist Revolution. Significant issues were at stake. Should mass social movements in the cities and the countryside be encouraged, or should they be suppressed lest they provoke a counterrevolutionary reaction that would prevent the national unification of China? And what was to be done about the grass-roots anti-imperialist movement? Should it be supported, or ought it to be stifled lest the foreign powers in China (Great Britain, Japan, the United States, France, and Italy) intervene and thwart the Nationalist Revolution?

The strategy adopted by the Soviet/Comintern political mission to the GMD was to channel popular antiforeign sentiment against Great Britain, the principal foreign power in China, rather than against the United States and France, the two other powers with important economic positions in China, and, above all, it was to avoid confrontation or conflict with Japan.[36] This strategy had been devised in the early stages of the Chinese Revolution, and it accorded well with the counter-British policy line articulated in RCP(B)/CPSU and Comintern resolutions since the beginning of the Dawes Plan-Locarno treaty capitalist stabilization era. It was moreover the policy recommended by the Politburo special committee on East Asian affairs in March 1926. With it came significant risks and dangers. Possibly, the British government could respond by intervening directly in the Chinese Revolution, or indirectly by rendering assistance to the warlords of north China, the principal potential military opposition to the Chinese Nationalist movement.

This strategy formed the basis of the activities continually advocated by Borodin in his advice to the left GMD-CPC regime in Wuhan. The leftists organized massive anti-British rallies there in December 1926 and January 1927 that resulted in the surrender of British concessions to Nationalist authorities. These events made the security of Shanghai a matter of concern for the China powers. The largest concentration of foreign residents in China resided in the International Settlement there, and the city was the center of British economic interests. To protect them, the government in London immediately dispatched to Shanghai a battalion of Indian troops from Hong Kong and made plans to send a cruiser squadron and an entire army division. While the threat of retaliation hung in the air, the ambassadors of Great Britain, the United States, Japan, France, and Italy met in Beijing. There they decided on a set of demands for retribution—without, however, being able to agree on any sanctions to enforce them.

The China policy that British governments followed for the next twenty years emerged from this crisis.[37] That policy took Bolshevik influence in China to be the fundamental problem faced by the British Empire in Asia, and it assumed that if Communism were defeated in China, the threat it posed to India would also be reduced. The most effective way to do this was to come to terms with the Chinese Nationalist movement, which was believed to possess a dynamic of its own that was not Communist and could not be controlled by Russians. In East Asia Austen Chamberlain and his advisers in the Foreign Office advanced a strategy that was remarkably similar to the one they pursued with Germany in Europe during the same period. In China as in Germany, British policy worked to conciliate nationalist political forces by the gradual revision of the system of unequal treaties, to promote a political regime that would regard Britain favorably, and to keep the country out of the clutches of the USSR. At the same time, the British Cabinet aimed to protect British life and property in the coastal areas of China accessible to British naval forces. Accordingly, British and other foreign troops and gunboats, along with Chinese police, defended European and American property and persons from popular anti-imperialist demonstrations. At the same time, action was taken directly against the Soviet advisers in China. With the permission of the foreign diplomatic corps, the Beijing metropolitan police on 6 April raided the compound of the Soviet embassy in that city[38] and there arrested twenty-two Russians and thirty-six GMD workers. They discovered and seized CPC and GMD documents, in all carting away seven truckloads of papers from the office of the Soviet military mission.

Parallel to these events, the antagonism between the two factions of the Chinese Nationalist movement became open and violent. Conservative and radical forces fought armed battles in major Chinese cities—Hangzhou, Nanchang, Shanghai, and Guangzhou. Radicals mounted propaganda campaigns, mobilized mass demonstrations, and denounced conservative GMD leaders. Uniformed and armed workers from the General Labor Union ("the inspection corps"), usually controlled by the CPC, protected the infrastructure of radical institutions and enforced strike orders. Conservative counterdemonstrations were organized under the slogans of "Uphold Commander-in-Chief Chiang" and "Expel Borodin." With the assistance of NRA troops, rival labor organizations attacked the headquarters of the General Labor Union, closed its offices, and disarmed "the inspection corps." On the orders of local military commanders, Communists were arrested and often summarily executed. The massacre of the Communists of Shanghai and of the workers they organized between 12 and 14 April marked the final break between Chiang and those allied with him, on the one hand, and Borodin, the Wuhan regime, and the CPC, on the other. Research done in the CPC Central Committee Archives has found that 30,000 to 40,000 people were killed as a result of anti-Communist terror,

3,000 to 4,000 of them party members. In all, 25,000 persons were arrested, and more than 30,000 were made refugees.[39] In a famous incident, the Comintern instructed the CPC in Shanghai to order the workers of the city to bury their weapons so as to avoid a conflict with Chiang's forces. Apparently the order was not carried out.[40]

The German Foreign Ministry in Berlin watched events in China with concern. An Anglo-Soviet conflict would confront the Wilhelmstrasse with the decision it wished above all others to avoid, that of having to choose to support one of its two most important treaty partners in opposition to the other. Could the Locarno relationship with Britain be sustained if Berlin did not side with London in the event of a diplomatic crisis, and would not the relationship with the USSR begun at Rapallo be damaged beyond all repair if it did? If England became involved in a war with Russia, would the Germans be able to remain neutral by citing the provisions of the Treaty of Berlin? They could do so only if Russia were attacked despite having maintained a peaceful stance. At this point the China crisis threatened to complicate German diplomacy severely. Would not Soviet support for the revolutionary forces that attacked British property in China be regarded as an act of provocation? If so, Stresemann would be compelled to make a decision of high policy, the seriousness of which would be apparent throughout Europe.

One way to stave off the dilemma of having to choose between England and the USSR was to mediate the Anglo-Russian conflict. The Wilhelmstrasse pondered this course of action beginning in January, and on 19 February Schubert formally instructed Brockdorff-Rantzau to suggest to the NKID—without proposing mediation as such—that the gains made by the advance of the revolution in China were not worth the risks Soviet involvement there imposed on both the USSR and Germany. Berlin was always disposed, Brockdorff was instructed to add, to make available its good offices to find a way out of the difficulties. Brockdorff, however, ignored these instructions and conveyed to Chicherin only part of what Schubert had instructed—an assurance that the Wilhelmstrasse would stand loyally behind the Berlin Treaty and a request for a regular exchange of information on the situation. Then, after Chamberlain made clear to Stresemann, at the March meeting of the League Council, that only his regard for Stresemann's dilemma prevented him from recommending to the Cabinet an immediate break in relations with Moscow, Stresemann returned to Berlin intent on insisting that Brockdorff propose to the NKID German mediation of the Anglo-Soviet conflict.[41] However, his plans were aborted by the rapid deterioration of relations between Moscow and London beginning with the Beijing raid in early April and culminating with an invasion of the offices of the Soviet trade delegation in London a month later, an event which set off a major war scare crisis in the USSR.

On 12 May, some 150 to 200 London police accompanied by interpreters from the Foreign Office raided the office of the Anglo-Russian Cooperative Society (ARCOS Ltd.) and entered the premises of the Soviet trade delegation next door, premises that were extraterritorial property and enjoyed diplomatic immunity. They searched at will for four days and removed numerous documents. Two weeks later the Baldwin government severed diplomatic relations with Moscow and terminated the Anglo-Soviet Trade Agreement entered into in 1921. An agreement recently concluded between the Soviet government and the Midland Bank extending credits for the purchase of British machinery was also canceled.[42] The break in relations with England exposed one of the basic contradictions inherent in Soviet foreign relations: Ultimately, the "united front" policy counteracted "peaceful coexistence." The British government, in effect and by intention, was refusing to allow Soviet Russia to support strikes by British coal miners and attacks on British property in China while at the same time conducting normal diplomatic relations and acquiring loans from London banks.

On 7 June, Petr Voikov, the Soviet *polpred* in Poland (1924–1927), was assassinated in the Warsaw central railway station by a nineteen-year-old counterrevolutionary Russian émigré named Boris Koverda.[43] On the same day, a bomb was set off at the Communist Party Clubhouse in Leningrad, an action planned, directed, and equipped from Paris by Russian émigré General Kutepov and executed by one of his six terrorist teams, called the Combat Corps, who infiltrated the USSR from Finland. The attack caused a dozen injuries. The OGPU responded by executing without trial twenty alleged enemy agents, five of whom were said to be working directly for British intelligence. A wave of OGPU house-to-house searches, arrests, deportations, and executions all over the USSR followed.[44] The OGPU reported to the Politburo that nationalist underground movements in Georgia and the Ukraine, which were believed to have ties to émigré organizations and to British intelligence, were making preparations for armed struggle. At the height of the crisis, articles positing the threat of imminent war filled the Soviet press. The German embassy in Moscow reported to Berlin, incorrectly, that the Red Army was concentrating troops and equipment in battle positions on the western frontier of the USSR. The NKID made representations abroad linking the events in China, London, and Warsaw to a "systematic and organized struggle against the USSR by the dark forces of world reaction and the enemies of peace."[45] The Politburo seems to have become confused and disoriented and, above all, anxious. The population at large engaged in panic buying and hoarding.

It was Stalin who articulated what would become the official account of the war scare crisis in a statement to the Central Committee in late July: The British bourgeoisie and its general staff, the Conservative party, were creating a coalition of imperialist powers to make war on the USSR. They struck their first blow with a raid on the embassy in Beijing designed to discover evidence of subversion and to provoke the USSR into war over China. They struck their second blow in London, a move aimed at drawing the other powers of Europe into a diplomatic blockade of the USSR. The third blow, the assassination of Voikov in Warsaw, was intended "to play a role similar to that of the Sarajevo assassination" and embroil the USSR in a war with Poland. In preparation for this war the British government was organizing a financial blockade of the USSR, subsidizing underground movements in the Ukraine, Georgia, Azerbaijan, and Armenia, and financing "bands of spies and terrorists, who blow up bridges, set fire to factories and commit acts of terrorism against USSR ambassadors."[46]

However, if we consider the events of the war scare in the broader context of Soviet foreign relations, politics, and ideology, the dynamics of the crisis look remarkably different. By 1927 the strategy of the "united anti-imperialist front," developed over the preceding six years, had become an important measure of political integration, or "solidarity" in Leninist terms. It was the ideological vehicle by which the exploited of Europe, the oppressed of Asia, and the peoples of the USSR were identified with the revolution in Russia, the Soviet regime, and the leadership of the CPSU. To promote that identification, party and Comintern spokesmen repeatedly issued urgent appeals to the Soviet population, to foreign Communist parties, and to the workers of Europe to mobilize to resist the imperialist drive toward war—even when they discounted the imminent threat of war, as they did in the winter of 1926–27. With solidarity and security so closely related, any struggle among the leadership for the allegiance of the party cadres and the international Communist movement could become an ideological struggle over foreign policy. And it did. The contradictory complex of foreign relations with which Stalin and Bukharin had identified themselves in their struggle with the Opposition, and for which they had taken responsibility since late 1926, was vulnerable to criticism on grounds of both ideology and policy. This is what happened. The foreign relations reversal in China revived the Opposition, which launched an attack on the foreign and domestic policies of Stalin and Bukharin. This attack coincided with the ARCOS raid (12–15 May) and with the action of the British government in breaking off relations with Moscow. All this surprised the

NKID and discombobulated the Politburo, which responded by proclaiming that Britain was preparing for war against the USSR and by introducing measures of preventative political and social terror.

Some members of the Central Committee, led by Stalin, advocated a hard-line response to the external-internal threat and directed a get-tough policy against the USSR's perceived enemies both at home and abroad. This response combined repressive OGPU terror measures at home, threats and near ultimatums delivered to Warsaw, and a series of provocative notes to the European powers whose wording increased the level of international tension.[47] Because Chicherin was in Germany and on the French Riviera when the crisis began, seeking rest and treatment for the effects of his ailments (diabetes and polyneuritis), Soviet diplomacy lacked the subtlety, nuance, and complexity he customarily gave to it. Litvinov felt Chicherin's absence both in the conduct of foreign policy and in the management of the NKID's relations with the Politburo.[48]

Crisis Diplomacy

The problems confronting Soviet diplomacy were compounded by a wave of anti-Communist sentiment that swept France following the Beijing raid. On 22 April, Albert Sarraut, the minister of the interior, charged the "directors of Muscovite communism" with subversion in Algeria, concluding his public speech praising the virtues of the French Empire with the Gambetta-like battle cry, "Communism, there is the enemy."[49] The minister of justice, Louis Barthou, then informed the Council of Ministers on 10 May that he would seek to revoke the parliamentary immunity of the leaders of the French Communist Party (PCF) for advocating that French soldiers refuse to participate in military operations in the colonies. (They were incarcerated in July.) A week later, *L'Avenir* called for reinforcement of the Entente with England and for Anglo-French cooperation against the USSR everywhere in the world, particularly China. Even de Monzie became annoyed with what he regarded as Soviet interference in the internal affairs of France. Whatever popular sympathy for the Soviet regime may have resulted from the ARCOS raid and England's precipitous break in diplomatic relations evaporated with the executions in Moscow. Berthelot told the British chargé that if they continued, French public opinion would demand the severing of relations with Russia.[50] Normal relations between Russia and Europe and America depended significantly on the West's belief that the USSR was becoming a normal and humane state. The relapse into OGPU terror in the summer of 1927 was a setback in the NKID's campaign to establish that belief. Clearly, the quest for agreements with Europe and America was at risk, and Soviet diplomacy was in an extremely delicate situation.

As a crisis in international relations, the war scare did not escalate beyond this point. The Baldwin government had no intention of organizing a second war of intervention; nor did Chamberlain try to form an overt diplomatic coalition in opposition to the USSR. Paris and Warsaw separated themselves from the events in London and assured the NKID that they would not sever relations with Moscow. Stresemann told the British ambassador that Germany would honor the Treaty of Berlin to the letter, and he assured Chicherin personally, when the two of them met in Baden-Baden, that Germany would not be "dragged into a struggle against the Soviet Union."[51]

At the League Council meeting in Geneva during the second week of June, the foreign ministers of the five principal Allied powers of the World War (Britain, France, Italy, Belgium, and Japan) and of Germany met to discuss the crisis. Chamberlain explained to the others the background of the breach in relations, and he denied that London had any hostile intentions toward the USSR or plans to form the Locarno powers into an anti-Soviet bloc. He asked Stresemann to explain London's peaceful intentions to Chicherin and to caution Moscow in the name of the six powers against escalating the crisis with Poland. Remarkably, Stresemann agreed to do so, thereby putting at risk both Germany's diplomatic neutrality and its relationship with the USSR. However, to have refused Chamberlain's request would have placed him in a difficult tactical position, and he too was indignant over the executions in Moscow. The message was conveyed through diplomatic channels, although the fact that it emanated from a six-power discussion was not. Chicherin accepted it as friendly advice and promised to try to influence his government in the direction of diplomatic moderation, something toward which he was already disposed.[52]

Within the Politburo, Stalin's hard line was opposed by Rykov, Tomskii, and Kalinin. And it was criticized by Chicherin on his return to Moscow around 15 June following his stay in Europe. At a joint session of the Politburo and Sovnarkom, he reported on his conversations with European leaders and presented his analysis of the situation.[53] In doing so, he took aim at the policy that had first rendered assistance to the Chinese revolutionaries and British coal miners and had then adopted an aggressive response to the break in relations with England. It was not possible to have two foreign policies, Chicherin insisted—a Comintern policy and a government policy. The activities of the OGPU had made things worse; the shooting of hostages had aroused universal indignation in the West. Although there was no immediate danger of war, the USSR was threatened with diplomatic isolation and an economic blockade that threatened the survival of the regime. The Politburo must decide, he said, between executions and foreign investment, put an end to the terror, reaffirm the precrisis foreign policy course, and make an effort to reduce the level of conflict with England. Chicherin supplemented his statement by a memorandum that was distributed afterwards and by his threat to resign.

Chicherin occupied a strong position. To have accepted the resignation of the figure most closely associated with the treaties of Rapallo and Berlin would have signaled a sharp devaluation of Soviet relations with Germany, something the USSR could ill afford so soon after the break with England. And Chicherin's recommendations found support among those members of Sovnarkom responsible for economic matters who acknowledged the dangers of an economic blockade. Stalin had to back down. By the end of the month, the Politburo had approved Chicherin's recommendations in a modified form and decided to sustain the previous direction of foreign policy. In July it renounced OGPU executions and repudiated the hard-line, get-tough measures. Led by Stalin, the majority leadership reaffirmed the importance of "peaceful coexistence" and of conventional diplomacy in defense of the security of the USSR.[54] Despite the alarms sounded regarding the foreign threat, and despite differences within the Politburo over strategy, no one either in the Central Committee majority or in the United Opposition was willing to risk a war or even heightened diplomatic isolation.[55]

Soviet diplomats reaffirmed Moscow's desire for international cooperation and for agreements with Europe and America. In accordance with the precepts of *politika dogovorennost,* they used foreign trade to improve political relations. Orders for machinery and other producer goods required by the industrialization drive were increasingly "diverted" from Germany to Britain and the United States. Purchases from the United States were aimed at breaking down long-standing resistance to more favorable political relations with the USSR. In Britain orders were, as one Soviet official explained later, part of a policy "to prevent a worsening of relations through economic concessions."[56]

Most of all, Moscow went the limit to improve relations with France and to prevent Paris from joining London in an anti-Communist and anti-Soviet rapprochement.[57] Even before the war scare crisis reached its most acute phase, the Quai d'Orsay had predicted that the growing hostility between London and Moscow would force the Russians to make additional concessions in the Franco-Soviet debt-loan-trade negotiations, provided the French delegation stood firm. And it was right. By late June the majority leadership, with its turn away from the hard-line response to the war scare, began to see a prompt debt settlement with Paris as a way to deny London a partner in a possible anti-Soviet coalition. As the policy was subsequently explained in *Pravda,"*we *buy* the possibility of peaceful economic relations with one of the capitalist countries in Europe, and France *sells* us this possibility." An offer to pay the tsarist debt, *Izvestiia* added, "is one of the most important prerequisites for the postponement of the moment of intervention." Hence Rakovskii addressed a memorandum to de Monzie on 30 June formally requesting that the Franco-Soviet conference be convened in plenary session to consider the Soviet offer. The Poincaré government rejected the initiative, however, having no interest in providing Rakovskii with a public forum in which to advertise the value of Soviet concessions. In mid-August, Rakovskii was authorized to propose a Franco-Soviet political treaty to the French government, and again he played the security card in Paris, proposing a Franco-Russian nonaggression pact, exploring the possibility of a similar treaty with Poland, and suggesting a multilateral accord that would include Paris, Moscow, and Warsaw. The policy of "buying off France" culminated on 21 September when Litvinov announced a new set of concessions, adding incentives to Moscow's standing offer of July 1926 (60 million gold francs annually for sixty-two years) and significantly reducing the size of the loan the USSR asked in return.[58]

Yet the international situation did not improve. The aggressive position taken in early June had damaged the effectiveness of Soviet diplomacy, as did mounting speculation within and among the foreign services of Europe that there would soon be a change of leadership in Moscow. Most of all, Franco-Soviet relations deteriorated sharply beginning in late August with a strident anti-Soviet campaign in the French press. Even the moderate *Le Temps* called upon the government to adopt an anti-Communist policy and to break off relations with Moscow. Much of the attack was directed at Rakovskii himself and demanded his recall to Moscow. The *polpred* was a leading member of the United Opposition, and he had signed the "Statement of the Thirteen" calling for workers and soldiers in capitalist countries to contribute to the defeat of "their own" governments in the event of a war with the USSR.[59] The Council of Ministers was divided. Poincaré favored a break in relations; Herriot and Painlevé were opposed. Briand was willing to consider the "Statement of the Thirteen" a matter of intraparty struggle, as had Mussolini in the instance of Kamenev, who was *polpred* in Rome at the time and who also signed the statement. Poincaré insisted on Rakovskii's recall, apparently intending thereby to scuttle the debt-loan-security negotiations. Briand countered by declaring Rakovskii persona non grata in mid-October, thereby forcing his recall to Moscow but keeping Franco-Soviet relations intact.[60]

Relations with Germany also worsened as the possibilities for further loan guarantees from the German government dimmed.[61] German industrialists complained to the Foreign Ministry in Berlin about the negative effects of the war scare crisis on the investment climate in the USSR and about the restrictions imposed on foreign enterprise by bureaucratic centralization in Russia and the government monopoly on foreign trade. Above all, they accused Moscow of using trade for political influence and of "diverting" machinery orders from Germany to the United States, Britain, and France. German-Soviet relations were affected most detrimentally and profoundly when, in a speech before the Reichstag on 24 June, Stresemann made public the warning he had conveyed to Moscow on behalf of the six powers at Geneva. Despite repeated efforts, Stresemann had never succeeded in justifying his *Westorientierung* to the NKID, and now, at what Moscow regarded as a most dangerous moment in its foreign relations, Berlin was compromising the neutrality on which Soviet security counted by defending Poland on behalf of a group of powers including England, and doing so with great publicity. Fears that Germany was drifting further westward diplomatically, leaving the USSR alone to face a hostile coalition, were magnified. Chicherin informed Brockdorff-Rantzau that "forcing Poland back to its ethnographical borders" was compromised as a goal of the Soviet-German relationship. And his relationship with the Politburo, he complained, was now jeopardized.[62]

At the end of July the Revolutionary Military Council renewed its request for a full acceleration of the collaboration between the Reichswehr and the Red Army. Unszlicht again traveled to Berlin. There he informed German generals and diplomats that the USSR expected to be attacked by Poland and Romania within months, and he revived the proposal for joint weapons production that he had made initially in the spring of 1926. As they had previously, the Germans showed little interest in rearming Russia. The uncertain international situation of the spring and summer of 1927 dictated to Berlin a policy of marking time on military collaboration. Even the Reichswehr minister, Otto Gessler, did not favor any extension of collaboration with the Red Army at a time of international crisis. Together, the German Reichswehr and the Foreign Ministry rejected the proposal.[63]

However, Stresemann did reassure Moscow. In mid-August he authorized Brockdorff-Rantzau to transmit to the NKID his final and formal approval of the establishment of the tank base at Kazan that had been agreed upon in March 1926. This was an action of considerable political significance. The German Foreign Ministry had previously been highly circumspect about involving any sector of the German government other than the Reichswehr Ministry directly in the covert military collaboration with the USSR—thereby allowing Stresemann to maintain "plausible deniability" in any discussions with his colleagues of Locarno, Chamberlain and Briand. Now Stresemann was implicated. The approval signaled an upswing in the level of Soviet-German military collaboration within the limits prescribed by the German side.[64] The exchange of officers at annual maneuvers continued. And Soviet officers now went through extended general staff training with the Reichswehr, studying German methods of training, organization, mobilization, and supply.[65]

Trotsky, Stalin, and China

In Moscow, the events in China set off a major foreign relations debate as the United Opposition, which had been quiet since late 1926, coalesced around an attack on the policy of Stalin and Bukharin.[66] Trotsky and Zinoviev led the Opposition, the membership of which included leading Bolsheviks like Radek, economists such as Sokolnikov, Preobrazhenskii, and Georgi Piatakov, and prominent representatives of Soviet policy abroad including Kamenev, Rakovskii, Krestinskii, and Ioffe. As provost of Sun Yat-sen University, Radek had access through Chinese students there to information on the situation in China. And thus informed, he criticized Stalin and Bukharin for their China policy—or their lack of one, as he put it—in an open debate at the Communist Academy a month before the Shanghai massacre. There he predicted that Chiang Kai-shek would turn on the CPC and betray the Chinese Revolution at the first opportunity.[67] Following the debacle in Shanghai, eighty-four party members—and eventually hundreds—signed a declaration identifying themselves with the now vastly expanded United Opposition and submitted it to the Politburo.[68] Zinoviev made an unauthorized speech censuring Bukharin and Stalin, and Trotsky forced a debate before the Eighth ECCI Plenum (18–30 May) at which he criticized their China policy in two vehement speeches.[69] Trotsky, a candidate member of the ECCI, appeared as a nonvoting delegate. Zinoviev, president of the ECCI little more than six months earlier, was excluded from the meeting. The struggle between the Opposition and the Central Committee majority continued throughout the summer and peaked in October–November. As it did so, the three members of the Opposition who held diplomatic posts in Europe conferred in Berlin. Kamenev and Rakovskii advocated direct action and mass demonstrations against the Central Committee majority; Krestinskii favored continued maneuvering within the party leadership. In an act of protest against the majority, Ioffe committed suicide.

The Opposition issued its indictment in a series of manifestos beginning in May and continuing until the Fifteenth Party Congress the following December and beyond. Although it centered on "the Chinese question," the indictment included the whole package of economic and foreign policies with which Stalin and Bukharin had identified themselves since the inception of "temporary capitalist stabilization" and "socialism in one country." They were attacked for their optimism and complacency, their belief that relations with the capitalist world were stabilized, their pursuit of "peaceful coexistence," their efforts to extend and consolidate "the breathing space," their failure to warn the workers of the world of the danger of imminent war with the imperialist powers, and their neglect of the task of sabotaging the war effort of the (prospective) interventionists. Criticizing the basic principles of the Stalin-Bukharin foreign policy, the Opposition charged the duumvirate with bringing the world revolutionary process to the brink of disaster with their "united front" strategy. This had failed not only in China but also in England, where the working class had reacted with passive indifference to the break in relations with the USSR. Russia, they charged, had lost the support of the international working class by sacrificing their interests to a foreign relations of power politics and maneuver with the capitalist states.

Rakovskii was both a leading member of the United Opposition and *polpred* in Paris. From the Fourteenth Party Congress in December 1925 to the Fifteenth Congress in December 1927, he consistently articulated the Opposition position in the intraparty debate: The breathing space was not being extended; capitalism and socialism could not coexist peacefully any better in 1927 than they could in 1917; the foreign policy that Stalin conducted was "fundamentally wrong." Because Stalin had rejected the imperatives of the world revolutionary process (at least for the near term), the international working class had lost faith in the Socialist Republic, and "the Soviet Union had ceased to represent an ideological danger for the capitalist states." Not surprisingly, Rakovskii concluded, the capitalist press feared not Stalin but the Opposition.[70]

Rakovskii had adopted a conciliatory stance in the debt settlement negotiations with France in 1926. Trotsky had too, hoping for access to European technology and capital. Stalin was publicly pledged to autarky. The war scare crisis turned the settlement with France into a point of contention in the leadership struggle, and both sides shifted positions.[71] Seeking a way out of the crisis into which their confrontationist response to the reversals in China, Britain, and Poland had led them, Stalin and the Politburo openly committed themselves to "buying" peaceful relations with Europe, and with France in particular. Trotsky then made their inconsistency an issue. The foreign policy of the USSR, he charged, had been distorted by the doctrine of "socialism in one country." In 1926, Stalin and Bukharin had disregarded "our world economic ties and our economy's dependence on the world market" and had failed to obtain an agreement with France at a time when the French were in a position of weakness (owing to financial crisis and governmental instability) and when the USSR could have bargained from a position of strength within world politics (because of the advancing revolution in China). Then, pressured by the war scare a year later, Trotsky continued, Bukharin and Stalin undertook what Trotsky called "super-hasty, exceptional measures to revive the negotiations," with France which resulted only in a tougher stance in Paris and "an intensification of pressure against us."[72] Countering Trotsky's attack, Stalin cited Rakovskii's support for a prompt debt settlement, and Trotsky responded by writing Rakovskii in Paris asking him to keep in mind that the policy he advocated in Paris had become an issue in the intraparty struggle.[73] Rakovskii was caught in a three-way conflict between his duties as *polpred*, his loyalty to the Opposition, and the desire of the Poincaré government to get rid of him. He could not have been unhappy about leaving his post in Paris.

The primary target of the Opposition attack was the China policy with which Stalin and Bukharin had openly identified themselves since the Seventh ECCI Plenum, and which had suffered such disastrous reversals.[74] The exchanges between Stalin and Trotsky over the tactics of revolution to be used in China are best known as the beginnings of a prolonged doctrinal dispute that their followers and supporters sustained for decades. Long after the battle for control of the Communist International and the Communist Party of the Soviet Union had been decided, that dispute remained at the heart of the battle for leadership of the international Communist movement. However, the intraparty China debate also constituted a significant event in the history of early Soviet foreign relations. There was a long-standing agreement among the Bolsheviks not to inject foreign relations into the party struggles among themselves, nor to dispute openly regarding foreign policy within the ranks of the Comintern.[75] This convention was broken in 1927 as the debate over China became the most visible feature of a wide-ranging intra-Bolshevik conflict.

Ignoring the norms of foreign policy formation and openly criticizing the policy of the Politburo during a time of war danger left the United Opposition open to charges of disloyalty. To such charges Trotsky replied that, as was the case with Georges Clemenceau in France in 1917, critics of a government could become the most effective fighters against the enemy— suggesting thereby that in the event of a direct military threat to the USSR, it might become necessary to oppose the Stalin-Bukharin leadership and take over direction of the war. With these words, which came to be known as his "Clemenceau thesis,"[76] Trotsky at last put himself forward openly as the political alternative to Stalin. Neither previously nor thereafter was the confrontation between the two men more direct. The climax came at a joint plenum of the Central Control Commission and the Central

Committee held between 24 July and 8 August. There Stalin exploited the war scare to defeat the Opposition. Previously he had been the member of the collective leadership who most denigrated the seriousness of the war threat. Now he spoke of "the real and actual threat of a new war," "not a matter of some vague and immaterial 'danger.'" He ridiculed and denounced the Opposition for their "attacks on the Party" and for their "cowardice" and "desertion" in the face of danger from without.[77]

All the Opposition's criticism was then summed up in a lengthy political platform,[78] which the thirteen members of the Opposition on the Central Committee submitted to the Politburo in September for discussion at the impending Fifteenth Party Congress. The Central Committee majority defied party rules, however, and refused to have it distributed to the party membership. When members of the Opposition attempted to reproduce it themselves, utilizing three or four typewriters,[79] the OGPU seized this "secret printing press," as they called it, and credited themselves with having exposed "an Opposition plot." Stalin ridiculed Zinoviev for having predicted the outbreak of war, at first for the spring and then for the autumn, and he characterized the Opposition as "hysterics."[80] When Trotsky and Zinoviev attempted—unsuccessfully—to organize worker support in Leningrad and Moscow during the celebrations of the tenth anniversary of the October Revolution, the OGPU suppressed them and recommended that the leadership of the Opposition be eliminated "at one stroke."[81] In mid-November, Trotsky and Zinoviev were charged with organizing counterrevolutionary demonstrations and expelled from the party.[82] The United Opposition split. In December, Zinoviev and Kamenev conceded to the majority leadership, leaving the followers of Trotsky alone in opposition. With Trotsky unable to participate, Rakovskii acted as spokesman for the Opposition at the Fifteenth Party Congress.[83] The delegates there passed a resolution making opposition incompatible with party membership, thus beginning what has been called "the complete ideological disarmament" of party members with heterodox views.[84] Rakovskii and seventy-five other Trotskyists were expelled from the party. And when these measures did not fully subdue the Opposition, Stalin submitted to the Central Committee proposals that in effect made opposition an unequivocal political crime. Persons holding Opposition views were to be regarded as accomplices of internal and external enemies and to be sentenced as "spies" by administrative decree of the OGPU.[85] Although the Politburo as a whole did not completely agree with Stalin regarding the specific police measures and punishments to be used against the Opposition, it did agree to the principle that the OGPU would be employed in suppressing it.

10 Economy, Politics, and Diplomacy in Crisis

The Grain Crisis and the Search
for Foreign Investment

At the time of the Fifteenth Party Congress, the two largest problems facing Soviet foreign relations and economic development—the agrarian problem and the trade deficit—seemed resolved in spite of the war scare and the break in relations with Britain. The grain harvested in the USSR in 1926/27 set a postrevolution record, and grain exports helped to push the country's trade surplus to near-record levels. The USSR received relatively substantial medium-term loans guaranteed by the German (1926) and the Austrian (1927) governments, and some American banks—Chase National and Equitable Trust—began to expand their short-term financing of purchases. Foreign loans for the year 1926/27 reached a level that had not been attained since the October Revolution, and one that would not be repeated until the years 1941–1945.[1] Short-term credits were negotiated to cover trade deficits, and loans were dedicated to a new and, at the time, distinctively Soviet style of technology transfer, described as "the direct purchase of technical assistance including foreign designs and foreign built factories, the direct hiring of foreign engineers and technicians, and the import of modern equipment both for production and for use and as a prototype to be copied for domestic production."[2] For the year 1926/27, machine and engineering imports reached 58 percent of the 1913 level in real terms. When combined with increased domestic machine production, the installation of new capital equipment exceeded the 1913 level by 15 percent. To both party leaders and nonparty economic planners it seemed as if the industrialization drive, first announced in late 1925, could now be undertaken and carried out without serious difficulty.

In August 1927, in the midst of the war scare crisis and the campaign against the United Opposition, the Politburo made the crucial decision implementing the industrialization drive. It approved new construction projects in major industries and allocated increased funds to industrial construction from the state budget. Thereby it sided with Vesenkha, which insisted that overtaking the economies of Europe necessitated increased industrial investment, and against those nonparty economic experts who argued that further drafts from the budget would endanger the country's economic equilibrium. As a result of this decision, capital investment in Vesenkha-planned industry increased by 50 percent during the economic years 1927/28 and 1928/29. By mid-1929 it had reached a level 70 percent higher than total capital investment in 1913. In the two years 1927/28 and 1928/29, the state budget grew by 60 percent, and 50 percent of this was allocated to industry and collective agriculture. This "triumph of rapid industrialization," as it has been called, was accompanied by a "socialist offensive," an effort to extinguish private enterprise, both rural and urban, by directing investment into the socialist sector of the economy.[3]

Optimism also pervaded the NKID Collegium. In late October 1927 it concluded that the worst of the tensions of the war scare crisis had dissipated. Chicherin sought and received—apparently at a joint meeting of the Politburo, Sovnarkom, and the Central Committee—a reendorsement of the policy of increased economic exchange and improved political relations with Europe and America. He predicted that relations could be improved, not only with France but with the United States and Britain as well. Investors in London and New York were showing interest in the USSR, he stated, and the governments of both countries were warming toward Moscow. If promoted, this interest "should not be without effect on the position of capitalist circles in other countries on the so-called Russian question," meaning that if Wall Street and the City could be won over to investing in Soviet Russia, the attitude of the government and business elites of the rest of the capitalist world would be transformed. There was a crucial proviso, however. New foreign investment would be forthcoming, Chicherin stated categorically, only if the foreign trade monopoly were relaxed or ended.[4]

At the same time, the policy of participation in the organizations and agreements of multilateral international cooperation was implemented as Litvinov went to Geneva in late November, where, as leader of the Soviet delegation to the Fourth Session of the Preparatory Commission on Disarmament, he proposed "immediate, complete, and general disarmament."[5] With him he took "the general line" of foreign policy that Stalin had articulated in a speech to a joint plenum of the Central Committee and the Central Control Commission on 23 October[6]: The USSR was the one power which for the sake of all humanity worked to preserve world peace against the preparations for war and the provocations of the imperialists, and it was the only honest advocate of disarmament, the one country truly interested in lifting the burden of arms from the backs of the exploited workers of Europe and the oppressed peoples of Asia. Late 1927 was the time when much of what would be sloganized for both domestic and foreign consumption over the next sixty years as "the struggle for peace" or as "the struggle for peace and disarmament" was formalized. Not coincidentally, "peaceful coexistence" was dogmatized at this time, with the term officially installed in party usage, ending what had been the practice since 1920 of using the terms "peaceful coexistence" and "peaceful cohabitation" interchangeably.[7]

In that same speech to the Central Committee, Stalin again articulated the autarkical strategy of economic development he had defended since 1925. Foreign concessions, he argued, subjected the Soviet proletariat to conditions of tsardom and slavery; the USSR could and would "re-equip our industry on the basis of internal accumulations." Such statements were rhetorically consistent with "socialism in one country." And they could hardly be abandoned at a time when Trotsky stood for more foreign concessions and expanded foreign trade, and when the platform of the United Opposition criticized the present and projected tempo of industrialization as inadequate, called for an abridgement of the government monopoly on foreign trade, and urged the payment of tsarist debts so as to encourage foreign loans. Such statements did, however, put the party's officially announced strategy of economic development (autarky) in direct contradiction to the government's de facto foreign relations (a search for loans from New York and London).

This discrepancy between rhetoric and policy continued even after the leadership of the United Opposition was on its way into exile. In a secret memorandum to the Politburo written in late December, Stalin revealed an economic foreign policy that drew heavily on the Opposition's strategy of development. He declared that the reconstruction of the economy, "the socialist construction of our state," and the "realization of the economic dictatorship of the proletariat" were "impossible without the help of foreign capital." "We are suffering from a chronic lack of money and a lack of intelligent economic forces so that we are unable to carry out our program with our own resources alone." After what he characterized as "long talks with Comrade Chicherin," Stalin urged a relaxation of the foreign trade monopoly, a proposal he claimed to have favored for months. The monopoly was a relic of War Communism, he stated, and, praising Lenin's concept of tactical retreat, he declared that "the period of War Communism is over."

If the trade monopoly were relaxed, "the prospects for coming to an agreement with the English and the Americans, that is, of obtaining the needed means for reconstruction, become much more favorable." And when London and New York were won over, Stalin stated in support of Chicherin's argument, the policy of the entire capitalist world would surely be transformed.[8]

The Stalin-Chicherin proposals were accepted in principle by the Politburo, and the relaxation of the foreign trade monopoly was discussed on repeated occasions in late 1927 and early 1928. These discussions were kept secret, and in public the majority leadership affirmed the importance of the foreign trade monopoly and denounced reports of pending modifications in it. In December 1927, while Stalin was urging the Politburo to relax the monopoly, and when the matter was near the top of the national policy agenda, Anastas Mikoian, people's commissar of foreign and internal trade (1925–30), told the Fifteenth Party Congress that the monopoly was "the impregnable condition of the building of socialism in a capitalist environment." The following February, while Litvinov instructed Soviet diplomats to suggest in foreign capitals that the monopoly was about to be relaxed, the ECCI announced through the Communist press abroad that modification of the trade monopoly was out of the question.[9]

By this time, however, a state of emergency gripped the country, the result of a crisis in economic development, foreign relations, and high politics. In October–December 1927, as the Opposition was defeated and as Trotsky and Rakovskii were sent into exile, the condition of the economy, which had been stable and growing since 1926, became critical. And in the months that followed, the Politburo initiated "extraordinary economic measures." A highly publicized show trial was conducted, presided over by Andrei Vishinskii. The Stalin-Bukharin coalition, which had governed the party for three years, disintegrated and the collective leadership of the CPSU split into "moderate" and proto-Stalinist groups. "Peaceful coexistence," international cooperation, and efforts at making agreements with the capitalist powers all failed to bring about significant new foreign investment. Economic policy took a leap forward into coerced collectivization and rapid industrialization.

What initially sent the economy and the politics of the USSR into crisis was a sharp decline in extra-rural grain marketings beginning in October 1927.[10] War rumors and fear of another famine discouraged the peasantry from selling grain and caused a rush of panic buying at consumer cooperative stores. By November–December, peasant grain sales to official collection agencies had dropped to one-half of what they had been for the same period the previous year. Peasants concealed grain in huge pits; speculation increased; government stocks became depleted; and the food supply to the towns, the industrial centers, and the Red Army was threatened.

The European and American scholars who have examined the causes of this crisis have attributed it to a whole complex of factors including chronic low productivity, low state grain prices, a shortage of goods for purchase, and insecurities aroused by the war scare.[11] Certainly the causes were systemic. With the decision for industrialization, the party had aimed at what Bukharin subsequently described as "maximum accumulation in socialist industry, maximum development in agriculture, and maximum consumption by the working class and the working masses in general."[12] Choosing among these objectives seemed unnecessary at first, as it was assumed that the agricultural sector could do everything—supply raw materials for industry, provide the exports to pay for imported industrial goods, contribute the labor force for industrial expansion, and furnish the food for the growing urban industrial population. These objectives would be accomplished, it was further assumed, through the operation of the price-managed market, without additional forms of incentive or coercion. The grain crisis decisively undermined these assumptions and confronted the party leadership with difficult choices.

The decision that shaped the party's response to the crisis and the future of the USSR was taken on 6 January 1928. Following a Politburo resolution, the Central Committee directed party organizations to use "all means" to bring about "a revolution in the grain collections" in the shortest possible time. Local party leaders were made personally responsible for the success of the campaign, and they were urged to enforce Article 107 of the Russian Criminal Code providing for the punishment of speculators and the confiscation of their grain stocks.[13] Over the next three months, 30,000 urban party cadres led by senior party officials went to the grain-growing areas to oversee the procurement campaign. Leading members of Sovnarkom and the Central Committee Secretariat toured the most crucial areas.

Stalin spent the last two weeks of January in Siberia, where he supervised the confiscation of surpluses from kulaks and the purge of local party and government apparatchiki. By the time he arrived he had decided that the crisis was the result of "sabotage" committed by kulaks, who aimed to force up prices by withholding their surpluses from the market and who encouraged smaller peasants to do the same. In Siberia he told party members of his conviction that this "kulak sabotage" posed a direct threat to the party's plans to finance accelerated industrial investment out of grain export surpluses and that the threat would continue as long as there were kulaks.[14] If the surpluses necessary to industrialize the USSR were to be made available to the state, and if socialism was to be constructed in Russia, he concluded, then small-scale private peasant farming would have to be replaced by an agriculture of large collective and state farms.

Implementation of these "extraordinary measures" in the countryside brought a torrent of peasant complaints flooding into local party offices. The leadership in Moscow became alarmed; Rykov clashed with Stalin upon his return; and by early February an atmosphere of imminent disaster pervaded the capital. The Politburo, Sovnarkom, and Central Committee meeting together heard Valerian Kuibyshev (chairman of the Supreme Economic Council) describe the situation in the darkest of terms:[15] What was happening to the economy was not reconstruction, he stated, but "slow death." Only one remedy was possible—further relaxation of the trade monopoly in order to secure "generous and long-term credits" from abroad. Meeting separately on 8 February, Sovnarkom agreed, declaring that the situation was very dangerous and adopting a resolution stating that the government did not at the moment have the resources to overcome the crisis.

Rykov informed Litvinov of the results of the meeting, and the next day the NKID notified missions abroad that the economy had been "very gravely shaken by the events of the past few months," that the situation had "deteriorated sharply" during the last few days, and that it was now "exceedingly serious." "We need money and/or credits," Litvinov wrote, "but we must not forget that we need this money or credit at an extremely unfavorable moment." Because of the deepening economic crisis, opinion in Europe and America, which had seemed disposed to loan and trade agreements in October and early November, had now become reserved and restrained, Litvinov explained. Since the beginning of January, negotiations with American, German, and French companies had come to a standstill. This was the result, the NKID believed, of an effort to take advantage of the dire economic and financial situation in the USSR and to gain further concessions before concluding agreements. Litvinov instructed Soviet diplomats abroad to respond to such hesitations "in an adroit and tactful manner" and, without "any open display of haste or insistence," to "speak out vigorously in favor of agreements." Confidentially, unofficially, and noncommittally, they were to suggest that the government was on the verge of relaxing the trade monopoly. "You must exert all your strength to persuade the forces that are interested in our market that it would be quite profitable for them to help in the reconstruction of our country and that the worker's and peasant's government is willing to make further concessions on the question of the foreign trade monopoly in the interest of the reconstruction of the country."[16]

This initiative was one of a series of measures adopted in mid-February to ease the economic crisis and to sustain the industrialization drive without completely sacrificing the interests of the peasantry.[17] Another was the reassurance given the peasantry that NEP was *not* about to be abolished combined with a warning to all party organizations against the excessive application of Article 107. The backbone of support for the February effort to restore allocation of resources based on market equilibrium was made up of Rykov, Bukharin, and Tomskii, men who believed the grain crisis to be the result of low productivity and bad price management rather than "kulak sabotage." Stalin went along with this easing of the coercive measures in the countryside, again backing away from confrontation, as he had the previous summer from the get-tough response to the war scare. Therefore, the initial imposition of "extraordinary measures" did not lead immediately and directly either to the end of NEP or to a permanent schism within the Politburo. However, it did open a rift among the leadership of the Central Committee majority for a second time. In the months that followed, this rift would open still wider as more objections were voiced in response to the arbitrary nature of Stalin's actions, to the way he shifted the blame for a complex crisis onto local officials, and to his proposals for the collectivization of agriculture.

Diplomatic Isolation and the Beginnings of Stalinism

Michael Reiman has argued that the Opposition remained a crucial factor in Soviet politics for some time after December 1927, when Zinoviev and Kamenev surrendered to the Stalin-Rykov-Bukharin leadership, and the recalcitrant Trotsky and seventy-five of his followers were expelled from the CPSU. In the winter of 1928, the struggle with the Opposition decisively influenced consideration within the Politburo of the strategies necessary to secure urgently needed foreign financial assistance. On the one hand, the requisites of international politics suggested that the Politburo would do well to eliminate the Opposition completely, once and for all. Signs of political instability in the USSR only made the Americans and the British hesitant about concluding agreements. On the other hand, open repression such as the executions that took place at the height of the war scare crisis would produce a negative reaction in the West and endanger the prospects for getting foreign loans and credits. Rykov, Stalin, and Kuibyshev were particularly concerned with securing foreign loans. Liquidating the Opposition was of lower priority for them, and they were inclined to believe that it did not continue to represent a serious danger.[18] Viacheslav Menzhinskii, the chairman of the OGPU (1926–34), on the other hand, argued that the Opposition could still make a comeback from remaining centers of resistance within the USSR.[19] And Bukharin was alarmed at the prospect that Communist political figures linked with the Opposition might make substantial gains in the national elections pending in France and Germany. Should they be victorious, they might challenge the domination of the Bukharin-led Russian delegation within the Communist International.

In the economic dislocation and political turmoil of the winter of 1928, fear of the Opposition prevailed within the Politburo. There was a realignment of forces, and Stalin joined with Menzhinskii and Bukharin in their drive to suppress what remained of it in Russia. Since late 1926 his support for relaxing the foreign trade monopoly had been crucial to the search for agreements with Europe and America. Now he moved away from that position, concluding that loans and credits from capitalist states were of less urgency than the complete defeat of the Opposition. At a decisive meeting of the Politburo held on 26 February, the Menzhinskii-Bukharin-Stalin group defeated the position held by Chicherin, who argued against any change in the direction of foreign policy. Proposals for extensive relaxation of the trade monopoly were withdrawn lest they provide ammunition to the Opposition. Instead, the Opposition was to be blamed for the condition of the economy. Within days, Sovnarkom declared that Opposition activities in particular were responsible for the economic crisis, that any and all economic sabotage would be punished, and that the OGPU would be given powers of surveillance over both the economy and the party organization.[20]

Suppressing opposition could not relieve the economic crisis, however, and the emergency measures for grain procurement did not. Although the grain procurement rate rose dramatically in February, in March it slowed and in April it dropped severely. For the 1927/28 economic year, grain exports declined to 410,000 metric tons from a level of 2.256 million metric tons in 1926/27. Increased export of industrial raw materials, timber, oil, sugar, ores, and furs compensated for this decline, all of them—with the exception of furs—being priced at below world and domestic market levels. As a result, the total volume of exports actually increased by 12.7 percent for the year 1927/28. However, imports, largely of industrial equipment, increased even more substantially, resulting in a negative trade balance. Gold and foreign exchange reserves were exported and short-term loans negotiated to cover the 247-million-ruble deficit.[21]

The prospect of a persistent grain procurement crisis brought Soviet domestic and foreign economic policy to an impasse in the spring of 1928. As that impasse was perceived by those who would come to be called the "Stalinists," either imports of the technology and foreign industrial raw materials on which the industrialization drive was premised had to be sacrificed or the market relations in the countryside that were central to the New Economic Policy must end for the sake of increased industrial investment. It was out of this Stalinist-defined impasse that the Stalinist solution eventually emerged—forcible mass collectivization of agriculture, rapid industrialization keyed to heavy industry, preemptive internal state terror, and the cult of the leader.[22]

In the 1970s, Moshe Lewin and others argued that this outcome was not a socioeconomic necessity; the problems of agriculture need not have meant the end of the New Economic Policy. Economic development might have continued under some version of NEP if the impact of the crisis upon the peasantry had been eased by a combination of grain and goods imports and an increase in procurement prices.[23] Lewin's argument has been extended by some economists who have asserted that the rates of economic growth achieved during the 1930s could have been duplicated within the framework of NEP. Others have contended in opposition that the New Economic Policy constituted an economic blind alley: NEP could not extract surplus grain from the peasantry, and it was fundamentally incapable of supporting industrialization. Both these hypotheses have been rejected by Davies, Wheatcroft, and Cooper, who have argued that by 1926/27, resource allocation and capital investment within the framework of NEP were sufficient to produce a level of industrial growth equal to or better than 1909–13 levels, but not an expansion equal to that achieved by the mid-1930s.[24]

In actuality, extraeconomic, political considerations determined the way out of the impasse. In 1927, Stalin had been a strong voice within the Politburo for the search for agreements with Europe and America, despite his public rhetoric. Foreign capital and technology, he maintained, were indispensable to the industrialization drive and to the construction of socialism in the USSR, which he called "the economic dictatorship of the proletariat." To gain foreign assistance he pressed harder than any other member of the collective leadership at the time for a policy of concessions to capitalism. As the economic crisis worsened in the late spring of 1928, however, Stalin and those who became aligned with him became convinced that the pace of industrialization must be sustained despite the agrarian problem, even if it meant shortages, inflation, and disequilibrium in the internal market. He became convinced that the economic crisis could not be resolved within the framework of the market mechanisms of the New Economic Policy and that the search for foreign credits to finance industrialization was destined to fail. At this point, Bukharin broke with Stalin and joined with Rykov and Tomskii, who, along with Kalinin and Voroshilov, formed a moderate majority of five within the Politburo—a grouping that persisted off and on until the latter two joined the Stalin group later in the year. Stalin responded by abandoning the consensus-building procedures by which the collective leadership had operated up to that time. Increasingly he resorted to making decisions either unilaterally or in consultation with his own group alone. In May and June the hard-line solution to the grain procurement problem, the punitive extraordinary measures, were reintroduced, apparently on Stalin's personal initiative.[25] Soon Bukharin and Stalin were no longer on speaking terms.

Gradually the Rykov-Bukharin group and the Stalin group compiled antithetical strategies for leading the country out of its economic impasse and foreign relations dilemma. Stalin advocated a program of industrialization through a "tribute" or "supertax" extracted from the peasantry by a purged and rejuvenated party and state apparatus. The moderates lined up behind the advice advanced by the nonparty economic experts of the People's Commissariat of Finance (Narkomfin), which included cancellation of "the extraordinary measures," no further increases in capital expenditure, and restoration of market equilibrium. They also supported the foreign policy advocated by Narkomindel—the continued search for economic and political agreements with Europe and America and participation in organized multilateral cooperation. The central role played by imports, both in the agricultural strategy and in the industrial strategy of the moderate program, made the quest for foreign credits and the search for agreements a crucial factor in determining the future course of economic development and the outcome of the struggle among the collective leadership for control of the instruments of political decision making.

What stood in the path of the search for agreements with Europe and America in the spring of 1928 was the Shakhty case. On 10 March, *Pravda* announced that the OGPU had uncovered a large-scale and long-standing conspiracy of engineers in the coal-mining industry in the Shakhty region of the north Caucasus and the nearby Donets Basin of the Ukraine. More than fifty engineers, including three Germans, were accused of sabotage and treason, their acts ranging from what the prosecutor at the trial called "irrational construction projects," "unnecessary waste of capital," and criminal waste of foreign currency to the flooding of mines and the wrecking of equipment. All this was done allegedly in collaboration with former mine owners who had close connections with agents of German firms and the Polish, German, and French intelligence services.[26] The show trial that began on 18 May was not the first in Soviet history, but it was the most highly dramatized and widely publicized one up to that time. Some among the party/state leadership feared the economic and political consequences of the affair and worked to limit the scope of the prosecution. Among them were Kuibyshev and Rykov, who reminded Menzhinskii that "the Central Committee has declared that the reconstruction of the socialist economy is not possible without the help of foreign capital and foreign experts"; the activities of the OGPU, he added, were "likely to sabotage not only our foreign policy position but also our entire economic life."[27] Chicherin informed the head of the OGPU that the arrest of German engineers threatened to bring economic negotiations in Berlin to a halt and that it only assisted the efforts of "hostile bourgeois elements in foreign countries, who for weeks have been working quite openly to try to win Germany definitely to a Western orientation and include it in the English front."[28] Others, however, sought to extend the scope of the affair— Menzhinskii himself and, above all, Stalin, who saw in Shakhty another example (following "the grain strike") of bourgeois counterrevolution, this time aided by Western European economic intervention against socialist industrialization, all of which he used as a confirmation of his doctrine that class struggle would intensify during the building of socialism, requiring, accordingly, greater use of police measures and state terror.[29] The Shakhty affair sustained the war scare mentality of suspicion and blame, a mentality that within months would lay responsibility for all that went wrong with the industrialization drive at the feet of "bourgeois specialists."

International reaction to the arrest and trial of the German engineers was both immediate and vigorous. A month earlier, German and Soviet negotiators had begun trade and credit discussions in Berlin.[30] To entice the Germans into an agreement, the Soviet delegation promised that orders amounting to 600 million marks would be placed in Germany over the next two years if Berlin granted a 600-million-mark credit, made additional long-term loans, and opened German financial markets to Soviet bonds. German industrial, commercial, and banking circles were not disposed toward an easy agreement, however. They had assumed that, as a result of the German-Soviet commercial agreement of October 1925 and the government-guaranteed 300-mark credit, they would have an increased share of Soviet foreign purchases. Instead, cash orders that had previously gone to Germany were diverted to England and the United States.[31] Germany's total share of Soviet imports had not increased, and the hopes of German business for an even greater share of the Russian market (of which they controlled the largest portion) went unfulfilled. In preparation for the trade negotiations, they had prepared a list of complaints and demands, including a demand for relaxation of the government foreign trade monopoly, which in their opinion placed cumbersome and arbitrary restrictions on German commerce.

At the German Foreign Ministry also this was a time of agonizing reappraisal. Many of the expectations of 1926 had evaporated. The Wilhelmstrasse could no longer assert with confidence that ties to the USSR would directly improve Germany's international position as Berlin shepherded an increasingly pragmatic and moderate Soviet regime out of isolation. In the aftermath of the war scare crisis, it could not even hope that German diplomacy would be able to abate that isolation. Russia's economic difficulties and diplomatic isolation meant that the Rapallo-Berlin relationship was not likely to be of immediate use, either in an effort to revise the postwar settlement in Eastern Europe or as a card to play at this time as the Stresemann-Schubert Foreign Ministry pressed for negotiations with the Allied powers on a definitive reparations agreement, an end to the military occupation of the Rhineland and what came to be called "the final settlement of the war."[32] However, no other strategy was available to the German Foreign Ministry. It therefore encouraged the trade talks with Moscow lest a refusal by German banks to extend new loans to the USSR, what Stresemann referred to as a "withdrawal of German business from Russia," jeopardize German-Soviet political relations.[33] The arrest of the German engineers, however, infuriated both public opinion and business interests, and on 15 March, Berlin broke off the trade talks.

In Moscow, a parallel policy review took place. Since early 1927 the Soviet military leadership had been concerned that Germany seemed to be moving into the British orbit, thereby creating the danger that intelligence gathered by German officers in the USSR would fall into the hands of Russia's enemies. To prevent security leaks, they pondered gradually severing relations with the Reichswehr.[34] Similar concerns were apparently raised in the Politburo as a result of the Shakhty affair, and it appointed a special commission to review cooperation between the Red Army and the Reichswehr and to propose whether it should be continued. Informed of this, Krestinskii complained directly to Stalin. In an appeal paralleling that made by Kuibyshev and Rykov, he argued that military collaboration with the Germans was the only way "to overtake and surpass European military technology" and that it directly increased Soviet security. German military officers in Russia could see firsthand the strength of the Red Army, he wrote, and, as a result, estimation of Soviet military power would be raised throughout Europe. This would, he maintained, "reduce the danger of attack on us." All this was achieved at bargain rates, Krestinskii added, because "we take more than we give."[35]

Elsewhere, the arrest of the German engineers was regarded as proof that one could not do business with Communists, and suspension of the trade negotiations in Berlin was applauded. Relations with France, in which

Chicherin had placed considerable hope, now quickly deteriorated. In a move that displayed little interest in improving them, the French government renewed its demands for the return of the French gold held in the Soviet state bank since the revolution.[36] With such unfavorable turns in relations with both Berlin and Paris, the diplomatic and economic isolation of the USSR deepened. Russia's situation in international politics was reminiscent of what it had been at the time of the war scare crisis. New rumors of an impending Polish-Soviet war circulated. And what hope there remained for the policy of agreements depended on the United States.

As "the most technologically advanced capitalist country" (as it was termed in the Soviet debate on economic development), the United States occupied a highly significant place in the Bolshevik concept of economic foreign relations, both as a source of technology and machinery and as a model of large-scale standardized production, assembly-line techniques, economies of scale, worker productivity, and high growth rates. So important was America to Soviet economic development that the Soviet government made an exception to its standard practice and traded with the United States even in the absence of official diplomatic relations.[37] Soviet engineers, designers, and planners preferred American technology to that of Germany, and by 1928 the American model of steel making, rather than the smaller German blast furnaces, had become the model for Soviet installations.[38] Nevertheless, after having led the world in exports to the USSR in 1924/25, the United States thereafter fell to second place behind Germany. As viewed from Moscow, the policy of the U.S. government was responsible for this. While the German government had bolstered trade with the USSR by guaranteeing long-term credits, Washington refused to discuss credits and withheld diplomatic recognition, permitting only private trade contracts to be entered into by American firms. In turn, the NKID stopped asking Washington for diplomatic recognition after 1923, although Litvinov made known Moscow's desire for normal relations through occasional statements before the Central Committee.[39]

According to calculations made by the NKID Collegium in the summer of 1928, however, the prospects for improving relations with Washington were growing. The November presidential elections would bring a change of administration, and the election of Herbert Hoover, they thought, would mean a shift in American policy toward the USSR. Such a shift would in turn influence the governments of Western Europe.[40] In an effort to gain access to American policymakers and to influence American policy attitudes, the Soviet government indicated its interest in ratifying the peace pact proposed by Frank B. Kellogg, the American secretary of state (1925–29), and in attending the signing ceremony in Paris. The Kellogg pact was another instance of multilateral international cooperation—following the Geneva Economic Conference and the Preparatory Disarmament Commission—where Soviet spokesmen could impress European and American policymakers with the sincerity of their "peace policy" and with the prospects for profit through economic exchange with the USSR. Diplomatically, participation in the pact was essential. To sign it would reduce the level of Soviet isolation; to remain outside could only solidify the capitalist powers into an anti-Soviet bloc.[41]

The German Foreign Ministry played a mediating role in the negotiations leading to the Kellogg-Briand Peace Pact. In its continuing effort to shepherd the USSR out of isolation, the Wilhelmstrasse used its influence in Washington, London, and Paris to gain admission for the USSR to the group of nations signing the agreement. In response, articles appeared in the Moscow press encouraging the German Foreign Ministry in its efforts to bridge the diplomatic gap between Russia and the West and looking forward to a new era in German-Soviet political relations.[42] In what may well have been a signal to Berlin and the other European capitals of a renewed desire for rapprochement and agreement, the Politburo liquidated the Shakhty case expeditiously and freed the German engineers.

In the Politburo, the decision to join the peace pact figured strongly in the efforts of the moderate group to rescue NEP through the financial assistance of Europe and America. This was not the only policy consideration however. Soviet participation in the pact was a way of continuing "the struggle for peace"—in this case, not only peace between the USSR and the capitalist world but also peace among the capitalist powers themselves—and of thereby preventing a repetition of the general European war of 1914. Inherent in this stance was acknowledgment that a second total war would inflict destruction on Russia as well as on Europe, on the bastion of socialism as well as on the centers of capitalism. In that sense, it represented a departure from the Leninist doctrine that counted on the antagonisms among the imperialists to promote the security of the Soviet state. Some substantiality is given to this interpretation of Russia's Kellogg pact policy by the way the supporters and defenders of the peace pact lined up as it was being formulated. Litvinov and Bukharin supported the idea of signing the pact, arguing that the USSR should be associated with any project that offered the possibility of establishing international peace. Chicherin, on the other hand, was critical, maintaining that it would allow the major powers to interfere in Russia's foreign affairs.[43]

In what was probably the last dispute between him and Litvinov, Chicherin lost out in the decision. In September he left Moscow for a second extended period of medical treatment in Germany. Litvinov was appointed acting commissar and took over operational leadership of the NKID. Chi-cherin was in effect leaving the Foreign Commissariat forever.[44] Although he returned in June 1930 with some of his previous energy restored, he resigned the next month to be succeeded by Litvinov. What combination of ill health, discouragement at the course of Soviet foreign relations, rivalry with Litvinov, and the problems associated with conducting a consensus foreign policy for an internally conflicted party leadership led to the demise of Chicherin has not been documented. Sheinis suggests that the internal conflicts, along with his failing health, constituted the crucial factor in the erosion of Chicherin's position in policy making and his eventual resigna-tion. Although Litvinov lacked Chicherin's powers of policy conception, he was well suited to dealing with the party leadership. He was less outwardly emotional than Chicherin, stronger-willed, and more capable of concealing his personal policy preferences. Above all, he was less confrontational and less demanding in his relations with the Central Committee.[45] Typically, Chicherin's last interventions in policy formation were directed at repri-manding Comintern spokesmen for making public statements that he considered damaging to relations with Germany.[46] He regarded Weimar Germany and Kemalist Turkey as the anchors of Soviet policy in Europe and Asia, respectively; promoting favorable relations with them was his major achievement as commissar and his chief legacy.

Washington meanwhile rejected the idea of Soviet participation in the ceremonies held in Paris on 27 August to sign the Kellogg-Briand Peace Pact. (The United States, the Locarno powers, Czechoslovakia and Poland, the British Commonwealth, and Japan attended.) It did agree, however, to a formula stating that no future distinction would be made between the original and subsequent signatories. Of the latter, the USSR was the first to adhere to the pact. The NKID also seized that opportunity to improve Russia's stalemated relations with Poland. In December, Litvinov proposed to Warsaw an agreement to bring the peace pact into force separately and in advance of its ratification by the original signatories. Warsaw agreed but insisted that the Baltic states and Romania be included too. Russia, Poland, Estonia, Latvia, and Romania signed the "Litvinov Protocol" (officially the Moscow Protocol) in Moscow on 9 February 1929. By April, Turkey, Persia, Lithuania, and the Free City of Danzig had also joined.[47]

In the immediate aftermath of the Kellogg Pact negotiations, the Soviet government took steps to indicate to the United States and Europe the economic potential of improved relations. In September 1928, it authorized an easing of the regulations governing the granting of concessions to foreign entrepreneurs and approved a list of enterprises, including large-scale enterprises and municipal ventures, that foreign businesses might take over. If the right offers were made, this move suggested, favorable deals could be concluded. The Soviet diplomatic offensive of the summer of 1928 was besieged with difficulties however. Foreign governments were well aware of the economic difficulties prevailing in the USSR and were reserved about signing trade or credit agreements. At the same time, the NKID suspected that an exhibition of too much eagerness for economic agreements would only bring increased pressure from Europe and America for more favorable terms. The proposed changes in the concessions policy yielded no new economic negotiations with the Americans, the French, or the British. Trade talks with Germany resumed, but Berlin avoided any discussion of new credits, and it made the outcome of negotiations dependent on payment of the first two installments on the credits the Soviets had received in 1926.

After 1928 the Soviets deemphasized foreign concessions as a channel for technology transfer. They had proved unpopular with foreign investors, and the economic benefits they yielded were offset by the threat they posed to socialist independence. Over 300 foreign concession contracts had been signed since 1920; in July 1928, 97 still operated—among them, 31 German, 14 American, 10 British, 6 French, and 5 Austrian. In 1929 only 59 of these still existed, accounting for less than 1 percent of industrial production in the USSR.[48] During the period of the First Five-Year Plan, concessions were replaced by technical aid contracts, which foreign investors preferred because they were paid for in gold or foreign exchange and did not require long-term commitments.[49]

The End of NEP and the Failure of a Moderate Economic Foreign Policy

By the late summer of 1928 the quest for agreements and the pursuit of international cooperation undertaken almost two years earlier had not pried loose new loans and credits from Europe and America. Instead the USSR was confronted with diplomatic isolation and with what Chicherin called "an intensification of economic pressure on us." Meanwhile the resumption of "extraordinary measures" in May, "the second wave," had effectively destroyed the internal market for grain.[50] Rumors that NEP was to be abolished swept the countryside. Grain exports, which had formed the basis of the foreign trade expansion of the two previous years, collapsed. In 1926/27 they had amounted to 25 percent of 1913 levels; in 1927/28 they fell to 5 percent. Never afterwards would they play a positive role in the economic development of the USSR. By early July, Bukharin, Rykov, and Tomskii were able to persuade the Politburo to cancel the "extraordinary measures" and to raise grain prices. Nevertheless, at the Central Committee plenum that followed, Stalin spoke in favor of resuming the measures in the future if circumstances so required.

Out of this impasse emerged the alternative strategies for economic development and foreign relations that dominated intraparty discussions in 1928–29. Bukharin, the party's leading theoretician, and Rykov, the leading Bolshevik with the most practical knowledge of the workings of the economy, put forth one strategy. The policies they advocated have been summarized as follows: "Import grain from abroad in order to normalize the food situation in the cities; refrain resolutely from 'extraordinary measures'; comply with revolutionary legality; make use of a more flexible system of grain taxes and prices . . . ; and step up the output of the means of agricultural production."[51] With these policies, NEP could be rescued and sustained. And they were moreover measures that would facilitate the program of long-range economic development Bukharin articulated (if only partially) in his published writings of 1928–29. This program, which historical scholarship of the 1970s and 1980s called "the Bukharin alternative," would have encouraged small and medium-sized farms and directed investment toward both light and heavy industry in a program of balanced growth. Finally, they were measures that were consistent with what might be called "the Rykov alternative"—development of the economy within the framework of economic exchange with the capitalist world.

The key to the rescue of NEP proposed by Bukharin and Rykov was to import grain with which to provision the cities and the armed forces and to pacify the peasantry by a flexible system of prices and taxes. For an agrarian country to import grain, now for a second time since the end of the famine, amounted to tacit recognition that NEP as it had been practiced since 1921 had ceased to work. And it was a highly problematical measure to propose, because in the absence of foreign credits, grain imports would absorb foreign currency otherwise allocated to the purchase of the advanced American and European technology necessary for accelerated industrial development.[52] Thus, adoption of the rescue measures would have amounted to a retreat, even if a temporary one, in the drive "to catch up and surpass." Without foreign credits, the moderates could point to no readily accessible exit from the impasse of 1928 other than a tactical retreat from socialist industrialization. In this manner, Russia's economic isolation both complicated the development strategy of those who sought to maintain NEP conditions and undermined their political position. They lost their hold on the management of the economy and on the direction of economic development and were reduced to criticizing and correcting the plans of the "Stalinists," which left them without the political currency they needed to stay in the contest for power.

The moderate road out of the impasse of 1928 constituted a temporary retreat from the socialist offensive, to be followed by balanced economic growth, gradual industrialization, and smooth socialization—what Bukharin called "more or less crisis free development." The other road, the one actually taken, was "the great leap forward" in economic development embraced by Stalin. His first step in that direction came with the "extraordinary measures" of grain collection in December. He took a second step when he decided that defeating the Opposition was of greater importance than were loans and credits from Europe and America; his reaction to the Shakhty affair indicated his willingness to write off foreign financial assistance to the industrialization of the USSR.

In the program Stalin was adopting, the only way to finance the foreign machinery and technical assistance required by the projected Five-Year Plan was to acquire hard currency through vastly increased grain exports and expend it on machinery imports. The need to export grain, he told a closed Central Committee plenum in July 1928, was why the collectivization of agriculture—and the control over the production and distribution of grain that came with it—was so necessary.[53] And, of course, the grain imports advocated by Bukharin and Rykov were out of the question as far as Stalin was concerned; importing grain simply squandered the foreign currency needed for machinery purchases. After mid-1928, Stalin did not urge concessions to capitalism in the face of continued economic quarantine; he openly opposed any relaxation of the foreign trade monopoly; and he returned to the view that the USSR should remain independent of the ties that came with foreign involvements.

As the moderates lost control over the formulation of economic policy, they were excluded from political power as well.[54] The struggle between Stalin and his allies, on the one hand, and the moderates, on the other, began in the spring of 1928 over the intensification of "the extraordinary measures." It continued as Stalin clearly abandoned some of the central tenets of NEP, including independent peasant agriculture, and called both for more rapid industrialization funded by "tribute" collected from the peasantry and for intensification of collectivization as the solution to Russia's problems of economic development. His confrontation with the technostructure, his doctrine of increasing class struggle, and his promotion of a permanent crisis atmosphere extended and broadened the conflict. The moderates recognized "Stalin's new program"[55] as a departure from the consensus on industrialization that had formed around the "catch up and surpass" slogan in 1926, and Bukharin, supported by Rykov and Tomskii, said so in memoranda to the Politburo in May and June. Although the moderates succeeded in getting "the second wave of extraordinary measures" cancelled in July, they lost their majority on the Politburo, as Kalinin and Voroshilov went over to Stalin's side. The struggle began in September—at the time of the diplomatic effort to open political and financial doors in Europe and America following the Kellogg-Briand Peace Pact. Bukharin openly attacked Stalin's economic policies with an article in *Pravda* entitled "Notes of an Economist"; the Politburo voted to condemn Bukharin's action over the objections of Rykov, Tomskii, and Bukharin himself. *Pravda*'s editorial board was altered to end Bukharin's control over editorial policy. The decisive battle—for control over the Moscow party organization, a moderate stronghold—was fought in October and won by the supporters of Stalin.[56] The moderates became demoralized and disposed to compromise. Bukharin lost his basis of support in the Comintern, as did Tomskii on the Trade Union Council. They made their last stand in January–February 1929 at meetings of the Politburo, where they ascribed to Stalin a policy of "military-feudal exploitation of the peasantry." The Politburo rejected this accusation as "slander" and reprimanded Bukharin. The defeat of the moderates was formalized in April at a joint plenum of the Central Committee and the Central Control Commission at which Stalin read a lengthy and insulting condemnation of "the group of Bukharin, Tomskii, and Rykov." The Bukharin-Rykov NEP rescue measures were rejected, and the "optimal variant" of the Five-Year Plan was adopted over their objections at the Sixteenth Party Congress. The latter constituted the single most crucial step toward Stalinist economic development, involving as it did drastic increases in capital investment, concentration on heavy industry, industrialization at a "furious pace" (Stalin's expression), development financed out of "tribute" collected from the peasantry (what Bukharin called War Communism "without a war"), coerced collectivization of agriculture, and assignment of blame for the economic crisis first to the Opposition and then to "bourgeois technical specialists."

As the moderates were crushed, foreign relations began to improve. In August 1928, German manufacturing firms, trading companies, and banks formed the *Russlandausschuss der deutschen Wirtschaft* to promote trade with Russia,[57] and economic negotiations resumed in November. On the Soviet side there were strong diplomatic incentives for making the trade talks a success, despite the high interest rates charged by German banks. Only the tie to Berlin saved the USSR from virtual isolation from the capitalist powers. The break in negotiations with Germany had naturally accentuated all the old shibboleths about the USSR in the centers of European and American capitalism—namely, that the USSR was a bad credit risk; that Moscow used trade for "political" purposes; that the foreign trade monopoly made doing business impossible; and that economic crisis and political strife were about to bring an end to the Soviet system.[58] And Germany was, of course, an important source for the technology required by the industrialization drive.

The way to a trade agreement was eased by the release of the German engineers imprisoned in the Shakhty case, by Soviet adherence to the Kellogg-Briand Peace Pact through German mediation, and by de facto tactical cooperation between the Soviet and German delegations at the Preparatory Commission on Disarmament in Geneva.[59] They reached agreement on all outstanding economic issues in late December amid statements released to the press speaking of "unanimous agreement" and "continued cooperation." A Soviet-German Conciliation Treaty, complete with machinery to resolve future commercial disputes, followed in January 1929. Herbert von Dirksen took over as German ambassador in Moscow that same month and proclaimed full German support for the industrialization drive, a message to which the Soviet press gave extensive publicity.[60] In 1930–31 he negotiated new long-term government-guaranteed credits for Soviet purchases, and, during the period of the First Five-Year Plan, Germany was the primary exporter to Russia, accounting for 47 percent of Russian imports in 1932.

Military relations improved at the same time. In the autumn of 1928, General Werner von Blomberg, head of the *Truppenamt,* headed a delegation of eight German officers who inspected the joint Soviet-German installations for the development of armor, aviation, and chemical warfare. They also attended the Red Army maneuvers in Kiev and met with Soviet military officers in Moscow. Blomberg consulted at length with Voroshilov, the head of the RMC, who, according to Blomberg's report, was an enthusiastic proponent of military collaboration with the Reichswehr and who took credit for overcoming resistance within the party leadership to continued cooperation.[61] Blomberg returned from Russia more convinced than ever that closer relations with a stronger Red Army were in Germany's interest, both as a way of developing weapons and as a way of gaining a future ally against Poland. As a result of his visit, many of the difficulties that had hampered collaboration between the Red Army and the Reichswehr since 1926 were ironed out, thus preparing the way for a significant increase in Soviet-German military cooperation. This flourishing military collaboration, along with formally correct diplomatic relations and the trade relations crucial to both countries, kept the Berlin-Moscow connection alive during the years 1928–1932 even as political relations between the two countries were declining rapidly.[62]

The possibility of improved relations with England emerged in March

1929 when a group of leading industrialists from the export-oriented, depressed north of England arrived in Moscow to investigate trade possibilities. To them the president of the Russian State Bank promised orders of £150–200 million if diplomatic relations were restored. The visit played a role in the British elections of 1929, allowing the Labour Party to campaign on a platform of diplomatic recognition and increased trade with the USSR as means of increasing employment in Britain and establishing peace among nations. No mention was made of loans or credits.

The second Labour government, which took office in June, did not rush into diplomatic recognition, however. "Russia has brought us down once. We can't afford to let it happen twice," Arthur Henderson, the new foreign secretary, told his parliamentary secretary. MacDonald, who had recognized the USSR in 1924 over the objections of King George V and without consulting the Cabinet, now insisted that Parliament give its approval in advance.[63] The two countries exchanged representation at the ambassadorial level—for the first time—in October. Sokolnikov was appointed *polpred* in London, an action that the British press took as a certain indication of the prospects for improved economic and political relations between the two countries. So did the émigré liberal Russian press in Europe. In Paris, Pavel Miliukov, founder of the Constitutional Democratic Party and the leading postrevolutionary spokesman for Russian liberalism, called Sokolnikov "the only real statesman in Soviet Russia." Horrified by these tributes, Sokolnikov told his wife: "Stalin will never forgive me for this, and he will certainly take his revenge some day."[64]

However, it was in the United States that Soviet technology and credit requirements were met most immediately.[65] In October 1928, International General Electric (IGE) granted to Amtorg, the Soviet Trading Corporation in New York, a $25-million six-year credit for the purchase of electrical equipment. Owen D. Young, chairman of the company, feared that otherwise the Germans would dominate the Russian market for electrical goods. "If Russia adopted European standards," he informed Kellogg, "it would mean an added and perhaps impossible barrier to our future business with Russia in the electrical field."[66] In making the offer, IGE tacitly renounced its $2-million claim against the Soviet government for nationalizing Russian General Electric during the revolution. And by agreeing to higher-than-market interest rates on the loan, the Soviet government in effect indemnified IGE for its losses. This agreement represented a historic breakthrough in Soviet-American trade relations. Until this time, the USSR had been unable to obtain medium- and long-term loans in America because the Department of State permitted only short-term financing of sales to the USSR. The IGE credit was granted with the knowledge of the State Department (although not guaranteed by the United States government), giving rise to false rumors that Washington was about to grant diplomatic recognition to the Soviet regime. Other technical assistance contracts and loans followed over the next two years; these involved the Radio Corporation of America, Standard Oil of New Jersey, and General Electric, which signed a ten-year contract. In May 1929 the Ford Motor Company agreed to build, and to finance, a 100,000-unit-per-year factory in the USSR. In July–August a delegation of ninety American entrepreneurs spent a month in the USSR, exploring the prospects for Soviet-American trade—the first such organized American effort to do so. So extensive were America's economic relations with the USSR in 1928–29 that one Russian scholar has stated that they amounted to "economic recognition."[67]

By 1929/30, the United States, which had ranked second to Germany in exports to the USSR since 1925/26, had returned to first place—temporarily. The First Five-Year Plan relied on technology that came primarily from Germany and secondarily from the United States.[68] Michael Reiman has well stated the ironic outcome of the behavior of international capital at this point in Soviet history: "The ruling circles in the industrial countries, who only six months earlier had refused to lend their support to the possible victory of a moderate course in the USSR, were now ready . . . to finance Stalin's despotism. The planning bodies could count on international economic cooperation on a larger scale."[69] And they did.

When the First Five-Year Plan was announced to the public, it was wrapped in the rhetoric of autarky. In a heroic appeal to self-sufficiency, *Izvestiia* proclaimed that industrialization would be based "exclusively on domestic accumulation" and on the "enthusiasm of the millions."[70] In actuality, it was not until Soviet foreign trade collapsed in the years 1932–1934 that industrialization was switched over to the path of autarky. As set out in 1928–29, the Five-Year Plan assumed that technology imports would be financed by increased expenditures from the state budget and by renewed grain exports made possible by expanded foreign trade and improved ties to the world economy.

There were, however, good reasons to question whether grain exports and foreign trade could offer a stable basis for rapid industrial development. By 1928, foreign trade was the sector of the economy that had recovered least from the dislocations of 1914–20.[71] In 1927/28, exports equalled 32 percent of their 1913 level, and imports were 47 percent. Grain had fueled the engine of Russian foreign trade before 1914, accounting (on the average) for 50 percent of exports during the immediate postwar era. In

1926/27—one of the best years of the NEP period for grain exports—they were 25 percent of 1913 levels. In 1927/28 they were only 5 percent. Increases in other exports, mainly timber, oil, sugar, furs, and cotton cloth, did not make up the difference. On the other side of the equation, chronic shortages of imported raw materials, rather than plant capacity or labor supply, restricted the development of light industry, and by the late 1920s these shortages hampered the metalworking industries too. Concession enterprises contributed little to economic development, amounting to one-half of 1 percent for NEP as a whole.[72]

These conditions created significant problems for the modernization and expansion of heavy industry, which depended almost entirely on technology imported from the United States and Europe. Long-term development loans were not available, and the medium-term credits from Germany, England, and the United States during the 1926–1929 period could not make up the trade deficits of those years, which were financed by exporting gold, depleting foreign currency reserves, and increasing short-term debt. Thus the problem-plagued foreign trade sector of the economy hindered economic recovery, and in 1928 it threatened to bring the industrialization drive to a standstill. Why?

The chief model for a Soviet economy that was both stable and integrated into the world economy under NEP conditions was one in which exports and imports would be priced at world levels, in which foreign trade would be based on the principle of commercial profitability, and in which export/import choices would be controlled through the monopoly on foreign trade. Through policies and institutions like these, the government could secure the advantages of foreign markets for the Soviet economy without the disadvantages represented by foreign economic penetration, such as the selling off of important Russian assets and a domestic market flooded with foreign products extraneous to economic recovery and probably detrimental to the construction of socialism. By 1928, however, the mechanisms by which the Soviet economy was to be integrated into the world economy were not working, largely because the industrialization drive made heavy demands on grain exports and because central economic managers were unable to overcome the dilemmas of grain marketing. If they set prices high enough to encourage production and harvesting, this nourished inflation, and exports became commercially unprofitable. If they set grain prices below market levels to stabilize the currency and to ensure export profitability, the peasants withheld their grain from the government agencies, and shortages of goods resulted. Consequently, if they wanted to supply the expansion and modernization of industry with vast quantities of foreign technology and machinery and do so in the absence of long-term development loans, economic planners had two alternative solutions available to them. Either exports had to be structured away from a reliance on grain, or agriculture had to be restructured. This was one of several crucial choices that confronted the party/state elite of the USSR at what has been called "the great turning point" in the history of the Soviet Union.

11 Foreign Relations During "The Great Turn"

Alternative Futures for the USSR?

The approximately one-year period from the spring of 1928 to the spring of 1929—from the intensification of "the extraordinary measures" to the adoption of "the optimal variant," from the time when Bukharin, Rykov, and the "moderates" separated from Stalin to the time when they were finally defeated—is sometimes referred to by scholars as "the great turning point" in Soviet history or, more briefly, as "the great turn." At this time the economic and political system of the USSR was set on a course of development, elements of which persisted for as long as the Soviet Union lasted. "The great turn," therefore, was one of the more significant events in the history of the twentieth century. Explaining how and why that turn was taken has been, and remains, an important endeavor.

One explanation has emphasized the potentialities and the failures of "the Bukharin alternative," or "moderate course," of gradual and harmonious economic development. Three elements comprise that explanation. First, the grain procurement crisis and the collapse of NEP did not constitute two elements of a single inevitable process. Both resulted from policy choices at the highest levels. The agrarian crisis could have been avoided, or its impact certainly mitigated, had different decisions regarding prices, imports, and exports been made. Subsequently, the New Economic Policy came to an end when Stalin and the "Stalinists" decided—without having any known feasible alternative in view—that they could not procure sufficient grain to accelerate industrialization under the partial market conditions of NEP.[1]

Second, the process of economic development undertaken by the Stalin-led Central Committee beginning in 1928–29—rapid and ultimately autonomous industrialization financed by "tribute" brutally extracted from the peasantry—was neither necessary nor efficacious, nor even feasible. It was a process that has been described as one "in which willful exhortations displaced actual planning, impossible goals were semi-achieved at unnecessarily great and enduring costs, and peasant agriculture was needlessly destroyed by a kind of collectivization that gave nothing to industrialization and probably impeded it."[2] The results endured for sixty years. The Soviet economy was "plagued from the very beginning," Holland Hunter has stated, "by poor quality, a slow rate of innovation, sluggish management, and a repressed labour force."[3] During the decade from 1927 to 1937, remarkable and even "dazzling" increases in gross industrial production were achieved, but they came with great difficulty and at tremendous cost, not only to the peasants, who were subjected to deportation, starvation, and death, but to the industrial working class as well. The period of the First Five-Year Plan was a time of critical economic instability, and the years 1932–1933 in particular were a time of acute crisis managed by the OGPU. Terror and repression were directed at factory managers and government and party officials alike, as they were removed from their posts, purged from the party, arrested, imprisoned, and put before firing squads. The costs of industrial production rose; labor productivity declined; national consumption fell. Hiroaki Kuromiya has determined that the real wages of Moscow industrial workers in 1932 came to only 53 percent of the 1928 level.[4]

Third, Stalinist industrialization and collectivization were not the only possible strategies of economic development open to the USSR. Other potentially viable modes of socialist construction existed within the discourse conducted among the party/state leadership during the years 1925–1929. Bukharin in his writings put forth one such strategy. He conceived his theory of development and corresponding economic policies in opposition to the programs for rapid industrialization put forth first by Trotsky and the Opposition between 1924 and 1926 and then by Stalin in 1928–29. During the earlier period, Bukharin's affinity for gradualism and moderation and his dislike of coercion led him to disregard the imperatives for vigorous, state-directed industrialization. By 1928–29, however, he had rethought his development strategy. In a series of publicized statements made between November 1928 and January 1929—while the moderates stood on the verge of decisive political defeat—he criticized Stalin's notions of rapid industrialization and forced collectivization and espoused a program of accelerated but controlled and balanced economic growth.[5]

These lines of interpretation are of historical as well as historiographical significance. During the thaw (1956–64), introduced by Khrushchev's denunciation of Stalin at the Twentieth and Twenty-second Party Congresses, scholars in the USSR undertook an extensive criticism of the rapid and forced collectivization of the 1930s. Subsequently, between 1969 and 1973, Moshe Lewin and Stephen Cohen discovered the full extent of "the Bukharin alternative." This was revealed most fully in Cohen's biography of Bukharin, a work translated in the West into the Russian language and then circulated privately in the USSR. In the 1970s and 1980s, Bukharin's program for evolutionary industrialization and socialization out of the conditions of NEP came to be viewed by some non-Soviet scholars, by East European reformers, and by dissident intellectuals in the Russia of Mikhail Suslov and Leonid Brezhnev not only as the alternative to Stalinist repression and brutality but also as the model for a reformed Communism, one that would support the relative political relaxation, semimarket economy, social diversity, cultural pluralism, intellectual flowering, and scientific progress they associated with the Soviet Union of the 1920s.

During *glasnost* a number of Soviet writers, mainly playwrights and novelists, frankly espoused some of Bukharin's views as constituting both a humane and a viable alternative to Stalinism.[6] Similar discussions took place among academicians who were largely unaware of the more technical and complex debates in America and Europe over the causes of the grain procurement crisis and the feasibility of the Five-Year Plan.[7] Bukharin was legally rehabilitated and reinstated in the Communist Party in February 1988, and soon thereafter a number of his writings were republished in the USSR. During the three and one-half years that preceded the August 1991 coup, NEP was enshrined in party publications as the true Leninist way to socialism (along with "peaceful coexistence"),[8] and Bukharin was held up as the most legitimate Leninist of the 1920s, one who at the same time appreciated the capabilities of capitalism—as opposed to Trotsky, Zinoviev, and Stalin, all of whom regarded capitalism as "rotten," "decadent," and "moribund."[9]

The rehabilitation of NEP did not go uncriticized, however. Even before the end of *perestroika*, some Soviet scholars argued that Lenin had no substantive notion of a humane road to socialism through a "social order of civilized cooperaters," or through any version of market socialism, and that he had no coherent idea of a developed socialism evolving out of NEP from which "the Bukharin alternative" could have been launched.[10] Other Soviet scholars questioned whether a "Bukharin alternative" actually existed in the real world of policy choices, that is, whether he had any clearly defined plans for the economic future of the USSR.[11] Still other scholars recalculated production figures for the years of NEP and demonstrated the sharp decrease in industrial productivity achieved by the end of the 1920s when compared to 1913 and concluded that the late NEP situation was one of economic stagnation, unemployment, and low living standards.[12]

Viewed from a post-Soviet historical perspective, there are good reasons to doubt whether NEP in actuality ever constituted a viable option for agriculture and economic foreign relations. Close examination of these two sectors of the economy indicates that the NEP crisis did not begin in November 1927. Rather "a cumulative series of converging crises" plagued NEP from the time it was instituted.[13] The foreign sector of the economy never recovered from the dislocations of the years 1914–1920; and only in 1923/24 and 1926/27 could grain be exported at a level sufficient to fulfill the trade plan for the year.[14] Responsibility for this has been laid at the door of those who planned and managed the economy in that they failed to develop an efficient system for marketing grain and goods and made repeated and disastrous errors in the pricing of both. Even more fundamental, however, were the refusal to recognize foreign debts, the persistence of the foreign trade monopoly, the fixed prices, the unrealistic exchange rate, and the unconvertible currency—all inimical to participation in a world market and to the development of an internal market economy as well.[15]

Historically, the foreign relations and economic crisis of 1927–29 exposed the two irreconcilable notions of NEP that prevailed within the party. The backers of one of them were willing to subordinate plans to acquire advanced foreign technology to the market of peasant proprietorship, to social and economic equilibrium, and to the evolutionary construction of socialism. The supporters of the other viewed agriculture as the sector of the economy from which the capital for the technology of a rapid-tempo industrialization was to be derived. This conflict over strategies of economic development was not resolved, as it might have been under different political conditions, by the dictates of cost-effectiveness and rational resource allocation. Instead, factional conflict within the CPSU made reasoned argument and rational problem solving impossible. Consideration of economic policy was transformed into a war of competing doctrines, the outcome of which was determined in the realm of intraparty political infighting.[16]

A second explanation for the direction taken at "the great turn" posits that the decisive factors in the outcome of the leadership struggle, and therefore of the economic crisis, were Stalin's assets and advantages. He seemed to be pragmatic, sober-minded, and responsible. His politics combined resolution, reassurance, and optimism; socialism *could* be constructed in the USSR, and in a comparatively short period of time. By contrast, the Trotsky-Zinoviev Opposition seemed rash and extremist, while the moderates, with their conciliation of kulaks, Nepmen, and foreign capitalists, stood discredited by what appeared to be their timidity. The development path of "revolution from above," on which Stalin embarked beginning with his tour of Siberia in January 1928, had a particular appeal to that generation of party officials which had come of political age during War Communism. To them, Communism meant "martial zeal, revolutionary voluntarism and *élan,* readiness to resort to coercion, rule by administrative fiat . . . , centralized administration, summary justice, and no small dose of . . . Communist arrogance."[17] Determined to "catch up and surpass" Europe and America as quickly as possible, they found the crisis of 1927–28 frustrating, and a return to a smoothly functioning NEP unappealing. NEP signified to them inequality of opportunity and living standards, profiteering Nepmen, a disunited leadership, and a suspicion that the movement had lost its purpose and direction and become mired in stagnation. With their belief in the continuing revolutionary transformation of Soviet society, they could not accept the New Economic Policy as the outcome and the end of the October Revolution.

What has been largely missing from the scholarly discussion of the alternatives available at the time of "the great turn" is an extended investigation of all the elements present within the programs discussed among the Soviet leadership during the years 1925–1929. Not only were contrasting strategies of industrialization debated during those years, but opposing conceptions of Russia's relations with the world economy and of Soviet foreign relations were also under consideration.[18] One strategy of economic foreign relations aimed at liberation from the influences of the world market. Another involved encouraging foreign states to participate in the Soviet economy and sought to integrate Russia into the world market. The latter was the strategy of technology transfer, capital imports, and trade treaties—the policy of Sokolnikov and Krasin, of Trotsky in 1925 to 1926, of Stalin from late 1926 to early 1928, and the one of which Rykov spoke unremittingly. One set of international relations would revive revolutionary internationalism, increase the level of militancy among the parties of the Comintern, and appeal to German nationalism as a weapon against international capitalist stability. The other aimed at détente with England, America, and France, and at cultivating their moral support for the Soviet regime.

Admittedly relations with Europe and America were no panacea for Soviet economic development.[19] Capitalist penetration posed a significant threat to the construction of socialism in the USSR, with or without the foreign trade monopoly. The integrative foreign trade model that NEP borrowed from the tsarist regime, based as it was on grain exports, had worked before 1914 only by means of an exploited peasantry. A regime that had repudiated the debts of the Russian past could not expect much in the way of long-term loans from Europe and America. The rhetoric of "world revolution" and the subversive activities of the Comintern, ineffective and unsuccessful as they were, perpetuated ideological opposition and provided nourishment for anti-Communism both in capitalist Europe and national- ist Asia. The doctrine of "peaceful coexistence," with its notion of a world divided into two irreconcilable camps, and "the struggle for peace," which aimed at the unilateral political/ideological disarmament of the other side, placed strict limitations on any possible socialist accommodation with the imperialist powers. The dual policy caused problems for Russia's relations with the world economy that could not be overcome by Soviet diplomacy.

What was the alternative to the foreign relations of "world revolution" and "peaceful coexistence" that Lenin and his successors adopted in the USSR during the years 1920–1929? Soviet policymakers might have de- veloped an appreciation of the inevitably destructive costs of a second round of twentieth-century total warfare to all participants, capitalist and socialist alike. They might have recognized in defeated Germany the larg- est potential contributor to the aggravation of those conflicts among na- tions that could lead to such a war. The ECCI might have ceased proclaim- ing that the German problem was insoluble, and the NKID and the RMC might have weaned themselves from dependency on the Rapallo relation- ship, together with the surreptitious military collaboration and occasional hints at cooperation against Poland that sustained it. The attention of Soviet foreign policy could have been moved westward from Berlin and oriented toward security guarantees for continental Europe.

In actuality, such a policy course could have been implemented only if significant ideological alterations had been made in both the capitalist and socialist worlds. Ideological alteration in Moscow would have entailed renunciation of the "catastrophic premise," with its set of optimistic expec- tations for a second round of imperialist wars, as the basis of Comintern and CPSU pronouncements on foreign relations. The "struggle for peace" might then have been reformulated accordingly.

For Lenin the "struggle for peace" was subject to the class struggle: War was inherent in the highest stage of capitalism; only with the global triumph of socialism would peace be assured. Stalin departed from this conception. In a statement to the Eighth ECCI Plenum in May 1927, he subordinated the "struggle for peace" to the inevitability of imperialist wars and defined it in terms of the threat to the security of the USSR. By the time of the Sixth Comintern Congress in 1928, the "struggle for peace" referred to a campaign conducted by foreign proletarian forces to protect the USSR against the dangers inherent in the conflict among nations.[20] The alternative, which was denounced in the CI during the years 1929–1933 as "petit bourgeois pacifism," was one that turned the "struggle for peace" into an effort to establish conditions of genuine peace on a global scale for the sake of humanity. This kind of a peace program would have encompassed more than "peaceful coexistence" between socialism and capitalism. Being based on acknowledgment that war between any two European states could engulf many, as it had in the World War, it would have aimed at creating conditions of peace among the capitalist states.

A program such as this would have departed from the foreign relations concept derived from Lenin's *Imperialism*. And it sounds utopian. However, it also resembles at some points the policies proposed by Litvinov in December 1933, a policy course approved by the Politburo and conducted by the NKID in the period that followed—although it ran directly counter to Stalin's own personal foreign policy conception.[21] Known as "collective security" in the 1930s, some elements of it had been advanced by Litvinov as early as 1922 in his objections to the pro-German Rapallo line adopted by the NKID at that time, and other elements appeared in his public statements five years later as Russia joined the League's Preparatory Commission on Disarmament.[22]

Bukharin too voiced an alternative to mainline Leninist-Stalinist foreign relations. In late 1926 and early 1927, he called for what would have amounted to a reconsideration of the "catastrophic premise." Doctrinally he moved Germany from the group of powers that were the oppressed victims of the imperialist victors of the World War into the camp of the imperialists themselves, and he also indicated the potential danger Germany posed to the peace of Europe. He suggested a new international politics in which the efforts of the Soviet government and the Communist International would be coordinated and directed toward preventing what he predicted would be a new and greater world war and toward establishing a generalized peace.[23] Neither Bukharin nor Litvinov looked sanguinely upon a second round of general warfare, and their collaboration in favor of the Kellogg-Briand Peace Pact in 1928 may well be explained by their shared aversion to a security policy premised on perpetual interimperialist conflict.

However, Bukharin failed to oppose with any consistency the two closely related concepts of international relations with which his opponents in the Comintern were associating themselves in 1928—that the world verged on "a second round of wars," and that therefore international capitalism was too hostile and too moribund to be a suitable partner to socialist development through peaceful international economic interdependence. Although he was the leading exponent of evolutionary socialization and balanced economic development among them, he remained the most autarkic of the Bolsheviks.[24] The theoretical legitimization Bukharin provided for "socialism in one country" made it difficult for him to develop a coherent alternative to the Stalinist course.[25] Although he became openly critical of forced-pace industrialization and coerced collectivization beginning in September 1928, he seems never to have rejected the assumption that self-sufficient economic development was both necessary and desirable.[26] His vision of Russia's economic future was thereby limited; possible cooperation on his part with integrationist economists was restricted; and he was left partially disarmed in his criticism of those who would abandon both the rationality of the market and the rationality of the plan and leap forward into forced collectivization and furious industrialization. Nor did Bukharin overtly oppose what became the central principle of Stalinist foreign policy, the idea that an ominous "foreign threat" confronted the USSR. Indeed, simultaneously with the warnings regarding the dangers of a new world war that he issued at the end of 1926, he became the earliest and most prominent spokesman within the party leadership for the alarmist statements which provoked the full-scale war scare crisis that climaxed six months later.[27] The significance of the "foreign threat" at the time of "the great turn" is considered next.

The "Foreign Threat" and Rearmament

One feature of the doctrine of war devised by Lenin before the October Revolution was the notion that armed struggle between the forces of the victorious proletarian revolution and the imperialist states was unavoidable. Although the Civil War seemed to validate this notion, Lenin's pronouncements on the international situation in the years immediately following the Civil War emphasized respite from imperialist onslaught, capitalist-socialist equilibrium, and the possibilities for "peaceful coexistence" between the two systems. This post–Civil War doctrine was undermined beginning in 1926. In the cooperation among the Locarno powers, in the statements of the diehards in London, and in Pilsudski's seizure of power in Warsaw, the Soviet leadership found substantiation for the belief that a capitalist coalition was organizing for an attack on the USSR. The foreign relations crisis the next year convinced the entire party leadership that the threat was actual. Representatives of both the Stalin-Bukharin-Rykov majority and the Trotsky-Zinoviev Opposition spoke of war breaking out within months.

Voroshilov, the commissar for military and naval affairs and head of the Revolutionary Military Council, was slightly more prudent. He informed the Soviet people at the height of the war scare crisis that "after the break in diplomatic relations, the next logical step would be an open military assault on us." The country should be ready, he warned, for an attack that might be launched "in two years, one year, or possibly, though very unlikely, in a few months." A special message of the Central Committee to the Soviet population on 1 July was even less definite regarding the time frame for capitalist aggression: "We do not know and we can not know when the enemy will attack the USSR openly with the bayonet. Yet there may be no shadow of a doubt that English imperialism is working ever harder to bring such a deadline closer."[28] Then in December, the resolutions of the Fifteenth Party Congress spoke of "the immediate threat of an imperialist attack from the outside."[29] Statements such as these suggested that the "foreign threat" was close at hand even if an actual attack was not imminent. They also extended the threat years into the future.

However, from the time of the war scare crisis, no one among the party leadership maintained with confidence that a restabilized system of capitalist states could continue to coexist peacefully with the Soviet Union for an indefinite period of time. At the height of the crisis, Tomskii proclaimed what he termed "the beginning of the end of the breathing space." As the crisis subsided, the Political Report of the Central Committee to the Fifteenth Party Congress announced that the period of " 'peaceful coexistence' [was] receding into the past, giving way to a period of imperialist assaults and preparation for intervention against the USSR." Events since the previous party congress two years earlier were ushering in a changed mode of relations between the USSR and the capitalist world, and at the same time a new era in the development of capitalism was beginning. "The stabilization of capitalism," the report stated, "is becoming more and more rotten and unstable."[30] With these notions, the Bolshevik concept of international relations was transformed. During "the great turn," the menace of war and the condemnation of "imperialist pacifism" became the guiding principles of Soviet foreign relations doctrine. As such, they strongly influenced economic policy, defense policy, and domestic politics.[31]

In the spring of 1926, when the Revolutionary Military Council first approached the German government regarding collaboration on the construction of a modern weapons industry in Russia, defense spending in the USSR was one-half of what it had been in peacetime, prerevolutionary Russia. This changed over the next three years as plans for industrial development evolved. Defense requirements—justified by the "foreign threat"—played an important role in these plans, and the war scare in particular was used to dramatize the urgency of military preparedness. Two days after Britain broke off relations with the USSR, the commissar for finance called on the population to make special efforts to strengthen the country both militarily and economically. Within three weeks, a "national defense week" was declared to proclaim the need for massive economic mobilization.[32] The isolation of the USSR, as demonstrated by the events of the summer of 1927, was the most significant immediate factor influencing the leadership when it implemented the industrialization drive in October. The rapid development of heavy industry was imperative, Kalinin stated at this time, even though there was little probability of a British "declaration of war tomorrow." Britain's "incessant and systematic preparation of such a war" made it necessary.[33] Thus, the war scare turned the *dognat i peregnat* slogan into a national security imperative. Either the USSR acquired the technology and industrial base for defense or, as Stalin subsequently stated, "we will be wiped out."[34]

Even as the "war menace" subsided, the "foreign threat" remained an incentive to rearmament and a means of mass mobilization. The Fifteenth Party Congress resolved: "Bearing in mind the possibility of a military attack it is essential in elaborating the Five-Year Plan to devote maximum attention to a most rapid development of those branches of the economy in general and industry in particular on which the main role will fall in securing the defense and economic stability of the country in wartime."[35] As the First Five-Year Plan was prepared, there was no wavering in the drive to construct a defense industry capable of providing the arms to defend the USSR, and successive drafts of the plan stressed the need for an arms industry that could produce technically advanced weapons. This development culminated in the summer of 1929 when the Politburo and Sovnarkom resolved to revise the Five-Year Plan in the direction of producing modern artillery, tanks, armored cars, and airplanes and approved an extensive program intended to develop a modern war industry that could support the conduct of war under conditions of economic blockade.[36]

The Shakhty trial in the spring of 1928 joined the "foreign threat" to the "internal class enemy." The OGPU and Andrei Vishinskii, the presiding judge at the trial, linked the indicted engineers conspiratorially to hostile foreign capitalists and their agents who allegedly sought to weaken the USSR in preparation for a future war of intervention. Stalin expressed the tie between the two doctrines most fully in a classic statement made at the time of the trial:

> It would be foolish to believe that international capital will leave us in peace. No, comrades, that is not true. Classes exist, international capital exists, and it cannot look on calmly at the development of the country that is building socialism. Formerly, international capital thought it could overthrow the Soviet regime by means of outright armed intervention. The attempt failed. Now it is trying, and will go on trying, to undermine our economic strength by means of inconspicuous, not always noticeable but quite considerable, economic intervention, organizing sabotage, engineering all sorts of "crises" in

this or that branch or industry, and thereby facilitating the possibility of armed intervention in the future. All this is woven into the web of the class struggle of international capital against the Soviet regime, and there can be no question of anything accidental here.[37]

Fused together in what Stalin called "the class struggle of international capital against Soviet power," the "foreign threat" and the "internal class enemy" were powerful ideological weapons. They justified the wider use of coercive measures against the residual Opposition, and they facilitated the defeat of the moderates and their nonparty supporters in government agencies who regarded the abilities of the old technical intelligentsia as necessary to the industrialization drive.

The "foreign threat" and the "internal class enemy" became two halves of the policy basis for Stalinist economic and political development. From the "foreign threat" was constructed what Sheila Fitzpatrick has called the "perpetual wartime-like crisis atmosphere" that prevailed during the years of the First Five-Year Plan. "Class enemies" were the substance of what Hiroaki Kuromiya has termed "the class warfare ideology of Stalin's industrialization."[38] The war menace allowed the emerging Stalinist leadership to push through an agenda of hurried industrialization and forced collectivization at any cost. Class warfare ideology inspired the sacrificial and superhuman efforts of "Stalin's industrial revolution." The presence of internal "class enemies" distracted attention from the blunders of the leadership during the years of the First Five-Year Plan and provided scapegoats for their mistakes. Not coincidentally, the "foreign threat" emerged at a time when economic development had reached the point where marketization under NEP had to be either extended or abolished. The extension of the market and the development of conditions of peaceful trade would eventually have made obsolete and irrelevant the combative party elite that had risen to prominence during the Civil War. Abolishing NEP and unleashing a new civil war, on the other hand, allowed that elite to survive and to continue asserting its control over Soviet society. The vast majority of those who had become party functionaries during the decade following the revolution had no choice but to support the Stalinist course with its doctrine of "foreign threats" and "class enemies."

Was the invocation of a "foreign threat" simply cynicism? Had it no basis in reality? On the one hand, the Red Army was poorly equipped and badly prepared. On the other, relations with the capitalist powers were improving in early 1929, and America and Europe were more forthcoming with loans and technology during the period of the First Five-Year Plan than they had been at the time of NEP. The proponents of the "foreign threat" did not analyze these phenomena according to the categories of political realism, however. Rather, their conviction that politics were to be understood in the terms of class analysis led them to look for the fundamental social forces that made up international relations. In doing so, they linked up the opposition that came from foreign governments and banks with the opposition that came from within the country and from inside the party itself. The result was a particularly virulent fear that the class base of Soviet power was weakening, that elements of the leadership were wavering, that the achievement of socialism was at risk, and that enemies abroad were ready to strike.

Diplomacy and "The Great Turn"

In his report on the international situation to the assembled delegates of the Sixth Comintern Congress held between July and September 1928, Bukharin discussed the changes that had taken place since the last congress in 1924. The era of "temporary capitalist stabilization" was coming to an end, he announced, and a "third period" in the history of the world since the October Revolution was beginning.[39] As the congress took place at the height of the struggle between Bukharin and Stalin, there was considerable conflict between the supporters of each leader as the two sides of the divided CPSU struggled for control of the international Communist movement. Much of that battle was fought over the final form of the "Program of the Communist International," in which social democracy was denounced and bracketed with Fascism as a tool of the bourgeoisie.[40] By contrast, the documents on international relations and the world political economy adopted by the congress reaffirmed the general line that Bukharin, with Stalin's support, had propounded regularly since late 1926. This line expressed their belief that the contradictions to which imperialism was subject, both among nation states and within particular national economies, were sharpening at an accelerated rate[41] and that, as this happened, the masses of Europe and Asia were becoming increasingly radicalized, and the USSR was becoming more and more threatened. The "third period" was, and would be, a time of crisis. This crisis was both systemic and international, one of both intensified class struggle and renewed imperialist war. As outlined in the "Resolution on the Measures of Struggle against the Dangers of Imperialist War" adopted by the congress, the future was defined in catastrophic terminology as a time of increasingly open imperialist hostility toward the Soviet Union and China, a time when "two imperialist groups of states" would clash "in a struggle for world hegemony," and a time when "a mighty revolutionary movement" would rise up.[42]

Adoption of this general line was one of several interrelated developments that took place in 1928–29. A "socialist offensive" was undertaken in the USSR against both independent peasant agriculture and private-enterprise small business. Stalin became a spokesman for the view that the Soviet Union was surrounded by foreign enemies, linked to enemies at home, who were plotting the ruination of the industrialization drive and the downfall of the Soviet regime. Within the leadership of the CPSU, the moderate group was defeated, and Stalin—and those who agreed with him or did not oppose him—gained control of the Central Committee. They put the First Five-Year Plan into effect and launched "Stalin's industrial revolution" with its "class war ideology." The official foreign policy conception of the Central Committee majority was transformed from one centered on an indeterminate period of "peaceful coexistence" to one premised on the approach of a new imperialist war and a mounting "foreign threat" to the USSR. One would normally expect to see such momentous changes—in party leadership, in strategies of economic development, in social policy, in the tactics of the international Communist movement, and in foreign policy conception—accompanied by diplomatic innovation, that is, by a change in the conduct of foreign relations and in particular in a shift in policy toward the major capitalist powers. There was none.

"People often forget," *Izvestiia* stated in May 1929, "that the Five Year Plan defines our foreign policy" and that this plan makes it necessary "to delay the war threat and make use of . . . world markets."[43] Rykov, the perpetual integrationist and the last remaining member of Lenin's Politburo (other than Stalin), stated the case for peaceful relations in his report to the Fifth Soviet Congress that same month:

> Comrades, the fulfillment of the Five Year Plan is bound up with an enormous development in our exports and imports, the import of a vast mass of equipment for our industry, agriculture, and transport. Therefore we are not less, but more interested than before in the development of peaceful relations and trade agreements. The fulfillment of the Five Year Plan demands consistent and systematic work over a number of years. Therefore in international relations we are trying for such solidarity and firmness in relations with individual states that no setback or loss will occur from that quarter in carrying out the colossal schemes of works laid down in the plan.[44]

Official government pronouncements such as these stressed the continuity of foreign policy through the radical transformations of 1928–29. The search for agreements with the capitalist powers went on, and the "struggle for peace and disarmament" was doctrinalized as the general line of Soviet diplomacy. Both government and party assemblies continued to affirm this slogan as the basic principle of Soviet foreign policy despite the "foreign threat." The explanation given was that the more provocative the capitalist powers became, the more necessary it was for the USSR to continue the "struggle for peace." Thus, although the new course of diplomatic initiatives first undertaken in 1926 had not achieved the positive results expected of them, there was no shift in the intentions and conduct of foreign relations with Europe and America at a time when nearly everything else in the USSR was becoming more militant and confrontational.

One solution to this puzzle states that the Sixth Comintern Congress adopted the "third period" doctrine, with its "new era of revolutions and wars," solely to explain class relations within capitalism. The doctrine was of importance largely for tactical purposes in the struggle between the emerging Stalinists and the supporters of Bukharin, and it was of consequence mainly for the tactics of the German Communist Party in its relations with the German Social Democratic Party. Stalin and the Stalinists did not really believe that war was imminent in 1928–29, this argument continues; in actuality, they expected a long period of peace while they loudly proclaimed the contrary.[45] Nevertheless it was contradictory to have counted on implementing the First Five-Year Plan with expanded foreign trade at a time when the entire capitalist system was proclaimed to be on the verge of collapse. A second solution to the puzzle suggests that Stalin himself took little interest in foreign relations in general and that he shunned diplomacy in particular.[46] He simply stuck with the foreign policies already in place in 1928 until forced into a policy shift in late 1933 by the threat a National Socialist Germany posed to Soviet security. For this reason, he induced no radical transformation of foreign relations at the time of "the great turn" comparable to what took place in other policy areas.

The scholarship of Robert Tucker contradicts both these theories. Stalin, he insists, was vitally interested in international relations largely because he was convinced that the USSR would be involved in another war within the space of a few years. The whole of the "policy program" that he implemented in his "revolution from above" was shaped by his concept of Russia's situation in world politics. Well before 1928, Stalin had decided that Russia's "backwardness" and isolation necessitated the construction of "socialism in one country." "To transform NEP Russia into a socialist Russia," Tucker argues, "was to construct an industrially and militarily powerful Soviet Russian state owning the instruments of production and capable of fending for itself in a hostile world." The requirements of national defense were primary for Stalin. "All else," according to Tucker, "had to be subordinated to the one great task of amassing military-industrial power in a hurry."[47]

Stalin made war preparedness the national priority because, in his mind, war was both inevitable and imminent. In the doctrine of war and peace that he developed during the period of "temporary capitalist stabilization" and "socialism in one country," he distinguished between imperialist and interventionist wars, just as Lenin had done in 1916. He viewed both as inevitable, and he saw either as a threat to the USSR. Indeed, the central concern that he voiced in the years 1925–1929 was that conflict between rivals within the capitalist camp would develop into an anti-Soviet war as the imperialist powers, either as a consequence of war with each other or as prelude to it, attempted to thwart the threat posed to international capitalism by a USSR-based international socialist revolution. At the same time, he decided that the international situation of the Locarno era strongly resembled the one in which the World War had begun—with developing anticolonial movements and great power rivalries in East Asia, North Africa, and the Balkans. It portended, he thought, a second imperialist war, "not tomorrow or the day after," in his own words, "but in a few years time."[48] And because Stalin believed that war among the imperialists would be accompanied by a war of intervention against the USSR, the threat to Russia was close at hand.

The international situation confronting the USSR, Stalin thought, made the development of a modern arms industry imperative. He first put forth his doctrine of impending war in a Central Committee discussion of appropriations for the Red Army in 1925, and he was the leading proponent on the Politburo of secret military collaboration with Germany. In turn, the construction of a socialist military-industrial complex carried foreign relations imperatives of its own, that is, a period of international peace. At the time of the 1927 war scare crisis, he stated: "We can and must build socialism in the USSR. But in order to build socialism we first of all have to exist. It is essential that there be a respite from war, that there be no attempts at intervention, that we achieve some minimum of international conditions indispensable for us so we can exist and build socialism."[49] The crucial task of extending the respite from war was assigned by Stalin to Soviet diplomacy.

Soviet diplomacy could operate effectively within the capitalist world system, Lenin had "taught," because of the contradictions inherent in the relations among the imperialists. To exploit those contradictions was the central precept of Leninist diplomacy as practiced at Brest-Litvosk and Genoa/Rapallo (in both cases by aligning Russia with Germany), and as adopted by Stalin. Like Lenin, Stalin regarded the first task of Soviet diplomacy to be that of preventing the formation of anti-Soviet coalitions and forestalling any coordinated intervention by the imperialist states and their clients while socialism—and the heavy industry and modern military capacity that accompanied it—was constructed in the USSR. Extending the interwar truce by diplomatic means, called "stretching out the breathing space," became the central tenet of Soviet foreign relations as "the great turn" was taken into "the new era of war and revolution."[50] Consequently, diplomatic relations with Europe and America did not take on the aggressive and confrontational tone otherwise characteristic of the policies and relations of "the great turn."

Nevertheless, the increasingly confrontational statements made by the leadership to CPSU and Comintern cannot be dismissed as merely tactical, ideologically delusionary, or meaninglessly rhetorical. A more reasonable understanding of the shift from "capitalist stabilization," "international equilibrium," and "peaceful coexistence" to "a new era of wars and revolutions" requires seeing it as a means to both national integration and national security. At a time when the membership of the Soviet and foreign Communist parties included those who sympathized with the Opposition or with the moderate group, an internal and an international Communist consensus, or "solidarity," might be formed in opposition to a "foreign threat" to the socialist homeland. That same "foreign threat," along with domestic "class enemies," could be used within the USSR as a new basis for social cohesion at a time when the tempo of collectivization and industrialization divided Soviet society. At a time when the USSR was without stable diplomatic alliances, the support of an international working class alerted to the threat of an imperialist attack on the USSR provided one of the few measures of preparedness available. And at a time when the Soviet defense establishment was unprepared for all-out warfare, the slogan "a new era of wars and revolutions" stood as a warning to the capitalist powers and as a deterrent against attack: "War against us will bring revolution to you."[51]

Conclusion

By the time of the 1928–29 "great turn" from the New Economic Policy to Stalinist economic and political development, many of the fundamental institutions, methods, and doctrines of Soviet national security were fixed in a form they would retain for decades. First, the drive for industrialization was launched, aimed at the creation of a self-sufficient military-industrial complex that would provide Soviet armed forces with weapons of current design and would be given first claim on national income and natural resources. Beginning in 1927, the project was justified by a high-range estimate of the magnitude of the "foreign threat" to the security of the USSR, and in 1928 it was joined to the use of preemptive state terror in defiance of internationally accepted humanitarian and democratic norms. Soon it came to have priority above all other economic, social, human, and environmental needs.

Second, in 1922 Soviet diplomacy had become discouraged about the prospects of a comprehensive post-revolutionary settlement between the socialist and capitalist camps. The diplomatic aspect of the special relationship with Germany had eroded seriously after 1925. Beginning in 1926, the efforts of the NKID were no longer aimed at obtaining dramatic breakthroughs to favorable relations with any of the capitalist powers but were concentrated on making gradual improvements in the tenor of relations and on concluding agreements piecemeal.

Third, the doctrine that informed foreign relations in 1928–29 reasserted that the capitalist world order was incapable of any prolonged stabilization and affirmed the concept that the greater the coherence demonstrated by the capitalist order, the greater the dangers that confronted the USSR. The Soviet Union would, nevertheless, be made more secure, the doctrine continued, by participating in world politics than it would be by remaining apart from them. However, any rapprochement between the USSR and the capitalist world could go no further than a "peaceful coexistence" standoff.

Institutions, methods, and doctrines such as these were not inherent in the revolutionary origins of the regime, nor were they taken directly from pre–World War I Marxism-Leninism. They were formed out of the international experience of the Soviet Union as it entered world politics during the years between the Bolshevik and Stalinist revolutions. Explaining the development of the foreign relations of the USSR during this period of formation is the project undertaken in this book, the argument of which can be stated in the form of the following propositions.

1. Soviet foreign relations were founded on twin principles. One was that the revolution begun in Russia could be continued by building an international Communist movement and aligning it with mass-based noninsurrectionary proletarian organizations in Europe and nationalist movements in Asia. The other was that the survival of the socialist republics in the lands of the former Russian Empire depended on protecting them against foreign intervention and on reconstructing and restructuring the Russian economy. To these ends, the Soviet leadership sought to obtain the technology of the advanced industrial countries, to construct protective zones on the frontiers of the USSR made up of stable states independent of the great powers, and to find a secure position for Soviet Russia within the capitalist world order. As the means to that stability, security, and technology, those who made the October Revolution established conventional commercial and diplomatic relations with the governments of the capitalist states of Europe and with the authoritarian modernizers of Asia, none of which were particularly sympathetic to the international Communist movement.

2. Internationalizing the October Revolution while normalizing relations with European capitalists and Asian nationalists was no simple task. The two efforts complicated each other in many ways. The series of trade and recognition agreements negotiated by the NKID beginning in 1921 restricted the dissemination of revolutionary propaganda. The ideological isolation into which their commitment to global revolution put the Bolsheviks posed a formidable obstacle to Soviet diplomacy in its efforts to establish normal relations with Europe and America. The search for trade and loan agreements presupposed a stable and prosperous system of capitalist states ready to transfer technology and to make loans; but internationalizing the October Revolution in Europe, Islamic Asia, or China threatened international capitalist stabilization. The financial aid given to

the General Strike in England and the political and military assistance sent to the Nationalist Revolution in China provoked Soviet Russia's most severe foreign relations crisis during the period between the end of the Civil War and the German invasion twenty years later. The Comintern's ideological attack on the Treaty of Versailles—an effort to promote solidarity with the German proletariat in opposition to the reparations-collecting European bourgeoisie—indirectly encouraged revanchist forces in Germany, diminished the prospects for international stability in Europe, and eventually ruined the system of security begun by Soviet diplomacy in the 1920s. In circumstances such as these, efforts to sharpen social conflict in Europe and nationalist conflict in Asia, and thereby to promote the global revolution on which the security of socialist revolution was presumed ultimately to depend, increased directly the isolation and insecurity of the Soviet state.

Neither half of "the dual policy" could be renounced, however. "The world revolutionary process" was the means by which the first and only socialist regime would reproduce itself; "peaceful coexistence" allowed the regime to survive until it did. Accordingly, while the Foreign Commissariat announced that socialism and capitalism could exist side by side to their mutual benefit, Comintern manifestos proclaimed the violent demise of capitalism and the inevitability of proletarian revolution in Europe. The two modes of early Soviet foreign relations could not be integrated into a coherent grand strategy, and in actuality no reliable method was found both to participate in and to overthrow capitalist international relations. Nor, despite Chicherin's repeated efforts to do so, were the two projects effectively separated from each other within Soviet policy making, either institutionally or rhetorically.

3. When Bolshevik assistance to revolutionary movements in Asia is regarded from a global perspective, it does not seem to have been a substitute for proletarian insurrection in Europe. On both continents similar strategies for internationalizing the October Revolution developed simultaneously—from revolution by local initiative in 1918–19, to revolution on the frontiers of the Civil War under the protection of the Red Army, to revolution by cadres coordinated from within the Comintern Executive Committee, to subversion through Soviet embassies abroad, to the elaborate missions of political guidance and military assistance dispatched to both Germany and China in 1923. Researchers in the archives of the Central Committee may or may not find a comprehensive plan for global revolution conceived in the Kremlin. However, the patterns of insurrectionary advance, retreat, and advance again were sufficiently simultaneous in both regions to undermine decisively the credibility of the notion that

national liberation in Asia was a form of strategic compensation for the recession of proletarian insurrection in Europe.

4. How the first socialist society acquired the means of production was a matter of foreign relations. Any of the various strategies posited in the industrialization debate that was conducted among the party/state leadership during the 1920s were to be achieved most fully by importing advanced technology from America and Europe. This was obscured by the rhetoric of autarky deployed in the debate itself, and it has been largely overlooked in the discussion of the problem by scholars. To fund technology import, two fundamentally different methods were potentially possible during the era of the New Economic Policy. One of them envisaged significant advances of capital from Europe and America. The feasibility of this method depended, however, on political prerequisites set forth in London, Paris, Brussels, and Washington: The leadership of the USSR must recognize the debts of previous Russian regimes and behave both internationally and at home as would pragmatic politicians at the head of a normal state. However, their involvement in nationalist struggles in Asia, the encouragement they gave to civil disobedience within the armed forces of Europe, and their repression of dissent and opposition within the USSR precluded the Bolsheviks from doing so. The other way to pay for imported technology looked to compulsory loans from the populace and to party/state control over the production and sale of grain as a way of acquiring revenue and foreign exchange for foreign purchases. Significantly, opting for one method or the other had consequences for the constitutional development of the USSR. Whereas international loans depended on favorable world opinion, internal borrowing and state grain controls not only freed the construction of socialism from foreign capital, it also allowed the regime to defy international public opinion and perpetuate and extend the use of preemptive state terror as the way to resolve internal political conflict.

5. Neither Genoa nor Rapallo provided a base for Soviet relations with the capitalist powers. The potential for a general peace treaty between socialist Russia and the capitalist powers that was projected at the Genoa Conference foundered on the complexity of the issues involved in a comprehensive multilateral East-West settlement, on disagreement on all sides over what debts of the Russian past were to be paid, and on reciprocal ideological antagonism. The Rapallo-based relations that Russia developed with Germany from 1922 to 1926 were based on full diplomatic recognition followed by a treaty of neutrality, on mutual cancellation of debts and reparations, on trade agreements and medium-term credits, and on the willingness of Weimar governments to forgo "punishing" the Soviet gov-

ernment for Communist insurrections in Germany. They remained "special" to these two countries, however. Although London and Paris recognized the Soviet regime in 1924, subsequent bilateral negotiations never got beyond the no-debt-payment/no-loan impasse, and die-hard anti-Communism brought Soviet relations with both Britain and France to a crisis within three years. When Germany and the Allied powers assembled at The Hague in 1929–30 to arrange what was called at the time "the final liquidation of the war," the USSR was not present. Not until 1943, after the Red Army had stopped the Wehrmacht, was the Soviet Union admitted to the councils of the world powers, and the USSR did not attend an international megaconference similar in size and scope to Genoa until the Helsinki Conference convened fifty years afterwards.

6. The world order that emerged with the liquidation of the Ruhr invasion in 1924 was defined in reports to congresses of the Comintern and the RCP(B)/CPSU as "the international stabilization of capitalism." The term signified the restoration of stability and productivity to bourgeois Europe by means of American capital achieved at the cost of the economic and political subordination of Britain and the Continent to the United States. In this world order the USSR was recognized diplomatically as the successor to the regime of the tsars by most of the nations of Europe, Asia, and Latin America. However, it remained in virtual diplomatic isolation. The governments of Britain, France, and Germany resolved their outstanding postwar conflicts and regularized their relations with the United States by means of a series of agreements on reparations, war debts, trade, and security. At the same time they suspended negotiations with the Soviet Union or kept them on a strictly tentative basis. It was in the context of these international developments that the crucial debates among the Soviet leadership on the construction of industrial socialism in Russia took place. And these developments constituted the international environment in which a Central Committee majority formed around Stalin and Bukharin and asserted at least officially that the achievement of socialist industrialization in Russia did not depend on either the proletarians or the capitalists of Europe.

7. During the era of "socialism in one country," Soviet foreign relations doctrine separated into two opposing conceptions, each with its own analysis of the international situation, its own predictions for the future, and its own prescriptions for policy. One conception posited that Euro-American capitalism and the proletarian regime in Russia were stabilizing simultaneously, that this dual stabilization would govern world politics for some time to come, and that it would offer to the USSR a "prolonged period of respite" from involvement in imperialist warfare. This respite, which would last for

years, even decades, would permit the USSR to consolidate its alliances with the proletariat of Europe and the peoples of Asia, to industrialize, and to construct socialism. The other conception denied that a protracted respite was in the offing and asserted categorically the "precarious" and "temporary" character of capitalist stabilization. Within this conception, the May 30th movement in China became the beginning of "a new era of wars and revolutions," and from the international conferences and treaties of 1925, and from the campaigns conducted by die-hard anti-Communists in Europe, it was concluded that the imperialist powers were arming themselves, encircling the USSR, and preparing for military conflict. A war could begin in a few years time and be accompanied by, or preceded by, a preemptive military strike against the Soviet Union. In 1925–26 these two contradictory prognostications coexisted within the Soviet discourse on the international situation. At times both were asserted in the same doctrinal pronouncements without the contradiction between the two of them being explicitly resolved.

8. In public statements and private conversations alike, both Chicherin and Litvinov carefully separated the NKID from the "foreign threat" prognostication, and during the second half of 1926, the Foreign Commissariat reformulated actual Soviet foreign policy according to the "whole period of respite" scenario. As was the industrialization strategy adopted at the same time, foreign policy was premised on the assumption that proletarian rule in the USSR had achieved stability both domestically and internationally and that socialism would be constructed gradually out of the conditions of NEP. In one of the heretofore least understood developments in the history of early Soviet foreign relations, the expectation of rapid breakthroughs to comprehensive settlements, either on the multilateral Genoa model or on the bilateral Rapallo model, was abandoned in favor of a search for piecemeal arrangements that included foreign trade agreements designed to improve, restore, or establish political relations with the major capitalist powers, bilateral neutrality treaties with states bordering the USSR, and participation in the instruments of multilateral international cooperation.

9. Lenin brought Soviet Russia into world politics in 1921 with a foreign policy conception composed largely of those of his pre-1917 ideas about the development of the early twentieth-century global political economy that seemed to have been confirmed by the course of international politics during the three years following the revolution. To wit, conflicts among the imperialist powers and between the capitalist and socialist "camps" were inevitable until the world order was transformed by proletarian revolution in Europe. Until then, coalitions of capitalist states

represented a particular threat to "proletarian power" in Russia. The block-ade and intervention of the period 1918–1920 were possible because the capitalist powers had been able to act together. On the other hand, "breath-ing space" was created when they were divided among themselves and at war with one another. Insofar as the capitalist world system offered any security to the Russian and other Soviet republics, it was because the postwar antagonisms inherent in the relations among the imperialist pow-ers could be counted on to prevent them from acting on their basic antago-nism toward "proletarian power" and taking united action against the Russian and other Soviet republics. Soviet security was best ensured, therefore, by participating in capitalist international relations and using the conflicts present in the postwar situation to prevent the formation of anti-Soviet coalitions—military, commercial, financial, or diplomatic.

The failure of the Genoa Conference and the conclusion of the Rapallo Treaty in 1922 seemed to validate Lenin's belief that antagonisms among the capitalist powers favored the survival of the Soviet republics. However, the Dawes Plan and the Locarno Treaties undermined the supposition that the capitalist powers could not overcome their postwar differences and that the divisions and antagonisms among them could be counted on to protect socialist Russia from their combined opposition. In this manner, the agree-ments of international stabilization concluded among Britain, France, Ger-many, and the United States between 1924 and 1926 represented a funda-mental challenge to the most basic precepts of Leninist foreign relations.

One possible response to that challenge was to abandon the premise that not only international proletarian revolution, but Soviet security as well, always benefited from conflict among the capitalist powers—and to adopt instead the alternative doctrine of foreign relations proposed on occasion during the post-Locarno era in both Comintern circles and the Foreign Affairs Commissariat. This doctrine held that "peace is indivisible," that another conflict anywhere in Europe could escalate into a second total war, a war that would devastate both capitalist and proletarian nations. The task of both the NKID and the Comintern was, therefore, not to add to the tensions that contributed to interimperialist conflict or to the antagonisms between the capitalist and socialist camps, but, rather, to work to reduce them.

10. Both the doctrine of "indivisible peace" and the prognostication of "prolonged respite" were casualties of the 1927 war scare and the extended crisis it touched off. The notion that capitalist coalescence threatened the USSR was reasserted amid cries of alarm over the foreign threat. No longer did any member of the party leadership, whether from the Opposition, the moderate group, or the future Stalinists, contend that the post-1923 world

order was one in which a restabilized system of capitalist states could continue to coexist for an indefinite period of time with stabilized proletarian power in the USSR. Instead, the foreign relations doctrine of both the CPSU and the Comintern stated dogmatically that the capitalist world order was incapable of any prolonged stabilization, that it was becoming increasingly "rotten and unstable," and that a new era in the history of international capitalist development was beginning that would bring cataclysmic war and revolution. To be sure, the idea that another total war in Europe would devastate both capitalist and socialist civilization would be revived to underpin Litvinov's security policy from 1934 to 1939, and the belief that capitalism and socialism could coexist at peace indefinitely would serve as the basis of post–World War II détentes between East and West. However, many of the more antagonistic conclusions drawn from the first era of Soviet foreign relations would exert a powerful hold on the national political imagination for almost as long as there was a Soviet Union.

Notes

INTRODUCTION

1. George F. Kennan, *Russia and the West under Lenin and Stalin* (Boston: 1961), 223.

2. Louis Fischer, *The Soviets in World Affairs: A History of the Relations between the Soviet Union and the Rest of the World* (London: 1930); Theodore H. von Laue, "Soviet Diplomacy: G. V. Chicherin, People's Commissar for Foreign Affairs, 1918–1930," in *The Diplomats, 1919–1939*, ed. Gordon A. Craig and Felix Gilbert (Princeton, N.J.: 1953; reprint, New York, 1963); Kennan, *Russia and the West*; Adam Ulam, *Expansion and Coexistence: The History of Soviet Foreign Policy, 1917–1967* (New York: 1968).

3. Teddy J. Uldricks, "Russia and Europe: Diplomacy, Revolution, and Economic Development in the 1920s," *International History Review* 1 (1979): 55–83; also his *Diplomacy and Ideology: The Origins of Soviet Foreign Relations, 1917–1930* (London and Beverly Hills, Calif.: 1979).

4. Two of the earliest works were the third volume of E. H. Carr's *Socialism in One Country, 1924–1926* (New York: 1964) and Harvey L. Dyck's *Weimar Germany and Soviet Russia, 1926–1933: A Study in Diplomatic Instability* (London: 1966). The method was perfected in two works of Richard K. Debo, *Revolution and Survival: The Foreign Policy of Soviet Russia, 1917–18* (Toronto: 1979) and *Survival and Consolidation: The Foreign Policy of Soviet Russia, 1918–1921* (Montreal and Kingston: 1992). Both works are based on a combination of archival and printed sources from the governments of Great Britain, France, Germany, Italy, and the United States, as well as on published Russian sources.

5. The publication of Moshe Lewin's *La paysannerie et le pouvoir soviétique* (Paris: 1966) marked the beginning of this development. The literature that followed is too vast to discuss here. For a compilation of research on NEP society and culture made in 1986, at the beginning of

perestroika, see Sheila Fitzpatrick, Alexander Rabinowich, and Richard Stites (eds.), *Russia in the Era of NEP: Explorations in Soviet Society and Culture* (Bloomington, Ind.: 1991). A summary of research on the economy prior to the dissolution of the USSR in 1991 is presented in R. W. Davies (ed.), *From Tsarism to the New Economic Policy: Continuity and Change in the Economy of the USSR* (Ithaca, N.Y.: 1991).

6. This research is described in R. W. Davies, *Soviet History in the Gorbachev Revolution* (London: 1989), 27–46.

7. See, for example, R. W. Davies' observation in the introduction to *From Tsarism to the New Economic Policy*, pp. 25–26, that consideration of the international situation of the USSR has played little part in the debates among economic historians regarding the breakdown of NEP; and V. A. Shishkin's statement that "The study and elucidation of the country's socioeconomic development in the 1920s are carried out without taking into consideration the country's interactions and relationships with the world economy": "The external factor in the country's socioeconomic development," in "The Soviet Union in the 1920s: A Roundtable," *Soviet Studies in History* 28 (1989): 48.

8. L. N. Nezhinskii, "Istoriia vneshnei politiki SSSR: poiski novykh podkhodov," *Novaia i noveishaia istoriia* (1990:4): 3.

9. Zinovii Sheinis, *Maxim Litvinov* (Moscow: 1990); original Russian edition, 1989.

10. A. A. Galkin, "Nekotorye voprosy istorii Kominterna," *Novaia i noveishaia istoriia* (1989:2): 83.

11. Shishkin, "External factor," 54.

12. Jon Jacobson, "Is There a New International History of the 1920s?" *American Historical Review* 88 (1983): 617–45. See also Donald Cameron Watt, "The New International History," *International History Review* 9 (1987): 518–52; Alexander de Conde, "On the Nature of International History," *International History Review* 10 (1988): 282–301; and Stephen Pelz, "On Systematic Explanation in International History," *International History Review* 12 (1990): 763–81.

1. IDEOLOGICAL AND POLITICAL FOUNDATIONS

1. Margot Light, *The Soviet Theory of International Relations* (Brighton, England: 1988), 27–28, 149–51; Allen Lynch, *The Soviet Study of International Relations* (New York: 1987), 8–18; V. Kubálková and A. A. Cruickshank, *Marxism and International Relations* (Oxford and New York: 1985), 76–77.

2. *Imperialism, the Highest Stage of Capitalism*: V. I. Lenin, *Collected Works* (Moscow: 1960–70), 22: 266 (hereafter cited as *CW*).

3. Lynch, *Soviet Study of International Relations*, 13.

4. Marx quoted in Fernando Claudin, *The Communist Movement: From Comintern to Cominform* (New York: 1975), 20.

5. Lenin quoted in Debo, *Revolution and Survival*, 408. Together, this work and Debo's *Survival and Consolidation* provide a full narrative of Soviet foreign policy from the October Revolution to the settlements of March 1921.

6. Piotr S. Wandycz, *Soviet-Polish Relations, 1917–1921* (Cambridge, Mass.: 1969), brought the diplomacy of the Soviet-Polish war into critical scholarship. Norman Davies, *White Eagle, Red Star: The Polish-Soviet War, 1919–20* (New York: 1972), chronicles the military events. In "The Genesis of the Polish-Soviet War, 1919–20," *European Studies Review* 5 (1975): 47–67, and "The Missing Revolutionary War: The Polish Campaigns and the Retreat from Revolution in Soviet Russia, 1919–21," *Soviet Studies* 27 (1975): 178–95, Davies draws out the interpretive implications of his research, one of them being that the war was a Bolshevik revolutionary offensive by military means, something that Lenin strongly favored. Thomas C. Fiddick, in *Russia's Retreat from Poland, 1920: From Permanent Revolution to Peaceful Coexistence* (London: 1990), looks into the diversity of policies preferred and activities undertaken by the major Bolshevik actors in 1920. He does so with remarkable depth and clarity and denies that revolutionary war was Lenin's policy. Debo, in *Survival and Consolidation*, 408–412, agrees that Soviet policy in Poland was not a revolutionary crusade. Rather, as the Red Army drove back the Polish forces from the Ukraine, the Bolsheviks rethought their entire foreign policy. Lenin included, they abandoned the cautious and realistic diplomacy they had pursued since Brest-Litvosk. Instead, Debo speculates, they were attracted to the possibility of dividing up Polish territory with Germany and forcing Britain and France into an international conference to revise the peace settlement in Eastern Europe. James M. McCann, "Beyond the Bug: Soviet Historiography of the Soviet-Policy War of 1920," *Soviet Studies* 36 (1984): 475–93, analyzes Soviet scholarship prior to *glasnost* and also comments on Euro-American historiography. Vladlen Sirotkin, "The Riga Peace Treaty," *International Affairs* (Moscow) (1989:9): 128–43, extols Lenin's realism and his 1921 turnabout leading to the adoption of the Riga Treaty, NEP, and "the high road" to world revolution, as opposed to Trotsky's notion of "direct revolution." A. Ya. Manusevkch, "Trudnyi put' k Rizhskomu mirnomu dogovoru 1921 g.," *Novaia i noveishaia istoriia* (1991:1): 19–43, reads like unreconstructed "old political thinking" despite the date of publication.

7. Fiddick, *Russia's Retreat from Poland*, 26–27.

8. Teddy J. Uldricks, "Russia and Europe: Diplomacy, Revolution, and Economic Development in the 1920s," *International History Review* 1 (1979): 55–83.

9. Major programmatic statements by Lenin on which the following analysis is based include: speech delivered to the Moscow Gubernia Conference of the RCP(B), 21 November 1920, Lenin, *CW*, 31: 408–415; report on concessions delivered to the RCP(B) group at the Eighth Congress of

Soviets, 21 December 1920, Lenin, *CW*, 31: 463–86; report on the political work of the CC of the RCP(B) to the Tenth Party Congress, 8 March 1921, Lenin, *CW*, 32:179–83; report of the Central Executive Committee and the Council of People's Commissars to the Ninth Congress of Soviets, 23 December 1921, Lenin, *CW*, 33: 143–61.

10. Branko Lazitch and Milorad Drachkovitch, *Lenin and the Comintern* (Stanford, Calif.: 1972), 532–45.

11. Report to the Tenth Party Congress, 8 March 1921, Lenin, *CW*, 32: 180.

12. Trotsky quoted in E. H. Carr, *The Bolshevik Revolution, 1917–1923* (New York: 1950–53), 3: 383.

13. Piero Melograni, *Lenin and the Myth of World Revolution: Ideology and Reasons of State, 1917–1920* (Atlantic Highlands, N.J.: 1989).

14. Lazitch and Drachkovitch, *Lenin and the Comintern*, 523, 546.

15. For the argument of M. M. Gorinov and S. V. Tasakunov that the New Economic Policy was forced on the party leadership by local Bolshevik chiefs, who, in confronting the realities of war-torn Russia and demands for food supplies from the cities, began working out tentative compromises with the peasantry as early as the autumn of 1918, see "Leninskaia kontseptsiia NEPa: stanovlenie i razvitie," *Voprosy istorii* (1990:4): 20–21.

16. Speech to the Plenary Session of the Moscow Soviet, 20 November 1922, Lenin, *CW*, 33: 441.

17. R. W. Davies, *Soviet History in the Gorbachev Revolution*, 119.

18. Samuel Farber, *Before Stalinism: The Rise and Fall of Soviet Democracy* (Oxford: 1990), 195–99.

19. Lenin quoted in N. V. Zagladin, *Istoriia uspekhov i neudach sovetskoi diplomatii: politologicheskii aspekt* (Moscow: 1990), 22–23.

20. Franklyn Griffiths, "Origins of Peaceful Coexistence: A Historical Note," *Survey*, no. 50 (January 1964): 195–201; Stephan Horak, "Lenin on Coexistence: A Chapter in Soviet Foreign Policy," *Studies on the Soviet Union* 3 (1964): 20–30; V. Kubálková and A. A. Cruickshank, "The Soviet Concept of Peaceful Coexistence: Some Theoretical and Semantic Problems," *Australian Journal of Politics and History* 24 (1978): 184–98; Warren Lerner, "The Historical Origins of the Soviet Doctrine of Peaceful Coexistence," *Law and Contemporary Society* 29 (1964): 865–70. Griffiths, 195–96, distinguishes carefully between "peaceful cohabitation" (*mirnoe sozhitelstvo*) and "peaceful coexistence" (*mirnoe sosushchestvovanie*) as terms used by the party/state leadership from 1917 to 1921; the former, he states, "suggests more active participation," but the latter "is more stable, less transitory." Light, *Soviet Theory of International Relations*, 42, does not regard the distinction as significant. The practice I have adopted here is to use "peaceful coexistence" and to rely on the political context to make clear its various connotations. The official historiography of the CPSU did not credit Trotsky with first usage of the term, or with any other achievements

as the first *narkom* for foreign affairs. The initial breakdown of this interpretation can be observed in A. V. Pantsov, "Brestskii mir," *Voprosy istorii* (1990:2): 60–79, which criticized the pre-*glasnost* line and used materials authored by Trotsky; the latter had been taboo up to that time.

21. Lenin and Chicherin quoted in Zagladin, *Istoriia uspekhov i neudach*, 50–51, and Griffiths, "Origins of Peaceful Coexistence," 197–98. For the negotiations with Estonia, see Debo, *Survival and Consolidation*, 124–46.

22. Fiddick, *Russia's Retreat from Poland*, 36–37, 41.

23. Ibid., 274.

24. V. G. Sirotkin, "Ot grazhdanskoi voiny k grazhdanskomu miru," in *Inogo ne dano*, ed. Iu. N. Afanaseva (Moscow: 1988), 371.

25. Report on Concessions at the Eighth Congress of Soviets, 21 December 1920, Lenin, *CW*, 31: 463–86; quotations on 471 and 480; report to the Tenth Party Congress, 8 March 1921, Lenin, *CW*, 32: 182–83.

26. Research into the articulation of NEP is discussed in V. P. Dmitrenko, "Certain Aspects of the New Economic Policy in Soviet Historical Scholarship of the 1960s," *Soviet Studies in History* 11 (1972–73): 224–25.

27. Quoted in Carr, *Bolshevik Revolution*, 3: 289.

28. Zinovii Sheinis, *Maxim Litvinov*, 153.

29. Anthony J. Heywood, "Trade or Isolation? Soviet Imports of Railway Equipment, 1920–1922," in *Contact or Isolation? Soviet-Western Relations in the Interwar Period*, ed. John Hiden and Aleksander Loit (Studia Baltica Stockholmiensia) 8 (Stockholm: 1991), 137–60; Christine A. White, " 'Riches have Wings,' The Use of Russian Gold in Soviet Foreign Trade, 1918–1922," ibid., 117–36.

30. Roger Pethybridge, *One Step Backwards, Two Steps Forward: Soviet Society and Politics in the New Economic Policy* (Oxford and New York: 1990), 94.

31. Charles M. Edmondson, "The Politics of Hunger: The Soviet Response to Famine, 1921," *Soviet Studies* 29 (1977): 506–518.

32. Lenin quoted in Edmondson, "Politics of Hunger," 516.

33. "Report by the RSFSR People's Commissariat of Foreign Affairs for the Ninth Congress of Soviets, December 1921," *International Affairs* (Moscow) (1990:2): 138, 144.

34. Benjamin M. Weissman, *Herbert Hoover and Famine Relief to Soviet Russia, 1921–1923* (Stanford, Calif.: 1974).

35. "Report by the RSFSR People's Commissariat of Foreign Affairs for the Ninth Congress of Soviets, December 1921," 146.

36. Report by Lenin to the RCP(B) Group at the Eighth Congress of Soviets, 22 December 1920, Lenin, *CW*, 31: 493.

37. Pethybridge, *One Step*, 232–33.

38. John Quigley, *The Soviet Foreign Trade Monopoly: Institutions and Laws* (Columbus, Ohio: 1974), 3–36.

39. V. L. Genis, "Upriamyi narkom s Ilinki," in *Otkryvaia novye stra-*

nitsy. Mezhdunarodnye voprosy: sobytiia i liudi, ed. A. A. Iskenderov (Moscow: 1989), 233.

40. Timothy Edward O'Connor, *The Engineer of Revolution: L. B. Krasin and the Bolsheviks, 1870–1926* (Boulder, Colo.: 1992), 166–220.

41. Report by Lenin to the RCP(B) Group at the Eighth Congress of Soviets, 21 December 1920, Lenin, *CW,* 31: 463–86, quotations on 485–86.

42. Widely quoted; see Light, *Soviet Theory of International Relations,* 28.

43. V. G. Sirotkin, *Vekhi otechestvennoi istorii* (Moscow: 1991), 175. In true *perestroika* fashion, the work gives high marks to the pragmatists of early Soviet politics—Lenin, Krasin, Chicherin, the NKID in general, and, later, Radek and Trotsky—contrasting them with the doctrinaire Zinoviev, Stalin, and Dzerzhinskii. The author is a historian at the Diplomatic Academy of the Russian Foreign Ministry. During the *glasnost* era, he was the one who proposed that the secret protocols to the Nazi-Soviet Nonaggression Pact be sought out in the archives and published immediately.

44. "Resolution of the All Russian Central Executive Committee on the Report of the Work of the Russian Delegation at Genoa and the Treaty with Germany signed at Rapallo," 18 May 1922, printed in Henri Barbusse, ed., *The Soviet Union and Peace: The Most Important of the Documents Issued by the Government of the USSR Concerning Peace and Disarmament from 1917 to 1929* (New York: [1929?]), 196.

45. On this point, see Kubálková and Cruickshank, *Marxism and International Relations,* 77, and "Soviet Concept," 185.

46. Barbusse, *The Soviet Union and Peace.*

47. Nikita Khrushchev, *Report of the Central Committee of the Communist Party of the Soviet Union to the 20th Party Congress,* 14 February 1956 (Moscow: 1956), 38–46, and "On Peaceful Co-existence," *Foreign Affairs* 38 (1959): 1–18. On the sometimes subtle adaptations of "peaceful coexistence" during the Stalin, Khrushchev, and Brezhnev eras, see V. Kubálková and A. A. Cruickshank, *Marxism-Leninism and Theory of International Relations* (London and Boston: 1980), 148–54, 165–67; and Light, *Soviet Theory of International Relations,* 31–68.

48. This line was sustained with increasingly ponderous repetition after 1968. See, for instance, K. P. Ivanov, *Leninism and Foreign Policy of the USSR* (Moscow: ca. 1971); and Mikhail I. Trush, *Soviet Foreign Policy: Early Years* (Moscow: ca. 1970). Numerous articles on the topic appeared in *International Affairs* (Moscow), the last of them being published in June 1987: Nikolai Yermoshkin, "Peaceful Coexistence: A Universal Norm of International Relations," *International Affairs* (Moscow) (1987:6): 71–78. See also Vilnis Sipols, *Soviet Peace Policy, 1917–1939* (Moscow: 1988).

49. A. E. Bovin, *Mirnoe sosushchestovnie: istoriia, teoriia, politika* (Moscow: 1988); A. O. Chubarian, *Mirnoe sosushchestvovanie: teoriia i praktika* (Moscow: 1976).

50. "Lenin's Legacy," *International Affairs* (Moscow) (1990:5): 71–74.

51. Zagladin, *Istoriia uspekhov i neudach sovetskoi diplomatii*, 11.

52. Barrington Moore, Jr., *Soviet Politics; the Dilemma of Power: The Role of Ideas in Social Change* (Cambridge, Mass.: 1959).

53. See, especially, Debo, *Revolution and Survival* and *Survival and Consolidation;* and Fiddick, *Russia's Retreat from Poland.*

54. The function of ideology in Soviet politics and foreign policy has received extensive coverage in European and American scholarship, much of it during the late 1960s. Opinion has varied widely. See the works discussed in Stephen White, "Ideology and Soviet Politics," in *Ideology and Soviet Politics,* ed. Stephen White and Alex Pravda (New York: 1988), 1–20, and in "Communist Ideology, Belief Systems, and Soviet Foreign Policy," in *The Conduct of Soviet Foreign Policy,* ed. Erik P. Hoffmann and Frederic J. Fleron, Jr. (2d ed.; New York: 1980), 91–97. Also Jonathan Harris, *Ideology and International Politics: An Introduction to Soviet Analysis* (Pittsburgh: 1970).

55. Graeme Gill, *The Origins of the Stalinist Political System* (Cambridge: 1990), 172–98; and "Ideology and System-Building: The Experience under Lenin and Stalin," in *Ideology and Soviet Politics,* 59–82.

56. For ideology and Soviet international relations doctrine, see Teddy J. Uldricks, *Diplomacy and Ideology: The Origins of Soviet Foreign Relations, 1917–1930* (London and Beverly Hills, Calif.: 1979), 143–55.

57. For the inevitability of war and the dilemma of peaceful coexistence, see Frederic S. Burin, "The Communist Doctrine of the Inevitability of War," *American Political Science Review* 57 (1963): 334–54; and Light, *Soviet Theory of International Relations,* 209–215.

2. INTERNATIONALIZING THE OCTOBER REVOLUTION

1. James W. Hulse, *The Forming of the Communist International* (Stanford, Calif.: 1964); Jules Humbert-Droz, *L'origine de l'internationale communiste: de Zimmerwald à Moscou* (Neuchâtel: 1968).

2. E. H. Carr's history of the Soviet Union is an encyclopedia of knowledge about the Communist International and about Bolshevik relations with the other national Communist parties. No other single work compares with it for comprehensiveness and detail: see *The Bolshevik Revolution 1917–1923* (New York: 1950–53), vol. 3, chaps. 23, 25, 30, and 31; *Socialism in One Country, 1924–1926* (New York: 1958–64), vol. 3, chaps. 27–28, 30–31, 35, 43, and 46; and, with Robert W. Davies, *Foundations of a Planned Economy, 1926–1929* (New York: 1969–78), vol. 3, chaps. 66–72 and 76–81. The most nuanced and coherent study is Fernando Claudin's *The Communist Movement: From Comintern to Cominform* (New York: 1975). The history of the Comintern was fully deployed by the followers of Trotsky in their struggle with Stalin and his supporters. The major Trotskyist work is Pierre Frank, *Histoire de l'Internationale commu-*

niste, 1919–1943 (Paris: 1979). Trotsky's own account is to be found in *The First Five Years of the Communist International* (New York: 1945–53); and in *Die Internationale Revolution und die Kommunistische Internationale* (Berlin: 1929) and *l'Internationale communiste après Lénine* (Paris: 1930), which were published together as *The Third International after Lenin* (London: 1974).

3. The initial phase of the Comintern's development (1919–1928) has been the subject of several outstanding monographs, for example, the works of Hulse and Humbert-Droz, noted above; Lazitch and Drachkovitch, *Lenin and the Comintern* (Stanford, Calif.: 1972); and Kermit McKenzie, *Comintern and World Revolution, 1928–1943: The Shaping of Doctrine* (London and New York: 1964).

4. Discussion of these contradictions has been a prominent feature of the scholarship of Euro-American critics of the Communist International. See, for example, Claudin, *Communist Movement*, 126. Soviet writers, including official historians of the Comintern, recognized them during *perestroika*. I. M. Krivoguz, in "Sud'ba i nasledie Kominterna," *Novaia i noveishaia istoriia* (1990:6): 9, expressed the view that the tragedy of the Comintern was to be found in the continual incongruence of its ideology and political strategies with historical reality, despite frequent attempts to adjust the former to the latter. F. I. Firsov, "Komintern: mekhanizm funktsionirovania," *Novaia i noveishaia istoriia* (1991:2): 37, stated that the "centralizing line" of the Comintern did much harm at a time when there was "a decline in revolutionary activities in the capitalist countries, when the tasks of daily work were moving to the first priority, and when specific national conditions were consequently becoming more important."

5. *"Left-Wing" Communism—An Infantile Disorder*, April–May 1920: Lenin, *CW*, 31: 17–117.

6. "Theses on the Conditions of Admission to the Communist International," Alan Adler, ed., *Theses, Resolutions, and Manifestos of the First Four Congresses of the Third International* (London and Atlantic Highlands, N.J.: 1980), 92–97; hereafter referred to as *First Four Congresses*. For their authorship, see John Riddell, ed., *Workers of the World and Oppressed Peoples Unite! Proceedings and Documents of the Second Congress, 1920* (New York: 1991), 1011–12; hereafter cited as *Second Congress*. Richard Lowenthal, in "The Rise and Decline of International Communism," *Problems of Communism* 12 (1963): 19–29, analyzes the conditions perceptively. Milorad Drachkovitch and Branko Lazitch, "The Third International," in *The Revolutionary Internationals, 1864–1943*, ed. Milorad M. Drachkovitch (Stanford, Calif.: 1966), 159–202, is uncompromisingly critical of the Bolshevik stamp Lenin and Zinoviev imprinted on the international movement.

7. This stage of development began in 1921 when the Third Congress elaborated on the "Twenty-one Conditions" in a lengthy "monster resolu-

tion," a set of theses entitled "Organizational Structure of the Communist Parties, the Methods and Content of their Work": See *First Four Congresses,* 234–61; Carr, *Bolshevik Revolution,* 3: 390. The second stage began in 1924–25 when the Fifth Congress, followed by the Fifth ECCI Plenum, decided in favor of the "Bolshevization" of the national parties. The transformation culminated in 1928 when the Sixth Congress adopted an organizational statute, long in preparation, which codified and extended the changes of the previous years: See Jane Degras, ed., *The Communist International, 1919–1943: Documents* (London and New York: 1956–65), 2: 464–71; hereafter cited as *Communist International;* and McKenzie, *Comintern and World Revolution,* 31–35, 55–56.

8. As early as January 1921, Clara Zetkin, a member of the German delegation to the Second Congress, complained to Lenin regarding the authoritarian demeanor of the ECCI: "Sometimes they are overtly rude and interventionist while genuine knowledge of the situation is absent." Quoted in Firsov, "Komintern: mekhanizm funktsionirovania," 35.

9. For a list of early interventions, see Souvarine to French Communist Party, 28 September 1921, in Siegfried Bahne et al., eds., *Archives de Jules Humbert-Droz* (Dortrecht: 1970–81), vol. 1, no. 37. Also Branko Lazitch, "Two Instruments of Control by the Comintern: The Emissaries of the ECCI and the Party Representatives in Moscow," in *The Comintern: Historical Highlights, Essays, Recollections, Documents,* ed. Milorad M. Drachkovitch and Branko Lazitch (New York: 1966), 45–65.

10. Carr, *Foundations,* 3: 128–29.

11. Geoff Eley, in "Reviewing the Socialist Tradition," presented at the symposium "The Crisis of Socialism in Eastern and Western Europe" held in Chapel Hill, N.C., in April 1990, pointed to the complexity of revolutionary possibilities in the years 1917–1923 in an effort to reconstruct the historical significance of the October Revolution in the wake of the events of 1989 in Eastern Europe.

12. Carr, *Bolshevik Revolution,* 3: 446.

13. Claudin, *Communist Movement,* 76–77.

14. A somewhat different sequence of stages is presented in Franz Borkenau's perceptive and caustic criticism of Comintern strategies of revolution—the CI as the instrument of revolution, as the tool of factional struggles within the RCP(B), and as the instrument of Russian foreign relations: See *World Communism: A History of the Communist International* (Ann Arbor, Mich.: 1962), 419.

15. Carr, *Bolshevik Revolution,* 3: 201.

16. Jules Humbert-Droz, *De Lénine à Staline. Dix ans au service de l'internationale communiste, 1921–1931* (Neuchâtel: 1971), and, even more, the memoirs of Aino Kuusinen, *Before and after Stalin: A Personal Account of Soviet Russia from the 1920s to the 1960s* (London: 1974), are informative on matters of Comintern organizational apparatus and personnel. So too is

Carr, *Socialism in One Country,* 3: 898–913. Branko Lazitch's *Biographical Dictionary of the Comintern* (rev. ed., Stanford, Calif.: 1986) contains over 700 biographies of Comintern figures. Vilem Kahan, "The Communist International, 1919–43: The Personnel of Its Highest Bodies," *International Review of Social History* 21 (1976): 151–85, verifies the names of Comintern participants. (CI records often did not list first names or pseudonyms).

17. Some of the initial activities and responsibilities of the Presidium are outlined in a letter from Boris Souvarine to the French Communist Party, 28 September 1921, in *Archives de Jules Humbert-Droz,* vol. 1, no. 37.

18. Geoff Eley, "Some Unfinished Thoughts on the Comintern," presented at the symposium "Fifty Years of the Popular Front," University of Michigan, November 1985.

19. Carr, *Bolshevik Revolution,* 3: 200–204.

20. Kuusinen to Humbert-Droz, 5 February 1923, *Archives de Jules Humbert-Droz,* vol. 1, no. 143.

21. The reprinting of those Comintern documents that were public when they originally appeared—theses, resolutions, manifestos, published statements, and open letters to national Communist parties—has been undertaken more widely in Europe and America than in the USSR. *The Communist International,* ed. Degras, is the fullest general collection of Comintern documents in English, or any language. There are more exhaustive collections of materials for specific congresses, such as John Riddell, ed., *The German Revolution and the Debate on Soviet Power: Documents, 1918–1919. Preparing the Founding Congress* (New York: 1986) and *Founding the Communist International: Proceedings and Documents of the First Congress, March 1919* (New York: 1987), and of the *Second Congress;* and Adler, ed., *First Four Congresses.* Vilem Kahan, in *Bibliography of the Communist International (1919–1979)* (Leiden and New York: 1990), lists more than 3,000 publications issued by the CI, including stenographic records and minutes, theses, resolutions, and manifestos of the world congresses and of plenary sessions of the ECCI. Included also are secondary publications concerning these meetings published between 1919 and 1979. The ECCI published two periodicals, *Kommunisticheskii Internatsional,* representing official views on current matters, and *International Press Correspondence,* which publicized news items of interest to the national Communist parties.

22. Some internal documents remained in national Communist party archives and in private collections, the most important being the *Archives de Jules Humbert-Droz.* Humbert-Droz was a founder of the Swiss Communist Party who attended the second and all subsequent congresses of the Comintern. As director of the Comintern's Latin Secretariat during the years 1921–1930, he carried out multiple confidential missions for the Comintern in France, Italy, Spain, and Portugal. The documents he retained are informative regarding the work of those parties, but they tell less

about the particulars of policy formulation at the center. In this regard, his memoirs, *De Lénine à Staline,* are more interesting and valuable. From 1926 to 1928 he was a member of the ECCI Presidium and Political Secretarat. He aligned himself with the moderate opposition to Stalin, became a confidant of Bukharin's, and—after engaging in public self-criticism and supporting the Stalinist position—lived to tell about it: *De Lénine à Staline,* 284–86.

23. In his speech on the seventieth anniversary of the October Revolution (November 1987), Mikhail Gorbachev stated that the "true history" of the CI had yet to be written: "We have to restore the truth about it. Despite all the fallacies and draw-backs in its actions, and however bitter could be the recalling of some of the pages of its history, the Comintern is part of the great past of our movement." See M. S. Gorbachev, *Oktiabr i perestroika: revoliutsiia prodolzhaetsia* (Moscow: 1987), 55.

Subsequently, the CPSU Central Committee adopted new procedures for the utilization of the Comintern archives, the purpose of which was to "help uproot Stalinism completely and restore and develop further Lenin's concept of the Communist movement." See Fridrikh J. Firsov, "What the Comintern Archives Will Reveal," *World Marxist Review* 32, 1 (1989): 52–57. A round-table discussion was held at the Institute of Marxism-Leninism in June 1988 to undertake the reevaluation of the theoretical and political work of the Comintern and of Stalin's role in it. Much of the opinion expressed at this meeting displayed considerable professional-political discomfort regarding the task. Stalin was to be criticized fully. Zinoviev, Trotsky, and Bukharin were said to have played a somewhat positive role in the affairs of the ECCI; however, their mistakes, especially those of Trotsky, were not to be minimized. It was necessary, one contributor stated, "to keep the proper balance," and "Bukharin, of course, cannot be idealized." The project was to be undertaken by professional academics who knew the archives and who would produce a scientifically balanced judgment. If left to others, the rewriting of the history of the Comintern would become a witch-hunt. The Western social democratic interpretation, which condemned the Comintern completely, was to be opposed. It was, after all, the survival of social democracy as the dominant political force among the working classes of Western Europe that had "doomed Communists to the dogmatic-sectarian positions" characteristic of Stalinism: See "Nekotorye voprosy istorii Kominterna," *Novaia i noveishaia istoriia* (1989:2); quotations, 76–79.

With a few notable exceptions, which I discuss elsewhere in this work, the initial reevaluations of Comintern history published during *perestroika* did not reflect extensive "new political thinking" and are both historiographically and politically cautious. For instance, in B. N. Ponomarev, "Stranitsy deiatel'nosti Kominterna," *Novaia i noveishaia istoriia* (1989:2): 118–30, the famous academic historian, principal editor of some two hundred works, and a member of Brezhnev's Politburo, "share[d] his reminiscences" of the Comintern in which he had worked on the staff of the ECCI under Georgii Dimitrov in the years 1937–1943. He criticized Stalin but praised the Comintern for its "glorious past," calling it the "great school" for all Communists (119–20). In Krivoguz, "Sudba i nasledie Kominterna," 3–20, one of the official historians of the Comintern issued what was called "a newly improved, balanced view." He identified Bukharin as "a complex personality," who, though not without faults, was nevertheless a great Communist. He chronicled Stalin's mistakes, but praised the Comintern as the place where the masses of the world were organized for the struggle for democracy and social justice and against Fascism. I. N. Undasynov and Z. P. Iakhimovich, *Kommunisticheskii Internatsional: dostizheniia, proschety, uroki* (Moscow: 1990), relied on monographic literature published in the USSR in the 1960s and 1970s and was intended as a "popular short review" for a *perestroika*-era audience. It attempted to rescue the reputation of the Comintern by blaming Stalin, by characterizing Zinoviev, Trotsky, and Bukharin as dangerous confusionists, and by attributing the salvation of the international Communist movement to the genius of Lenin and those who faithfully followed his teaching.

24. Claudin, *Communist Movement*, 65–67.

25. *First Four Congresses*, 184–203, 274–99, 383–88.

26. Karl Radek, *Der Kampf der Kommunistischen Internationale gegen Versailles und gegen die Offensive des Kapitals* (Hamburg: 1923).

27. Carr, *Bolshevik Revolution*, 3: 449–50; *Socialism in One Country*, 3: 283–93, 490–95; *Foundations*, 3: 144–45; McKenzie, *Comintern and World Revolution*, 51–52.

28. "To the Fourth Congress of the Communist International," 4 November 1922, Lenin, *CW*, 33: 430–32.

29. Bukharin quoted in Sirotkin, "Ot grazhdanskoi voiny k grazhdanskomu miru," 380.

30. Carr, *Bolshevik Revolution*, 3: 443.

31. Moshe Lewin, *Lenin's Last Struggle* (New York: 1968), first indicated the historical importance of these writings. V. I. Startsev, "Political Leaders of the Soviet State in 1922 and Early 1923," *Soviet Studies in History* 28 (1989–90): 5–40, chronicles the vicissitudes of Lenin's physical condition and demonstrates their impact on the struggle for succession among the RCP(B) leadership. For Lenin's reconceptualization of the postwar international situation, see Claudin, *Communist Movement*, 66–71.

32. "Better Fewer, but Better," 2 March 1923, Lenin, *CW*, 33: 487–502.

33. The concept of "achieving genuine communism" that emerged from Lenin's final writings is that of a long transition period, an entire historical epoch of a decade or two or more, during which the prerequisites for genuine Communism would develop. Lenin called these "civilization,"

by which he meant industrial technology and a culturally advanced and civic-minded population. See Lenin, "Better Fewer, but Better," *CW*, 33: 500–501; Lewin, *Lenin's Last Struggle*, 108, 114; Stephen F. Cohen, *Bukharin and the Bolshevik Revolution: A Political Biography, 1888–1938* (New York: 1975), 134–38; and Robert C. Tucker, *Stalin as Revolutionary, 1879–1929: A Study in History and Personality* (New York: 1973), 368–72.

34. "Better Fewer, but Better," Lenin, *CW*, 33: 500–502.

35. Report by Lenin to the Tenth Party Conference, 28 March 1921, *CW*, 32: 437.

36. L. N. Nezhinskii, "Vneshniaia politika sovetskogo gosudarstva v 1917–1921 godakh: kurs na 'mirovuiu revoliutsiu' ili na mirnoe sosushchestvovanie?" *Istoriia SSSR* (1991:6): 3–27.

37. For the incompetencies and failures of the CI, see Alexander Dallin, "The Soviet Union as a Revolutionary Power," in *Perestroika: The Historical Perspective*, ed. Catherine Merridale and Chris Ward (London and New York: 1991), 220–21, 224.

38. Theses and Resolutions of the Third Congress, 29 June–17 July 1921, *Communist International*, 1: 255–56.

39. Speech by Lenin to the Fourth All-Russian Congress of Garment Workers, 6 February 1921, Lenin, *CW*, 32: 113–14; report by Lenin to the Ninth All-Russian Congress of Soviets, 23 December 1921, Lenin, *CW*, 33: 145.

40. Lazitch and Drachkovitch, *Lenin and the Comintern*, 529–30.

41. Helmut Gruber, *International Communism in the Era of Lenin: A Documentary History* (Ithaca, N.Y.: 1967), 316.

42. Werner T. Angress, *Stillborn Revolution: The Communist Bid for Power in Germany, 1921–1923* (Princeton, N.J.: 1963), 109–110.

43. Theses and Resolutions of the Third Congress, 29 June–17 July 1921, *Communist International*, 1: 230, 238, 242–43.

44. The premises on which "united fronts" were to be based were discussed at the Third Comintern Congress in June–July 1921. The strategy was adopted by the ECCI in December 1921. The "Theses on the United Front" were published by the Fourth Comintern Congress in November–December 1922. See *First Four Congresses*, 400–409.

45. For Radek's reports, see Dietrich Möller, *Karl Radek in Deutschland: Revolutionär, Intrigant, Diplomat* (Cologne: 1976), nos. 23, 28–29; also Warren Lerner, *Karl Radek: The Last Internationalist* (Stanford, Calif.: 1970), 112–17.

46. For the theory and strategy of the "united front," see Claudin, *Communist Movement*, 145–53; Wolfgang Eichwede, *Revolution und Internationale Politik: Zur kommunistischen Interpretation der kapitalistischen Welt, 1921–1925* (Cologne: 1971), 7–19; Frank, *Histoire de l'Internationale Communiste*, 223–29. F. I. Firsov, "K voprosu o taktike edinogo fronta v

1921–1924 gg," *Voprosy Istorii KPSS* (1987:10): 113–27, is based on materials in the Central Party Archives of the Institute of Marxism-Leninism. It was actually written in 1964, near the end of the Khrushchev thaw, by one of the leading official party specialists on Comintern history. The tone and approach are those of the confining Brezhnev conservative orthodoxy emerging at that time, rather than those of *glasnost*, which was emerging when it was finally printed.

47. Lenin quoted in Carr, *Foundations*, 3: 157.

48. Zinoviev quoted in Carr, *Bolshevik Revolution*, 3: 420.

49. Theses and Resolutions of the Third Congress, 29 June–17 July, 1921, *Communist International*, 1: 256.

50. Zinoviev and Stalin first associated social democracy with Fascism in January 1924 during the reaction against Socialist-Communist "united fronts from above" that took place in the wake of the abortive Communist revolution in Germany the previous November. Stalin stated at this time that "there had occurred a major shift of the petty bourgeois social-democratic forces to the side of counterrevolution, into the fascist camp." From this he concluded that the best tactic for the Comintern to adopt was "not a coalition with social democracy but lethal battle against it, as the pillar of fascisized power." See Firsov in "Nekotorye voprosy istorii Kominterna," 89. At the Fifth Comintern Congress in June–July, the leadership of the Russian party led a chorus of denunciation that would last for years. Zinoviev: "The Fascists are the right hand and the Social Democrats are the left hand of the bourgeoisie." Stalin: "Social Democracy is objectively *the moderate wing of Fascism*." See Claudin, *Communist Movement*, 152–53. The exact term *social-fascism* was first used in April 1929, in an editorial in *Kommunisticheskii Internatsional*, according to Firsov, "Nekotorye voprosy istorii Kominterna," 89.

51. Sirotkin, "Ot grazhdanskoi voiny k grazhdanskomu miru," 384; Lenin quoted in Lazitch and Drachkovitch, *Lenin and the Comintern*, 534.

52. Chicherin quoted in S. Iu. Vygodskii, *Vneshniaia politika SSSR, 1924–1929* (Moscow: 1963), 292. A well-documented monograph, Vygodskii's work reflected the Khrushchev thaw (1956–64) and the revitalization of the doctrine of peaceful coexistence at this time. It superseded the faithful Stalinist work on this period, A. A. Troianovskii, *Vneshniaia politika SSSR, 1924–1926* (Moscow: 1945). And it is a bolder and livelier work than the diplomatic history done by party scholars during the Brezhnev-Suslov period that followed, for example, A. A. Gromyko and B. N. Ponomarev (eds.), *Istoriia vneshnei politiki SSSR 1917–1980* (Moscow: 1980–81); English translation, *Soviet Foreign Policy, 1917–1980* (Moscow: 1981). Initial discussions concerning a replacement for this work, one that would be informed by the values of *glasnost*, took place in 1988. See "Kompleksnaia programma 'Istoriia vneshnei politiki SSSR i mezhdunarodnykh otnoshenii,'" *Novaia i noveishaia istoriia* (1988:2): 63–81.

3. REVOLUTIONARY RUSSIA AND ISLAMIC ASIA

1. V. I. Lenin, *The National Liberation Movement in the East* (3d rev. ed.; Moscow: 1969). Stalin's writings on "the national and colonial question" actually predate those of Lenin: Demetrio Boersner, *The Bolsheviks and the National and Colonial Question 1917–1928* (Westport, Conn.: 1981), 32–58; hereafter cited as *National and Colonial Question*.

2. "The Socialist Revolution and the Right of Nations to Self-determination: Theses," April 1916, Lenin, *CW*, 22: 150–52.

3. This point is stressed by R. A. Ulyanovskii in the preface to Ulyanovskii, ed. *The Comintern and the East: The Struggle for the Leninist Strategy and Tactics in National Liberation Movements* (Moscow: 1979), 6–9.

4. A. B. Reznikov, *The Comintern and the East: Strategy and Tactics in the National Liberation Movement* (Moscow: 1984), 50–51.

5. Boersner, *National and Colonial Question*, 38–39, 45.

6. Bukharin's statement to the Eighth Party Congress, March 1919: Boersner, *National and Colonial Question*, 62.

7. Alexandre A. Bennigsen and S. Enders Wimbush, *Muslim National Communism in the Soviet Union: A Revolutionary Strategy for the Colonial World* (Chicago: 1979), 51–57.

8. "Theses on the National and Colonial Question" (original draft version), Lenin, *CW*, 31: 144–51.

9. A complete record of the deliberations of the Second Comintern Congress, including relevant reports, theses, and the stenographic record of the proceedings, has been published in *Second Congress*. In the 1970s, Soviet scholars reexamined the debate on "the national and colonial question" at the Second Congress on the basis of archival research: see A. B. Reznikov, *Comintern and the East*, 51–87.

10. Charles B. McLane, *Soviet Strategies in Southeast Asia: An Exploration of Eastern Policy under Lenin and Stalin* (Princeton, N.J.: 1966), 12–24, offers a penetrating analysis of the issues debated at the Second Congress.

11. Minutes of the meeting of the Commission on the National and Colonial Questions, 25 July 1920, *Second Congress*, 865–66; also Roy's revised supplementary theses and report, 26 July 1920, *Second Congress*, 218–24.

12. For Roy's original draft supplementary theses, see Gangadhar M. Adhikari, ed., *Documents of the History of the Communist Party of India* (New Delhi: 1971), 1: 173–88.

13. Sobhanlal Datta Gupta, *Comintern, India, and the Colonial Question, 1920–37* (Calcutta: 1980), 14–51, examines the Lenin-Roy debate from a close reading of the major and minor texts.

14. Stenographic record of debate, 28 July 1920, *Second Congress*, 227.

15. On this and other views on revolution in Asia expressed by Lenin at

the congress, see his "Report on the National and Colonial Questions," *Second Congress*, 211–22.

16. Reznikov, *Comintern and the East*, 74–75.

17. Datta Gupta, *Comintern, India, and the Colonial Question*, 21–70, emphasizes the persistence with which Roy held to and developed the views he first expressed in embryonic form at the Second Comintern Congress.

18. Quoted in Stephen White, *Britain and the Bolshevik Revolution: A Study in the Politics of Diplomacy, 1920–1924* (London: 1979), 120.

19. Lenin's revised theses, adopted 28 July 1920, *Second Congress*, 283–90; Lenin's report on National and Colonial Questions," 26 July 1920, *Second Congress*, 213.

20. *Second Congress*, 846–55.

21. Trotsky quoted in Boersner, *National and Colonial Question*, 66.

22. Light, *Soviet Theory of International Relations*, 81–90.

23. See, for example, Donald M. Lowe, *The Function of "China" in Marx, Lenin, and Mao* (Berkeley, Calif.: 1966), 54–81. The exception is Stanley W. Page, whose thesis is that sometime in the summer or fall of 1919 "Lenin arrived at a concept regarding the course of world revolution differing radically from that which he had previously held." He became an "Easterner" who believed that the revolution in Europe could not succeed unless and until it was preceded by revolution in Asia: "Lenin, Prophet of World Revolution from the East," *Russian Review* 11 (1952): 67–75; *Lenin and World Revolution* (New York: 1959), 143, 152; *The Geopolitics of Leninism* (Boulder, Colo. and New York: 1982), 167–68, 187–88.

24. A. B. Reznikov, "Strategy and Tactics of the Communist International in the National and Colonial Question," in R. A. Ulyanovskii, ed., *Comintern and the East*, 154–55; and Reznikov, *Comintern and the East*, 87.

25. "Report on the Tactics of the RCP" to the Third Congress of the Communist International, 5 July 1921, Lenin, *CW*, 32: 478–79, 481–82.

26. "The Question of Nationalities or 'Autonomisation,' " 30–31 December 1922, Lenin, *CW*, 36: 605–611.

27. Quoted in Ronald G. Suny, "Don't Paint Nationalism Red. National Revolution and Socialist Internationalism: The Comintern and the Baku Congress of the Peoples of the East," paper delivered to the American Historical Association, December 1989, p. 29.

28. Appeal to the Muslims of Russia and the East, 3 December 1917: Basil Dmytryshyn and Frederick Cox, *The Soviet Union and the Middle East: A Documentary Record of Afghanistan, Iran, and Turkey, 1917–1985* (Princeton, N.J.: 1987), 3–6; hereafter cited as *Soviet Documents on the Middle East*.

29. Suny, "Don't Paint Nationalism Red," 1–2.

30. Debo, *Survival and Consolidation*, 176–80; Lenin quoted, 177.

31. A. N. Kheifets, *Sovetskaia Rossiia i sopredelnye strany Vostoka, 1918–1920* (Moscow: 1964), 135, 159–60.

32. Ronald Grigor Suny, *The Making of the Georgian Nation* (Bloomington, Ind. and Stanford, Calif.: 1988), 207–219.

33. Seymour Becker, *Russia's Protectorates in Central Asia: Bukhara and Khiva, 1865–1924* (Cambridge, Mass.: 1968), 273–95; Hélène Carrère d'Encausse, *Islam and the Russian Empire: Reform and Revolution in Central Asia* (London: 1988), 148–66. Dov. B. Yaroshevski, "The Central Government and Peripheral Opposition in Khiva, 1910–24," in *The USSR and the Muslim World: Issues in Domestic and Foreign Policy,* ed. Yaacov Roi (London: 1984), utilizes Russian/Soviet archival sources.

34. Sultan Galiev quoted in Bennigsen and Wimbush, *Muslim National Communism,* 54–55.

35. Appeal to the peoples of the Middle East, September 1920: *Soviet Documents on the Middle East,* 7–15.

36. Stephen White, "Communism and the East: The Baku Congress, 1920," *Slavic Review* 33 (1974): 491–514; hereafter "Baku Congress"; Suny, "Don't Paint Nationalism Red," 20–29.

37. White, "Baku Congress," 506–510.

38. Bennigsen and Wimbush, *Muslim National Communism,* 57.

39. Richard H. Ullman, *Anglo-Soviet Relations, 1917–1921* (Princeton, N.J.: 1961–72), 3: 350–54.

40. For renunciation of the Anglo-Russian Agreement of 1907, 27 January 1918, see *Soviet Documents on the Middle East,* 244–46; for renunciation of all tsarist claims on Persia and the appeal for friendly relations, 26 June 1919, ibid., 246–49. Also Harish Kapur, *Soviet Russia and Asia, 1917–1927: A Study of Soviet Policy towards Turkey, Iran, and Afghanistan* (Geneva: 1966), 160–67.

41. Trotsky to Lenin and Chicherin, 20 April 1920: Lev Trotskii, *The Trotsky Papers, 1917–1922,* ed. Jan M. Meijer (The Hague: 1964–71), vol. 2, no. 522, p. 147; hereafter *Trotsky Papers.*

42. Ullman, *Anglo-Soviet Relations,* 3: 262–67; Debo, *Survival and Consolidation,* 184–87.

43. M. I. Volodarskii, *Sovety i ikh iuzhnye sosedi Iran i Afganistan 1917–1933* (London: 1985). The author is a Soviet émigré historian.

44. Volodarskii, *Sovety i ikh iuzhnye sosedi,* 65–66; Bennigsen and Wimbush, *Muslim National Communism,* 79–80, 218–19; Sepeher Zabih, *The Communist Movement in Iran* (Berkeley, Calif.: 1966), 13–45.

45. Kuchik Khan quoted in Kapur, *Soviet Russia and Asia,* 175. During the World War, Kuchik Khan had been armed and funded by the Germans and the Turks; he had purchased weapons from the troops of the defeated and retreating tsarist army in 1917; he had made previous contact with the *Adalet* and *Hummet,* the Bolshevik-leaning Azeri, and Persian communist organizations in Baku.

46. Trotsky quoted in Kapur, *Soviet Russia and Asia,* 176.

47. Volodarskii, *Sovety i ikh iuzhnye sosedi,* 69.

48. Trotsky to Chicherin, 4 June 1920: *Trotsky Papers,* vol. 2, nos. 556, 209.

49. Volodarskii, *Sovety i ikh iuzhnye sosedi,* 68–69.

50. The Tehran government protested angrily. The NKID's reply was astutely employed by Chicherin to expose the complicity of Stalin and his group: Volodarskii, *Sovety i ikh iuzhnye sosedi,* 69–72.

51. Bennigsen and Wimbush, *Muslim National Communism,* 80.

52. Volodarskii, *Sovety i ikh iuzhnye sosedi,* 68–69.

53. Kapur, *Soviet Russia and Asia,* 177–81.

54. Stephen White, "Soviet Russia and the Asian Revolution, 1917–1924," *Review of International Studies* 10 (1984): 223–25.

55. Volodarskii, *Sovety i ikh iuzhnye sosedi,* 75–81, 92–93; Kapur, *Soviet Russia and Asia,* 182–88. For the treaty negotiations, see Debo, *Survival and Consolidation,* 368–71.

56. Treaty between Russian Socialist Republic and Persia, 26 February 1921: *Soviet Documents on the Middle East,* 262–63.

57. Volodarskii, *Sovety i ikh iuzhnye sosedi,* 72.

58. Volodarskii, *Sovety i ikh iuzhnye sosedi,* 95; Kapur, *Soviet Russia and Asia,* 178–81; Bennigsen and Wimbush, *Muslim National Communism,* 80; Martin Sicker, *The Bear and the Lion: Soviet Imperialism and Iran* (New York: 1988), 45.

59. White, "Baku Congress," 512–13.

60. On Soviet-Afghan relations, see Volodarskii, *Sovety i ikh iuzhnye sosedi,* and "First Steps in Soviet Diplomacy towards Afghanistan, 1917–21," in *The USSR and the Muslim World,* ed. Yaacov Roi, 215–25; Ludwig W. Adamec, *Afghanistan, 1900–1923: A Diplomatic History* (Berkeley, Calif.: 1967) and *Afghanistan's Foreign Affairs to the Mid-Twentieth Century: Relations with the USSR, Germany, and Britain* (Tucson, Ariz.: 1974); and Kapur, *Soviet Russia and Asia.* The Soviet work is L. B. Teplinskii, *Sovetsko-Afganskie otnosheniia, 1919–1987* (Moscow: 1988).

61. Curzon quoted in White, *Britain and the Bolshevik Revolution,* 91.

62. Adamec, *Afghanistan, 1900–1923,* 115.

63. Mark Jacobsen, "The Modernization of the Indian Army, 1925–1939," doctoral dissertation, University of California, Irvine, 1979, 119–33.

64. Volodarskii, "First Steps," 217.

65. Red forces isolated in Tashkent actually transmitted the texts by radio before the letters reached their destinations: Volodarskii, *Sovety i ikh iuzhnye sosedi,* 161–62.

66. Note on the establishment of diplomatic relations, 27 May 1919: *Soviet Documents on the Middle East,* 87–88.

67. First Soviet technological assistance to Afghanistan, 29 May 1920: *Soviet Documents on the Middle East,* 89.

68. Volodarskii, "First Steps," 218.

69. After having been one of the blank spots in Soviet history for decades, the life and career of Raskolnikov became the object of considerable attention during *glasnost*. See, for instance, V. K. Arkhipenko, "Fedor Raskolnikov" in *Otkryvaia novye stranitsy: Mezhdunarodnye voprosy: sobytiia i liudi*, ed. A. A. Iskenderov (Moscow: 1989), 309; also Branko Lazitch, *Biographical Dictionary of the Comintern* (Stanford, Calif.: 1973), 331–32, 337.

70. Lenin quoted in Volodarskii, "First Steps," 218.

71. Treaty between Russian Socialist Federative Republic and Afghanistan, 28 February 1921: *Soviet Documents on the Middle East*, 90–94.

72. Volodarskii, *Sovety i ikh iuzhnye sosedi*, 168.

73. Kapur, *Soviet Russia and Asia*, 228–29.

74. Milan Hauner, *What Is Asia to Us? Russia's Asian Heartland Yesterday and Today* (Boston: 1990), 90.

75. Glenda Fraser, "Basmachi I," *Central Asian Survey* 6, 1 (1987): 1–73, and "Basmachi II," *Central Asian Survey* 6, 2 (1987): 7–42, utilizes British Foreign Office records of reports by special agents and informants on the scene to reconstruct the events of the *basmachi* rebellion in considerable detail. See also Alexandre A. Bennigsen et al., *The Soviet Union and Muslim Guerrilla Wars, 1920–1981: Lessons for Afghanistan* (Santa Monica, Calif.: 1981).

76. Enver quoted in Fraser, "Basmachi I," 58–59, and "Basmachi II," 37–38.

77. Quoted in Volodarskii, *Sovety i ikh iuzhnye sosedi*, 178.

78. Ibid., 180.

79. Volodarskii, *Sovety i ikh iuzhnye sosedi*, 180–81.

80. Vartan Gregorian, *The Emergence of Modern Afghanistan: Politics of Reform and Modernization, 1880–1916* (Stanford, Calif.: 1969), 239–61.

81. Kapur, *Soviet Russia and Asia*, 222, 238–39; Volodarskii, *Sovety i ikh iuzhnye sosedi*, 182.

82. Compare Gregorian, *The Emergence of Modern Afghanistan*, 237–38.

83. Peter Hopkirk, *Setting the East Ablaze: Lenin's Dream of an Empire in Asia* (London: 1984).

84. For the Comintern, M. N. Roy, and India, see Gene D. Overstreet and Marshall Windmiller, *Communism in India* (Berkeley, Calif.: 1959), 21–81; Robert H. Donaldson, *Soviet Policy toward India: Ideology and Strategy* (Cambridge, Mass.: 1974), 13–18; John Patrick Haithcox, *Communism and Nationalism in India: M. N. Roy and Comintern Policy, 1920–1939* (Princeton, N.J.: 1971), 11–43; and M. N. Roy, *M. N. Roy's Memoirs* (Bombay and New York: 1964).

85. Hopkirk, *Setting the East Ablaze*, 108–22, is a highly readable account of Roy's activities; also Haithcox, *Communism and Nationalism in India*, 20–25.

86. Gregorian, *Emergence of Modern Afghanistan*, 235–36.

87. Donaldson, *Soviet Policy toward India*, 6–7.

88. Instructions to the Soviet Representative in Afghanistan, 3 June 1921: *Soviet Documents on the Middle East*, 95–98.

89. Volodarskii, *Sovety i ikh iuzhnye sosedi*, 173–74.

90. Quoted in Ullman, *Anglo-Soviet Relations*, 3: 342.

91. For Afghan negotiations with Britain and Russia, see Adamec, *Afghanistan, 1900–1923*, 136–66.

92. Quoted in Tilak Raj Sareen, *Russian Revolution and India: A Study of Soviet Policy towards the Indian National Movement, 1922–29* (New Delhi: 1978), 34–43; also Overstreet and Windmiller, *Communism in India*, 67–68, and Haithcox, *Communism and Nationalism in India*, 34–36.

93. White, *Britain and the Bolshevik Revolution*, 129.

4. FIRST DÉTENTE

1. Note from Chicherin to the Allied Powers, 18 October 1921, *Soviet Documents*, 1: 270–72. Chicherin's proposals were ratified by the Ninth Soviet Congress on 1 January 1922. In his report to the congress, he emphasized that the Russian government was not accepting the principle of war debt repayment but was, rather, offering an initial concession as a way of opening negotiations toward a comprehensive settlement with the Entente powers and the United States: Annual Report by the RSFSR People's Commissariat of Foreign Affairs for the Ninth Congress of Soviets (1920–1921), *International Affairs* (Moscow) (1990:2): 146. The Soviet government formally accepted the Allied invitation to a conference at Genoa on January 8: Note from Chicherin to the Supreme Allied Council, *Soviet Documents*, 1: 287–88.

2. Carole Fink, *The Genoa Conference: European Diplomacy, 1921–1922* (Chapel Hill, N.C.: 1984), and Stephen White, *The Origins of Détente: The Genoa Conference and Soviet-Western Relations, 1921–1922* (Cambridge and New York: 1985) both offer full narratives of the Genoa Conference and its antecedents based on admirable research. White focuses on relations between Russia and Europe, whereas Fink adopts an international/multinational approach. *Genoa, Rapallo, and European Reconstruction in 1922*, ed. Carole Fink, Axel Frohn, and Jurgen Heideking (Cambridge: 1991) incorporates the findings of an international group of scholars. Evgeny M. Chossudovsky's "Genoa Revisited: Russia and Coexistence," *Foreign Affairs* 50 (1972): 554–77, is an argument for détente written by a Soviet diplomat and senior member of the United Nations Secretariat.

3. Timothy Edward O'Connor, *Diplomacy and Revolution: G. V. Chicherin and Soviet Foreign Affairs, 1918–1930* (Ames, Iowa: 1988), 80; hereafter cited as *Chicherin*.

4. The projects of German industry and Walter Rathenau's Russian

policy are discussed in depth with precision and insight in Robert Himmer, "Rathenau, Russia, and Rapallo," *Central European History* 9 (1976): 146–83; Rathenau quoted, 171. See also Ernst Laubach, *Die Politik der Kabinette Wirth 1921/22* (Lubeck: 1968), and Hélène Seppain, *Contrasting US and German Attitudes to Soviet Trade, 1917–91: Politics by Economic Means* (London: 1992), 32–54.

5. On the international consortium project, see Himmer, "Rathenau, Russia, and Rapallo," 154–58; White, *Origins of Détente*, 38–51, 71–72; and Fink, *Genoa Conference*, 101–105.

6. Lloyd George's Grand Design is revealed fully in Carole Fink, "European Politics and Security at the Genoa Conference of 1922," in *German Nationalism and the European Response, 1890–1945*, ed. Carole Fink, Isabel V. Hull, and MacGregor Knox (Norman, Okla.: 1985), 136–37, 149, 151, and in *Genoa Conference* 191–97. Marc Trachtenberg has written that the readiness with which Lloyd George gave up on his Grand Design suggests that it may have been completely fatuous: See his review of Fink, *Genoa Conference*, in *Journal of Modern History* 58 (1986): 712. For the making of Britain's Genoa policy, see Andrew J. Williams, "The Genoa Conference of 1922: Lloyd George and the Politics of Recognition," in *Genoa, Rapallo, and European Reconstruction*, 29–47.

7. Widely discussed; see, in particular, Neil Harding, *Lenin's Political Thought* (New York: 1978), 2: 243–49.

8. Report by Lenin to the Eighth All-Russian Congress of Soviets, 21 December 1920, in Lenin, *CW*, 31: 475; Report by Lenin to the Ninth All-Russian Congress of Soviets, 23 December 1921, *CW*, 33: 146.

9. Robert C. Tucker, *The Soviet Political Mind: Stalinism and Post-Stalin Change* (rev. ed.; New York: 1971), 213.

10. Zinovii S. Sheinis, "Polpred B. E. Stein," *Novaia i noveishaia istoriia* (1991:1): 101, 107.

11. Chicherin to Lenin, 24 October 1921, first published in *Izvestiia Tsk KPSS* (1990:4): 189–90.

12. Zinovii S. Sheinis, *Maxim Litvinov* (Moscow: 1990), 151–60.

13. Lenin quoted in Carr and Davies, *Foundations of a Planned Economy, 1926–1929*, 3: 120.

14. For the Soviet negotiating stance, see report by Chicherin to the Central Executive Committee, 27 January 1922, *Soviet Documents*, 1: 291, and Chicherin's opening statement at Genoa, 10 April 1923, *Soviet Documents*, 1: 298–301. For Soviet strategy and preparations for Genoa, see Fink, *Genoa Conference*, 96–97; White, *Origins of Détente*, 107–109; O'Connor, *Chicherin*, 82–85; quotations from Walter C. Clemens, Jr., "Lenin on Disarmament," *Slavic Review* 23 (1964): 512–13.

15. For Lenin's recommendation of Keynes, see Ia. G. Temkin, "Marksisty i patsifisty (Iz opyta vzaimootnoshenii)," *Voprosy Istorii KPSS* (1987:8): 67.

16. Stephen A. Schuker, "American Policy toward Debts and Reconstruction at Genoa, 1922," in *Genoa, Rapallo, and European Reconstruction*, 95–122.

17. Himmer, "Rathenau, Russia, and Rapallo," 161–64, 169–70; White, *Origins of Détente*, 76–77, 151, 153; Chicherin quoted, 76.

18. *Pravda*, 15 October 1921, 11 November 1921, 3 January 1922; *Die Rote Fahne*, 3 December 1921: reprinted in Möller, *Karl Radek in Deutschland*, nos. 24–27; also Marie-Luise Goldbach, *Karl Radek und die deutschsowjetischen Beziehungen, 1918–1923* (Bonn-Bad Godesberg: 1973), 9–19, 109–116.

19. Anne Hogenhuis-Selverstoff, "French Plans for the Reconstruction of Russia: A History and Evaluation," in Fink, Frohn, and Heideking (eds.) *Genoa, Rapallo, and European Reconstruction*, 131–47.

20. For opposition to the Genoa project in Washington, Paris, and London, see Fink, *Genoa Conference*, 47–49, 82–87, 94, 97–100, 133–42; White, *Origins of Détente*, 68–70, 75–76, 83–94, 127–28.

21. For the major proposals and exchanges made during the Genoa Conference, see Allied Proposal to the Soviets, 15 April 1922, *Documents on British Foreign Policy, 1919–1939*, ser. 1, v. 19, no. 74 (appendix); and Chicherin's letter, 20 April 1922, no. 81 (appendix); hereafter cited as *DBFP*.

22. The Cannes resolutions, 6 January 1922: *DBFP*, ser. 1, v. 19, no. 6. The London Experts Report, 28 March 1922: *DBFP*, ser. 1, v. 19, no. 56 (appendix).

23. Soviet memorandum, 20 April 1922, quoted in White, *Origins of Détente*, 172.

24. For divisions within the Soviet delegation, see White, *Origins of Détente*, 39, 106, 112–13, 169–73, 180–81.

25. For Soviet counterproposals, 24 April 1922, see *Soviet Documents*, 1: 301–303; *DBFP*, ser. 1, v. 19, no. 91 (annex). For Chicherin's continued efforts to sustain negotiations, *Soviet Documents*, 1: 306–18.

26. Speech by Lenin to Congress of Metalworkers, 6 March 1922, in Lenin, *CW*, 33: 220–23.

27. Startsev, "Political Leaders of the Soviet State in 1922 and Early 1923," 7–9, 11.

28. Trush, *Soviet Foreign Policy*, 195–97; Lenin quoted in White, *Origins of Détente*, 181 (emphasis in original).

29. Fink, *Genoa Conference*, 303.

30. White, *Origins of Détente*, 210–12.

31. For antagonisms within the Entente, see Fink, *Genoa Conference*, 123; White, *Origins of Détente*, 28, 206.

32. White, *Origins of Détente*, 88, 95–96.

33. Ibid., 43, 92–93.

34. Lenin quoted in Sheinis, *Litvinov*, 158.

35. Press interview given by Chicherin, *Observer*, 20 August 1922, in *Soviet Documents*, 1: 328–29.

36. For the draft of the telegram submitted by Lenin to the Politburo on 9 May and sent to Genoa, see Trush, *Soviet Foreign Policy,* 196.

37. Sheinis, *Litvinov,* 175.

38. Resolution of the Central Executive Committee, 17 May 1922: *Soviet Documents,* 1: 318–20. In the writings of party historians during the 1960s, the Rapallo relationship became an example of the benefits the Federal Republic of Germany could gain from closer relations with the USSR: See George Ginsburgs, "The Theme of Rapallo in Post-War Soviet-West German Relations," *Soviet Union/Union Soviétique* 13 (1986): 357–66. Documents on the origins of the relationship were compiled from the archives of both the USSR and the German Democratic Republic: German Democratic Republic. Ministerium für Auswärtige Angelegenheiten der DDR. *Deutsch-sowjetische Beziehungen von den Verhandlungen in Brest-Litowsk bis zum Abschluss des Rapallovertrages; Dokumentensammlung* (Berlin: 1967–71).

39. For a to-the-point discussion of "the Rapallo legend" and of the significance of the treaty for German foreign relations, see Eberhard Kolb, *The Weimar Republic* (London and Boston: 1988), 172–74; also the highly nuanced discussion of the sources of German Rapallo policy in John Hiden, *Germany and Europe 1919–1939* (2d ed.; London and New York: 1993), 111–17. On German diplomacy, see the works discussed in Kolb, especially Hartmut Pogge von Strandmann, "Rapallo—Strategy in Preventative Diplomacy: New Sources and New Interpretations," in Volker R. Berghahn and Martin Kitchen, eds., *Germany in the Age of Total War* (London: 1981), 123–46, and Peter Krüger, "A Rainy Day, April 1922: The Rapallo Treaty and the Cloudy Perspective for German Foreign Policy," in Fink, Frohn, and Heideking, *Genoa, Rapallo, and European Reconstruction,* 49–64.

40. Startsev, "Political Leaders," 11–30.

41. Hugh D. Phillips, *Between the Revolution and the West: A Political Biography of Maxim M. Litvinov* (Boulder, Colo.: 1992), 71–85.

42. Phillips, *Between the Revolution and the West,* 73; compare Jiri Hochman, *The Soviet Union and the Failure of Collective Security, 1934–1938* (Ithaca, N.Y.: 1984), 31–33.

43. Sheinis, *Litvinov,* 182–83.

44. Ibid., 183–84.

45. Hodgson to Gregory, 29 September 1921, *DBFP,* ser. 1, vol. 20, no. 427.

46. During the Khrushchev thaw Chicherin's reputation was rescued by Andrei Gromyko from the oblivion to which it had been consigned during the Stalin era. His articles and speeches from the 1920s were published as Georgii Chicherin, *Stati i rechi po voprosam mezhdunarodnoi politiki* (Moscow: 1961), and two biographies were commissioned—S. V. Zarnitskii and A. N. Sergeev, *Chicherin* (Moscow: 1966), and I. Gorokhov, L. Zamiatin, and I. Zemskov, *G. V. Chicherin—Diplomat leninskoi shkoly* (Moscow: 1966). Nevertheless, Timothy O'Connor's *Chicherin* is unsurpassed; and

Evgeny M. Chossudovsky, "Lenin and Chicherin: The Beginnings of Soviet Foreign Policy and Diplomacy," *Millennium* 3 (1974): 1–16, remains a valuable contribution.

47. Gorokhov, Zamiatin, and Zemskov, *Chicherin*, 23.

48. Mikoian quoted in Sheinis, *Litvinov*, 152.

5. SOVIET RUSSIA AND THE BRITISH EMPIRE

1. Curzon quoted in Stephen White, *Britain and the Bolshevik Revolution* (London: 1979), 85–86.

2. Richard H. Ullman, *Anglo-Soviet Relations* (Princeton, N.J.: 1961–73), 3: 397–453, is effectively supplemented by Debo, *Survival and Consolidation*, 248–71, 314–19, and 328–37, particularly with regard to the formulation of Soviet policy, and by Timothy O'Connor, *The Engineer of Revolution: L. B. Krasin and the Bolsheviks, 1870–1926* (Boulder, Colo.: 1992), regarding relations between Krasin, who negotiated the treaty, and Lenin, Chicherin, Litvinov, and Kamenev.

3. Quoted in White, *Britain and the Bolshevik Revolution*, 91.

4. Curzon quoted in White, *Britain and the Bolshevik Revolution*, 86–87. For face-to-face negotiations between the British and Soviet delegations, 31 May–7 June, 29 June, and 21 December, see *DBFP*, ser. 1, vol. 8, chaps. 3, 6, and 15. Notes were exchanged on 30 June and 7 July 1920; additional notes were dispatched from Curzon to Chicherin on 1 and 9 October; and there was a final exchange of notes on 4 and 25 February 1921. The texts of these notes, which were made public at the time, are not reprinted in *Documents on British Foreign Policy*, for which see *DBFP*, ser. 1, vol. 12, 679–82. Narrative in Ullman, *Anglo-Soviet Relations*, 3: 399–401, 427–30, 443–44.

5. Text reprinted in Ullman, *Anglo-Soviet Relations*, 3: 474–78.

6. Also reprinted in Ullman, *Anglo-Soviet Relations*, 3: 479–82.

7. Debo, *Survival and Consolidation*, 317.

8. Quoted in White, *Britain and the Bolshevik Revolution*, 104.

9. Note to Soviet Government, 7 September 1921, *DBFP*, ser. 1, vol. 20, no. 414.

10. Ullman, *Anglo-Soviet Relations*, 3: 265–314.

11. Christopher M. Andrew, *Her Majesty's Secret Service: The Making of the British Intelligence Community* (New York: 1986), 262, 273; and Christopher M. Andrew and Oleg Gordievsky, *KGB: The Inside Story of Its Foreign Operations from Lenin to Gorbachev* (New York: 1990), 76–79.

12. "Memorandum by Earl Curzon on the Krasin Negotiations," ca. 14 February 1921, *DBFP*, ser. 1, vol. 12, no. 835; Ullman, *Anglo-Soviet Relations*, 3: 445–46.

13. Hopkirk, *Setting the East Ablaze*, chaps. 1–6.

14. Andrew, *Her Majesty's Secret Service*, 277, 280.

15. "Reply from Litvinov to Curzon's Note Alleging Soviet Violations of the Anglo-Russian Treaty," *Soviet Documents*, 1: 257–62.

16. Draft reply to the Soviet government, 27 October 1921, *DBFP*, ser. 1, vol. 20, no. 347. As a result of this incident the organizational structure of British intelligence was changed, and the procedures for interpreting intelligence were reformed: Andrew, *Her Majesty's Secret Service*, 280–85; White, *Britain and the Bolshevik Revolution*, 104–109.

17. Moscow Treaty between the Russian Socialist Republic and Persia, 26 February 1921, *Soviet Documents on the Middle East*, 262; treaty between the Russian Socialist Federative Republic and Afghanistan, 28 February 1921, *Soviet Documents on the Middle East*, 90.

18. Instructions to the Soviet Representative in Afghanistan, 3 June 1921, *Soviet Documents on the Middle East*, 97.

19. Stephen White, "Soviet Russia and the Asian Revolution, 1917–1924," *Review of International Studies* 10 (1984): 220–21; "Baku Congress," 504.

20. Lenin and Kamenev voted in favor of Chicherin's request; Molotov abstained; Zinoviev was absent: "From the Party Archives," *Izvestiia TsK KPSS* 1990, no. 4, p. 181.

21. Andrew, *Her Majesty's Secret Service*, 291–92.

22. Mikhail I. Volodarskii, *Sovety i ikh iuzhnye sosedi Iran i Afganistan, 1917–1933* (London: 1985), 87.

23. John D. Gregory quoted in White, *Britain and the Bolshevik Revolution*, 157–58. Gregory's memoirs, *On the Edge of Diplomacy: Rambles and Reflections, 1902–1928* (London: 1929), are not revealing on matters of policy formulation.

24. Curzon to Hodgson, 2 May 1921, *DBFP*, ser. 1, vol. 25, no. 53.

25. Andrew, *Her Majesty's Secret Service*, 292–93.

26. Hodgson to Curzon, 10 May 1923, *DBFP*, ser. 1, vol. 25, no. 60.

27. Hodgson to Curzon, 13 May 1923, *DBFP*, ser. 1, vol. 25, no. 68.

28. Hodgson to Curzon, 13 May 1923, *DBFP*, ser. 1, vol. 25, no. 67.

29. For Curzon's meeting with Krasin, 17 May 1923, see *DBFP*, ser. 1, vol. 25, no. 72; O'Connor, *Engineer of Revolution*, 275–76.

30. Gregory to Krasin, 29 May 1923, *DBFP*, ser. 1 vol. 25, no. 80.

31. Krasin to Curzon, 9 June 1921, *DBFP*, ser. 1, vol. 25, no. 94. Chicherin made one exception. He refused to withdraw Raskolnikov and Shumiatskii—even when offered ingenious face-saving measures by the Foreign Office. He regarded this demand as an unacceptable infringement on the right of the Soviet government to control the conduct of its foreign relations. Shumiatskii remained at his post in Tehran. Raskolnikov, against whom the most serious charges contained in the ultimatum were made, was not recalled officially, but he was transferred to another post: Memorandum from Curzon to Krasin, 13 June 1923, *DBFP*, ser. 1, vol. 25, no. 100.

32. White, *Britain and the Bolshevik Revolution*, 168.

33. Andrew, *Her Majesty's Secret Service,* 296, citing intercepts by British intelligence.

34. Trotsky to Chicherin, 4 June 1920, *Trotsky Papers,* vol. 2, no. 556, p. 209.

35. Chicherin quoted in Fiddick, *Russia's Retreat from Poland,* 51.

36. For Lenin's mediation of the disagreement between Krasin and Chicherin, see Debo, *Survival and Consolidation,* 315–19, 328–33; Chicherin quoted on 329.

37. Chicherin quoted in Ullman, *Anglo-Soviet Relations,* 3: 427, citing an intercept by British intelligence.

38. Bennigsen and Wimbush, *Muslim National Communism,* 75–77.

39. Ibid., chap. 4.

40. Bennigsen, *Soviet Strategy and Islam* (New York: 1989), 8–22.

41. This is the central conclusion of Stephen White's research on the topic; see especially his "Soviet Russia and the Asian Revolution."

42. The treaties are reproduced in *Soviet Documents on the Middle East,* 90–94, 260–71, and 473–80.

43. White, "Soviet Russia and the Asian Revolution"; *Britain and the Bolshevik Revolution,* 134–38.

44. Tareq Y. Ismael and Rifa 'at El-Sa'id, *The Communist Movement in Egypt, 1920–1988* (Syracuse, N.Y.: 1990), 12–31; Joel Beinin and Zachary Lockman, *Workers on the Nile: Nationalism, Communism, Islam, and the Egyptian Working Class, 1882–1954* (Princeton, N.J.: 1987), 140–54.

45. Ullman, *Anglo-Soviet Relations,* 3: 377–85.

46. Ibid., 3: 388.

47. Volodarskii, *Sovety i ikh iuzhnye sosedi,* 102–106.

48. Ervand Abrahamian, *Iran between Two Revolutions* (Princeton, N.J.: 1982), 118–48; Werner Zurrer, *Persien zwischen England und Russland 1918–1925: Grossmachteinflusse und nationaler Wiederaufstieg am Beispiel des Iran* (Bern: 1978), 368–99.

49. Kemal quoted in Alexander N. Kheifets, *Sovetskaia Rossiia i sopredelnye strany Vostoka v gody grazhdanskio voiny, 1918–1920* (Moscow: 1964), 135. This work and the author's *Sovetskaia diplomatiia i narody Vostoka, 1921–1927* (Moscow: 1968) were researched during the Khrushchev thaw and based on the party's archives in Moscow, Baku, Tashkent, Irkutsk, and elsewhere, on the NKID archives, the military archives, and the Central State Archive of the October Revolution—as well as on contemporary published sources and the memoirs of Soviet diplomats. Both works carefully trace the development of Soviet foreign policy toward the Asian districts of the former Tsarist Empire and the neighboring countries of Turkey, Persia, Afghanistan, Mongolia, and China.

50. Kheifets, *Sovetskaia Rossiia i sopredel'nye strany Vostoka,* 139.

51. Ibid., 168.

52. Ibid., 164–66.

53. White, "Soviet Russia and the Asian Revolution," 227–29.

54. Datta Gupta, *Comintern, India, and the Colonial Question*, 45–70; Reznikov, *Comintern and the East*, 93–103, 242–43.

55. This analysis follows Boersner, *National and Colonial Question*, chap. 5, who uses the words *Eastern* and *Western* to refer to nationalist revolutions and proletarian revolutions, respectively.

56. Boersner, *National and Colonial Question*, 141–42.

57. *Izvestiia* quoted in R. A. Mirovitskaia, *Sovetskii Soiuz v strategii Gomindana (20–30-e gody)* (Moscow: 1990), 214–15.

58. On the origins of Soviet-Chinese diplomatic relations, see Allen S. Whiting, *Soviet Policies in China, 1917–1924* (New York: 1953), 131–235.

59. V. V. Sokolov, "Polpred v Kitae Lev Karakhan," in *Otkryvaia novye stranitsy. Mezhdunarodnye voprosy: sobytiia i liudi*, ed. A. A. Iskenderov (Moscow: 1989), 208. The author is director of the Archives of the USSR Ministry of Foreign Affairs. Although he gives no references, his work obviously draws on archival transcripts from the 1920s.

60. Lee Feigon, *Chen Duxiu: Founder of the Chinese Communist Party* (Princeton, N.J.: 1983), 137–65.

61. Arif Dirlik, *The Origins of Chinese Communism* (New York: 1989), 149–51, 191–95, 201–8.

62. Feigon, *Chen Duxiu*, 170–71.

63. C. Martin Wilbur and Julie Lien-ying How, *Missionaries of Revolution: Soviet Advisers and Nationalist China, 1920–1927* (Cambridge, Mass.: 1989), 27–28, 50; hereafter cited as *Soviet Advisers*.

64. "ECCI Resolution on the Relations between the Chinese Communist Party and the Kuomintang," 12 January 1923, and "ECCI Instructions to the Third Congress of the Chinese Communist Party," May 1923: *The Communist International* 2: 5–6, 25–26.

65. Hans J. van de Ven, *From Friend to Comrade: The Founding of the Chinese Communist Party, 1920–1927* (Berkeley, Calif.: 1991), 123–26, 130, 134–36; V. I. Glunin, "The Comintern and the Rise of the Communist Movement in China, 1920–1927," in R. A. Ulyanovskii, ed., *The Comintern and the East* (Moscow: 1979), 280–344.

66. Mirovitskaia, *Sovetskii Soiuz v strategii Gomindana*, 22–23. This work by a veteran scholar and member of the Institute of the Far East demonstrates the full impact of "the new political thinking" of the Gorbachev-Shevardnaze era on the academic study of Sino-Soviet relations. The author utilizes both Chinese Nationalist and Communist historiography, deals evenhandedly with both movements, and renders balanced judgments. One axiom of the study is that the GMD was of revolutionary value, just as was the CPC, the former being referred to as "a party of the new type" (21)—a term normally reserved in Soviet historiography for Communist parties with strict "revolutionary discipline" and "democratic centralism." A second axiom is that "national interests" can be distinguished from "class

relations," that they are worthy of investigation, and that it may be progressive to pursue the former as well as to conduct the latter (3–20).

67. Chicherin to Sun Yat-sen, 21 August 1921, quoted in Mirovitskaia, *Sovetskii Soiuz v strategii Gomindana*, 23.

68. Mirovitskaia, *Sovetskii Soiuz v strategii Gomindana*, 45, 47.

69. Wilbur and How, *Soviet Advisers*, 60–62.

70. Taiwanese historiography emphasizes Sun Yat-sen's drive to create a political party and organs of state power independently of the inspiration of the Russian Revolution and the urgings of Soviet advisers: See Mirovitskaia, *Sovetskii Soiuz v strategii Gomindana*, 31.

71. In *Soviet Advisers*, Wilbur and How have reconstructed the history of the Soviet aid mission in south China from primary documents—chiefly, but not exclusively, those seized by the Beijing police during the raid on the Soviet embassy compound in April 1927. The discussion of Soviet activities in China that I present here depends on their account and on the eighty-one documents printed in their work. The memoirs of numerous Soviet advisers were published in the 1960s and 1970s as part of the Soviet anti-Maoist campaign of that time. Some have been translated into English, including those of A. V. Blagodatov, A. I. Cherepanov, S. A. Dalin, M. I. Kasanin, V. M. Primakov, and Vera Vladimirovna Vishnyakova-Akimoval. Some of these, as well as the memoirs of other advisers, appear in Y. V. Chudodeyev, ed., *Soviet Volunteers in China, 1925–1945; Articles and Reminiscences* (Moscow: 1980).

72. For a brief period during 1926, two other officers substituted for Bliukher—first Nikolai Kuibyshev, formerly commandant and commissar of Kronshtadt (1922–23) and assistant commander of the Turkistan Front (1925–26), who was the brother of Valerain Kuibyshev, and then V. A. Stepanov. In China, Kuibyshev was code-named "Kisanka" (literally, "Pussycat").

73. Mirovitskaia, *Sovetskii Soiuz v strategii Gomindana*, 39.

74. Lydia Holubnychy, *Michael Borodin and the Chinese Revolution, 1923–1925* (Ann Arbor, Mich.: 1979) utilizes published Comintern documents and the works of Soviet historians with access to archival sources in the USSR; Dan N. Jacobs, *Borodin: Stalin's Man in China* (Cambridge, Mass.: 1981) is also based on published Comintern documents as well as on contemporaneous accounts, both Euro-American and Soviet.

75. Mirovitskaia, *Sovetskii Soiuz v strategii Gomindana*, 50, citing unpublished reports by Borodin and the published memoirs of A. I. Cherepanov.

76. Y. V. Chudodeyev, "Soviet Volunteers in the Chinese Revolution and War of Liberation," in *Soviet Volunteers in China*, 9.

77. Mirovitskaia, *Sovetskii Soiuz v strategii Gomindana*, 28–29, citing data in the possession of historians at the Institute for the History of the Mongolian People's Revolutionary Party in Urga.

78. McLane, *Soviet Strategies in Southeast Asia,* 37–43, analyzes the relative importance of Europe and the various regions of Asia in Comintern grand strategy.

79. Nine articles were published in 1923; eighteen in 1924; ninety-five in 1925: See Heng-yü Kuo, *Die Komintern und die Chinesische Revolution: Die Einheitsfront zwischen der KP Chinas und der Kuomintang 1924–1927* (Paderborn, Germany: 1979), 296–300.

80. Compare Boersner, *National and Colonial Question,* 180–81, who maintains that by the time of the Fifth Congress the strategic concept of the Comintern had undergone a complete reorientation from one aimed at the proletarians of Europe to one directed at the democratic nationalists of Asia.

6. THE CHALLENGES OF CAPITALIST STABILIZATION

1. In the historical scholarship on early Soviet foreign relations, works on relations between Russia and Germany predominate. Germany was important both to the revolutionary expectations of the Bolsheviks and to their efforts to break out of diplomatic and commercial isolation. But Germany did not have the singular importance one might assume from the large number of works devoted to Soviet-German relations listed in Robert H. Johnston, *Soviet Foreign Policy, 1918–1945: A Guide to Research and Research Materials* (Wilmington, Del.: 1991), 155–60. The accessibility of archival sources from Germany before similar sources became available in England, France, and Russia permitted an extensive investigation of Soviet-German relations. A significant portion of the work of E. H. Carr for this period is devoted to Soviet-German relations, for example, *The Interregnum, 1923–1924* (New York: 1954), chaps. 5, 7, 9, and *Socialism in One Country,* 3: 46–62. Martin Walsdorff, *Westorientierung und Ostpolitik: Stresemanns Russlandpolitik in der Locarno Ära* (Bremen: 1971), 29–42, achieved a breakthrough toward a fuller understanding of both Soviet and German policy. Gunter Rosenfeld's *Sowjetrussland und Deutschland, 1917–1922* and *Sowjetunion und Deutschland, 1922–1933* (Cologne: 1984) are based on archival sources in the former Soviet Union and the former German Democratic Republic and on printed sources published in German, Russian, and English. Although the work utilizes "bourgeois" as well as "socialist" scholarship, it sustains a pervasive Marxist-Leninist interpretation. The Soviet work in the field is A. A. Akhtamzian, *Rapallskaia politika: sovetsko-germskie diplomatichoskie otnosheniia v 1922–1932 gg* (Moscow: 1974). The author's *glasnost*-era publications based on unpublished archival materials are significant contributions to scholarship: "Sovetsko-Germanskie ekonomicheskie otnosheniia v 1922–1932 gg," *Novaia i noveishaia istoriia* (1988:4): 42–56, and "Voennoe sotrudnichestvo SSSR i Germanii v 1920–1933 gg," *Novaia i noveishaia istoriia* (1990:5): 3–24.

2. Kurt Rosenbaum, *Community of Fate: German-Soviet Diplomatic*

Relations, 1922–1928 (Syracuse, N.Y.: 1965) demonstrates the personal relationship between Brockdorff and Chicherin. So too does Timothy Edward O'Connor, *Diplomacy and Revolution: G. V. Chicherin and Soviet Foreign Affairs, 1918–1930* (Ames, Iowa: 1988), 95–96 (hereafter cited as *Chicherin*).

3. Brockdorff-Rantzau quoted in Valeri A. Shishkin, "The USSR and Western Countries in the Mid-1920s. An Experience of Political and Economic Relations in Connection with *de jure* Recognition," in *Contact or Isolation?* ed. John Hiden and Aleksander Loit (Stockholm: 1991), 110.

4. The torture of Krestinskii was established juridically in 1957 during "the Khrushchev thaw," but it was revealed publicly in the USSR only during *glasnost:* See N. V. Popov, "Byl i ostaius' kommunistom," in *Otkryvaia novye stranitsy,* ed. Akhmed A. Iskenderov (Moscow: 1989), 244–51.

5. Helmut Grieser, "Die Rapallo-Politik in sowjetischer Sicht: Zur Beurteilung der deutschen Aussenpolitik 1922–1932 in der zeitgenössischen sowjetischen Presse," in *Historisch-politische Streiflichter: Geschichtliche Beiträge zur Gegenwart,* ed. Kurt Jürgensen and Reimer Hansen (Neumünster: 1971), 159–68; and *Die Sowjetpresse über Deutschland in Europa 1922–1932. Revision von Versailles und Rapallo-Politik in sowjetischer Sicht* (Stuttgart: 1970). Also, Klaus Hildebrand, *Das Deutsche Reich und die Sowjetunion im internationalen System, 1918–1932. Legitimität oder Revolution?* (Wiesbaden: 1977), 9–15.

6. On the Ruhr occupation, see the works of Denise Artaud, Jacques Bariety, Walter McDougall, Charles Maier, Hermann Rupieper, Stephen Schuker, and Marc Trachtenberg discussed in Jon Jacobson, "Strategies of French Foreign Policy after World War I," *Journal of Modern History* 55 (1983): 82–83, 89. Contemporary Soviet reactions are explained in Eichwede, *Revolution und Internationale Politik,* 154–75.

7. For the Central Executive Committee's condemnation of the Ruhr occupation, 13 January 1923, see *Soviet Documents,* 1: 368–70. For the Soviet warning to Poland, see *Izvestiia,* 21 January 1923, in Xenia Eudin and Harold H. Fischer, eds., *Soviet Russia and the West, 1920–1927: A Documentary Survey* (Stanford, Calif.: 1957), no. 55. For the possibility of renewed intervention, see press interview by Chicherin in *Manchester Guardian,* 24 December 1923, *Soviet Documents,* 1: 422. For the report on the Soviet diplomatic offensive, see speech by Kamenev to the Second Congress of Soviets of the USSR, *SRW,* no. 78. See Wolfgang Ruge, *Die Stellungnahme der Sowjetunion gegen die Besetzung des Ruhrgebiets: zur Geschichte der deutsch-sowjetischen Beziehungen von Januar bis September 1923* (Berlin: 1962), 32–59, for the fullest scholarly discussion.

8. For the "German October," see Angress, *Stillborn Revolution,* chaps. 11–13, especially 394–405 (decision and preparation), 319, 365–69 (hesitations of Radek and Brandler), and 417–20 (military provisions).

9. This was the objective of the "Schlageter line" strategy devised by

Radek and presented to the Third ECCI Plenum on 12 June 1923: See Möller, *Karl Radek in Deutschland*, no. 31. Discussion in Angress, *Stillborn Revolution*, 327–50; Eichwede, *Revolution und Internationale Politik*, 38–52; and Warren Lerner, *Karl Radek: The Last Internationalist* (Stanford, Calif.: 1970), 119–23.

10. Angress, *Stillborn Revolution*, 378, 398.

11. Kuusinen, *Before and after Stalin*, 63.

12. Uldricks, *Diplomacy and Ideology*, 159–60, and "Russia and Europe," 64–66.

13. The apology was made for a raid by the Berlin police on the Soviet Trade Delegation in May 1924—"the Bozenhardt incident": See Rosenbaum, *Community of Fate*, 87–112; O'Connor, *Engineer of Revolution*, 281–86.

14. For British recognition, see Resolution of the Second Congress of Soviets, 2 February 1924, *Soviet Documents*, 1: 422–23; for the note from Rakovskii to MacDonald, 8 February 1924, *Soviet Documents*, 1: 426–27; for interview by Litvinov in *Pravda*, 14 February 1924, *Soviet Documents*, 427–29; and Gabriel Gorodetsky, *The Precarious Truce: Anglo-Soviet Relations, 1924–27* (Cambridge and New York: 1977), 7–13.

15. Shishkin, "The USSR and Western Countries," 109.

16. For the de jure recognitions of 1924, see Carr, *Interregnum*, 243–53.

17. Francis Conte, *Un révolutionnaire-diplomate: Christian Rakovski. L'Union soviétique et l'Europe, 1922–1941* (Paris and New York: 1978), credits Rakovskii's "personal skill" with winning for the USSR the maximum concessions possible in the negotiations with both Britain and France. The English translation of Conte's work—*Christian Rakovski (1873–1941): A Political Biography* (Boulder, Colo. and New York: 1989)—"does not do justice to the competent analysis of the original French version," as Michael Carley has stated in a review published in *International History Review* 12 (1990): 604. Gus Fagan, ed., *Christian Rakovsky: Selected Writings on Opposition in the USSR 1923–30* (London: 1980), 35–45, briefly sketches Rakovskii's career as a diplomat as well as his role in Bolshevik intraparty politics. Rakovskii was the number-two man in the Trotsky opposition, and he spoke for Trotsky at the Fifteenth Party Congress in December 1927. For sixty years thereafter his name was expunged from the record of Soviet foreign relations. This situation began to change in May 1988 at a discussion of Soviet history of the 1920s held under the auspices of the leading Soviet historical journal, *Voprosy istorii*. There V. A. Shishkin, a corresponding member of the USSR Academy of Sciences, stated that the reinclusion of Rakovskii in the history of Soviet diplomacy would be one of the most significant steps that could be taken toward ending the prolonged depersonalization (*obezlichivanie*) of the history of Soviet foreign policy. A move in this direction was taken by Dimiter Stanischev, in "Khristian Rakovsky: His Life and Work," *International*

Affairs (Moscow) (1989:1): 90–95. Written by the secretary of the CC of the Bulgarian Communist Party, this work is a *glasnost*-era tribute to "an honest and selfless man, a well-educated Marxist devoted to the cause of the revolution, an associate of Lenin in the bitter struggle to found, consolidate, and develop the Soviet state." See also N. A. Paniev, "Bolgarskii revoliutsioner i sovetskii polpred," in *Otkryvaia novye stranitsy,* ed. A. A. Iskenderov (Moscow: 1989), 278–80.

18. For Chicherin's telegram to Paris welcoming recognition by France, 28 October 1924, see *Soviet Documents,* 1: 473–75. The archives of the French Foreign Ministry have yet to be used extensively for the study of Franco-Soviet relations during the 1920s, but see Michael Jabara Carley, "From Revolution to Dissolution: The Quai d'Orsay, the Banque Russo-Asiatique, and the Chinese Eastern Railway, 1917–1926," *International History Review* 12 (1990): 721–61. Anne Hogenhuis-Seliverstoff, *Les relations franco-soviétiques, 1917–1924* (Paris: 1981) argues that French policy was inspired by considerations of grand diplomatic strategy—the fear of a German-Russian alliance and an unwillingness not to follow the British lead—rather then by economic interests. Similarly, Kalervo Hovi, "The French Alliance Policy 1917–1927: A Change of Mentality," in *Contact or Isolation?* ed. Hiden and Loit, 93–99, contends that anti-Bolshevik ideology was not an important consideration in French foreign policy after the autumn of 1920, policymakers being overcome by a concern for security against Germany.

19. Stuart R. Schram, "Christian Rakovskij et le premier rapprochement franco-soviétique," *Cahiers du Monde Russe et Soviétique* 1 (1960): 214–17; hereafter cited as "Rapprochement franco-soviétique."

20. Schram, "Rapprochement franco-soviétique," 230.

21. Report by Stalin at the Central Committee Courses for Secretaries of Uezd Party Committees, 17 June 1924, in Josef Stalin, *Works* (Moscow: 1952), 6: 248.

22. For the Anglo-Soviet Conference, 14 April–12 August 1924, see *DBFP,* ser. 1, v. 25, ch. 3. For the speech by Rakovskii, 14 April 1924, *Soviet Documents,* 1: 441–47; for press interviews by Rakovskii, 26 April and 1 June 1924, *Soviet Documents,* 1: 449–52; for the draft text of the Anglo-Soviet Treaty, 8 August 1924, *Soviet Documents,* 1: 453–59, and *DBFP,* ser. 1, v. 25, no. 293. Also, Gorodetsky, *Precarious Truce,* 13–32; Conte, *Rakovski,* 120–32; David Marquand, *Ramsay MacDonald* (London: 1977), 361–63; and Shishkin, "The USSR and Western Countries," 106–107.

23. This is the standard interpretation. Compare the counterargument in Andrew J. Williams, *Labour and Russia: The Attitude of the Labour Party to the USSR, 1924–34* (Manchester and New York: 1989), 13–16, which states that MacDonald did attach great importance to the meetings; he truly was busy with other duties, and Ponsonby was the best-suited person with whom to entrust the work of the conference.

24. Speech by Chicherin to the special plenary session of the Moscow Soviet, 20 August 1924, *SRW*, no. 94; report by Chicherin to the Central Executive Committee, 18 October 1924, *Soviet Documents*, 1: 466.

25. For the Dawes Plan, see Jon Jacobson, "The Reparation Settlement of 1924," in *Konsequenzen der Inflation*, ed. Gerald D. Feldman et al. (Berlin: 1989), 79–108.

26. Jürgen Spenz, *Die diplomatische Vorgeschichte des Beitritts Deutschlands zum Völkerbund, 1924–1926. Ein Beitrag zur Aussenpolitik der Weimarer Republik* (Göttingen, Berlin, Frankfurt, Zürich: 1966), 33–34; Christoph M. Kimmich, *Germany and the League of Nations* (Chicago: 1976), 54–61.

27. Report by Chicherin to the Central Executive Committee, 18 October 1924, *Soviet Documents*, 1: 463.

28. Marquand, *Ramsay MacDonald*, 364–78. Allegedly under pressure from the left wing of the Labour Party, MacDonald persuaded the attorney general to drop the charges lodged under the Incitement to Mutiny Act against J. R. Campbell, the temporary editor of the official organ of the British Communist Party (CPGB), the *Worker's Weekly*. Campbell had allowed publication of an article calling on soldiers in the British army to let it be known that they would not turn their guns on their fellow workers in case of either a foreign war or a class war at home.

29. Marquand, *Ramsay MacDonald*, 381–89.

30. Andrew, *Her Majesty's Secret Service*, 298–313, suggests that the published letter was a composite of leaks from a genuine original authored by Zinoviev, and that its publication was an effort by Tory diehards within the intelligence community to bring down the Labour government, which it considered soft on Communism and a threat to the intelligence service itself.

31. The case for forgery is put forth most fully in Lewis Chester, Stephen Fay, and Hugo Young, *The Zinoviev Letter* (Philadelphia: 1968), with significant emendations by Gabriel Gorodetsky, *The Other "Zinoviev Letters": New Light on the Mismanagement of the Affair*, Slavic and Soviet Series, no. 3, Russian and East European Research Center of Tel-Aviv University, 1976. According to this explanation, the letter was manufactured by a group of White Russian émigrés in Berlin and fed to the Foreign Office through the efforts of some members of the Central Office of the Conservative Party and of the Special Intelligence Service. No one in the Foreign Office regarded it as having any special significance except for Eyre Crowe, who took an extraordinary interest in the document. Being critical of the Russia policy of the Labour government and knowing that the *Daily Mail* was about to publish the letter, Crowe released it to the press before its authenticity could be confirmed or denied by the Soviet government and without clear authorization from MacDonald, who was slow to recognize the impact it would have on the electoral campaign. A thorough criticism of

the forgery thesis, and an attempted exoneration of Crowe, is to be found in Sybil Crowe, "The Zinoviev Letter: A Reappraisal," *Journal of Contemporary History* 10 (1975): 407–432.

32. Note from Rakovskii to MacDonald, 25 October 1925, *Soviet Documents,* 1: 471–73; NKID reply to British note, 27 October 1924, *Soviet Documents,* 1: 473; note from Rakovskii to Chamberlain, 28 November 1924, *Soviet Documents,* 1: 477–80; interview by Chicherin, *Pravda,* 22 March 1928, *Soviet Documents,* 2: 296–99.

33. Notes from Chamberlain to Rakovskii, 21 November 1924, *DBFP,* ser. 1, v. 25, nos. 266, 267. For the official position of the British government on the "Zinoviev letter," see Foreign Office memorandum, 11 November 1924, *DBFP,* ser. 1, v. 25, no. 264.

34. For the Chamberlain-Herriot meeting, see memorandum by Chamberlain, 5 December 1924, *DBFP,* ser. 1, vol. 26, no. 608. For other contemporaneous Anglo-French conversations, see Clemens A. Wurm, *Die französische Sicherheitspolitik in der Phase der Umorientierung 1924–1926* (Frankfurt a.M., Bern, and Las Vegas: 1979), 218.

35. Kuusinen, *Before and after Stalin,* 51.

36. Report by Chicherin to the Central Executive Committee, 18 October 1924, *Soviet Documents,* 1: 461, 465–67.

37. Jon Jacobson, "Is There a New International History of the 1920s?" *American Historical Review* 88 (1983): 643–45.

38. Indeed, because Chamberlain was careful to keep London's relations with Moscow formally correct, the NKID was unable to find direct evidence that the British government had undertaken a policy hostile to the Soviet Union or was leading the rest of Europe toward one: See report by Chicherin to the Third Soviet Congress, 14 May 1925, *Soviet Documents,* 2: 38–43.

39. Stephen F. Cohen, *Bukharin and the Bolshevik Revolution* (New York: 1975), 147–48, 162, 186–88; Tucker, *Stalin as Revolutionary,* 377–94. Tucker maintains (399) that it was Stalin who insisted that international proletarian revolution be retained as a second stage of development in the formulation of "socialism in one country." Cohen attributes this idea to Bukharin (187).

40. The role played by the debate over the doctrines of "socialism in one country," "permanent revolution," and "revolutionary internationalism" in the Lenin succession is discussed in Richard Day, *Leon Trotsky and the Politics of Economic Isolation* (Cambridge: 1973), 3–16, 98–101, and in Anthony D'Agostino, *Soviet Succession Struggles: Kremlinology and the Russian Question from Lenin to Gorbachev* (Boston: 1988), 75–105. Both works correct the notion that Bolshevik intraparty politics of 1925 to 1927 are to be understood as a confrontation between Stalin and "socialism in one country," on the one hand, and Trotsky and "permanent revolution" on the other. Isaac Deutscher, *The Prophet Unarmed: Trotsky, 1921–1929* (Lon-

don and New York: 1959), 157–63, 201–70, discusses Trotsky's absence from the debate during the important period from January 1925 to April 1926. For Trotsky's writings and politics during these years, see Pierre Broue, *Trotsky* (Paris: 1988), 441–73.

41. For the implications of the doctrine of "socialism in one country" for international relations theory, see V. Kubálková and A. A. Cruickshank, *Marxism and International Relations* (Oxford and New York: 1985), 85–86; quotation, 82; Allen Lynch, *The Soviet Study of International Relations* (New York: 1987), 18–19.

42. Report by Stalin to the Moscow Party Organization on the results of the Fourteenth Party Conference, 9 May 1925, in Stalin, *Works,* 7: 95.

43. Richard B. Day, *The Crisis and the Crash: Soviet Studies of the West (1917–1939)* (London: 1981), 77–81; and *Leon Trotsky,* 130.

44. "The International Situation and the Tasks of the Communist Parties," *Pravda,* 22 March 1925, Stalin, *Works,* 7: 51–57; Report to the Moscow Party Organization, 9 May 1925, Stalin, *Works,* 7: 90–134; Political Report of the Central Committee to the Fourteenth Party Congress, 18 December 1925, Stalin, *Works,* 7: 267–403; Resolutions, Decisions, and Directives of the Fourteenth Party Congress, December 1925, in *Resolutions and Decisions of the Communist Party of the Soviet Union: The Early Soviet Period: 1917–1929,* ed. Richard Gregor (Toronto and Buffalo: 1974), 2: 258–60, hereafter cited as *Resolutions and Decisions.*

45. Stalin, *Works,* 7: 51, 92–95, 302–304. For Marx, Lenin, and Bukharin on the theory of "capitalist stabilization" and its implications for the doctrine of "socialism in one country," see Day, *The Crisis and the Crash,* 73–77.

46. Stalin, *Works,* 7: 51–52.

47. Ibid., 272–73.

48. Ibid., 98.

49. Ibid., 99–100.

50. Ibid., 52.

51. Ibid., 276.

52. Ibid., 53–55, 290–94.

53. Ibid., 98–99, 273–74, 278–79. The Soviet/Comintern economist Eugen Varga also maintained that the Dawes Plan would not stabilize the international economy: See Day, *The Crisis and the Crash,* 70–72. His argument was the conventional one. France and Britain could not accept German exports at the level required for Germany to create the surplus necessary to make reparations payments.

54. "Concerning the International Situation," *Bolshevik,* 20 September 1924, Stalin, *Works,* 6: 289–99, 303.

55. Stalin, *Works,* 7: 279–83.

56. Anna di Biagio, "Bukharin's International Alternative," in *The Ideas of Nikolai Bukharin,* ed. A. Kemp-Welch (Oxford: 1992), 116–20.

57. Report by Stalin to the Moscow Party Organization, 27 January 1925, Stalin, *Works*, 7: 25–29.

58. Resolutions of the Fourteenth Party Congress, *Resolutions and Decisions*, 258–60.

59. Speech by Stalin to the Central Committee Plenum, 19 January 1925, Stalin, *Works*, 7: 9–14; "The Prospects of the Communist Party of Germany and the Question of Bolshevization," *Pravda*, 3 February 1925, in Stalin, *Works*, 7: 34–41; Political Report of the Central Committee to the Fourteenth Party Congress, 18 December 1925, Stalin, *Works*, 7: 279–83, 287; Robert C. Tucker, "The Emergence of Stalin's Foreign Policy," *Slavic Review* 36 (1977): 563–64, 565–66. Stalin's analysis and his prescription were supported by M. V. Frunze, who replaced Trotsky as commissar for military and naval affairs in January 1925. Frunze warned that "the danger of war . . . has not diminished . . . as a result of our economic consolidation, it has increased." "Nothing but the development of our military power will prevent our enemies from attacking us": Speech by Frunze to the Moscow Garrison, *Pravda*, 16 February 1925, *SRW*, no. 104.

60. Stalin, *Works*, 7: 12–13, 34.

61. Resolutions of the Third Soviet Congress, 16 May 1925, *Soviet Documents*, 2: 45; Resolutions of the Fourteenth Party Congress, *Resolutions and Decisions*, 258.

62. Cohen, *Bukharin*, 179, 246–47; Day, *Leon Trotsky*, 101–104, 118–21.

63. Resolutions of the Fourteenth Party Congress, *Resolutions and Decisions*, 258; Stalin quoted in Day, *Leon Trotsky*, 120. Tucker, *Stalin as Revolutionary*, 377, contends that "Stalin made no particular contribution to the industrialization debate in its earlier phases. He echoed the Bukharinist position." Cohen, *Bukharin*, 215, states that "while Stalin sometimes eulogized industrialism . . . and the virtues of Soviet economic autarky more than did Bukharin, he did not seem to harbor a separate industrial or agrarian program."

64. Stalin, *Works*, 7: 279; Day, *The Crisis and the Crash*, 71–72; also the statement by Ia. Rudzutak quoted from the Stenographic Report of the Fourteenth Party Congress in S. Iu. Vygodskii, *Vneshniaia politika SSSR, 1924–1929 gg* (Moscow: 1963), 85: "The Dawes plan is aimed at converting Russia into an agrarian appendage, even Germany's, . . . at squeezing pennies [out of the Russian working people] to pay German reparations to the USA. That is not our way, comrades!"

65. Stalin quoted in Day, *Leon Trotsky*, 121.

66. For the discussion of Trotsky's strategy of economic development and economic foreign policy, see Day, *Leon Trotsky*, 126–78, and "Leon Trotsky on the Dialectics of Democratic Control," in *The Soviet Economy on the Brink of Reform: Essays in Honor of Alec Nove*, ed. Peter Wiles (Boston: 1988), 17–24.

67. Hodgson (Moscow) to Chamberlain, 25 August 1925, *DBFP*, ser. 1, vol. 25, no. 326.

68. Day, *Leon Trotsky*, 131, 169.

69. On Preobrazhenskii see M. M. Gorinov and S. V. Tsakunov, "The Life and Works of Evgenii Alekssevich Prebrazhenskii," *Slavic Review* 50 (1991): 286–96, and Alexander Erlich, *The Soviet Industrialization Debate, 1924–1928* (Cambridge, Mass.: 1960), 31–60.

70. Richard Day demonstrates convincingly that although Preobrazhenskii and Trotsky both favored rapid industrialization, Trotsky wanted to fund it with foreign capital rather than by expropriating the accumulations of the peasantry. Moreover, unlike Preobrazhenskii, Trotsky favored balanced industrial growth rather than giving priority to heavy industry: *Leon Trotsky*, 146–47. Compare Erlich, *Soviet Industrialization Debate*, in which the Preobrazhenskii road and the Bukharin road are viewed as the two primary alternative industrialization paths.

7. NARKOMINDEL AND EUROPEAN SECURITY

1. Raymond J. Swinder, *Soviet Military Reform in the Twentieth Century: Three Case Studies* (Westport, Conn.: 1992), 23–73; John Erickson, *The Soviet High Command: A Military-Political History, 1918–1941* (New York: 1962), 164–213. For the composition of the committee, see Grigori Alimurzayev, "A Shield or a Sword? History of Soviet Military Doctrine," *International Affairs* (Moscow) (1989:5): 102.

2. Jacob W. Kipp, "Soviet Military Doctrine and the Origins of Operational Art, 1917–1936" in *Soviet Military Doctrine from Lenin to Gorbachev, 1915–1991*, ed. Willard C. Frank, Jr., and Phillip S. Gillette (Westport, Conn.: 1992), 85–131.

3. Stuart R. Schram, "Christian Rakovskij et le premier rapprochement franco-soviétique," *Cahiers du Monde Russe et Soviétique* 1 (1960): 208–210; hereafter cited as "Rapprochement franco-soviétique."

4. For Stresemann, Locarno, and the strategies and objectives of German revisionism, see Jon Jacobson, *Locarno Diplomacy: Germany and the West, 1925–1929* (Princeton, N.J.: 1972); Peter Krüger, *Die Aussenpolitik der Republik von Weimar* (Darmstadt: 1985); Klaus Megerle, *Deutsche Aussenpolitik 1925: Ansatz zu aktivem Revisionismus* (Bern: 1974); and Wolfgang Michalka and Marshall M. Lee, *Gustav Stresemann* (Darmstadt: 1982).

5. Jürgen Spenz, *Die diplomatische Vorgeschichte des Beitritts Deutschlands zum Völkerbund, 1924–1926*, 41–43; hereafter cited as *Beitritts Deutschlands*; Gorodetsky, *Precarious Truce*, 78–79.

6. On the December initiative and its sequel, see note by Brockdorff-Rantzau on a conversation with Victor Kopp, 4 December 1924; letter from Brockdorff-Rantzau to Stresemann, 29 December 1924; Brockdorff's note on a conversation with Chicherin, 25/26 December 1924; and his note on

additional conversations with Chicherin, 9 March 1925, in Walsdorff, *Westorientierung und Ostpolitik*, 214–16, 219–23, 225–27, 228. This study is the central work on Soviet-German relations during the Locarno era. In it are reproduced the texts of the major documents from the German Foreign Ministry. These not only form the basis for analysis of German policy but offer insight into Soviet policy as well. For discussion of the alliance offer, see pp. 15–77. Earlier work on the subject also remains valuable, e.g., Hans W. Gatzke, "Von Rapallo nach Berlin: Stresemann und die deutsche Russlandpolitik," *Vierteljahreshefte für Zeitgeschichte*, 4 (1956): 1–19; Zygmunt J. Gasiorowski, "The Russian Overture to Germany of December 1924," *Journal of Modern History* 30 (1958): 99–117, and also his "Stresemann and Poland before Locarno," *Journal of Central European Affairs* 18 (1958): 25–47; and "Stresemann and Poland after Locarno," *Journal of Central European Affairs* 18 (1958): 292–317; Schram, "Rapprochement franco-soviétique"; Spenz, *Beitritts Deutschlands*, 48–50—all based on the records of the German Foreign Ministry.

7. Carr, *Socialism in One Country*, 3: 257.

8. Karl Dietrich Erdmann, "Das Problem der Ost oder Westorientierung in der Locarno-Politik Stresemanns," *Geschichte in Wissenschaft und Unterricht* 6 (1966): 133–62, and "Die Geschichte der Weimarer Republik als Problem der Wissenschaft," *Vierteljahreshefte fur Zeitgeschichte* 3 (1955): 1–19; Herbert Helbig, *Die Träger der Rapallo-Politik* (Göttingen: 1958); Theodor Schieder, "Die Entstehungsgeschichte des Rapallo-Vertrags," *Historische Zeitschrift* 204 (1967): 545–609.

9. Note by Brockdorff-Rantzau on a conversation with Rykov, 24 February 1925, Walsdorff, *Westorientierung und Ostpolitik*, 223–25.

10. On the "forcing back Poland" question, see Walsdorff, *Westorientierung und Ostpolitik*, 63–70, 76–77, 133–38; and Carr, *Socialism in One Country*, 3: 254–57, 275–76. Stresemann subsequently repudiated Brockdorff-Rantzau's statement in a conversation with Chicherin: Walsdorff, *Westorientierung und Ostpolitik*, 133–35.

11. Spenz, *Beitritts Deutschlands*, 46–47.

12. For the initial German response to the Soviet alliance offer—Maltzan to Brockdorff-Rantzau, 13 December 1924; Schubert to Brockdorff-Rantzau, 29 December 1924—see Walsdorff, *Westorientierung und Ostpolitik*, 216–19; discussed in Walsdorff, 78–107, and in Carr, *Socialism in One Country*, 3: 260–62.

13. Walsdorff, *Westorientierung und Ostpolitik*, 109.

14. For the Western European security pact negotiations from the German initiative to the conclusion of the Locarno agreements, see Jacobson, *Locarno Diplomacy*, chap. 1.

15. Walsdorff, *Westorientierung und Ostpolitik*, 117.

16. For German-Soviet negotiations from Stresemann's Rhineland pact proposal in January 1925 to the commercial treaty in October, see Walsdorff, *Westorientierung und Ostpolitik*, 71–132.

17. Francis Conte, *Un révolutionnaire-diplomate: Christian Rakovski,* 163; hereafter cited as *Rakovski.*

18. Walsdorff, *Westorientierung und Ostpolitik,* 74–75, 108–109, 122, 135.

19. For Soviet overtures to Poland and the reaction of Warsaw and Berlin, see Carr, *Socialism in One Country,* 3: 274–75, 432–33, 436, 444–47; Walsdorff, *Westorientierung und Ostpolitik,* 103–104, 110–13, 132–33, 174–75, 179–80, 195.

20. Report by Chicherin to the Fourteenth Party Congress, December 1925, *Kentavr,* October–December 1991, 121.

21. Report by Chicherin to the Third Soviet Congress, 14 May 1925, *Soviet Documents,* 2: 37.

22. Schram, "Rapprochement franco-soviétique," 234, 236–37.

23. Chicherin's press interview while in Warsaw, 28 September 1925, *Izvestiia,* 4 October, in *Soviet Documents,* 2: 55–56.

24. Schram, "Rapprochement franco-soviétique," 222–23.

25. Conte, *Rakovski,* 140.

26. Brockdorff-Rantzau to Stresemann, 29 December 1924: Walsdorff, *Westorientierung und Ostpolitik,* 68. On the French card, which Chicherin played more than once, and the reaction at the Wilhelmstrasse, see Walsdorff, *Westorientierung und Ostpolitik,* 63–64, 70–73, 132; and Spenz, *Beitritts Deutschlands,* 46.

27. Kalervo Hovi, "The French Alliance Policy 1917–1927," 93–99.

28. Schram, "Rapprochement franco-soviétique," 225, 226.

29. Ibid., 585.

30. Chicherin's statement to the press, 15 December 1925, *Izvestiia* and *Le Temps,* 17 December, in *Soviet Documents,* 2: 66–67. He reportedly told the French ambassador to Berlin, Pierre de Margerie, in early October that he preferred an agreement with France to one with Germany and that he wished to come to Paris to meet with Briand: Memo by Chamberlain on a conversation with Briand, 13 October 1925, *DBFP,* ser. 1, v. 25, no. 332.

31. Rakovskii quoted in Carr, *Socialism in One Country,* 3: 423.

32. Brockdorff-Rantzau to Berlin, 3 April 1926, *Akten zur deutschen Auswärtigen Politik, 1918–1945,* ser. B, v. 2, pt. 1, no. 105; hereafter cited as *ADAP;* Schubert to Moscow, 8 April 1926, *ADAP,* ser. B, v. 2, pt. 1, no. 115. Philippe Berthelot, secretary-general at the Quai d'Orsay, told Leopold von Hoesch, the German ambassador in Paris, that Chicherin, Rakovskii, and Herbette were "crazy about the idea" of a "continental bloc": Walsdorff, *Westorientierung und Ostpolitik,* 175.

33. For the Franco-Russian Conference, February–July 1926, see Rakovskii's speech at the opening of Franco-Soviet negotiations, 25 February 1926, *Izvestiia,* 27 February, *Soviet Documents,* 2: 92–95; Litvinov's report to the Central Executive Committee, 24 April 1926, *Soviet Documents,* 2: 109. The most complete account is Schram, "Rapprochement franco-soviétique," 587–623, the sources for which include de Monzie's personal

papers and a long report written by de Monzie for Briand, which the author discovered in the archives of the German Foreign Ministry.

34. Schram, "Rapprochement franco-soviétique," 588.

35. Daladier quoted in Conte, Rakovski, 186.

36. Alan Cassels, "Repairing the Entente Cordiale and the New Diplomacy," Historical Journal 23 (1980): 133–53; Stephen A. Schuker, The End of French Predominance in Europe: The Financial Crisis of 1924 and the Adoption of the Dawes Plan (Chapel Hill, N.C.: 1976), 237–45, 256–63; Jacobson, "Is There a New International History of the 1920s?" 41–42.

37. Brian Bond, British Military Policy between the Two World Wars (Oxford: 1980), 82.

38. John Robert Ferris, The Evolution of British Strategic Policy, 1919–1926 (London: 1989), 154–55.

39. Jacobson, Locarno Diplomacy, 21–22.

40. Christopher M. Andrew, "British Intelligence and the Breach with Russia in 1927," Historical Journal 25 (1982): 957–59.

41. Memorandum by Chamberlain, 10 June 1925, DBFP, ser. 1, v. 25, no. 317. For the fullest exposition of the Foreign Office's policy of "masterly inactivity" with regard to the USSR, see memorandum by Gregory, 1 November 1925, DBFP, ser. 1A, v. 1, no. 46. Gorodetsky, Precarious Truce, 53–67, 71–85, 258–61, offers a fascinating look into Soviet as well as British policy; quotations from pp. 71, 136. See also Andrew, Her Majesty's Secret Service, 315–81; Harriette Flory, "The Arcos Raid and the Rupture of Anglo-Soviet Relations, 1927," Journal of Contemporary History 12 (1977): 707–723; and Roger Schinness, "The Conservative Party and Anglo-Soviet Relations, 1925–7," European Studies Review 7 (1977): 393–407.

42. Chicherin interview in Izvestiia, 23 December 1925, Soviet Documents, 2: 77.

43. Chamberlain to Hodgson (Moscow), 1 April 1925, DBFP, ser. 1, v. 25, no. 308; Chamberlain to Peters (Moscow), 5 November 1925, DBFP, ser. 1A, v. 1, no. 65; Chamberlain to G. Clerk (Prague), 13 April 1926, DBFP, ser. 1A, v. 1, no. 418.

44. Gorodetsky, Precarious Truce, 84. "The Soviet government has offered and continues to offer the hand of peace to England, but it is left in the air": Chicherin interview in Izvestiia, 8 December 1926, Soviet Documents, 2: 145.

45. On the foreign policy of the diehards and Chamberlain's response, see Gorodetsky, Precarious Truce, 62–67; 175–79, 181–82; 213, 219, 228–29; Jacobson, Locarno Diplomacy, 123; note from Litvinov to London, 26 February 1927, Soviet Documents, 161. There is still no definitive study of the General Strike. The work done in the 1970s does not seem to have exhausted the possibilities of the archives, e.g., Christopher Farman, The General Strike: May 1926 (London: 1972); Patrick Renshaw, The General Strike (London: 1975). Fortunately, Soviet involvement has been carefully

studied: See, for instance, Daniel F. Calhoun, *The United Front!: The TUC and the Russians, 1923–1928* (Cambridge and New York: 1976), 233–54; Gabriel Gorodetsky, "The Soviet Union and Britain's General Strike of May 1926," *Cahiers du Monde russe et soviétique* 17 (1976): 292–300, and *Precarious Truce*, 145–59. For the explanation of the NKID, 27 June 1926, see *Soviet Documents*, 2: 120–23. There is no recent archive-based study of Joynson-Hicks.

46. Gorodetsky, *Precarious Truce*, 84–85, 144–45, 181, 261.

47. Conte, *Rakovski*, 193.

48. Jacobson, *Locarno Diplomacy*, 130–34.

49. On the "united front" policies of the Comintern, see Calhoun, *United Front!;* Goredetsky, "The Soviet Union and Britain's General Strike," and *Precarious Truce*, 86–133, 204–205, 263–64.

50. Stalin quoted in Daniel F. Calhoun, "Trade Union Internationalism in the 1920s: Personalities, Purposes, Premises," in *Contact or Isolation?* 258.

51. Leon Trotsky, *Leon Trotsky on Britain* (New York: 1973), Part I.

52. Carr, *Socialism in One Country*, 3: 494.

53. Trotsky, *On Britain*, Part III.

54. Statements by Stalin quoted in Claudin, *Communist Movement*, 153 and n. 51; Goredetsky, "The Soviet Union and Britain's General Strike," 305; *SRW*, no. 118.

55. For example, Karl Radek in *Izvestiia*, 22 October 1925, *SRW*, no. 106.

56. Report of the Central Committee to the Fourteenth Party Congress, 23 December 1925, *Resolutions and Decisions*, 258.

57. For Chicherin's pre-Locarno negotiations with Stresemann, see Walsdorff, *Westorientierung und Ostpolitik*, 133–38; for Stresemann's Ost-politik at Locarno, Walsdorff, *Westorientierung und Ostpolitik*, 139–56.

58. Report by Chicherin to Fourteenth Party Congress, December 1925: *Kentavr*, October–December 1991, 117–19, 121, 124. Also press interviews by Chicherin, 15 and 21 December 1925, in *Soviet Documents*, 2: 67, 78. For his earlier statements, see report by Chicherin to the Central Executive Committee, 4 March 1925, *Soviet Documents*, 2: 17; speech by Chicherin to Third Soviet Congress, 14 May 1925, *Soviet Documents*, 2: 42.

59. Report by Chicherin to Fourteenth Party Congress, December 1925, *Kentavr*, October–December 1991, 117.

8. RUSSIA, EUROPE, AND ASIA AFTER LOCARNO

1. Report by Chicherin to Fourteenth Party Congress, December 1925, *Kentavr*, October–December 1991, 122–23.

2. Ibid.

3. Treaty of Friendship and Neutrality between Turkey and the Union of Soviet Socialist Republics, 17 December 1925, *Soviet Documents on the*

Middle East, 525–28; Pagman Treaty of Neutrality and Nonaggression between the USSR and Afghanistan, 31 August 1926, *Soviet Documents on the Middle East,* 101–6; Treaty of Guarantee and Neutrality between Persia and the Union of Soviet Socialist Republics, 1 October 1927, *Soviet Documents on the Middle East,* 288–92.

4. Editorial in *Izvestiia,* 29 September 1926, *SRW,* no. 113; report by Chicherin to Fourteenth Party Congress, December 1925, *Kentavr,* October–December 1991, 119; report by Litvinov to Central Executive Committee, 24 April 1926, *Soviet Documents,* 2: 107.

5. Statement by Rakovskii, n.d., *SRW,* no. 107; statement by Chicherin in *Izvestiia,* 8 December 1926, *Soviet Documents,* 2: 146; statement by Litvinov in *Pravda,* 24 December 1925, *Soviet Documents,* 2: 79–80.

6. This is the interpretation of Harish Kapur, *Soviet Russia and Asia,* 78–79, 212, 214.

7. Kapur, *Soviet Russia and Asia,* 139–40.

8. Chicherin to Agent and Consul-General of the USSR in Hejaz, Comrade Khakimov, n.d.: "Chicherin and the Foundations of Soviet-Arab Relations," *Vestnik,* November 1990, 66–67; hereafter cited as "Soviet-Arab Relations." This article reproduces previously unpublished documents from the USSR Foreign Policy Archives.

9. "Soviet-Arab Relations," 66–67.

10. Aleksandr N. Kheifetz, *Sovetskaia diplomatiia i narody Vostoka, 1921–1927* (Moscow: 1968), 313–14.

11. Igor P. Senchenko, *Persidskii zaliv: vzgliad skvoz stoletie: Ot "novogo kursa" Peterburga do politiki novogo myshleniia* (Moscow: 1991), 95.

12. Chicherin to Yurenev, 3 April 1924, "Soviet-Arab Relations," 65–66.

13. Senchenko, *Persidskii zaliv,* 98.

14. Chicherin to the Politburo and Central Committee of the CPSU, 13 February 1926, "Soviet-Arab Relations," 68.

15. Chicherin to Khakimov, 31 October 1926, "Soviet-Arab Relations," 69–70.

16. Kheifetz, *Sovetskaia diplomatiia,* 315–16.

17. Senchenko, *Persidskii zaliv,* 98.

18. Volodarskii, *Sovety i ikh iuzhnye sosedi Iran i Afganistan,* 115.

19. Georgii S. Agabekov, *OGPU, the Russian Secret Terror* (New York: 1931), 97.

20. Sicker, *The Bear and the Lion,* 48.

21. Volodarskii, *Sovety i ikh iuzhnye sosedi,* 120–23.

22. Official Soviet Summary of Relations with Persia for the Year 1927, *Soviet Documents on the Middle East,* 214–317.

23. Soviet policy leading to the Treaty of Berlin in April 1926 is revealed in Chicherin's conversation with Stresemann and Schubert in Berlin

in December 1925 and in his conversations with Brockdorff-Rantzau in Moscow in March 1926: See *ADAP*, ser. B, vol. 2, pt. 1, nos. 12, 15, 54, 75, 79, 84. For the text of the Treaty of Berlin, see *ADAP*, ser. B, vol. 2, pt. 1, no. 168. On Soviet-German negotiations, October 1925–April 1926, see Walsdorff, *Westorientierung und Ostpolitik*, 157–89; Spenz, *Beitritts Deutschlands*, 109–21; and Rosenfeld, *Sowjetunion und Deutschland*, 166–81.

24. For Germany's Polish policy after Locarno, see Harald von Riekhoff, *German-Polish Relations, 1918–1933* (Baltimore: 1971), 120–30, 226–94; Walsdorff, *Westorientierung und Ostpolitik*, 171–74.

25. Gorodetsky, *Precarious Truce*, 139–41; Jacobson, *Locarno Diplomacy*, 81–82.

26. Piotr S. Wandycz, *The Twilight of French Eastern Alliances 1926–36: French-Czechoslovak-Polish Relations from Locarno to the Remilitarization of the Rhineland* (Princeton, N.J.: 1988), 40–42.

27. Litvinov's report to Central Executive Committee, 24 April 1926, *Soviet Documents*, 2: 106–108. For evaluations of the significance of the Treaty of Berlin for Soviet foreign relations, see Walsdorff, *Westorientierung und Ostpolitik*, 187–89; Gorodetsky, *Precarious Truce*, 242–43 (Radek quoted).

28. John Hiden, *Germany and Europe, 1919–1939* (London and New York: 1993), 121–22.

29. For the texts of the German proposals, see Walsdorff, *Westorientierung und Ostpolitik*, 228–29, 232–39.

30. Walsdorff, *Westorientierung und Ostpolitik*, 169. Litvinov himself announced before the Central Executive Committee Moscow's willingness to renew negotiations with London without delay and to conduct them to a favorable conclusion in a businesslike manner: Gorodetsky, *Precarious Truce*, 144–45.

31. The possibility of a Soviet-Polish rapprochement may have been a factor that the German Foreign Ministry was required to integrate into its policy calculations, but the Wilhelmstrasse did not feel particularly pressed by Chicherin's efforts with Warsaw. The German ambassador to Poland, Ulrich Rauscher, calmly and repeatedly predicted that a real rapprochement between Poland and the USSR could never take place. And the Soviet experts at the Wilhelmstrasse—both Erich Wallroth and Herbert von Dirksen—became indignant and intransigent rather than compliant in response to NKID overtures to Warsaw: See Wallroth to Moscow, 6 March 1926, *ADAP*, ser. B, vol. 2, pt. 1, no. 76; Dirksen to Moscow, *ADAP*, ser. B, vol. 2, pt. 1, no. 78.

32. Brockdorff-Rantzau to Berlin, 4 March 1926, *ADAP*, ser. B, vol. 2, pt. 1, no. 75. For the nonaggression pact proposal, see *Izvestiia*, 28 August 1926, *Soviet Documents*, 2: 130; Harvey L. Dyck, *Weimar Germany and Soviet Russia, 1926–1933: A Study in Diplomatic Instability* (London: 1966), 33–38.

33. Memorandum by Stresemann, 25 March 1926, *ADAP*, ser. B, vol. 2, pt. 1, no. 91; memorandum by Schubert, *ADAP*, ser. B, vol. 2, pt. 1, no. 96.

34. Statement by Litvinov, *Izvestiia*, 13 October 1926, *Soviet Documents*, 2: 140–41; message from Litvinov to Stresemann, 16 April 1927, *Soviet Documents*, 2: 181–82.

35. Litvinov's report to Central Executive Committee, 24 April 1926, *Soviet Documents*, 2: 111–12.

36. NKID statement on Soviet proposal, *Izvestiia*, 28 August 1926, *Soviet Documents*, 2: 130.

37. Walsdorff, *Westorientierung und Ostpolitik*, 194–96.

38. On the Baltic bloc and European diplomacy, see John Hiden, "On the Edge of Diplomacy? Britain, the Baltic and East-West Relations between the Wars," in *Contact or Isolation?* 311–19; Merja-Liisa Hinkkanen, "Bridges and Barriers, Pawns and Actors. The Baltic States in East-West Relations in the 1920s," in ibid., 431–42; Patrick Salmon, "Perceptions and Misperceptions: Great Britain and the Soviet Union in Scandinavia and the Baltic Region 1918–1939," ibid., 415–29.

39. Richard W. Rigby, *The May 30 Movement: Events and Themes* (Canberra: 1980).

40. Gregorii Zinoviev, "The Epoch of Wars and Revolutions," *Inprecor* 55 (1925): 745–47, quoted in Haithcox, *Communism and Nationalism in India*, 58.

41. The major Soviet documentary source is M. L. Titarenko, ed., *Kommunisticheskii Internatsional i kitaiskaia revoliutsiia. Dokumenty i materialy* (Moscow: 1986), which includes individual Comintern documents published in the USSR since the 1960s. Kuo Heng-yü, *Die Komintern und die Chinesische Revolution* examines printed Comintern documentation. Reznikov, *Comintern and the East*, 209, discusses the "Hands Off China" campaign.

42. Both Karakhan and Borodin played important roles in the project to provide the Chinese Revolution with professionally trained cadres. Radek was director of the KUTV; Pavel Mif assisted him. See Sokolov, "Polpred v Kitae Lev Karakhan," 208; Mirovitskaia, *Sovetskii Soiuz v strategii Gomin'dana*, 80; Jacobs, *Borodin*, 144.

43. "Prospects for Further Work in the South, or the Grand Plan of Kuomintang Military Activity for 1926," in Wilbur and How, *Missionaries of Revolution: Soviet Advisers and Nationalist China*, Document 7, 508–16; also 158–60; hereafter cited as *Soviet Advisers*.

44. "Report of Soviet adviser 'L. Grey' in Canton on Kuomintang military aviation," in Wilbur and How, *Soviet Advisers*, Document 35, 640–43; also 233–34.

45. Wilbur and How, *Soviet Advisers*, 216–17, 428; compare Erickson, *Soviet High Command*, 232–33.

46. "Problems of Our Policy with Respect to China and Japan, 25 March 1926," in Leon Trotsky, *Leon Trotsky on China*, ed. Les Evans and Russell Block (New York: 1976), 102–10.

47. Mirovitskaia, *Sovetskii Soiuz v strategii Gomindana*, 34–35, 204.

48. Wilbur, *The Nationalist Revolution in China*, 47–49; Wilbur and How, *Soviet Advisers*, 252–73.

49. See the discussion of Trotsky's China policy at this time in Anthony D'Agostino, *Soviet Succession Struggles: Kremlinology and the Russian Question from Lenin to Gorbachev* (Boston: 1988), 98–100. From research in party archives, A. I. Kartunova, "Kitaiskaia revolutsiia: diskussii v Kominterne," *Voprosy istorii KPSS* (1989:6): 59, reports that "unfounded attacks by Trotsky and Zinoviev" at this time "obstructed discussion in the Comintern."

50. Wilbur and How, *Soviet Advisers*, 272.

51. Stepanov's "Report on the March Twentieth Incident," ca. 2 April 1926, and his "Report to a Meeting of the Soviet Group at Canton," ca. 10 April 1926, in Wilbur and How, *Soviet Advisers*, Documents 50 and 51. V. A. Stepanov led the Soviet mission in south China from 24 March to early May 1926.

52. The Opposition's critique was sustained by both Trotskyist and non-Marxist scholarship. During the Cold War, American scholars labeled Soviet participation in the Nationalist Revolution in China "Stalin's Far Eastern Program," "Stalin's Chinese Adventure," or "Stalin's Failure in China." Meanwhile, pre-1987 official party scholarship in the USSR condemned the politics of Trotsky and Zinoviev and affirmed the course of policy taken by "the Comintern" without crediting Stalin and/or Bukharin with it: See Reznikov, *Comintern and the East*, 214–29; Glunin, "Comintern and the Rise of the Communist Movement in China." During *perestroika* it was admitted that Trotsky's role in Soviet history had been underrepresented and dealt with in an overtly biased manner: See, for instance, N. A. Vasentskii, "L. D. Trotskii: politicheskii portret," *Novaia i noveishaia istoriia* (1989:3), 142. And one of the principal official specialists on the history of the Communist International, K. K. Shirinia, attempted to come to a balanced view of Trotsky's Comintern policy in "Trotskii i Komintern," *Novaia i noveishaia istoriia* (1991:1). However, there were few important new revelations, and many older concepts were preserved, including complete lists of the mistakes attributed to Trotsky in pre-1987 Soviet scholarship.

53. Analyzed in McLane, *Soviet Strategies in Southeast Asia*, 57–59.

54. Drachkovitch and Lazitch, "The Third International," 182–83.

55. Glunin, "Comintern and the Rise of the Communist Movement in China," 335–36.

56. Wilbur, *Nationalist Revolution in China*, 55–63, and Wilbur and How, *Soviet Advisers*, chap. 6.

57. Lengthy extracts from the "Resolution on the Chinese Situation," 16 December 1926, are printed in *Communist International*, 2: 336–48.

58. Conrad Brandt, *Stalin's Failure in China, 1924–1927* (New York: 1966), 95–101.

59. Reznikov, *Comintern and the East*, 218–19.

60. Hans J. van de Ven, *From Friend to Comrade: The Founding of the Chinese Communist Party, 1920–1927* (Berkeley, Calif.: 1991), 214–15.

61. 30 November 1926, "The Prospects of the Revolution in China," speech to Chinese Commission of the Seventh ECCI Plenum, Stalin, *Works*, 8: 373–91.

62. Kartunova, "Kitaiskaia revolutsiia," 58–72, demonstrates some of the effects of the Gorbachev-Shevardnadze-era "new political thinking" on the study of Soviet-Chinese relations. The author praises Chinese Communist Party historians for their attention to Comintern issues and urges scholarly cooperation with them. At the same time, she expresses some remarkably conservative opinions: "Any attempts to ascribe the fault for the defeat of the revolution of 1925–1927 to the Comintern should be dismissed, whoever tries to do it" (70).

63. For instance, Robert C. North, *Moscow and Chinese Communists* (Stanford, Calif.: 1963), 90; Brandt, *Stalin's Failure in China*, 103.

64. Interview by Chicherin, *Izvestiia*, 6 April 1926, *Soviet Documents*, 2: 102–103; report by Litvinov to Central Executive Committee, 24 April 1926, *Soviet Documents*, 2: 104. For the crisis over German membership in the League Council, see David Carlton, "Great Britain and the League Council Crisis," *Historical Journal* 11 (1968): 354–64; and Christoph M. Kimmich, *Germany and the League of Nations* (Chicago: 1976), 78–89.

65. Conte, *Rakovski*, 166.

66. See Chicherin's discussion in *Izvestiia*, 8 December 1926, *Soviet Documents*, 2: 147.

67. On Soviet League policy, see press interview by Chicherin, *Izvestiia*, 23 December 1925, *Soviet Documents*, 2: 77–78; press interview by Chicherin, 27 February 1926, *Soviet Documents*, 2: 96–97; Chicherin's notes to Geneva, 16 January and 7 April 1926, in Barbusse, *Soviet Union and Peace*, 128–33; statement by Litvinov to the press, 22 November 1927, ibid., 134–37. Carr, *Socialism in One Country*, 3: 450–62 provides the fullest account in any language. G. I. Morozov, "Liga natsii: vzgliad cherez polveka," *Voprosy istorii* (1992:2–3): 162–67, revises orthodox Soviet historiography, suggesting that the effectiveness of the League of Nations might have been increased had the USSR taken a more favorable attitude toward it during the 1920s.

68. Georgi Dragunov, "Vorovski's Assassination: New Facts," *International Affairs* (Moscow) (1989:5): 116–27.

69. V. L. Genis, "Upriamyi narkom s Il'inki," in *Otkryvaia novye stra-*

nitsy Mezhdunarodnye voprosy: sobytiia i liudi, ed. A. A. Iskenderov (Moscow: 1989), 234.

70. Kathryn Davies, *The Soviets at Geneva: The USSR and the League of Nations, 1919–1933* (Westport, Conn.: 1977), 208.

71. Gorodetsky, *Precarious Truce,* 180, 184–88, 217, 266.

72. William G. Ratliff, *Faithful to the Fatherland: Julius Curtius and Weimar Foreign Policy* (New York: 1990), 41–42.

73. On the Thoiry conference, see Jacques Bariety, "Finances et relations internationales: à propos du 'plan du Thoiry'; septembre 1926," *Relations internationales* 21 (1980): 51–70; Jon Jacobson and John T. Walker, "The Impulse for a Franco-German Entente: The Origins of the Thoiry Conference, 1926," *Journal of Contemporary History* 10 (1975): 157–81; Heinz-Otto Sieburg, "Les Entretiens de Thoiry, 1926," *Revue d'Allemagne* 4 (1972): 520–46.

74. Hiden, *Germany and Europe,* 123–24.

75. Dyck, *Weimar Germany and Soviet Russia,* 46–63.

76. Michael Reiman, *The Birth of Stalinism: The USSR on the Eve of the "Second Revolution"* (Bloomington, Ind.: 1987), vii–viii, 9.

77. "Fully approving of this peace policy, the Congress charges the Soviet government to continue in the future steadily to pursue this policy and to aim at the establishment and reinforcement of friendly relations with foreign states. The Congress notes with satisfaction that these aspirations of the USSR have found a response in certain states, and the development of economic ties with them, which is the best evidence of the correctness of this policy": Resolution of the Fourth Congress of Soviets, 19 April 1927, in Barbusse, *Soviet Union and Peace,* 134.

78. Press statement by Chicherin, 6 December 1926, *Izvestiia,* 8 December 1926, *Soviet Documents,* 2: 147.

79. Isaac Deutscher, *The Prophet Unarmed. Trotsky: 1921–1929* (London and New York: 1959), 262–310; Medvedev, *Let History Judge,* 159–69.

80. Anna di Biagio, "Bukharin's International Alternative," in *The Ideas of Nikolai Bukharin,* ed. A. Kemp-Welch (Oxford and New York: 1992), 123.

81. Carr and Davies, *Foundations of a Planned Economy,* 3: 123–24.

82. Chicherin quoted in Zagladin, *Istoriia uspekhov i neudach Sovetskoi diplomatii,* 82.

9. THE DRIVE FOR INDUSTRIALIZATION

1. For the Soviet economy in 1926/27, see Robert W. Davies, *The Soviet Economy in Turmoil, 1929–1930* (Cambridge, Mass.: 1989), 37–42; hereafter cited as *Turmoil;* S. G. Wheatcroft, R. W. Davies, and J. M. Cooper, "Soviet Industrialization Reconsidered: Some Preliminary Conclusions

about Economic Development between 1926 and 1941," *Economic History Review*, 2d. ser., 39 (1986): 264–72.

2. On the industrialization drive, see Davies, *Turmoil*, 46–50; Wheatcroft, "Soviet Industrialization Reconsidered," 268–69; Carr, *Socialism in One Country*, 1: 352–53, and *Foundations*, 1: 287–88.

3. G. A. Bordiugov and V. A. Kozlov, "The Turning Point of 1929 and the Bukharin Alternative," *Soviet Studies in History* 28 (Spring 1990): 9.

4. Carr, *Socialism in One Country*, 1: 445–54, and *Foundations*, 1: 705–718; resolution quoted, 710; Davies, *Turmoil*, 32–37.

5. The analysis here follows M. R. Dohan, "Foreign Trade" in *From Tsarism to the New Economic Policy: Continuity and Change in the Economy of the USSR*, ed. R. W. Davies (Ithaca, N.Y.: 1991), 212–33.

6. Michael R. Dohan, "Foreign Trade and Soviet Investment Strategy for Planned Industrialization, 1928–1938," in *Soviet Investment for Planned Industrialization, 1929–1937: Policy and Practice*, ed. R. W. Davies (Berkeley, Calif.: 1984), 114.

7. Dohan, "Foreign Trade" (1991), 229; Davies, *Turmoil*, 33–34; Day, *Leon Trotsky*, 114–15, 151–52.

8. "Opyt proshlykh ekonomicheskikh reform," *Voprosy ekonomiki* (1988:2): 63–64.

9. V. A. Shishkin, "The external factor in the country's socioeconomic development," in "The Soviet Union in the 1920s: A Roundtable," *Soviet Studies in History* 28 (1989), 52.

10. Day, *Leon Trotsky*, 153–59; Carr, *Foundations*, 1: 851–54.

11. Day, *Leon Trotsky*, 167–68.

12. Cohen, *Bukharin*, 247; Uldricks, "Russia and Europe," 69; Rykov quoted in Carr, *Foundations*, 1: 712.

13. On *politika dogovorennost* and Stalin's views on foreign investment and the government foreign trade monopoly, see memorandum from Stalin to the Politburo, 27 December 1927, in Reiman, *Birth of Stalinism*, 128–33; also 9. Reiman's work makes use of highly secret Soviet documents that were sent to Herbert von Dirksen of the German Foreign Ministry in 1927–28 and that the author discovered in the Political Archives of the German Foreign Ministry. They include correspondence among Politburo members, party directives, Central Committee and government protocols, and letters from NKID officials in Moscow to Soviet representatives in Berlin. The work offers a view into Soviet decision making at the highest level.

14. Erickson, *Soviet High Command*, 301–303.

15. Anthony C. Sutton, *Western Technology and Soviet Economic Development* (Stanford, Calif.: 1968), 258–66.

16. A. A. Akhtamzian, "Voennoe sotrudnichestvo SSSR i Germanii," 3–24. This work, authored by the leading Soviet specialist on relations with Germany during the 1920s, is based on extensive archival research spon-

sored by the Ministry of Foreign Affairs of the USSR during the tenure of Shevardnadze. Some of the documents dating from the years 1926–1929 have been published in English translation: "Soviet-German Military Cooperation, 1920–1933," *International Affairs* (Moscow) (1990:7): 95–113; hereafter, "Military Cooperation." These publications represent the first documentation of Soviet-German military cooperation from the Foreign Policy Archives of the USSR (FPA-USSR). Official confirmation of these contacts were first made in the October 1989 issue of *Vestnik MID SSSR*, which printed a letter written by Chicherin dated 17 June 1927. The fullest discussion of the 1926-and-after phase of military collaboration is based on the records of the German Foreign Ministry: Erickson, *Soviet High Command*, 247–82. The pioneering work was done from French sources by Georges Castellan, *Le réarmement clandestin du Reich, 1930–1935, vue par le 2e Bureau de l'État-Major Français* (Paris: 1954), and from German sources by Hans W. Gatzke, "Russo-German Military Collaboration during the Weimar Republic," *American Historical Review* 63 (1958): 565–97.

17. Letter from Krestinskii to Unszlicht, 1 February 1926, Akhtamzian, "Military Cooperation," 97–100; Akhtamzian, "Voennoe sotrudnichestvo," 11.

18. Akhtamzian, "Military Cooperation," 100.

19. Walsdorff, *Westorientierung und Ostpolitik*, 170–71.

20. Dyck, *Weimar Germany and Soviet Russia*, 19–27, 76–77; Dirksen quoted, 76.

21. Akhtamzian, "Voennoe sotrudnichestvo," 12.

22. Memorandum by Unszlicht on negotiations with the Reichswehr, ca. April 1926, Akhtamzian, "Military Cooperation," 100–102; unsigned memorandum, January 1927, Akhtamzian, "Military Cooperation," 103–105.

23. Erickson, *Soviet High Command*, 225–57.

24. Unsigned memorandum, January 1927, Akhtamzian, "Military Cooperation," 104.

25. Krestinskii to Litvinov, 18 January 1927, Akhtamzian, "Military Cooperation," 105; quotation from Akhtamzian, "Voennoe sotrudnichestvo," 14–15.

26. Unsigned memorandum, January 1927, Akhtamzian, "Military Cooperation," 104.

27. Ibid., 103.

28. Dyck, *Weimar Germany and Soviet Russia*, 96–98, 188–90.

29. Letter from Trotsky to Central Committee, 27 June 1927, in Deutscher, *Prophet Unarmed*, 339.

30. Erickson, *Soviet High Command*, 288–90.

31. On the war scare crisis of 1927 and its antecedents, see Alfred G. Meyer, "The War Scare of 1927," *Soviet Union/Union Soviétique*, 5 (1978): 1–25, which regards the war scare as spurious, inspired by Bukharin and

used by Stalin in the battle against Trotsky and Zinoviev. John P. Sontag, "The Soviet War Scare of 1926–27," *Russian Review* 34 (1975): 66–77, rightly interprets the war scare as "the result of confusion and uncertainty as well as of cool, sober calculation." Sheila Fitzpatrick, "The Foreign Threat during the First Five Year Plan," *Soviet Union/Union Soviétique,* 5 (1978): 26–35, finds in the scare the beginnings of mass mobilization. Reiman, *Birth of Stalinism,* 11–18, examines the interactions of the Soviet leadership. Gorodetsky, *Precarious Truce,* 182–83, 211–40, defines the diplomatic context and emphasizes the crucial role played by the break in relations with London in setting off the crisis. During *perestroika,* leading Soviet scholars rejected the idea that there was any real basis for the war scare in the international relations of the time. "It seems to me that an analysis of the events gives no ground for such a conclusion": Valeri A. Shishkin, "External factor," 54. L. N. Nezhinskii, "Byla li voennaia ugroza SSSR v kontse 20-kh—nachale 30-kh godov?" *Istoriia SSSR* (1990:6): 14–30, concludes from an examination of the international situation in the years 1927–1933 that the menace of a major war against the Soviet Union did not exist.

32. Wandycz, *Twilight of French Eastern Alliances,* 47–50.

33. Speech by Stalin to Fifteenth Party Conference, 1 November 1926, *Izvestiia,* 5 November 1926, *SRW,* no. 116; speech by Stalin to workers of the Stalin Railway Workshops, October Railway, 1 March 1927, *Works,* 9: 173; speech by Bukharin to Fifteenth Moscow Party Conference, *Izvestiia,* 13 January 1927, *SRW,* no. 119; report by Rykov to Fourth Soviet Congress, 18 April 1927, *Soviet Documents,* 2: 182, 192. Stalin's statement of 1 March that war would not occur in the spring or autumn was contradicted by Bukharin's speech of 13 January in which he stated that there was no guarantee that war would not break out within that time frame. Meyer, "War Scare," 2–6, regards Bukharin as the primary instigator of the war scare.

34. Litvinov reportedly agreed with the British representative in Moscow that the war scare was "stupid": Hodgson (Moscow) to Chamberlain, 11 February 1927, *DBFP,* ser. 1a, vol. 3, no. 11.

35. Wilbur, *Nationalist Revolution in China,* 77–117.

36. On the Northern Expedition and international relations, see Wilbur, *Nationalist Revolution,* 68–77; Wilbur and How, *Soviet Advisers,* 367–71.

37. Edmund S. K. Fung, *The Diplomacy of Imperial Retreat: Britain's South China Policy, 1924–1931* (Hong Kong and New York: 1991).

38. C. Martin Wilbur and Julie Lien-ying How, *Documents on Communism, Nationalism, and Soviet Advisers in China 1918–1927: Papers Seized in the 1927 Peking Raid* (New York: 1956), 8–9.

39. Van de Ven, *Friend to Comrade,* 193, citing the statistical research of Zaho Bu.

40. Wilbur, *Nationalist Revolution*, 108.

41. Schram, "Rapprochement franco-soviétique," 605–606.

42. NKID account of the ARCOS raid and the rupture of Anglo-Soviet relations, 7 June 1927, *Soviet Documents*, 2: 221–27; formal Soviet protest against the raid, 12 May 1927, *Soviet Documents*, 2: 202–204; supplementary note by Litvinov, 17 May 1927, *Soviet Documents*, 2: 204–208; note from Chamberlain to Rosengloz severing relations, 26 May 1927, *DBFP*, ser. 1a, vol. 3, no. 215; statement by Litvinov, 26 May 1927, *Soviet Documents*, 2: 209–212. For historical accounts, see Gorodetsky, *Precarious Truce*, 221–31; Andrew, "British Intelligence and the Breach with Russia," 957–64; Flory, "Arcos Raid"; and Schinness, "Conservative Party," 401–403.

43. Paul W. Blackstock, *The Secret Road to World War Two: Soviet versus Western Intelligence 1921–1939* (Chicago: 1969), 136–61.

44. The assassin, the son of a Russian monarchist émigré, was a journalist for the Vilnius newspaper *Bielorusskoe slovo*. He claimed to be avenging the execution of the Russian imperial family in which, he believed, Voikov had taken part. Privately Chicherin stated that the assassination "had no political significance" and was a "purely personal act": Wandycz, *Twilight of French Eastern Alliances*, 95. Nezhinskii, "Byla li voennaia ugroza," 17, affirms that Koverda was acting alone and not as part of a reactionary plot. For the initial protest by Litvinov, 7 June 1927, see *Soviet Documents*, 2: 220–21; subsequent note, 11 June 1927, *Soviet Documents*, 2: 228–31. On the assassination and the diplomacy of the war scare, see Josef Korbel, *Poland between East and West: Soviet and German Diplomacy toward Poland, 1919–1933* (Princeton, N.J.: 1963), 217–20.

45. Notes from Litvinov to the Polish Minister in Moscow, 7 and 11 June 1927, *Soviet Documents*, 2: 220–21, 228–31. On activities and reports of the GPU, see Reiman, *Birth of Stalinism*, 15, 16, 17; and on troop concentrations, Dyck, *Weimar Germany and Soviet Russia*, 97–98.

46. "The Threat of War," 28 July 1927, Stalin, *Works*, 9: 328–37.

47. Memorandum by Soviet government on the rupture in Anglo-Soviet relations, 7 June 1927, *Soviet Documents*, 2: 221–27; note from Litvinov to Polish Minister in Moscow, 11 June 1927, *Soviet Documents*, 2: 228–31.

48. Sheinis, *Litvinov*, 194.

49. Schram, "Rapprochement franco-soviétique," 607–610.

50. Note from Phipps (Paris) to Chamberlain, 13 June 1927, *DBFP*, ser. 1a, vol. 3, no. 231.

51. Memorandum by Stresemann, 7 June 1927, *ADAP*, ser. B, vol. 5, no. 209.

52. Memorandum by Stresemann, 15 June 1927, *ADAP*, ser. B, vol. 5, no. 236; Chamberlain (Geneva) to Tyrell, 16 June 1927, *DBFP*, ser. 1a, vol. 3, no. 240. On the international politics of the war scare, see Harvey L. Dyck, "German-Soviet Relations and the Anglo-Soviet Break, 1927," *Slavic Re-*

view 25 (1966): 67–83, and *Weimar Germany and Soviet Russia*, 87–94; Gorodetsky, *Precarious Truce*, 234–38; quotation, 236; Jacobson, *Locarno Diplomacy*, 131–34.

53. For the debate within the leadership over the future direction of Soviet foreign policy, see Reiman, *Birth of Stalinism*, 15–18.

54. Stalin, "The Threat of War," *Pravda*, 28 July 1927, *Works*, 9: 334; speech by Stalin to the joint plenum of the Central Committee and the Central Control Commission, 23 October 1927, Stalin, *Works*, 10: 205–206.

55. Meyer's work states that Moscow's willingness to appease France showed that the Bolshevik elite, with the possible exception of Bukharin, did not take the threat of war seriously but rather used it for the purposes of a factional political struggle: Meyer, "War Scare," 2, 10–11, 13. Sontag argues that the Soviet willingness to appease France shows how seriously they took the idea that Britain was lining up allies for an attack on the USSR: Sontag, "Soviet War Scare," 72–74.

56. Dyck, *Weimar Germany and Soviet Russia*, 122.

57. Schram, "Rapprochement franco-soviétique," 611–15; Conte, *Rakovski*, 193–96.

58. Soviet proposal, 21 September 1927, *Soviet Documents*, 2: 250–54; statements by Litvinov to the press, 16 September 1927, *Soviet Documents*, 2: 248–54; and 22 September 1927, *Soviet Documents*, 2: 255.

59. Statement of the Thirteen, 8 August 1927: Lev Trotskii, *The Challenge of the Left Opposition (1926–1927)* (New York: 1980), 291–95.

60. On the recall of Rakovskii, see press statement by Rakovskii, 4 September 1927, *Soviet Documents*, 2: 247–48; Chicherin's note to Paris, 4 October 1927, *Soviet Documents*, 2: 270; TASS statement in *Izvestiia*, 5 October 1927, *Soviet Documents*, 2: 270–71; Conte, *Rakovski*, 196–204; Schram, "Rapprochement franco-soviétique," 615–23.

61. Dyck, *Weimar Germany and Soviet Russia*, 94–96, 121–23.

62. Brockdorff-Rantzau to Stresemann, 27 August 1927, *ADAP*, ser. B, vol. 6, no. 146.

63. Dyck, *Weimar Germany and Soviet Russia*, 96–97.

64. Memorandum by Brockdorff-Rantzau, 24 July 1927, *ADAP*, ser. B, vol. 6, no. 60; Stresemann to Moscow, 12 August 1927, *ADAP*, ser. B, vol. 6, no. 108.

65. Krestinskii to Stalin, 28 December 1928, in Akhtamzian, "Military Cooperation," 107–108; Erickson, *Soviet High Command*, 258–61.

66. On China, the war scare, and the revival and suppression of the Opposition, see Reiman, *Birth of Stalinism*, 19–36; Deutscher, *Prophet Unarmed*, 316–79; Pierre Broué, *Trotsky* (Paris: 1988), 506–546; and Medvedev, *Let History Judge*, 169–75.

67. Lerner, *Karl Radek*, 141–43.

68. "Declaration of the Eighty-Four," May 1927: Trotsky, *Challenge of the Left Opposition (1926–1927)*, 224–39.

69. The minutes of the proceedings of the Eighth ECCI Plenum were not published—the first such suppression—and they have yet to be published in any language. The resolutions adopted were printed in *Inprecor* (9 and 12 June 1927), and an extract appears in Degras, ed., *Communist International*, 2: 382–90. Stalin's address of 24 May 1927, "The Revolution in China and the Tasks of the Comintern," appeared in *Bolshevik* on 31 May (1927:10) and is printed in Stalin, *Works*, 9: 288–318. Trotsky's speeches, along with his initial attack, "The Chinese Revolution and the Theses of Comrade Stalin" (7 May), appeared in Trotsky, *Problems of the Chinese Revolution* (New York: 1966), as did Zinoviev's "Theses on the Chinese Revolution." Other statements by Trotsky are collected in Trotsky, *Leon Trotsky on China*.

70. See, for example, the text of Rakovskii's speech to the Fifteenth Party Congress in Fagan, *Rakovsky*, 115–20.

71. Fagan, *Rakovsky*, 44.

72. "Recognition of the Tsarist Debts," 12 October 1927: Trotsky, *Challenge of the Left Opposition (1926–1927)*, 433–36.

73. Fagan, *Rakovsky*, 44.

74. Shirinia, "Trotskii i Komintern," credits Trotsky with perspicacity. "Always suspicious of the national bourgeoisie in the Guomindang, Trotsky was able to notice earlier than anyone else their turn to the right" (10). The work allows that Trotsky "may have been correct on some questions," but insists that the excessively sarcastic tone of Trotsky's interventions in the ECCI alienated many party members (12). On balance, Shirinia sustains the judgment of pre-*glasnost* Soviet scholarship, that Trotsky's position on the China question was marked by "simplification" and "left-dogmatism" (10). Trotsky himself later maintained that he had opposed the CPC's "bloc within" strategy since 1923. This claim, however, is not sustained by research in the Trotsky archives at Harvard, from which Brandt concludes that Trotsky paid little attention to the Chinese situation and knew little about it until March 1927: Brandt, *Stalin's Failure*, 155–58. Trotsky was apparently a party to the Politburo vote in May 1926 favoring the continuation of the "bloc within" strategy while Soviet advisers planned and supplied the Northern Expedition.

75. Carr, *Socialism in One Country*, 3: 491.

76. " 'Defeatism' and Clemenceau," 11 July 1927, and "The Clemenceau Thesis and the Party Regime," 24 September 1927, in Trotsky, *Challenge of the Left Opposition (1926–1927)*, 252–53, 395–404.

77. Stalin's statement was published in *Pravda* on 28 July 1927 as "Notes on Contemporary Issues: The Threat of War," *Works*, 9: 328, 336–37. It was incorporated into the resolutions of the Central Committee and the Central Control Commission as "the menace of counter-revolutionary war against the USSR is the most acute problem of the current period"; quoted in L. N. Nezhinskii, "Byla li voennaia ugroza v kontse 20-kh—

nachale 30-kh godov?" *Istoriia SSSR* (1990:6): 14. Trotsky's reply is published as "Speech to the Joint Plenum of the CC and the CCC," 6 August 1927, in Trotsky, *Challenge of the Left Opposition,* 270–90.

78. "The Platform of the Opposition: The Party Crisis and How to Overcome It," September 1927, in Trotsky, *Challenge of the Left Opposition,* 301–394.

79. Victor Serge and Natalia Sedova Trotsky, *The Life and Death of Leon Trotsky* (London: 1975), 148.

80. Speech by Stalin to the joint plenum of the Central Committee and Central Control Commission, 23 October 1927, Stalin, *Works,* 10: 206.

81. Memorandum by Menzhinskii, 10 November 1927, in Reiman, *Birth of Stalinism,* 124–26.

82. "Resolution on the expulsion of Comrades Zinoviev and Trotsky from the Central Committee," 23 October 1927, *Resolutions,* 306; "Resolution on the anti-party statements of the leaders of the Opposition," 14 November 1927, *Resolutions,* 306–308.

83. For the text of Rakovskii's speech, see Fagan, *Rakovsky,* 115–20.

84. Graeme Gill, *The Origins of the Stalinist Political System* (Cambridge and New York: 1990), 187.

85. Note from Stalin to the Central Committee, n.d., Reiman, *Birth of Stalinism,* 126–28.

10. ECONOMY, POLITICS, AND DIPLOMACY IN CRISIS

1. All in all, foreign lending (bank, corporate, and government-guaranteed) came to a roughly calculated one billion rubles for the years 1923/24–1926/27. As the USSR's foreign trade turnover equalled 4.8 billion rubles for the same period, approximately one-fifth of Soviet foreign trade was financed by loans from abroad: See Shishkin, "External factor," 50.

2. Dohan, "Foreign Trade" (1991), 231–32.

3. Davies, *Turmoil,* 34–45, 51–60, 67–70, 75–80; Dohan, "Foreign Trade and Soviet Investment Strategy," 114–15.

4. Chicherin cited reports from the Soviet ambassadors in London, Paris, and Berlin. Elements of his report are incorporated in Stalin's memorandum to the Politburo, 27 December 1927, in Reiman, *Birth of Stalinism,* 128–33. For foreign-policy decision making in October 1927, see pp. 38–40.

5. Statement by Litvinov to the press in Berlin, 22 November 1927, Barbusse, *Soviet Union and Peace,* 134–37; Declaration by the Soviet Delegation to the Fourth Session of the Preparatory Commission on Disarmament, 30 November 1927, ibid., 137–43.

6. Speech by Stalin to joint plenum of the Central Committee and Central Control Commission, 23 October 1927, Stalin, *Works,* 10: 204–206.

7. Griffiths, "Origins of Peaceful Coexistence," 195.

8. Memorandum from Stalin to Politburo, 27 December 1927, Reiman, *Birth of Stalinism*, 128–33.

9. Carr, *Foundations*, 1: 708; Reiman, *Birth of Stalinism*, 139–40.

10. On Soviet agriculture during the 1920s and the causes of the grain procurement crisis, see Moshe Lewin, *Russian Peasants and Soviet Power: A Study of Collectivization* (Evanston, Ill.: 1968); James Hughes, *Stalin, Siberia and the Crisis of the New Economic Policy* (New York: 1991); Davies, *Socialist Offensive*, 4–51.

11. For an extended analysis of the various factors involved in the procurement crisis, see Hughes, *Stalin, Siberia and the Crisis of the New Economic Policy*, 104–22; also Bordiugov and Kozlov, "Turning Point," 15, and Zagladin, *Istoriia uspekhov i neudach sovetskoi diplomatii*, 88.

12. Bukharin quoted in Carr, *Foundations*, 1: 315.

13. Reiman, *Birth of Stalinism*, 36–47; Hughes, *Stalin, Siberia and the Crisis of the New Economic Policy*, 121–33.

14. Hughes, *Stalin, Siberia and the Crisis of the New Economic Policy*, 137–48.

15. Speech by Kuibyshev at joint meeting of Politburo, Sovnarkom, and Central Committee Presidium, January 1928, Reiman, *Birth of Stalinism*, 135–38. On foreign-policy decision making in January–February 1928, see 46–50.

16. Note from Litvinov to Soviet representatives abroad, 9 February 1928, Reiman, *Birth of Stalinism*, 138–42.

17. Davies, *Turmoil*, 62–65; Hughes, *Stalin, Siberia and the Crisis of the New Economic Policy*, 155, 179.

18. Note from Stalin to the Central Committee, 11 November 1927, Reiman, *Birth of Stalinism*, 123–24; Political Report of the Central Committee to the Fifteenth Party Congress, 3 December 1927, Stalin, *Works*, 10: 296.

19. Speech by Menzhinskii at joint meeting of the Politburo, Sovnarkom, and Central Committee Presidium, January 1928, Reiman, *Birth of Stalinism*, 133–35.

20. Reiman, *Birth of Stalinism*, 49.

21. Davies, *Turmoil*, 71–75.

22. This is the central concept of Reiman, *Birth of Stalinism*.

23. Moshe Lewin, *The Making of the Soviet System: Essays in the Social History of Interwar Russia* (New York: 1985), 91–95, 114–20.

24. Davies, *Socialist Offensive*, 39–41; Robert W. Davies, and S. G. Wheatcroft, "Further Thoughts on the First Soviet Five Year Plan," *Slavic Review* 34 (1975): 798. Wheatcroft, Davies, and Cooper, "Soviet Industrialization Reconsidered," 264–94, presents some of the conclusions of the authors' research against a background of other scholarship. Bordiugov and Kozlov, "Turning Point," 11–15, examines the problems and tensions in-

herent in NEP, how they increased in the 1925–1927 period, and how they were overlooked by the Bukharin-Stalin-Rykov leadership as they announced the industrialization drive in 1926. The result, the authors maintain, was that the program of accelerated industrialization within NEP was "hardly possible." The views of other *perestroika*-era Soviet writers are discussed in Davies, *Soviet History in the Gorbachev Revolution* (London: 1989), 28–33.

25. For the conflict among the leadership and the struggle over economic and foreign policy, see Reiman, *Birth of Stalinism*, 67–71; Cohen, *Bukharin*, 276–86; Tucker, *Stalin as Revolutionary*, 409–416; Davies, *Turmoil*, 60–62, 459–61; and Hughes, *Stalin, Siberia and the Crisis of the New Economic Policy*, 181–83.

26. Kendall E. Bailes, *Technology and Society under Lenin and Stalin: Origins of the Soviet Technical Intelligentsia, 1917–1941* (Princeton, N.J.: 1978), chap. 3; Hiroaki Kuromiya, *Stalin's Industrial Revolution: Politics and Workers, 1928–1932* (Cambridge: 1988), 12–17.

27. Note from Rykov to Menzhinskii, 12 March 1928, Reiman, *Birth of Stalinism*, 145–47.

28. Note from Chicherin to Menzhinskii, 13 March 1928, Reiman, *Birth of Stalinism*, 147–49.

29. Report by Stalin to Moscow Party Organization, 13 April 1928, Stalin, *Works*, 11: 57–58; Tucker, *Stalin in Power*, 76–80.

30. Akhtamzian, "Sovetsko-Germanskie ekonomicheskie otnosheniia," 53; Dyck, *Weimar Germany and Soviet Russia*, 119–29.

31. According to statistics from Soviet sources, the volume of trade with Germany in 1924/25 was 149 million rubles; in 1925/26, 225.6 million rubles; in 1926–27, 264.3 million rubles; and in 1927/28, 364.7 million rubles. In terms of Germany's total foreign trade, these were negligible sums—1.4 percent of exports in 1924 and 3.3 percent in 1928; 1.4 percent of imports in 1924 and 2.7 percent in 1928: Akhtamzian, "Sovetsko-Germanskie ekonomicheskie otnosheniia," 48–49. This work by the leading Soviet expert on relations between Weimar Germany and the USSR is based in part on documents from the "Historical Diplomatic Archives," papers apparently taken from Germany during World War II and kept secret until the late 1980s. Published under the political influence of the Gorbachev-Reagan summit conference at Reykjavik, his work reflects partial "new political thinking." The author's final conclusion: "Historic experience has shown that successful cooperation is possible between two different social systems, if good will prevails" (56).

32. Jacobson, *Locarno Diplomacy*, 279–306.

33. Dyck, *Weimar Germany and Soviet Russia*, 144–46, 216.

34. Krestinskii to Litvinov, 18 January 1927, "Military Cooperation," 105.

35. Krestinskii to Stalin (with copies to Litvinov and Voroshilov),

28 December 1928, "Military Cooperation," 106–110; Akhtamzian, "Voennoe sotrudnichestvo SSSR i Germanii," 17, 22.

36. Reiman, *Birth of Stalinism*, 60–61.

37. Shishkin, "The USSR and Western Countries," 113–14.

38. Kendall E. Bailes, "The American Connection: Ideology and the Transfer of American Technology to the Soviet Union, 1919–1941," *Comparative Studies in Society and History* 23 (1981): 426–33, 439; also Sutton, *Western Technology and Soviet Economic Development*, 1: 276–79, 296–99.

39. Robert Paul Browder, *The Origins of Soviet-American Diplomacy* (Princeton, N.J.: 1953), 22–23.

40. On foreign-policy decision making in July–August 1928, see Reiman, *Birth of Stalinism*, 48, 61, 75–77. For Soviet-American trade, 1925–1928, see Joan Hoff-Wilson, *Ideology and Economics: U.S. Relations with the Soviet Union, 1918–1933* (Columbia, Mo.: 1974), 71–93; and Frank Costigliola, *Awkward Dominion: American Political, Economic, and Cultural Relations with Europe, 1919–1933* (Ithaca, N.Y.: 1984), 160. V. L. Malkov, "SShA: Ot interventsii k priznaniiu Sovetskogo Soiuza (1917–1933gg)," *Novaia i noveishaia istoriia* (1984:1): 125–46, looked back on the opening of diplomatic relations between the United States and the USSR in 1933 as a time of friendlier relations and expressed the hope that they would be restored to that level.

41. Statement by Chicherin in *Izvestiia*, 5 August 1928, *Soviet Documents*, 2: 322–25; Tass statement in *Izvestiia*, 28 August, *Soviet Documents*, 2: 333–35; note from Litvinov to Paris, 31 August 1928, *Soviet Documents*, 2: 335–39.

42. Dyck, *Weimar Germany and Soviet Russia*, 111–12, 139–43.

43. Phillips, *Between the Revolution and the West*, 102–103.

44. Sheinis, *Litvinov*, 204. Elsewhere Sheinis states that Chicherin abandoned the leadership of Soviet diplomacy in November 1926, at the time he began his first extended period of treatment in Germany, and that in September 1928 he was literally sent abroad: Sheinis, "Polpred B. E. Stein," *Novaia i noveishaia istoriia* (1991:1): 108.

45. Sheinis, *Litvinov*, 193; Sheinis, "Stein," 108.

46. When the Social Democratic Party became the main party in the coalition governing Germany in 1928, Comintern attacks on the SPD, labeling its leadership "social-fascist," posed renewed problems for Chicherin's diplomacy. In June 1929, at a time when he was seriously ill and recovering at a health spa in Germany, Chicherin addressed a protest to Stalin. The "social-fascist" line of the Comintern was, he wrote, in what would be one of his last political initiatives, "ridiculous nonsense," "based on falsehoods and propaganda rattling": Quoted by Firsov in "Nekotorye voprosy istorii Kominterna," *Novaia i noveishaia istoriia* (1989:2): 90.

47. Notes from Litvinov to Warsaw, 29 December 1928 and 11 January 1929, Barbusse, *Soviet Union and Peace*, Part IV; report by Rykov to Fifth

Soviet Congress, 20 May 1929, *Soviet Documents*, 2: 372–74; Phillips, *Between the Revolution and the West*, 103–105; Wandycz, *Twilight of French Eastern Alliances*, 135–36.

48. Akhtamzian, "Sovetsko-Germanskie ekonomicheskie otnosheniia," 53–54.

49. Bailes, "American Connection," 433.

50. Bordiugov and Kozlov, "Turning Point," 16–17; Shishkin, "External factor," 53.

51. Bordiugov and Kozlov, "Turning Point," 22.

52. Ibid., 21–22.

53. Tucker, *Stalin in Power*, 71.

54. On Stalin versus the moderates, see Reiman, *Birth of Stalinism*, 89–99; Medvedev, *Let History Judge*, 195–202; Cohen, *Bukharin*, 276–329.

55. Moshe Lewin, "The Disappearance of Planning in the Plan," *Slavic Review* 32 (1973): 279–80.

56. Catherine Merridale, "The Reluctant Opposition: The Right 'Deviation' in Moscow, 1928," *Soviet Studies* 41 (1989): 382–400.

57. Perrey, Hans-Jurgen, *Der Russlandausschuss der deutschen Wirtschaft. Die deutsche-sowjetischen Wirtschaftsbeziehungen der Zwischenkriegszeit. Ein Beitrag zur Geschichte des Ost-West-Handels* (Munich: 1985).

58. Litvinov complained before the Central Executive Committee on 10 December 1928 of "the periodical repetition and dissemination of legends about our difficulties, about alleged crises, catastrophes, insurrections, and the approaching end of the Soviet system": *Soviet Documents*, 2: 355–56.

59. On report by Litvinov to Fifteenth Party Congress, see Barbusse, *Soviet Union and Peace*, 159; Phillips, *Between the Revolution and the West*, 94, 96, 97, 101.

60. Dyck, *Weimar Germany and Soviet Russia*, 143–51.

61. Erickson, *Soviet High Command*, 263–68.

62. See the analysis in Hiden, *Germany and Europe*, 124–25, and compare Jiri Hochman, *The Soviet Union and the Failure of Collective Security, 1934–1938* (Ithaca, N.Y.: 1984), 15–36.

63. Donald N. Lammers, "The Second Labour Government and the Restoration of Relations with Soviet Russia, 1929," *Bulletin of the Institute of Historical Research* 37 (1964): 60–72; Williams, *Labour and Russia*, chaps. 6–7; Henderson quoted, 91.

64. Genis, "Upriamyi narkom s Ilinki," 235. When Sokolnikov returned to Moscow in September 1932, Stalin said to him (237): "I have heard, Grigori, that these gentlemen in England became so fond of you that they didn't want you to leave. Perhaps, it would have been better for you to have stayed with them?"

65. Costigliola, *Awkward Dominion*, 161–64; Hoff-Wilson, *Ideology and Economics*, 93–96; Nikolai V. Sivachev and Nikolai N. Yakovlev, *Russia and the United States* (Chicago: 1979), 86–89.

66. Bailes, "American Connection," 434–35.

67. Shishkin, "The USSR and Western Countries," 112.

68. Bailes, "American Connection," 440; cf. Sutton, *Western Technology*, 346–49. On German technological assistance and the First Five-Year Plan, see Werner Beitel and Jürgen Nötzold, *Deutsch-sowjetische Wirtschafts-beziehungen in der Zeit der Weimarer Republik* (Baden-Baden: 1979).

69. Reiman, *Birth of Stalinism*, 103.

70. *Izvestiia*, 7 December 1928, quoted in Sontag, "Soviet War Scare," 75.

71. For the analysis that follows, see Michael R. Dohan, "The Economic Origins of Soviet Autarky, 1927/28–1934," *Slavic Review* 35 (1976): 603–35; "Foreign Trade and Soviet Investment Strategy," 114–20; "Foreign Trade," 224–33.

72. Anders Johansson, "Swedish Concessionaires in Soviet Industry: Experiences of Foreign Participants in the Rise and Fall of NEP, 'the First Perestroika'" in *Contact or Isolation?* ed. Hiden and Loit, 189–207. Also, Alexander Kulikov, "Concessions of the 1920s," *International Affairs* (Moscow) (1989:4): 76–83.

11. FOREIGN RELATIONS DURING "THE GREAT TURN"

1. Lewin, *Making of the Soviet System*, 104–105. At the same time, the work is not uncritical of the economic strategies offered by the moderates in 1928–29.

2. Stephen F. Cohen, *Rethinking the Soviet Experience: Politics and History since 1917* (New York: 1985), 86.

3. For the critical examination of Stalinist industrialization, see Holland Hunter, "The Over-ambitious First Soviet Five-Year Plan," *Slavic Review* 32 (1973): 237–57, with comments by Robert Campbell, Stephen F. Cohen, Moshe Lewin, and a reply by Hunter, 258–91; quotation from review by Hunter in the *Journal of Economic History* 49 (1989): 221.

4. On the achievements, difficulties, and costs of the First Five-Year Plan, see Kuromiya, *Stalin's Industrial Revolution*, 287–96, 302–310. In the transformation of historical awareness that accompanied the Gorbachev revolution, "a new radical consensus" emerged in the summer of 1988. Although that consensus recognized the industrial achievements of the 1930s, it rejected the collectivization of agriculture and the administrative planning that had replaced the mixed market economy of NEP. The abandonment of Leninist principles in the political system was criticized, and the whole Stalinist period was regarded as "a substantial departure from the road to socialism." Gorbachev himself, in the report he gave on the occasion of the seventieth anniversary of the Bolshevik Revolution in November 1987, denounced Stalinist repression, condemned what he called the "administrative-command system of party-state management of the

country" initiated in the 1930s, and criticized its negative consequences for the democratization of Soviet society: See R. W. Davies, *Soviet History in the Gorbachev Revolution,* 135–36, 195.

5. Bukharin's development strategy, his criticism of what became Stalinist industrialization, and his appeal to Lenin's political testament are examined in Cohen, *Bukharin and the Bolshevik Revolution,* especially 312–22. The idea of a Bukharin road to socialism as an alternative to Stalinism is developed in Cohen's introduction to the 1980 edition of this work. See also the reviews of Cohen's work by Lewin in the *Journal of Modern History* 47 (1975): 373–83, and by Loren Graham in the *Russian Review* 33 (1974): 324–26.

6. Davies, *Soviet History in the Gorbachev Revolution,* 1–2, 32–38, 146–47.

7. On the "Bukharin alternative" and its impact on *perestroika,* see Peter Kneen, "The Background to *Perestroika:* 'Political Undercurrents' Reconsidered in the Light of Recent Events," in *Stalinism: Its Nature and Aftermath: Essays in Honour of Moshe Lewin,* ed. Nick Lambert and Gábor T. Rittersporn (Armonk, N.Y.: 1992), 243–59; "The Bukharin Alternative," *Soviet Studies in History* 28 (Spring 1990), edited with introduction by Lynne Viola. Sirotkin, "Ot grazhdanskoi voiny k grazhdanskomu miru," offers an appreciation of NEP as a program of socialization well thought out by Lenin and further developed by Bukharin in opposition to Trotsky.

8. G. M. Adibekov, "Tri krutykh povorota. (O vzaimosviazi vnutrennei i vneshnei politiki KPSS)," *Voprosy Istorii KPSS* (1990:3): 30–43.

9. A. G. Latyshev, "Bukharin—izvestnyi i neivestnyi," in *Otkryvaia novye stranitsy,* 328. Also L. K. Shkarenkov, "Nikolai Ivanovich Bukharin," *Voprosy istorii* (1988:7): 59–78; and N. V. Pavlov and M. L. Fedorov, "Nikolai Ivanovich Bukharin," *Voprosy istorii KPSS* (1988:10): 73–87; both are printed in translation in *Soviet Studies in History* 28 (Spring 1990): 40–97.

10. M. M. Gorinov and S. V. Tasakunov, "Leninskaia kontseptsiia NEPa: stanovlenie i razvitie," *Voprosy istorii* (1990:4): 20–39. Also Lars T. Lih, "Political Testament of Lenin and Bukharin and the Meaning of NEP," *Slavic Review* 50 (1991): 241–52.

11. Bordiugov and Kozlov, "Turning Point," 33–34.

12. G. I. Khanin, "Why and When did NEP Die? An Economist's Reflections," *Soviet Review* 31 (1990): 47–59; original Russian publication, "Pochemu i kogda pogib NEP? Razmyshleniia ekonomista," *Ekonomika i organizatsiia poromyslennogo proizvodstva* (1989:10): 66–83.

13. Hughes, *Stalin, Siberia and the Crisis of the New Economic Policy,* 99–104, 208–209; quotation from 209.

14. Dohan, "Foreign Trade," 232–33.

15. Khanin, "Why and When did NEP Die?" 59–62, argues that, so

essential were economic foreign relations to the long-term development of the economy that there was no possibility of solving Russia's economic problems within the framework of NEP once the decisions had been made in 1922 not to recognize fully the debts of previous regimes, not to relax the foreign trade monopoly, and not to alter the system of one-party dictatorship.

16. Gill, *Origins of the Stalinist Political System,* 18.

17. Tucker, "Stalinism as Revolution from Above," 89–94; quotation, 92.

18. D'Agostino, *Soviet Succession Struggles;* Day, *Leon Trotsky and the Politics of Economic Isolation.*

19. Gorinov and Tasakunov, "Leninskaia kontseptsiia NEPa."

20. Stephane Courtois, "Le système communiste international et la lutte pour la paix 1917–1939," *Relations internationales* 53 (1988): 7–10.

21. Tucker, *Stalin in Power,* 223–37.

22. Phillips, *Between the Revolution and the West,* 47–99.

23. di Biagio, "Bukharin's International Alternative," 123.

24. The major investigations into Bukharin's writings give little attention to the issue of foreign investment: Cohen, *Bukharin;* Lewin, *Political Undercurrents.* Discussions of the issue at the highest political levels, as opposed to the level of theoretical/ideological disputation, show little evidence of his influence: Reiman, *Birth of Stalinism.*

25. Michael Haynes, *Nikolai Bukharin and the Transition from Capitalism to Socialism* (London: 1985), chap. 6.

26. Bordiugov and Kozlov, "Turning Point," 23.

27. Meyer, "War Scare," 2–6.

28. Central Committee message quoted in Nezhinskii, "Byla li voennaia ugroza," 21; Voroshilov in *Izvestiia,* 11 June 1927, and Tomskii in *Izvestiia,* 12 June 1927, are quoted in Gorodetsky, *Precarious Truce,* 238.

29. Gregor, *Resolutions and Decisions,* 312–13.

30. Political Report of the Central Committee to the Fifteenth Party Congress, 3 December 1927, Stalin, *Works,* 10: 291–95. The congress resolution stated that "reactionary elements of the international bourgeoisie have started to prepare the ground for an armed assault on the USSR, after entangling it in a whole cluster of provocation (assaults on the USSR diplomatic representatives, murder of Soviet diplomats)": *Resolutions,* 313.

31. Manfred von Boetticher, *Industrialisierungspolitik und Vertiedigungskonzeption der UdSSR 1926–1930: Herausbildung des Stalinismus und "aüssere Bedrohung"* (Dusseldorf: 1979); Fitzpatrick, "Foreign Threat." Nezhinskii, "Byla li voennaia ugroza," 14–30, a work published during *perestroika* by a prominent Soviet scholar, constitutes a full refutation of the notion that "the foreign threat" proclaimed by Stalin had any real basis in international relations.

32. Gorodetsky, *Precarious Truce,* 238–39.

33. Statement by Kalinin in *Pravda,* 12 October 1927, quoted in Gorodetsky, *Precarious Truce,* 240.

34. Stalin's statement (November 1928) quoted in Reiman, *Birth of Stalinism,* 85–86.

35. Resolutions of Fifteenth Party Congress, December 1927, quoted in Davies, *Soviet Economy in Turmoil,* 442.

36. Davies, *Soviet Economy in Turmoil,* 441–45, 461–62; Carr, *Foundations,* 1: 872.

37. Report by Stalin to Moscow Party Organization, 13 April 1928, Stalin, *Works,* 11: 58. For Stalin's exploitation of the Shakhty case, see Bailes, *Technology and Society,* 84–89.

38. Fitzpatrick, "Foreign Threat," passim; also her *The Russian Revolution, 1917–1932* (Oxford: 1982), 110–13; Kuromiya, *Stalin's Industrial Revolution,* especially 310–18.

39. For Report by Bukharin on the International Situation and the Tasks of the Communist Parties, 18–19 July 1928, see Xenia J. Eudin and Robert M. Slusser, eds., *Soviet Foreign Policy, 1928–1934: Documents and Materials* (University Park, Pa.: 1967), 1: 106–120; hereafter, *SFP, 1928–1934;* Carr, *Foundations,* 3: 193–222.

40. Carr, *Foundations,* 3: 223–34.

41. Nicholas N. Kozlov and Eric D. Weitz, "Reflections on the Origins of the 'Third Period': Bukharin, the Comintern, and the Political Economy of Western Germany," *Journal of Contemporary History* 24 (1989): 387–401, demonstrates that Bukharin believed that capitalism was in crisis despite its relative stabilization, just as did Varga, Trotsky, Zinoviev, and Stalin. In fact, it was Bukharin who coined the term "third period" at the Seventh ECCI Plenum in November–December 1926. Where he differed from the others, who depicted capitalism as "decadent," "rotten," and "moribund," was in contending that capitalism's crisis developed from its progressive stabilization and continued advances in technology and organization rather than from its general decline. Stalin and Bukharin had a common hostility toward social democracy and a belief that the "third period" was one of wars and revolutions. However, as Day has demonstrated, Stalin defined the current *epoch* as one of "general crisis" and the *period* as one of wars and revolutions, meaning that war might occur in the immediate future. Bukharin, on the other hand, contended that the *epoch* was one of wars and revolutions, while the period was one of capitalist stabilization and reconstruction, meaning that there could be years of international peace: See Day, *Crisis and Crash,* 111.

42. "Measures of Struggle against the Danger of Imperialist War and the Tasks of the Communists," Sixth Comintern Congress, July–September 1928: *SFP, 1928–1934,* 1: 128.

43. *Izvestiia,* 23 May 1929, quoted in *SFP, 1928–1934,* 1: 4–5.

44. Report by Rykov to the Fifth Congress of Soviets, 20 May 1929, *Soviet Documents,* 2: 374.

45. See, for example, Ulam, *Expansion and Coexistence,* 183.

46. For example, Jonathan Haslam, *Soviet Foreign Policy, 1930–33: The Impact of the Depression* (London and New York: 1983), 18–20.

47. Robert C. Tucker, "Emergence of Stalin's Foreign Policy," 563–75; his *Stalin in Power,* 44–65, quotations on 45; and his "Stalinism as Revolution from Above," 77–108.

48. Speech by Stalin at Plenum of the Central Committee and the Central Control Commission, 27 January 1925, *Works,* 7: 13–14.

49. Stalin quoted in Meyer, "War Scare," 3.

50. "To stretch out the breathing space for as long as possible . . . is the foundation and the most essential formula of the foreign policy of the USSR": "Leninist Principles of Soviet Foreign Policy," *Izvestiia,* 22 January 1929, *SFP, 1928–1934,* 1: 160–61.

51. Antonio Carlo, "Structural Causes of the Soviet Coexistence Policy," in Jahn, ed. *Soviet Foreign Policy,* 65.

Glossary

Adalet.   Baku-based Social Democratic Party with branches in Central Asia; merged with RCP(B) and Persian Communist Party.

AEG.   German electrical cartel.

Amtorg Trading Corporation.   Corporation founded in New York and managed by the Soviet trade organization to conduct trade between the USSR and the United States.

ARCOS.   All-Russian Cooperative Joint Stock Company, an organization similar to Amtorg, operating in London.

ARJAC.   Anglo-Russian Joint Advisory Council.

CC.   Central Committee (of the Communist Party).

CEC.   Central Executive Committee (of the Congress of Soviets).

Chevonets.   Ten-ruble bank note backed by gold, introduced in the currency reform of 1922–24.

Comintern (CI).   Communist International.

CPC.   Chinese Communist Party.

CPGB.   Communist Party of Great Britain.

CPSU.   Communist Party of the Soviet Union. Not the official term until 1952, but used in this work instead of AUCP(B), All Union Communist Party, adopted at the Fourteenth Party Congress in December 1925.

Dognat i peregnat.   To catch up and surpass.

ECCI.   Executive Committee of the Communist International.

Gosplan.   State Planning Commission, under Sovnarkom.

Guomindang (GMD).   Chinese Nationalist Party.

KPD.   German Communist Party.

Kulak.   Rich peasant, rural trader, or entrepreneur.

Mirnoe sosushchestvovanie.   Peaceful coexistence.

Mirnoe sozhitelstvo.   Peaceful cohabitation.

Musavat (Muslim Democratic Party Musavat).   Azerbaijani nationalist party.

Narkom.   People's commissar.

Narkomfin (NKF).   People's Commissariat of Finance.

Narkomindel (NKID).   People's Commissariat of Foreign Affairs.

NEP.   New Economic Policy.

NRA.   National Revolutionary Army.

(O)GPU.   Soviet state security service (1922–34), successor to Cheka (1917–22) and predecessor of NKVD (1934–46), NKGB, MGB, MVD, and KGB (1954–91).

PCF.   French Communist Party.

Peredyshka.   Breathing space or respite.

Plenum.   General or full assembly.

Politburo.   Political Bureau of the Central Committee, the leading decision-making organ of the RCP(B)/CPSU.

Politika dogovorennost.   Politics of understanding.

Polpred.   Term for a Soviet diplomatic representative abroad.

Proderzhatsiia.   Holding out.

Profintern.   Red International of Trade Unions.

RCP(B).   Russian Communist Party.

RMC.   Revolutionary Military Council of the USSR.

RSFSR.   Russian Socialist Federated Soviet Republic.

Smychka.   Worker-peasant alliance or link between town and country.

Sovnarkom (SNK).   Council of People's Commissars of the USSR.

SPD.   German Social Democratic Party.

United Opposition.   Opposition to the Central Committee majority formed in April 1926.

Vesenkha (VSNKh).   Supreme Council of the National Economy.

Vneshtorg.   State foreign trade monopoly.

Soviet Government, Communist Party, and Comintern Officials

Bekzadian, Aleksandr, 1879–1938.   Revolutionary and diplomat. Member of the Transcaucasian Regional Committee of the RCP(B) (1919–20). Acting chairman of the Revolutionary Committee and people's commissar of foreign affairs of Soviet Armenia (1920–21). Worked in the Soviet Trade Agency in Germany (1922–26). Vice-chairman of the Council of People's Commissars and people's commissar of trade of the Transcaucasian SFSR (1926–30).

Bliukher, Vasilii, 1890–1938.   Military commander. Minister of war, commander, and president of the Military Council of the People's Army of the Far Eastern Republic (1921–22). Member of the RCP(B) Central Committee (1921–24). Chief of Soviet military mission in south China (1924–27). Commander of Special Far Eastern Army (1929).

Borodin, Mikhail (born Mikhail Grusenberg), 1884–1953.   Revolutionary and Comintern official. Comintern emissary to the United States who also served in Mexico and Spain (1919); emissary in Berlin (1921) and Britain (1922). Comintern envoy to the Chinese Communist Party and chief political adviser to the Central Committee of the Guomindang (1923–27).

Bubnov, Andrei, 1883–1940.   Revolutionary and party official. Served on the Revolutionary Military Council of the Northeastern Caucasus Military District and on the staff of the First Cavalry Army (1921–22). Chief of the Political Administration of the Red Army and member of the Revolutionary Military Council (1924–29). Full member of the RCP(B) Central Committee and Orgburo (1924); secretary of Central Committee (1925). Led Central Committee commission to investigate the situation in China (1926).

Bukharin, Nikolai, 1888–1938.   Revolutionary, party and Comintern leader. Member of RCP(B) Central Committee (1917–29); candidate (1919–24) and then full member (1924–29) of Politburo. Member of

ECCI Presidium (1920–29); vice-chairman of the ECCI (1925); then leader (1926–29). Editor of *Pravda* (1917–29) and *Izvestiia* (1934–37). Expelled from Politburo (1929). Tried and executed with Rykov (1938).

Chicherin, Georgii, 1872–1936.   Soviet diplomat. People's commissar for foreign affairs (1918–30); elected to RCP(B) Central Committee (1925, 1927).

Dzerzhinskii, Feliks, 1877–1926. Revolutionary and party leader. Founder and first chairman of Cheka (1917–19), GPU (1919–26), and OGPU (1926). Chairman of the Supreme National Economic Council and candidate member of the Politburo (1924–26).

Frunze, Mikhail, 1885–1925.   Military commander. Commanded Red Army in the Crimea and the Ukraine (1920). Member of RCP(B) Central Committee (1921–25). Elected Ukrainian representative to the ECCI (1924), then candidate member of ECCI Presidium. Deputy chairman of the Revolutionary Military Council (1924); chairman of RMC, chief of staff and people's commissar for military and naval affairs (1925).

Humbert-Droz, Jules, 1891–1971.   Comintern official. Cofounder of the Swiss Communist Party (1921). Assumed high Comintern functions (1922–28), becoming secretary to the ECCI; member of the Orgburo, the Political Secretariat, and the ECCI Presidium; and director of the Latin Secretariat.

Ioffe, Adolf (born Adolf Abramovich), 1883–1927.   Revolutionary and diplomat. *Polpred* in Germany (1918) and China (1922–23); deputy *polpred* in Britain (1924) and Austria (1924–25).

Kalinin, Mikhail, 1875–1946.   Revolutionary and party leader. Member of the RCP(B) Central Committee and candidate member of the Politburo (1919), then full member (1926–46). Chairman of Central Executive Committee (1919–38) and then of Presidium of Supreme Soviet (1938–46).

Kamenev, Lev (born Lev Rosenfeld), 1883–1936.   Revolutionary, party leader, and diplomat. Member of the RCP(B) Central Committee and Politburo (1917–27). Deputy chairman of the Council of People's Commissars (1922–25). Candidate member of the ECCI (1921); full member and candidate to the ECCI Presidium (1924). Soviet *polpred* in Austria (1918) and Italy (1926–27). Member of the triumvirate with Zinoviev and Stalin following Lenin's death, then joined Trotsky and Zinoviev in the Opposition. Expelled from offices (1926–27) and from party (1927), reinstated (1928), and expelled again (1932). Arrested and imprisoned following Kirov murder (1935); tried and executed with Zinoviev (1936).

Katayama, Sen, 1859–1933.   Comintern official. Member of the Comintern's American Bureau in Mexico (1921); elected to ECCI and its Presidium (1922–33).

Kopp, Victor, 1880–1930.   Diplomat. Soviet representative in Germany (1919–21); representative in negotiations with Poland (1923); member of NKID Collegium (1924–25); *polpred* in Japan (1925–27) and Sweden (1927–30).

Krasin, Leonid, 1870–1926.   Diplomat and government official. Conducted negotiations and signed trade agreement with England (1920–21); attended Genoa and Hague conferences (1922); participated in Anglo-Soviet negotiations (1923); *polpred* in France (1924–25) and England (1925–26).

Krestinskii, Nikolai, 1883–1938.   Revolutionary and diplomat. Member of RCP(B) Central Committee (1917–21). People's commissar of finance (1918–21). *Polpred* in Germany (1921–30).

Kuibyshev, Nikolai, 1893–1938.   Military commander. Infantry division commander on the Southern Front (1920), corps commander (1921). Commandant and commissar of Kronstadt (1922–23); head of the Higher Infantry School of the Soviet Army (1923–25). Assistant commander of the Turkistan Front (1925–26), then corps commander. Chief of the Command Directorate of the Red Army and assistant commander of the Moscow Military District (1927–28). Commander of the troops of the Siberian Military District (1928–36). Brother of V. Kuibyshev.

Kuibyshev, Valerian, 1888–1935.   State official and party leader. Deputy chairman of the Council of People's Commissars and the Council of Labor and Defense (1923–35). Chairman of the Supreme Economic Council (1926–30). Elected to Central Committee and Politburo (1927).

Kun, Béla, 1885–1937.   Revolutionary and Comintern official. Organized revolution in Budapest (1919); launched "March Action" in Germany (1921). Member or candidate member of ECCI Presidium (1921, 1926, 1931).

Kuusinen, Otto, 1881–1964.   Comintern official. Named secretary of the Comintern (1921); elected to ECCI and its Presidium (1922), positions that he retained until the Comintern's "dissolution" (1943).

Lenin, Vladimir (born Vladimir Ilyich Ulianov), 1870–1924.   Revolutionary and government, party, and Comintern leader. Founded Bolshevik wing of the Russian Social Democratic Party (1903); led Bolsheviks in overthrow of Provisional government (1917). Chairman of the Council of People's Commissars (1917–24). Founded Communist International (1919) and was active in Comintern affairs until incapacitated by a series of strokes (1922–23).

Litvinov, Maksim, 1876–1951.   Diplomat. Headed numerous special diplomatic missions in Western Europe (1917–21). Member of NKID Collegium (1918–34); deputy people's commissar for foreign affairs (1921–30). Member of Soviet delegation to Genoa Conference (1922); led delegation to Hague Conference (1922); chairman of Moscow Disarmament Conference (1922); led Soviet delegation to Preparatory Commission on Disarmament (1927–30); signed Moscow (Litvinov) Protocol (1929). People's commissar for foreign affairs (1930–39).

Manuilskii, Dmitrii, 1883–1959.   Comintern official. Secretary of the Ukrainian Communist Party Central Committee (1921). Member of the RCP(B) Central Committee (1923). Member of the ECCI and its Presidium (1924–43) and of the Comintern's Political Secretariat (1926–43).

Menzhinskii, Viacheslav, 1874–1934.   Party activist and government official. Head of the Cheka's Special Department (1920) and chief of the Secret Operational Department (1921). Deputy chairman of the (O)GPU (1923–26) and chairman of (O)GPU (1926–34). Member of the CPSU Central Committee (1927, 1930).

Mif, Pavel (born Mikhail Firman), 1899–1937.   Comintern official and specialist on Far Eastern revolutionary movements. Comintern representative in Shanghai (1926); deputy director of Sun Yat-sen University in Moscow (1927); director (1928).

Mikoian, Anastas, 1895–1978.   Government official and party leader. Candidate member of the Politburo and commissar of foreign and domestic trade (1926–30).

Molotov, Viacheslav (born Viacheslav Skryabin), 1890–1986.   Party leader. Candidate member of the RCP(B) Central Committee (1920); full member, member of the Central Committee Secretariat, and candidate member of the Politburo (1921); full member of Politburo (1925). Member of RCP(B) delegations to Third and Fifth Comintern congresses (1921, 1925); candidate member of ECCI Presidium (1926–28); member of Presidium and Secretariat (1928–1930).

Ordzhonikidze, Grigorii ("Sergo"), 1886–1937.   Revolutionary and party leader. Chairman of Military Revolutionary Council of the Caucasus Front (1920). Head of Transcaucasian Regional Committee of the RCP(B) (1922–26). Member of RCP(B) Central Committee (1921–26); candidate member of Politburo (1925); chairman of the party's Central Control Commission (1926).

Pavlov, Pavel, 1892–1924.   Military commander. Deputy commander in Bukhara, suppressing the *basmachi* (1922–23). Elected member of the Bukhara Central Committee (1923). Chief military adviser to Sun Yat-sen (1924).

Piatakov, Georgi, 1890–1937.   Party official. Candidate member of the RCP(B) Central Committee (1921), full member (1923). Attended Third ECCI Plenum as RCP(B) delegate and participated in preparations for the German October (1923).

Piatnitskii, Iosif (born Osip Aronovich), 1882–1939.   Comintern official.

Treasurer of the Comintern and chief of the OMS (1921); member of the Comintern Orgburo (1922–35); member of the ECCI Secretariat and candidate member of ECCI (1923–35).

Preobrazhenskii, Evgenii, 1886–1937. Economist and state and party official. Member of the RCP(B) Central Committee and of its Secretariat, Orgburo, Politburo, and Central Control Commission (1920); lost seats (1921). Vocal member of the Opposition (1921–26), publishing extensively on the Soviet economy. Chairman of the Central Committee's Finance Committee and Collegium member of the People's Commissariat of Finance. Expelled from the CPSU and exiled to Uralsk (1927–28) but readmitted in 1929.

Radek, Karl (born Karl Berngardovich), 1885–1939. Revolutionary and party leader. Member of the RCP(B) Central Committee (1919–24). Secretary of the Comintern, member of the ECCI (1920), and of the ECCI Presidium (1921–25). Head of Sun Yat-sen University (1926–27).

Rakovskii, Christian, 1873–1941. Revolutionary and diplomat. Prime minister of the Ukrainian government (1918–23). Cofounder of the Communist International (1919). Member of RCP(B) delegations to Second and Third congresses (1920, 1921). Member of RCP(B) Central Committee (1919–27). Soviet representative in England (1923–25), then in France (1925–27). Expelled from the CPSU and deported to Astrakhan (1927).

Raskolnikov, Fedor (aka Petrov), 1892–1939. Revolutionary and diplomat. Commander of Caspian Sea flotilla and of Baltic Fleet during the Civil War. *Polpred* in Afghanistan (1921–24). Candidate member of the ECCI and full member of its Orgburo (1924–27), during which time he was appointed director of the Eastern Department of the Comintern Secretariat and editor of the *Communist International.* Member of the ECCI Political Commission (1925) and Secretariat (1926).

Reisner, Larissa, 1895–1926. Revolutionary and poet. Commissar to Fifth Red Army during the Civil War. Married to Raskolnikov during his term in Afghanistan, separated in 1923. Accompanied Radek to Germany and acted as liaison between Comintern and KPD leaders during the German October (1923). Undertook other missions in the Urals, the Don Basin, and Persia.

Rothshtein, Fedor, 1871–1953. Diplomat and Comintern official. Confidential Comintern emissary in Great Britain (1919–20); Soviet *polpred* in Persia (1920). Member of NKID Collegium (1923–30). Appointed NKID press director (1925), and wrote for Comintern press.

Roy, Manabendra N., 1887–1954. Revolutionary and Comintern official. Delegate of the Mexican Communist Party to the Second Comintern Congress (1920). Headed the Far Eastern Bureau of the Comintern in Tashkent (1921). Member of the ECCI (1921–24), candidate member

(1924–25), member of the ECCI and its Presidium (1925–27). Replaced Borodin as head of Comintern delegation to China (1927). Expelled from Comintern (1929).

Rykov, Aleksei, 1881–1938. Revolutionary and government and party leader. Member of the RCP(B) Central Committee (1905–30) and Politburo (1924–30). Chairman of Supreme Council of the National Economy (1918–21). Chairman of the Council of People's Commissars (1924–30). Delegate to Second (1920) and Third (1921) Comintern congresses. Member of ECCI (1924–30). Lost important government, party, and Comintern positions (1930). Expelled from party (1937); tried, sentenced, and executed with Bukharin (1938).

Shumiatskii, Boris, 1886–? Comintern official and diplomat. Helped organize the Comintern Secretariat for the Far East in Irkutsk (1920–21) and attended Third Congress of Comintern as delegate thereof (1921). Secretary at the Congress of Revolutionary Organizations and Peoples of the Far East (1922). *Polpred* in Persia (1922–25).

Sneevliet, Hendricus (aka H. Maring), 1883–1942. Founding member of Indonesian Communist Party (1920). Member of ECCI (1920); Comintern emissary to China (1921–23). Assisted in founding Chinese Communist Party (1921). Worked in Far Eastern office of Comintern (1923). Active in Dutch Communist Party (1924–27).

Sokolnikov, Grigori, 1888–1939. Revolutionary, party leader, and government official. Member of the RCP(B) Central Committee (1917–27). Leader of various revolutionary military councils during Civil War. Deputy and then commissar of finance (1921–26). Delegate to Second Congress of the Comintern (1920). Sent to Turkistan as head of Central Asian Bureau of the Comintern (1920). Candidate member of the ECCI (1924). Participated in United Opposition. *Polpred* in England (1929–32).

Souvarine, Boris (aka Varine), 1895–? Comintern official. Founding member of the French Communist Party. French delegate to the Third Comintern Congress (1921); elected member of the ECCI, the Presidium, and, later, the Secretariat. Defended Trotsky and was expelled from all Comintern positions and from the PCF (1924).

Stalin, Josef (born Iosif Vissarionovich Dzhugashvili), 1879–1953. Revolutionary and party leader. Member of the Central Committee and Politburo (1917–53). Member of the Revolutionary Military Council (1920–23). People's commissar for nationalities (1921–23). General secretary of the Central Committee (1922). Active in Comintern affairs, particularly as member of the ECCI Presidium beginning with the Fifth Congress (1924). Following Lenin's death, combined with Zinoviev and Kamenev against Trotsky, and then with Bukharin against Zinoviev, Kamenev, and Trotsky (1926–27); led Central Committee majority that defeated Bukharin, Tomskii, and Rykov (1928–30).

Stasova, Elena, 1873–1966.   Comintern official. Member of the RCP(B) Central Committee (1917–20). Assisted in preparing the Congress of the Peoples of the East (1920). Appointed Comintern representative to the KPD, worked within the Orgburo of the KPD Central Committee (1921–26).

Surits, Yakov, 1882–1952.   Diplomat. *Polpred* in Afghanistan (1919–21). Member of the Turkistan Commission and commissar for foreign affairs for Turkistan and Central Asia (1921–22). *Polpred* in Norway (1922–23) and Turkey (1923–24).

Tomskii, Mikhail, 1880–1936.   Revolutionary and party and government leader. Member of the RCP(B) Central Committee (1919–29) and Politburo (1922–29). Chairman of the Central Council of Soviet Trade Unions (1919–28). Expelled from party (1928); subsequently recanted. Threatened with trial during the purges, he committed suicide (1936).

Trotsky, Leon (born Lev Davidovich Bronstein), 1879–1940.   Revolutionary and party leader. Member of the Central Committee and Politburo (1917–26). Commissar for foreign affairs (1917–18); commissar for military affairs (1918–25) and organizer of Red forces in the Civil War. Active in Comintern affairs beginning with the Third Congress (1921), first as candidate, then as full member of the ECCI until his removal (1927). Defeated in contest to succeed Lenin. Expelled from party (1927) and banished from USSR (1929). Murdered by Stalinist agent in Mexico (1940).

Tuchachevskii, Mikhail, 1893–1937.   Joined RCP(B) in 1918. Red Army commander in Civil War against Generals Kolchak and Denikin and against Poland. Chief of staff (1925–28).

Unszlicht, Józef, 1879–1937 or 1938.   Party activist and military expert. Representative of the Polish Communist Party at founding Congress of the Comintern (1919). Appointed deputy director of the (O)GPU (1921). Member of RCP(B) Control Commission (1924); candidate member of Central Committee (1925, 1927). Member of the Revolutionary Military Council and chief of logistics for the Red Army (1923–25); deputy chairman of RMC (1925–30).

Vishinskii, Andrei, 1883–1954.   Government official and diplomat. Public prosecutor of the Criminal-Judicial Collegium of the USSR Supreme Court (1923–25). Rector of Moscow State University (1925–28). Presiding judge at the Shakhty case (1928) and other show trials.

Voikov, Petr, 1888–1927.   Diplomat. *Polpred* in Poland (1924–27), murdered in Warsaw.

Voitinskii, Grigori, 1893–1953.   Comintern official. Chief of the Comintern's Far Eastern Secretariat (1921–24); Comintern emissary to China (1924–25, 1927).

Voroshilov, Kliment, 1881–1969. Military commander and party leader. Deputy commander on southern front during the Civil War; commander of the North Caucasus Military District (1921–24). Commander of the Moscow Military District and member of the Revolutionary Military Council (1924–25). People's commissar for military and naval affairs and chairman of the Revolutionary Military Council (1925–34). Member of the Central Committee of the RCP(B) (1921–61) and its Politburo (1926–60).

Vorovskii, Waclaw, 1871–1923. Revolutionary, Comintern official, and diplomat. Representative of the RCP(B) to the ECCI and the Comintern Secretariat (1919–20). *Polpred* in Italy (1921–23); secretary-general of the Soviet delegations at the Genoa and Lausanne conferences (1922–23); murdered in Lausanne (1923).

Yurenev, Konstantin. Diplomat. *Polpred* in Bukhara (1922–23), Latvia (1923–24), Czechoslovakia (1924–25), Italy (1925–27), and Persia (1927–33).

Zinoviev, Grigorii, 1883–1936. Revolutionary and party leader. Head of Petrograd/Leningrad Soviet and member of Politburo (1921–26). President of the ECCI (1919–26). Allied with Stalin and Kamenev against Trotsky following Lenin's death; then allied with Kamenev and Trotsky against Stalin and Bukharin (1926–27). Expelled from various offices and from party (1926–27); recanted and was readmitted to party (1928) but expelled again (1932). Imprisoned following Kirov murder (1935); tried, sentenced, and executed with Kamenev (1936).

Bibliography

Abrahamian, Ervand. *Iran between Two Revolutions.* Princeton, N.J.: 1982.

Adamec, Ludwig W. *Afghanistan, 1900–1923: A Diplomatic History.* Berkeley, Calif.: 1967.

———. *Afghanistan's Foreign Affairs to the Mid-Twentieth Century: Relations with the USSR, Germany, and Britain.* Tucson, Ariz.: 1974.

ADAP. See Germany. Auswärtiges Amt. *Akten zur Deutschen Auswärtigen Politik, 1918–1945.*

Adhikari, Gangadhar M. Editor. *Documents of the History of the Communist Party of India.* 8 vols. New Delhi: 1971–82.

Adibekov, G. M. "Tri krutykh povorota. (O vzaimosviazi vnutrennei i vneshnei politiki KPSS.") *Voprosy istorii KPSS* (1990:3): 30–43.

Adler, Alan. Editor. *Theses, Resolutions, and Manifestos of the First Four Congresses of the Third International.* London and Atlantic Highlands, N.J.: 1980.

Afanaseva, Iu. N. Editor. *Inogo ne dano.* Moscow: 1988.

Agabekov, Georgii S. *OGPU, the Russian Secret Terror.* New York: 1931.

Akhtamzian, Abdulkhan A. *Rapallskaia politika: sovetsko-germskie diplomatichoskie otnosheniia v 1922–1932 gg.* Moscow: 1974.

———. "Sovetsko-Germanskie ekonomicheskie otnosheniia v 1922–1932 gg." *Novaia i noveishaia istoriia* (1988:4): 42–56.

———. "Voennoe sotrudnichestvo SSSR i Germanii v 1920–1933 gg." *Novaia i noveishaia istoriia* (1990:5): 3–24. English edition: "Soviet-German Military Cooperation, 1920–1933." *International Affairs* (Moscow) (1990:7): 95–113.

Alimurzayev, Grigori. "A Shield or a Sword? History of Soviet Military Doctrine." *International Affairs* (Moscow) (1989:5): 100–109.

Andrew, Christopher M. "British Intelligence and the Breach with Russia in 1927." *Historical Journal* 25 (1982): 957–64.

———. *Her Majesty's Secret Service: The Making of the British Intelligence*

Community. New York: 1986. Original British edition: Secret Service: The Making of the British Intelligence Community. London: 1985.

Andrew, Christopher M., and Oleg Gordievsky. KGB: The Inside Story of Its Foreign Operations from Lenin to Gorbachev. New York: 1990.

Angress, Werner T. Stillborn Revolution: The Communist Bid for Power in Germany, 1921–1923. Princeton, N.J.: 1963.

Arkhipenko, Vladimir K. "Fedor Raskolnikov." In Otkryvaia novye stranitsy. Mezhdunarodnye voprosy: sobytiia i liudi. Edited by Akhmed A. Iskenderov. Moscow: 1989.

Bailes, Kendall E. "The American Connection: Ideology and the Transfer of American Technology to the Soviet Union, 1917–1941." Comparative Studies in Society and History 23 (1981): 421–48.

———. Technology and Society under Lenin and Stalin: Origins of the Soviet Technical Intelligentsia, 1917–1941. Princeton, N.J.: 1978.

Barbusse, Henri. Editor. The Soviet Union and Peace: The Most Important of the Documents Issued by the Government of the USSR Concerning Peace and Disarmament from 1917 to 1929. New York: [1929?].

Bazhanov, Boris. Bazhanov and the Damnation of Stalin. Translated by David W. Doyle. Athens, Ohio: 1990.

Becker, Seymour. Russia's Protectorates in Central Asia: Bukhara and Khiva, 1865–1924. Cambridge, Mass.: 1968.

Beinin, Joel, and Zachary Lockman. Workers on the Nile: Nationalism, Communism, Islam, and the Egyptian Working Class, 1882–1954. Princeton, N.J.: 1987.

Beitel, Werner, and Jürgen Nötzold. Deutsch-sowjetische Wirtschaftsbeziehungen in der Zeit der Weimarer Republik: ein Balanz im Hinblick auf gegenwärtige Probleme. Baden-Baden: 1979.

Bennigsen, Alexandre A. The Soviet Union and Muslim Guerrilla Wars, 1920–1981: Lessons for Afghanistan. Santa Monica, Calif.: 1981.

Bennigsen, Alexandre A., Paul B. Hinze, George K. Tanham, and S. Enders Wimbush. Soviet Strategy and Islam. New York: 1989.

Bennigsen, Alexandre A., and S. Enders Wimbush. Muslim National Communism in the Soviet Union: A Revolutionary Strategy for the Colonial World. Chicago: 1979.

Berghahn, Volker R., and Martin Kitchen. Germany in the Age of Total War. London: 1981.

Bessel, Richard, and E. J. Feuchtwanger. Social Change and Political Development in Weimar Germany. London and Totowa, N.J.: 1981.

Blackstock, Paul W. The Secret Road to World War Two: Soviet versus Western Intelligence, 1921–1939. Chicago: 1969.

Boersner, Demetrio. The Bolsheviks and the National and Colonial Question 1917–1928. 1957. Reprint. Westport, Conn.: 1981.

Bond, Brian. British Military Policy Between the Two World Wars. Oxford: 1980.

Bordiugov, G. A., and V. A. Kozlov. "The Turning Point of 1929 and the

Bukharin Alternative." *Soviet Studies in History* 28 (Spring 1990): 8–39. Original Russian publication: "Povorot 1929 goda i alternativa Bukharina." *Voprosy istorii KPSS* (1988:8): 15–33.

Borkenau, Franz. *World Communism: A History of the Communist International.* 1938. Reprint. Ann Arbor, Mich.: 1962.

Bovin, Aleksandr E. *Mirnoe sosushchestovnie: istoriia, teoriia, politika.* Moscow: 1988.

Brandt, Conrad. *Stalin's Failure in China, 1924–1927.* 1958. Reprint. New York: 1966.

Broué, Pierre. *Trotsky.* Paris: 1988.

Burin, Frederic S. "The Communist Doctrine of the Inevitability of War." *American Political Science Review* 57 (1963): 334–54.

Calhoun, Daniel F. "Trade Union Internationalism in the 1920s." In *Contact or Isolation? Soviet-Western Relations in the Interwar Period.* Edited by John Hiden and Aleksander Loit. Studia Baltica Stockholmiensia, no. 8. Stockholm: 1991.

———. *The United Front!: The TUC and the Russians, 1923–1928.* Cambridge and New York: 1976.

Carley, Michael Jabara. "From Revolution to Dissolution: The Quai d'Orsay, the Banque Russo-Asiatique, and the Chinese Eastern Railway, 1917–1926." *International History Review* 12 (1990): 721–61.

Carlo, Antonio. "Structural Causes of the Soviet Coexistence Policy." In *Soviet Foreign Policy: Its Social and Economic Conditions.* Edited by Egbert Jahn. New York: 1978.

Carr, Edward Hallett. *The Bolshevik Revolution, 1917–1923.* 3 vols. New York: 1950–53.

———. *The Interregnum, 1923–1924.* New York: 1954.

———. *Socialism in One Country, 1924–1926.* 3 vols. New York: 1958–64.

Carr, Edward Hallett, and Robert W. Davies. *Foundations of a Planned Economy, 1926–1929.* 3 vols. New York: 1969–78.

Carrère d'Encausse, Hélène. *Islam and the Russian Empire: Reform and Revolution in Central Asia.* Translated by Quintin Hoare. London: 1988. Original French edition: *Réforme et Révolution chez les Musulmans de l'Empire russe.* Paris: 1966.

Cassels, Alan. "Repairing the *Entente Cordiale* and the New Diplomacy." *Historical Journal* 23 (1980): 133–53.

Castellan, Georges. *Le réarmement clandestin du Reich, 1930–1935, vue par le 2e Bureau de l'Etat-Major Français.* Paris: 1954.

Champonnois, Suzanne. "The Baltic States as an Aspect of Franco-Soviet Relations 1919–1934. A Policy or Several Policies?" In *Contact or Isolation? Soviet-Western Relations in the Interwar Period.* Edited by John Hiden and Aleksander Loit. Studia Baltica Stockholmiensia, no. 8. Stockholm: 1991.

Chester, Lewis, Stephen Fay, and Hugo Young. *The Zinoviev Letter.* Philadelphia: 1968.

Chicherin, Georgii. *Stati i rechi po voprosam mezhdunarodnoi politiki.* Moscow: 1961.

"Chicherin and the Foundations of Soviet-Arab Relations." *Vestnik* (November 1990): 64–70.

Chossudovsky, Evgeny M. "Genoa Revisited: Russia and Coexistence." *Foreign Affairs* 50 (1972): 554–77.

———. "Lenin and Chicherin: The Beginnings of Soviet Foreign Policy and Diplomacy." *Millennium* 3 (1974): 1–16.

Chubarian, Aleksandr O. *Mirnoe sosushchestvovanie: teoriia i praktika.* Moscow: 1976.

Chudodeyev, Y. V. Editor. *Soviet Volunteers in China, 1925–1945: Articles and Reminiscences.* Moscow: 1980.

Churchill, Randolph S., and Martin Gilbert. *Winston Churchill.* Boston, Mass.: 1966–.

Claudin, Fernando. *The Communist Movement: From Comintern to Cominform.* New York: 1975. Original Spanish edition: *La Crisis del Movimiento Comunista.* Paris: 1970.

Clemens, Walter C., Jr. "Lenin on Disarmament." *Slavic Review* 23 (1964): 504–525.

Cohen, Stephen F. *Bukharin and the Bolshevik Revolution: A Political Biography, 1888–1938.* 1973. Reprint. New York: 1975.

———. *Rethinking the Soviet Experience: Politics and History since 1917.* New York: 1985.

Communist International. See Degras, Jane. Editor. *The Communist International, 1919–1943.*

Conte, Francis. *Un révolutionnaire-diplomate: Christian Rakovski. L'Union soviétique et l'Europe (1922–1941).* Paris and New York: 1978. English edition, *Christian Rakovski, 1873–1941: A Political Biography.* Boulder, Colo. and New York: 1989.

Costigliola, Frank. *Awkward Dominion: American Political, Economic, and Cultural Relations with Europe, 1919–1933.* Ithaca, N.Y.: 1984.

Courtois, Stephane. "Le système communiste international et la lutte pour la paix 1917–1939." *Relations internationales* 53 (1988): 5–22.

Crowe, Sybil. "The Zinoviev Letter: A Reappraisal." *Journal of Contemporary History* 10 (1975): 407–432.

Dadiani, Georgi. Editor. "Looking Back on the Vistula Miracle." *International Affairs* (Moscow) (1990:10): 104–113.

D'Agostino, Anthony. *Soviet Succession Struggles: Kremlinology and the Russian Question from Lenin to Gorbachev.* Boston: 1988.

Datta Gupta, Sobhanlal. *Comintern, India, and the Colonial Question, 1920–37.* Calcutta: 1980.

Davies, Kathryn. *The Soviets at Geneva: The USSR and the League of Nations, 1919–1933.* Westport, Conn.: 1977.

Davies, Norman. "The Genesis of the Polish-Soviet War, 1919–20." *European Studies Review* 5 (1975): 47–67.

——. "The Missing Revolutionary War: The Polish Campaigns and the Retreat from Revolution in Soviet Russia, 1919–21." *Soviet Studies* 27 (1975): 178–95.

——. *White Eagle, Red Star: The Polish-Soviet War, 1919–20.* New York: 1972.

Davies, Robert William. *The Socialist Offensive: The Collectivisation of Soviet Agriculture, 1929–1930.* Cambridge, Mass.: 1980.

——. *The Soviet Economy in Turmoil, 1929–1930.* Cambridge, Mass.: 1989.

——. *Soviet History in the Gorbachev Revolution.* London: 1989.

Davies, R. W. Editor. *From Tsarism to the New Economic Policy: Continuity and Change in the Economy of the USSR.* Ithaca, N.Y.: 1991.

——. *Soviet Investment for Planned Industrialization, 1929–1937: Policy and Practice: Selected Papers from the Second World Congress for Soviet and East European Studies.* Berkeley, Calif.: 1984.

Davies, R. W., and S. G. Wheatcroft. "Further Thoughts on the First Soviet Five Year Plan." *Slavic Review* 34 (1975): 790–802.

Day, Richard B. *The Crisis and the Crash: Soviet Studies of the West (1917–1939).* London: 1981.

——. *Leon Trotsky and the Politics of Economic Isolation.* Cambridge: 1973.

——. "Leon Trotsky on the Dialectics of Democratic Control." In *The Soviet Economy on the Brink of Reform: Essays in Honor of Alec Nove.* Edited by Peter Wiles. Boston, Mass.: 1988.

DBFP. See Great Britain. Foreign Office. *Documents on British Foreign Policy, 1919–1939.*

Debo, Richard. *Revolution and Survival: The Foreign Policy of Soviet Russia, 1917–18.* Toronto and Buffalo, N.Y.: 1979.

——. *Survival and Consolidation: The Foreign Policy of Soviet Russia, 1918–1921.* Montreal and Kingston: 1992.

Degras, Jane. Editor. *The Communist International, 1919–1943: Documents.* 3 vols. London and New York: 1956–65.

——. *Soviet Documents on Foreign Policy.* 3 vols. London and New York: 1951–53.

Deutscher, Isaac. *The Prophet Unarmed: Trotsky, 1921–1929.* London and New York: 1959.

di Biagio, Anna. "Bukharin's International Alternative." In *The Ideas of Nikolai Bukharin.* Edited by A. Kemp-Welch. Oxford and New York: 1992.

Dirlik, Arif. *The Origins of Chinese Communism.* New York: 1989.

Dmitrenko, V. P. "Certain Aspects of the New Economic Policy in Soviet Historical Scholarship of the 1960s." *Soviet Studies in History* 11 (1972–73): 213–51.

Dmytryshyn, Basil, and Frederick Cox. *The Soviet Union and the Middle*

East: A Documentary Record of Afghanistan, Iran, and Turkey, 1917–1985. Princeton, N.J.: 1987.

Dohan, Michael R. "The Economic Origins of Soviet Autarky, 1927/28–1934." *Slavic Review* 35 (1976): 603–35.

———. "Foreign Trade." In *From Tsarism to the New Economic Policy: Continuity and Change in the Economy of the USSR.* Edited by R. W. Davies. Ithaca, N.Y.: 1991.

———. "Foreign Trade and Soviet Investment Strategy for Planned Industrialization, 1928–1938." In *Soviet Investment for Planned Industrialization, 1929–1937: Policy and Practice: Selected Papers from the Second World Congress for Soviet and East European Studies.* Edited by R. W. Davies. Berkeley, Calif.: 1984.

Donaldson, Robert H. *Soviet Policy toward India: Ideology and Strategy.* Cambridge, Mass.: 1974.

Drachkovitch, Milorad M. Editor. *The Revolutionary Internationals, 1864–1943.* Stanford, Calif.: 1966.

Drachkovitch, Milorad M., and Branko Lazitch. "The Third International." In *The Revolutionary Internationals, 1864–1943.* Edited by Milorad M. Drachkovitch. Stanford, Calif.: 1966.

Drachkovitch, Milorad M., and Branko Lazitch. Editors. *The Comintern: Historical Highlights, Essays, Recollections, Documents.* New York: 1966.

Dragunov, Georgi. "Vorovski's Assassination: New Facts." *International Affairs* (Moscow) (1989:5): 116–27.

Dyck, Harvey L. "German-Soviet Relations and the Anglo-Soviet Break, 1927." *Slavic Review* 25 (1966): 67–83.

———. *Weimar Germany and Soviet Russia, 1926–1933: A Study in Diplomatic Instability.* London: 1966.

Edmondson, Charles M. "The Politics of Hunger: The Soviet Response to Famine, 1921." *Soviet Studies* 29 (1977): 506–18.

Eichwede, Wolfgang. "Der Eintritt Sowjetrusslands in die Internationale Politik, 1921–1927." In *Sowjetunion: Aussenpolitik 1917–1955.* Edited by Dietrich Geyer. 3 vols. Cologne: 1972–76.

———. *Revolution und Internationale Politik: Zur kommunistischen Interpretation der kapitalistischen Welt, 1921–1925.* Cologne: 1971.

Eley, Geoff. "Reviewing the Socialist Tradition." Paper presented before the UNC Planning Group for a Center for European Studies, April 1990, University of North Carolina.

———. "Some Unfinished Thoughts on the Comintern," Paper presented at the symposium "Fifty Years of the Popular Front," University of Michigan, November 1985.

Erdmann, Karl Dietrich. "Das Problem der Ost- oder Westorientierung in der Locarno-Politik Stresemanns." *Geschichte in Wissenschaft und Unterricht* 6 (1966): 133–62.

Erickson, John. *The Soviet High Command: A Military-Political History, 1918–1941.* New York: 1962.

Erlich, Alexander. *The Soviet Industrialization Debate, 1924–1928.* Cambridge, Mass.: 1960.

Eudin, Xenia J., and Harold H. Fischer. Editors. *Soviet Russia and the West, 1920–1927: A Documentary Survey.* Stanford, Calif.: 1957.

Eudin, Xenia J., and Robert M. Slusser. Editors. *Soviet Foreign Policy, 1928–1934: Documents and Materials.* University Park, Pa.: 1967.

Fagan, Gus. Editor. *Christian Rakovsky: Selected Writings on Opposition in the USSR 1923–30.* London: 1980.

Farber, Samuel. *Before Stalinism: The Rise and Fall of Soviet Democracy.* Oxford: 1990.

Farman, Christopher. *The General Strike: May 1926.* London: 1972.

Feigon, Lee. *Chen Duxiu: Founder of the Chinese Communist Party.* Princeton, N.J.: 1983.

Fiddick, Thomas C. *Russia's Retreat from Poland, 1920: From Permanent Revolution to Peaceful Coexistence.* London: 1990.

Filene, Peter G. *Americans and the Soviet Experiment, 1917–1933.* Cambridge, Mass.: 1967.

Fink, Carole. "European Politics and Security at the Genoa Conference of 1922." In *German Nationalism and the European Response, 1890–1945.* Edited by Carole Fink, Isabel V. Hull, and MacGregor Knox. Norman, Okla.: 1985.

——. *The Genoa Conference: European Diplomacy, 1921–1922.* Chapel Hill, N.C.: 1984.

Fink, Carole, Axel Frohn, and Jurgen Heideking. Editors. *Genoa, Rapallo, and European Reconstruction in 1922.* Cambridge: 1991.

Fink, Carole, Isabel V. Hull, MacGregor Knox. Editors. *German Nationalism and the European Response, 1890–1945.* Norman, Okla.: 1985.

Firsov, Fridrikh I. "K voprosu o taktike edinogo fronta v 1921–1924 gg." *Voprosy istorii KPSS* (1987:10): 113–27.

——. "Komintern: mekhanizm funktsionirovaniia." *Novaia i noveishaia istoriia* (1991:2): 32–47.

——. "Stalin i komintern." *Voprosy istorii* (1989:8): 3–23.

——. "What the Comintern Archives Will Reveal." *World Marxist Review* 32, 1 (1989): 52–57.

First Four Congresses. See Adler, Alan. Editor. *Theses, Resolutions, and Manifestos of the First Four Congresses of the Third International.*

Fischer, Louis. *Men and Politics; Europe between the Two World Wars.* 1941. Reprint. New York: 1966.

——. *The Soviets in World Affairs: A History of the Relations between the Soviet Union and the Rest of the World, 1917–1929.* 1930. Reprint. Princeton, N.J.: 1951.

Fitzpatrick, Sheila. "The Foreign Threat during the First Five Year Plan." *Soviet Union/Union Soviétique* 5 (1978): 26–35.

Fleron, Frederic J. Jr., Erik P. Hoffmann, and Robbin F. Laird. Editors. *Soviet Foreign Policy: Classic and Contemporary Issues.* New York: 1991.

Flory, Harriette. "The Arcos Raid and the Rupture of Anglo-Soviet Relations, 1927." *Journal of Contemporary History* 12 (1977): 707–723.

Fowkes, Ben. *Communism in Germany under the Weimar Republic.* London: 1984.

Frank, Pierre. *Histoire de l'Internationale communiste, 1919–1943.* Paris: 1979.

Fraser, Glenda. "Basmachi I." *Central Asian Survey* 6, 1 (1987): 1–73.

——. "Basmachi II." *Central Asian Survey* 6, 2 (1987): 7–42.

Fung, Edmund S. K. *The Diplomacy of Imperial Retreat: Britain's South China Policy, 1924–1931.* Hong Kong and New York: 1991.

Gasiorowski, Zygmunt J. "The Russian Overture to Germany of December 1924." *Journal of Modern History* 30 (1958): 99–117.

——. "Stresemann and Poland after Locarno." *Journal of Central European Affairs* 18 (1958): 292–317.

——. "Stresemann and Poland before Locarno." *Journal of Central European Affairs* 18 (1958): 25–47.

Gatzke, Hans W. "Von Rapallo nach Berlin: Stresemann und die deutsche Russlandpolitik," *Vierteljahreshefte für Zeitgeschichte* 4 (1956): 1–19.

——. "Russo-German Military Collaboration during the Weimar Republic." *American Historical Review* 63 (1958): 565–97.

Genis, V. L. "Upriamyi narkom s Ilinki." In *Otkryvaia novye stranitsy. Mezhdunarodnye voprosy: sobytiia i liudi.* Edited by A. A. Iskenderov. Moscow: 1989.

Germany. Auswärtiges Amt. *Akten zur Deutschen Auswärtigen Politik, 1918–1945,* Series B. 21 vols. Göttingen: 1966–83.

——. Ministerium für Auswärtige Angelegenheiten der DDR. *Deutsch-sowjetische Beziehungen von den Verhandlungen in Brest-Litowsk bis zum Abschluss des Rapallovertrages; Dokumentensammlung.* 2 vols. Berlin: 1967–71.

Geyer, Dietrich. Editor. *Sowjetunion: Aussenpolitik 1917–1955.* 3 vols. Cologne: 1972–76.

——. *Die Sowjetunion und Iran; eine Untersuchung zur Aussenpolitik der UdSSR im Nahen Osten, 1917–1954.* Tübingen: 1955.

Gill, Graeme. "Ideology and System-Building: The Experience under Lenin and Stalin." In *Ideology and Soviet Politics.* Edited by Stephen White and Alex Pravda. New York: 1988.

——. *The Origins of the Stalinist Political System.* Cambridge and New York: 1990.

Ginsburgs, George. "The Theme of Rapallo in Post-War Soviet-West German Relations." *Soviet Union/Union Soviétique* 13 (1986): 349–66.

Glunin, V. I. "The Comintern and the Rise of the Communist Movement in China (1920–1927)." In *The Comintern and the East: The Struggle for the Leninist Strategy and Tactics in National Liberation Movements.* Edited by R. A. Ulyanovskii. Moscow: 1979.

Goldbach, Marie-Luise. *Karl Radek und die deutsch-sowjetischen Beziehungen, 1918–1923*. Bonn-Bad Godesberg: 1973.

Gorbachev, Mikhail. *Oktiabr i perestroika: revoliutsiia prodolzhaetsia*. Moscow: 1987. English translation, *October and Perestroika: The Revolution Continues*. Moscow: 1987.

Gorinov, M. M., and S. V. Tasakunov. "Leninskaia kontseptsiia NEPa: stanovlenie i razvitie." *Voprosy istorii* (1990:4): 20–39.

——. "The Life and Works of Evgenii Alekssevich Preobrazhenskii." *Slavic Review* 50 (1991): 286–96.

Gorodetsky, Gabriel. *The Other "Zinoviev Letters": New Light on the Mismanagement of the Affair*. Slavic and Soviet Series, no. 3. Russian and East European Research Center at Tel-Aviv University, March 1976.

——. *The Precarious Truce: Anglo-Soviet Relations, 1924–1927*. Cambridge and New York: 1977.

——. "The Soviet Union and Britain's General Strike of May 1926." *Cahiers du Monde russe et soviétique* 17 (1976): 287–310.

Gorokhov, Ivan, Leonid Zamiatin, and Igor Zemskov. *G. V. Chicherin— Diplomat leninskoi shkoly*. 1966. Reprint. Moscow: 1974.

Great Britain. Foreign Office. *Documents on British Foreign Policy, 1919–1939*. 62 vols. London: 1946–85.

Gregor, Richard. Editor. *Resolutions and Decisions of the Communist Party of the Soviet Union: The Early Soviet Period: 1917–1929*. Toronto and Buffalo, N.Y.: 1974.

Gregorian, Vartan. *The Emergence of Modern Afghanistan: Politics of Reform and Modernization, 1880–1946*. Stanford, Calif.: 1969.

Gregory, John D. *On the Edge of Diplomacy: Rambles and Reflections, 1902–1928*. London: 1929.

Grieser, Helmut. "Die Rapallo-Politik in sowjetischer Sicht: Zur Beurteilung der deutschen Aussenpolitik 1922–1932 in der zeitgenössischen sowjetischen Presse." In *Historisch-politische Streiflichter: Geschichtliche Beiträge zur Gegenwart*. Edited by Kurt Jürgensen and Reimer Hansen. Neumünster: 1971.

——. *Die Sowjetpresse über Deutschland in Europa, 1922–1932. Revision von Versailles und Rapallo-Politik in sowjetischer Sicht*. Stuttgart: 1970.

Griffiths, Franklyn. "Origins of Peaceful Coexistence: A Historical Note." *Survey*, no. 50 (1964): 195–201.

Gromyko, A. A., and B. N. Ponomarev. Editors. *Soviet Foreign Policy, 1917–1980*. Moscow: 1981.

Grosup, V. Ya. "H. R. Rakovskii, revolucioner, diplomat i publicist." *Novaia i noveishaia istoriia* (1988:6): 151–75.

Gruber, Helmut. *International Communism in the Era of Lenin: A Documentary History*. Ithaca, N.Y.: 1967.

Haithcox, John Patrick. *Communism and Nationalism in India: M. N. Roy and Comintern Policy, 1920–1939*. Princeton, N.J.: 1971.

Harding, Neil. *Lenin's Political Thought.* New York: 1978.

Harris, Jonathan. *Ideology and International Politics: An Introduction to Soviet Analysis.* Pittsburgh: 1970.

Haslam, Jonathan. *Soviet Foreign Policy, 1930–33: The Impact of the Depression.* London and New York: 1983.

——. *The Soviet Union and the Struggle for Collective Security in Europe.* London: 1984.

——. *The Soviet Union and the Threat from the East, 1933–41: Moscow, Tokyo and the Prelude to the Pacific War.* London: 1992.

Hauner, Milan. *What Is Asia to Us? Russia's Asian Heartland Yesterday and Today.* Boston, Mass.: 1990.

Haynes, Michael. *Nikolai Bukharin and the Transition from Capitalism to Socialism.* London: 1985.

Helbig, Herbert. *Die Träger der Rapallo-Politik.* Göttingen: 1958.

Henshen, Folke. "Lenin in the Last Month of His Life." *International Affairs* (Moscow) (1991:10): 109–15.

Heywood, Anthony J. "Trade or Isolation? Soviet Imports of Railway Equipment, 1920–1922." In *Contact or Isolation? Soviet-Western Relations in the Interwar Period.* Edited by John Hiden and Aleksander Loit. Studia Baltica Stockholmiensia, no. 8. Stockholm: 1991.

Hiden, John. *Germany and Europe, 1919–1939.* 2d ed. London and New York: 1993.

——. "On the Edge of Diplomacy? Britain, the Baltic and East-West Relations between the Wars." In *Contact or Isolation? Soviet-Western Relations in the Interwar Period.* Edited by John Hiden and Aleksander Loit. Studia Baltica Stockholmiensia, no. 8. Stockholm: 1991.

Hiden, John, and Aleksander Loit. Editors. *The Baltic in International Relations between the Two World Wars.* Studia Baltica Stockholmiensia, no. 3. Stockholm: 1991.

——. *Contact or Isolation? Soviet-Western Relations in the Interwar Period.* Studia Baltica Stockholmiensia, no. 8. Stockholm: 1991.

Hildebrand, Klaus. *Das Deutsche Reich und die Sowjetunion im internationalen System, 1918–1932. Legitimität oder Revolution?* Wiesbaden: 1977.

Himmer, Robert. "Rathenau, Russia, and Rapallo." *Central European History* 9 (1976): 146–83.

Hinkkanen, Merja-Liisa. "Bridges and Barriers, Pawns and Actors. The Baltic States in East-West Relations in the 1920s." In *Contact or Isolation? Soviet-Western Relations in the Interwar Period.* Edited by John Hiden and Aleksander Loit. Studia Baltica Stockholmiensia, no. 8. Stockholm: 1991.

Hochman, Jiri. *The Soviet Union and the Failure of Collective Security, 1934–1938.* Ithaca, N.Y.: 1984.

Hoffmann, Erik P., and Frederic J. Fleron, Jr. Editors. *The Conduct of Soviet Foreign Policy.* 2d ed. New York: 1980.

Hoff-Wilson, Joan. *Ideology and Economics: U.S. Relations with the Soviet Union, 1918–1933.* Columbia, Mo.: 1974.

Hogenhuis-Seliverstoff, Anne. "French Plans for the Reconstruction of Russia: A History and Evaluation." In *Genoa, Rapallo, and European Reconstruction in 1922.* Edited by Carole Fink, Axel Frohn, and Jurgen Heideking. Cambridge: 1991.

———. *Les relations franco-soviétiques, 1917–1924.* Paris: 1981.

Holubnychy, Lydia. *Michael Borodin and the Chinese Revolution, 1923–1925.* Ann Arbor, Mich.: 1979.

Hopkirk, Peter. *Setting the East Ablaze: Lenin's Dream of an Empire in Asia.* London: 1984.

Horak, Stephan M. "Lenin on Coexistence: A Chapter in Soviet Foreign Policy." *Studies on the Soviet Union* 3 (1964): 20–30.

Hovi, Kalervo. "The French Alliance Policy 1917–1927: A Change of Mentality." In *Contact or Isolation? Soviet-Western Relations in the Interwar Period.* Edited by John Hiden and Aleksander Loit. Studia Baltica Stockholmiensia, no. 8. Stockholm: 1991.

Hughes, James. *Stalin, Siberia and the Crisis of the New Economic Policy.* New York: 1991.

Hulse, James W. *The Forming of the Communist International.* Stanford, Calif.: 1964.

Humbert-Droz, Jules. *Archives de Jules Humbert-Droz.* Edited by Siegfried Bahne. 2 vols. Dortrecht: 1970–81.

———. *De Lénine à Staline. Dix ans au service de l'internationale communiste, 1921–1931.* Neuchâtel: 1971.

———. *L'origine de l'internationale communiste: de Zimmerwald à Moscou.* Neuchâtel: 1968.

Hunter, Holland. "The Over-ambitious First Soviet Five-Year Plan." *Slavic Review* 32 (1973): 237–57.

Iskenderov, Akhmed A. Editor. *Otkryvaia novye stranitsy. Mezhdunarodnye voprosy: sobytiia i liudi.* Moscow: 1989.

Ismael, Tareq Y., and Rifa 'at El-Sa'id. *The Communist Movement in Egypt, 1920–1988.* Syracuse, N.Y.: 1990.

Ivanov, Konstantin P. *Leninism and Foreign Policy of the USSR.* Moscow: ca. 1971.

Jacobs, Dan N. *Borodin: Stalin's Man in China.* Cambridge, Mass.: 1981.

Jacobsen, Hans-Adolf. "Primat der Sicherheit, 1928–1938." In *Sowjetunion: Aussenpolitik 1917–1955.* Edited by Dietrich Geyer. 3 vols. Cologne: 1972–76.

Jacobson, Jon. "Is There a New International History of the 1920s?" *American Historical Review* 88 (1983): 617–45.

———. *Locarno Diplomacy: Germany and the West, 1925–1929.* Princeton, N.J.: 1972.

———. "The Reparation Settlement of 1924." In *Konsequenzen der Inflation.* Edited by Gerald D. Feldman et al. Berlin: 1989.

Jahn, Egbert. Editor. *Soviet Foreign Policy: Its Social and Economic Conditions.* New York: 1978.

Johansson, Anders. "Swedish Concessionaires in Soviet Industry: Experiences of Foreign Participants in the Rise and Fall of NEP, 'the First Perestroika.'" In *Contact or Isolation? Soviet-Western Relations in the Interwar Period.* Edited by John Hiden and Aleksander Loit. Studia Baltica Stockholmiensia, no. 8. Stockholm: 1991.

Johnston, Robert H. *Soviet Foreign Policy, 1918–1945: A Guide to Research and Research Materials.* Wilmington, Del.: 1991.

Kahan, Vilem. *Bibliography of the Communist International (1919–1979).* Leiden and New York: 1990.

———. "The Communist International, 1919–43: The Personnel of Its Highest Bodies." *International Review of Social History* 21 (1976): 151–85.

Kapur, Harish. *Soviet Russia and Asia, 1917–1927: A Study of Soviet Policy towards Turkey, Iran, and Afghanistan.* Geneva: 1966.

Kartunova, A. I. "Kitaiskaia revolutsiia: diskussii v Kominterne." *Voprosy istorii KPSS* (1989:6): 58–72.

Kemp-Welch, A. Editor. *The Ideas of Nikolai Bukharin.* Oxford and New York: 1992.

Kennan, George F. *Russia and the West under Lenin and Stalin.* Boston: 1961.

Khanin, G. I. "Why and When Did NEP Die? An Economist's Reflections," *Soviet Review* 31 (1990): 47–64.

Kheifets, Aleksandr N. *Sovetskaia diplomatiia i narody Vostoka, 1921–1927.* Moscow: 1968.

———. *Sovetskaia Rossiia i sopredelnye strany Vostoka v gody grazhdanskio voiny, 1918–1920.* Moscow: 1964.

Khrushchev, Nikita S. "On Peaceful Co-existence." *Foreign Affairs* 38 (1959): 1–18.

———. *Report of the Central Committee of the Communist Party of the Soviet Union to the 20th Party Congress, February 14, 1956.* Moscow: 1956.

Kimmich, Christoph M. *Germany and the League of Nations.* Chicago: 1976.

Kipp, Jacob W. "Soviet Military Doctrine and the Origins of Operational Art, 1917–1936." In *Soviet Military Doctrine from Lenin to Gorbachev, 1915–1991.* Edited by Willard C. Frank, Jr. and Phillip S. Gillette. Westport, Conn.: 1992.

Kneen, Peter. "The Background to *Perestroika*: 'Political Undercurrents' Reconsidered in the Light of Recent Events." In *Stalinism: Its Nature and Aftermath: Essays in Honour of Moshe Lewin.* Edited by Nick Lambert and Gábor T. Rittersporn. Armonk, N.Y.: 1992.

Kolb, Eberhard. *The Weimar Republic.* London and Boston: 1988. Original German edition: *Die Weimarer Republik.* Munich: 1984.

"Kompleksnaia programma 'Istoriia vneshnei politiki SSSR i mezhdunarodnykh otnoshenii," *Novaia i noveishaia istoriia* (1988:2): 63–81.

Korbel, Josef. *Poland between East and West: Soviet and German Diplomacy toward Poland, 1919–1933.* Princeton, N.J.: 1963.

Kozlov, Nicholas N., and Eric D. Weitz. "Reflections on the Origins of the 'Third Period': Bukharin, the Comintern, and the Political Economy of Western Germany." *Journal of Contemporary History* 24 (1989): 387–410.

Krivoguz, I. M. "Sudba i nasledie Kominterna." *Novaia i noveishaia istoriia* (1990:6): 3–20.

Krüger, Peter. *Die Aussenpolitik der Republik von Weimar.* Darmstadt: 1985.

——. "A Rainy Day, April 1922: The Rapallo Treaty and the Cloudy Perspective for German Foreign Policy." In *Genoa, Rapallo, and European Reconstruction in 1922.* Edited by Carole Fink, Axel Frohn, and Jurgen Heideking. Cambridge: 1991.

Kubálková, V., and A. A. Cruickshank. *Marxism and International Relations.* Oxford and New York: 1985.

——. *Marxism-Leninism and Theory of International Relations.* London and Boston: 1980.

——. "The Soviet Concept of Peaceful Coexistence: Some Theoretical and Semantic Problems." *Australian Journal of Politics and History* 24 (1978): 184–98.

Kulikov, Alexander. "Concessions of the 1920s." *International Affairs* (Moscow) (1989:4): 76–83.

Kuo Heng-yü. *Die Komintern und die Chinesische Revolution: Die Einheitsfront zwischen der KP Chinas und der Kuomintang 1924–1927.* Paderborn, Germany: 1979.

Kuromiya, Hiroaki. *Stalin's Industrial Revolution: Politics and Workers, 1928–1932.* Cambridge: 1988.

Kuusinen, Aino. *Before and after Stalin: A Personal Account of Soviet Russia from the 1920s to the 1960s.* London: 1974. Original German edition: *Der Gott stürzt seine Engel.* Vienna, Munich, Zurich: 1972.

Lambert, Nick, and Gábor T. Rittersporn. Editors. *Stalinism: Its Nature and Aftermath: Essays in Honour of Moshe Lewin.* Armonk, N.Y.: 1992.

Lammers, Donald N. "The Second Labour Government and the Restoration of Relations with Soviet Russia, 1929." *Bulletin of the Institute of Historical Research* 37 (1964): 60–72.

Latyshev, A. G. "Bukharin—izvestnyi i neivestnyi." In *Otkryvaia novye stranitsy. Mezhdunarodnye voprosy: sobytiia i liudi.* Edited by A. A. Iskenderov. Moscow: 1989.

Laubach, Ernst. *Die Politik der Kabinette Wirth 1921/22.* Lübeck and Hamburg: 1968.

Lazitch, Branko. *Biographical Dictionary of the Comintern.* Stanford, Calif.: 1973.

——. "Two Instruments of Control by the Comintern: The Emissaries of the ECCI and the Party Representatives in Moscow." In *The Comintern:*

Historical Highlights, Essays, Recollections, Documents. Edited by Milorad M. Drachkovitch and Branko Lazitch. Stanford, Calif.: 1966.

Lazitch, Branko, and Milorad Drachkovitch. *Lenin and the Comintern.* Stanford, Calif.: 1972.

Lenin, V. I. *Collected Works.* 45 vols. Moscow: 1960–70.

——. *The National Liberation Movement in the East.* 3d rev. ed. Moscow: 1969.

"Lenin's Legacy." *International Affairs* (Moscow) (1990:5): 71–74.

Lerner, Warren. "The Historical Origins of the Soviet Doctrine of Peaceful Coexistence." *Law and Contemporary Society* 29 (1964): 865–70.

——. *Karl Radek: The Last Internationalist.* Stanford, Calif.: 1970.

Lewin, Moshe. "The Disappearance of Planning in the Plan." *Slavic Review* 32 (1973): 271–87.

——. *Lenin's Last Struggle.* New York: 1968.

——. *The Making of the Soviet System: Essays in the Social History of Interwar Russia.* New York: 1985.

——. *Political Undercurrents in Soviet Economic Debates: From Bukharin to the Modern Reformers.* Princeton, N.J.: 1974.

——. *Russian Peasants and Soviet Power: A Study of Collectivization.* Evanston, Ill.: 1968. Original French edition: *La Paysannerie et le pouvoir soviétique.* Paris: 1966.

Light, Margot. *The Soviet Theory of International Relations.* Brighton, England: 1988.

Lindemann, Albert S. *The 'Red Years': European Socialism versus Bolshevism, 1919–1921.* Berkeley, Calif.: 1974.

Lowe, Donald M. *The Function of "China" in Marx, Lenin, and Mao.* Berkeley, Calif.: 1966.

Lowenthal, Richard. "The Rise and Decline of International Communism." *Problems of Communism* 12 (1963): 19–29.

Lynch, Allen. *The Soviet Study of International Relations.* New York: 1987.

McCann, James M. "Beyond the Bug: Soviet Historiography of the Soviet-Policy War of 1920." *Soviet Studies* 36 (1984): 475–93.

McFadden, David W. *Alternative Paths: Soviets and Americans, 1917–1920.* New York and Oxford: 1993.

Macfarlane, L. J. "Hands off Russia: British Labour and the Russo-Polish War, 1920." *Past and Present* 38 (1967): 126–52.

McKenzie, Kermit E. *Comintern and World Revolution, 1928–1943: The Shaping of Doctrine.* London and New York: 1964.

McLane, Charles B. *Soviet Strategies in Southeast Asia: An Exploration of Eastern Policy under Lenin and Stalin.* Princeton, N.J.: 1966.

Malkov, V. L. "SShA: Ot interventsii k priznaniiu Sovetskogo Soiuza (1917–1933gg)." *Novaia i noveishaia istoriia* (1984:1): 125–46.

Manusevkch, A. Ya. "Trudnyi put k Rizhskomu mirnomu dogovoru 1921 g." *Novaia i noveishaia istoriia* (1991:1): 19–43.

Marquand, David. *Ramsay MacDonald*. London: 1977.

Medvedev, Roy A. *Let History Judge: The Origins and Consequences of Stalinism*. Revised and expanded edition. New York: 1989.

Megerle, Klaus. *Deutsche Aussenpolitik 1925: Ansatz zu aktivem Revisionismus*. Bern: 1974.

Melograni, Piero. *Lenin and the Myth of World Revolution: Ideology and Reasons of State, 1917–1920*. Atlantic Highlands, N.J.: 1989. Original Italian edition: *Il mito della rivoluzione mondiale. Lenin tra ideologia e ragion di Stato, 1917–1920*. Rome: 1985.

Merridale, Catherine. "The Reluctant Opposition: The Right 'Deviation' in Moscow, 1928." *Soviet Studies* 41 (1989): 382–400.

Merridale, Catherine, and Chris Ward. Editors. *Perestroika: The Historical Perspective*. London and New York: 1991.

Meyer, Alfred G. "The War Scare of 1927." *Soviet Union/Union Soviétique* 5 (1978): 1–25.

Michalka, Wolfgang, and Marshall M. Lee. *Gustav Stresemann*. Darmstadt: 1982.

Mirovitskaia, Raisa A. *Sovetskii Soiuz v strategii Gomindana (20–30-e gody)*. Moscow: 1990.

Misiunas, Romuald. "The Role of the Baltic States in Soviet Relations with the West during the Interwar Period." In *The Baltic in International Relations between the Two World Wars*. Edited by John Hiden and Aleksander Loit. Studia Baltica Stockholmiensia no. 3. Stockholm: 1991.

Möller, Dietrich. *Karl Radek in Deutschland: Revolutionär, Intrigant, Diplomat*. Cologne: 1976.

Moore, Barrington, Jr. *Soviet Politics; the Dilemma of Power: The Role of Ideas in Social Change*. 1950. Reprint. Cambridge, Mass.: 1959.

Morozov, G. I. "Liga natsii: vzgliad cherez polveka." *Voprosy istorii* (1992:2–3): 162–67.

Nation, R. Craig. *Black Earth, Red Star: A History of Soviet Security Policy, 1917–1991*. Ithaca, N.Y.: 1992.

"Nekotorye voprosy istorii Kominterna." *Novaia i noveishaia istoriia* (1989:2): 75–107.

Nezhinskii, L. N. "Byla li voennaia ugroza v kontse 20-kh—nachale 30-kh godov?" *Istoriia SSSR* (1990:6): 14–30.

——. "Istoriia vneshnei politiki SSSR: poiski novykh podkhodov." *Novaia i noveishaia istoriia* (1990:4): 3–13.

——. "Vneshniaia politika sovetskogo gosudarstva v 1917–1921 godakh: kurs na 'mirovuiu revoliutsiu' ili na mirnoe sosushchestvovanie?" *Istoriia SSSR* (1991:6): 3–27.

North, Robert C. *Moscow and Chinese Communists*. 1953. Reprint. Stanford, Calif.: 1963.

North, Robert C., and Xenia J. Eudin. *M. N. Roy's Mission to China: The Communist-Kuomintang Split of 1927*. Berkeley, Calif.: 1963.

O'Connor, Timothy Edward. *Diplomacy and Revolution: G. V. Chicherin and Soviet Foreign Affairs, 1918–1930.* Ames, Iowa: 1988.

——. *The Engineer of Revolution: L. B. Krasin and the Bolsheviks, 1870–1926.* Boulder, Colo.: 1992.

"Opyt proshlykh ekonomicheskikh reform." *Voprosy ekonomiki* (1988:2).

Overstreet, Gene D., and Marshall Windmiller. *Communism in India.* Berkeley, Calif.: 1959.

Page, Stanley W. *The Geopolitics of Leninism.* Boulder, Colo. and New York: 1982.

——. "Lenin: Prophet of World Revolution from the East." *Russian Review* 11 (1952): 67–77.

——. *Lenin and World Revolution.* New York: 1959.

Paniev, N. A. "Bolgarskii revoliutsioner i sovetskii polpred." In *Otkryvaia novye stranitsy. Mezhdunarodnye voprosy: sobytiia i liudi.* Edited by A. A. Iskenderov. Moscow: 1989.

Pantsov, A. V. "Brestskii mir." *Voprosy istorii* (1990:2): 60–79.

Pavlov, N. V., and M. L. Fedorov. "Nikolai Ivanovich Bukharin." *Soviet Studies in History* 28 (Spring 1990): 74–97. Original Russian publication: *Voprosy istorii KPSS* (1988:10): 73–87.

Perrey, Hans-Jurgen. *Der Russlandausschuss der deutschen Wirtschaft. Die deutsche-sowjetischen Wirtschaftsbeziehungen der Zwischenkriegszeit. Ein Beitrag zur Geschichte des Ost-West-Handels.* Munich: 1985.

Pethybridge, Roger. *One Step Backwards, Two Steps Forward: Soviet Society and Politics in the New Economic Policy.* Oxford and New York: 1990.

Phillips, Hugh D. *Between the Revolution and the West: A Political Biography of Maxim M. Litvinov.* Boulder, Colo.: 1992.

Pogge von Strandmann, Hartmut. "Grossindustrie und Rapallopolitik: deutsch-sowjetische Handelsbeziehungen in der Weimarer Republik." *Historische Zeitschrift* 222 (1976): 265–341.

——. "Industrial Primacy in German Foreign Policy? Myths and Realities in German-Russian Relations at the End of the Weimar Republic." In *Social Change and Political Development in Weimar Germany.* Edited by Richard Bessel and E. J. Feuchtwanger. London and Totowa, N.J.: 1981.

——. "Rapallo—Strategy in Preventative Diplomacy: New Sources and New Interpretations." In *Germany in the Age of Total War.* Edited by Volker R. Berghanh and Martin Kitchen. London: 1981.

Ponomarev, B. N. "Stranitsy deiatelnosti Kominterna." *Novaia i noveishaia istoriia* (1989:2): 118–30.

Popov, N. V. "Byl i ostaius kommunistom." In *Otkryvaia novye stranitsy. Mezhdunarodnye voprosy: sobytiia i liudi.* Edited by Akhmed A. Iskenderov. Moscow: 1989.

Pozdnyakov, Elgz. "National and International in the Foreign Policy." *International Affairs* (Moscow) (1989:6): 3–13.

Quigley, John. *The Soviet Foreign Trade Monopoly: Institutions and Laws.* Columbus, Ohio: 1974.

Radek, Karl. *Der Kampf der Kommunistischen Internationale gegen Versailles und gegen die Offensive des Kapitals.* Hamburg: 1923.

Raleigh, Donald J. Editor. *A Russian Civil War Diary: Alexis Babine in Saratov, 1917–1922.* Durham, N.C.: 1988.

——. *Soviet Historians and Perestroika: The First Phase.* Armonk, N.Y.: 1989.

——. "The Soviet Union in the 1920s: A Roundtable." *Soviet Studies in History* 28 (1989). Original Russian publication: "Kruglyi stol: Sovetskii Soiuz v 20-e gody." *Voprosy istorii* (1988:9): 3–58.

Ratliff, William G. *Faithful to the Fatherland: Julius Curtius and Weimar Foreign Policy.* New York: 1990.

Reiman, Michael. *The Birth of Stalinism: The USSR on the Eve of the "Second Revolution."* Bloomington, Ind.: 1987. Original German edition: *Die Geburt des Stalinismus: Die UdSSR am Vorabend der "zweiten Revolution."* Frankfurt a.M.: 1979.

Renshaw, Patrick. *The General Strike.* London: 1975.

Resolutions and Decisions. See Gregor, Richard. Editor. *Resolutions and Decisions of the Communist Party of the Soviet Union: The Early Period: 1917–1929.*

Reznikov, Aleksandr B. *The Comintern and the East: Strategy and Tactics in the National Liberation Movement.* Moscow: 1984. Original, unabridged Russian edition: *Strategiia i taktika Kommunistichekogo Internatsionala po natsional no-kolonial nomu voprosu.* Moscow: 1978.

——. "Strategy and Tactics of the Communist International in the National and Colonial Question." In *The Comintern and the East: The Struggle for the Leninist Strategy and Tactics in National Liberation Movements.* Edited by R. A. Ulyanovskii. Moscow: 1979.

Riddell, John. Editor. *Founding the Communist International: Proceedings and Documents of the First Congress, March 1919.* New York: 1987.

——. *The German Revolution and the Debate on Soviet Power: Documents, 1918–1919. Preparing the Founding Congress.* New York: 1986.

——. *Workers of the World and Oppressed Peoples Unite! Proceedings and Documents of the Second Congress, 1920.* New York: 1991.

Rigby, Richard W. *The May 30 Movement: Events and Themes.* Canberra: 1980.

Roi, Yaacov. Editor. *The USSR and the Muslim World: Issues in Domestic and Foreign Policy.* London and Boston: 1984.

Rosenbaum, Kurt. *Community of Fate: German-Soviet Diplomatic Relations, 1922–1928.* Syracuse, N.Y.: 1965.

Rosenfeld, Gunter. *Sowjetrussland und Deutschland, 1917–1922.* Cologne: 1984.

——. *Sowjetunion und Deutschland, 1922–1933.* Cologne: 1984.

Roy, M. N. *M. N. Roy's Memoirs.* Bombay and New York: 1964.

RSFSR. People's Commissariat of Foreign Affairs. Annual Report for the Ninth Congress of Soviets (1920–1921). *International Affairs* (Moscow) (1990:2): 133–58.

Ruge, Wolfgang. *Die Stellungsnahme der Sowjetunion gegen die Besetzung des Ruhrgebiets: zur Geschichte der deutsch-sowjetischen Beziehungen von Januar bis September 1923.* Berlin: 1962.

Salmon, Patrick. "Perceptions and Misperceptions: Great Britain and the Soviet Union in Scandinavia and the Baltic Region 1918–1939." In *Contact or Isolation? Soviet-Western Relations in the Interwar Period.* Edited by John Hiden and Aleksander Loit. Studia Baltica Stockholmiensia, no. 8. Stockholm: 1991.

Sareen, Tilak Raj. *Russian Revolution and India: A Study of Soviet Policy towards the Indian National Movement, 1922–29.* New Delhi: 1978.

Schieder, Theodor. "Die Entstehungsgeschichte des Rapallo-Vertrags." *Historische Zeitschrift* 204 (1967): 545–609.

Schinness, Roger. "The Conservative Party and Anglo-Soviet Relations, 1925–7." *European Studies Review* 7 (1977): 393–407.

Schram, Stuart R. "Christian Rakovskij et le premier rapprochement franco-soviétique." *Cahiers du Monde Russe et Soviétique* 1 (1960): 205–237, 584–626 (two parts).

Schuker, Stephen A. "American Policy toward Debts and Reconstruction at Genoa, 1922." In *Genoa, Rapallo, and European Reconstruction in 1922.* Edited by Carole Fink, Axel Frohn, and Jurgen Heideking. Cambridge: 1991.

Second Congress. See Riddell, John. Editor. *Workers of the World and Oppressed Peoples Unite! Proceedings and Documents of the Second Congress.*

Senchenko, Igor P. *Persidskii zaliv: vzgliad skvoz stoletie: Ot "novogo kursa" Peterburga do politiki novogo myshleniia.* Moscow: 1991.

Seppain, Hélène. *Contrasting US and German Attitudes to Soviet Trade, 1917–91: Politics by Economic Means.* London: 1992.

Serge, Victor, and Natalia Sedova Trotsky. *The Life and Death of Leon Trotsky.* London: 1975. Original French edition: *Vie et mort de Leon Trotsky.* Paris: 1951.

SFP. See Eudin, Xenia J., and Robert M. Slusser. Editors. *Soviet Foreign Policy, 1928–1934. Documents and Materials.*

Sheinis, Zinovii S. *Maxim Litvinov.* Moscow: 1990. Original Russian edition: *Maksim Maksimovich Litvinov; revoliutsioner, diplomat, chelovek.* Moscow: 1989.

——. "Polpred B. E. Stein." *Novaia i noveishaia istoriia* (1991:1): 101–18.

Shirinia, K. K. "Trotskii i Komintern." *Novaia i noveishaia istoriia* (1991:1): 3–18.

Shishkin, Valeri A. "The external factor in the country's socioeconomic development." In "The Soviet Union in the 1920s: A Roundtable." *Soviet Studies in History* 28 (1989): 48–56. Original Russian publication: "Kruglyistol: Sovetskii Soiuz v 20-e gody." *Voprosy istorii* (1988:9): 3–58.

———. "The USSR and Western Countries in the Mid-1920s. An Experience of Political and Economic Relations in Connection with *de jure* Recognition." In *Contact or Isolation? Soviet-Western Relations in the Interwar Period.* Edited by John Hiden and Aleksander Loit. Studia Baltica Stockholmiensia, no. 8. Stockholm: 1991.

Shkarenkov, Leonid Konstantinovich. "Nikolai Ivanovich Bukharin." *Soviet Studies in History* 28 (Spring 1990): 40–73. Original Russian publication: *Voprosy istorii* (1988:7): 59–78.

Sicker, Martin. *The Bear and the Lion: Soviet Imperialism and Iran.* New York: 1988.

Siegelbaum, Lewis H. *Soviet State and Society between Revolutions, 1918–1929.* Cambridge and New York: 1992.

Sipols, Vilnis. *Soviet Peace Policy, 1917–1939.* Moscow: 1988.

Sirotkin, Vladlen G. "Ot grazhdanskoi voiny k grazhdanskomu miru." In *Inogo ne dano.* Edited by Iu. N. Afanaseva. Moscow: 1988.

———. "The Riga Peace Treaty." *International Affairs* (Moscow) (1989:9): 128–43.

———. *Vekhi otechestvennoi istorii.* Moscow: 1991.

Sivachev, Nikolai V., and Nikolai N. Yakovlev. *Russia and the United States.* Chicago: 1979.

Sokolov, V. V. "Polpred v Kitae Lev Karakhan." In *Otkryvaia novye stranitsy. Mezhdunarodnye voprosy: sobytiia i liudi.* Edited by A. A. Iskenderov. Moscow: 1989.

Sontag, John P. "The Soviet War Scare of 1926–27." *Russian Review* 34 (1975): 66–77.

Soviet Documents. See Degras, Jane. Editor. *Soviet Documents on Foreign Policy.*

Soviet Documents on the Middle East. See Dmytryshyn, Basil, and Frederick Cox. *The Soviet Union and the Middle East: A Documentary Record of Afghanistan, Iran, and Turkey, 1917–1985.*

Spenz, Jürgen. *Die diplomatische Vorgeschichte des Beitritts Deutschlands zum Völkerbund, 1924–1926. Ein Beitrag zur Aussenpolitik der Weimarer Republik.* Göttingen, Berlin, Frankfurt, Zürich: 1966.

SRW. See Eudin, Xenia J., and Harold H. Fischer. Editors. *Soviet Russia and the West, 1920–1927: A Documentary Survey.*

Stalin, Josef. *Works.* 13 vols. Moscow: 1952–55.

Stanischev, Dimiter. "Khristian Rakovsky: His Life and Work." *International Affairs* (Moscow) (1989:1): 90–95.

Startsev, V. I. "Political Leaders of the Soviet State in 1922 and Early 1923." *Soviet Studies in History* 28 (1989–90): 5–40. Original Russian publication: "Politicheskie rukovoditeli Sovetskogo gosudarstva v 1922-nachale 1923 goda." *Istoriia SSSR* (1988:5): 101–22.

Suny, Ronald Grigor. "Don't Paint Nationalism Red. National Revolution and Socialist Internationalism: The Comintern and the Baku Congress of the Peoples of the East." Paper delivered before the Annual Meeting of the American Historical Association, December 1989.

———. *The Making of the Georgian Nation.* Bloomington, Ind. and Stanford, Calif.: 1988.

Sutton, Antony C. *Western Technology and Soviet Economic Development.* 3 vols. Stanford, Calif.: 1968–73.

Swinder, Raymond J. *Soviet Military Reform in the Twentieth Century: Three Case Studies.* Westport, Conn.: 1992.

Temkin, Ia. G. "Marksisty i patsifisty (Iz opyta vzaimootnoshenii)." *Voprosy istorii KPSS* (1987:8): 56–68.

Teplinskii, Leonid B. *Sovetsko-Afganskie otnosheniia, 1919–1987.* Moscow: 1988.

Titarenko, M. L. Editor. *Kommunisticheskii Internatsional i kitaiskaia revoliutsiia. Dokumenty i materialy.* Moscow: 1986.

Trotsky, Leon. *The Challenge of the Left Opposition (1926–27).* New York: 1980.

———. *The First Five Years of the Communist International.* 2 vols. New York: 1945–53.

———. *Leon Trotsky on Britain.* New York: 1973.

———. *Leon Trotsky on China.* Edited by Les Evans and Russell Block. New York: 1976.

———. *Leon Trotsky on France.* Edited by David Aalmer. New York: 1979.

———. *The Permanent Revolution and Results and Prospects.* New York: 1969.

———. *Problems of the Chinese Revolution.* 3d ed. New York: 1966.

———. *The Third International after Lenin.* London: 1974. This includes *Die Internationale Revolution und die Kommunistische Internationale* (Berlin: 1929) and *L'Internationale communiste après Lénine* (Paris: 1930).

———. *The Trotsky Papers, 1917–1922.* Edited by Jan M. Meijer. 2 vols. The Hague: 1964–71.

Trush, Mikhail I. *Soviet Foreign Policy: Early Years.* Moscow: ca. 1970.

Tucker, Robert C. "The Emergence of Stalin's Foreign Policy." *Slavic Review* 36 (1977): 563–89.

———. *The Soviet Political Mind: Stalinism and Post-Stalin Change.* Revised edition. New York: 1971.

———. *Stalin as Revolutionary, 1879–1929: A Study in History and Personality.* New York: 1973.

———. *Stalin in Power: The Revolution from Above, 1928–1941.* New York: 1990.

———. "Stalinism as Revolution from Above." In *Stalinism: Essays in Historical Interpretation.* Edited by the author. New York: 1977.

Ulam, Adam. *Expansion and Coexistence: The History of Soviet Foreign Policy, 1917–1967.* New York: 1968.

Uldricks, Teddy J. *Diplomacy and Ideology: The Origins of Soviet Foreign Relations, 1917–1930.* London and Beverly Hills, Calif.: 1979.

——. "Russia and Europe: Diplomacy, Revolution, and Economic Development in the 1920s." *International History Review* 1 (1979): 55–83.

——. "Stalin and Nazi Germany." *Slavic Review* 36 (1977): 599–603.

Ullman, Richard H. *Anglo-Soviet Relations, 1917–1921.* 3 vols. Princeton, N.J.: 1961–73.

Ulyanovskii, R. A. Editor. *The Comintern and the East: The Struggle for the Leninist Strategy and Tactics in National Liberation Movements.* Moscow: 1979. Original Russian edition, 1969.

Undasynov, Iskander N., and Z. P. Iakhimovich. *Kommunisticheskii Internatsional: dostizheniia, proschety, uroki.* Moscow: 1990.

USSR. Ministry of Foreign Affairs. *Dokumenty vneshnei politiki SSSR.* 21 vols. Moscow: 1957–77.

——. Institute of Marxism-Leninism. "Nekotorye voprosy istorii Kominterna." *Novaia i noveishaia istoriia* (1989:2): 75–107.

van de Ven, Hans J. *From Friend to Comrade: The Founding of the Chinese Communist Party, 1920–1927.* Berkeley, Calif.: 1991.

Vasentskii, N. A. "L. D. Trotskii: politicheskii portret." *Novaia i noveishaia istoriia* (1989:3): 136–65.

——. "People's Commissar Trotsky." *International Affairs* (Moscow) (1991:2): 63–78.

Viola, Lynne. Editor. "The Bukharin Alternative." *Soviet Studies in History* 28 (Spring 1990): 3–97.

Volodarskii, Mikhail I. "First Steps in Soviet Diplomacy towards Afghanistan, 1917–21." In *The USSR and the Muslim World: Issues in Domestic and Foreign Policy.* Edited by Yaacov Roi. London and Boston: 1984.

——. *Sovety i ikh iuzhnye sosedi Iran i Afganistan, 1917–1933.* London: 1985.

von Boetticher, Manfred. *Industrialisierungspolitik und Verteidigungskonzeption der UdSSR 1926–1930: Herausbildung des Stalinismus und "aüssere Bedrohung."* Dusseldorf: 1979.

von Laue, Theodore H. "Soviet Diplomacy: G. V. Chicherin, People's Commissar for Foreign Affairs, 1918–1930." In *The Diplomats, 1919–1939.* Edited by Gordon A. Craig and Felix Gilbert. 1953. Reprint. New York: 1963.

von Riekhoff, Harald. *German-Polish Relations, 1918–1933.* Baltimore: 1971.

Vygodskii, Semen. Iu. *Vneshniaia politika SSSR, 1924–1929 gg.* Moscow: 1963.

Walsdorff, Martin. *Westorientierung und Ostpolitik: Stresemanns Russlandpolitik in der Locarno Ära.* Bremen: 1971.

Wandycz, Piotr S. *Soviet-Polish Relations, 1917–1921.* Cambridge, Mass.: 1969.

——. *The Twilight of French Eastern Alliances, 1926–1936: French-Czechoslovak-Polish Relations from Locarno to the Remilitarization of the Rhineland.* Princeton, N.J.: 1988.

Weissman, Benjamin M. *Herbert Hoover and Famine Relief to Soviet Russia, 1921–1923*. Stanford, Calif.: 1974.

Wheatcroft, S. G., R. W. Davies, and J. M. Cooper, "Soviet Industrialization Reconsidered: Some Preliminary Conclusions about Economic Development between 1926 and 1941." *Economic History Review*, 2d ser., 39 (1986): 264–94.

White, Christine A. " 'Riches have Wings,' The Use of Russian Gold in Soviet Foreign Trade, 1918–1922." In *Contact or Isolation? Soviet-Western Relations in the Interwar Period*. Edited by John Hiden and Aleksander Loit. Studia Baltica Stockholmiensia, no. 8. Stockholm: 1991.

White, Stephen. *Britain and the Bolshevik Revolution: A Study in the Politics of Diplomacy, 1920–1924*. London: 1979.

——. "Colonial Revolution and the Communist International, 1919–1924." *Science and Society* 40 (1976): 173–93.

——. "Communism and the East: The Baku Congress, 1920." *Slavic Review* 33 (1974): 491–514.

——. "Communist Ideology, Belief Systems, and Soviet Foreign Policy." In *The Conduct of Soviet Foreign Policy*. Edited by Erik P. Hoffmann and Frederic J. Fleron, Jr. 2d ed. New York: 1980.

——. "Ideology and Soviet Politics." In *Ideology and Soviet Politics*. Edited by Stephen White and Alex Pravda. New York: 1988.

——. *The Origins of Détente: The Genoa Conference and Soviet-Western Relations, 1921–1922*. Cambridge and New York: 1985.

——. "Soviet Russia and the Asian Revolution, 1917–1924." *Review of International Studies* 10 (1984): 219–32.

White, Stephen, and Alex Pravda. Editors. *Ideology and Soviet Politics*. New York: 1988.

Whiting, Allen S. *Soviet Policies in China, 1917–1924*. New York: 1953.

Wilbur, C. Martin. *The Nationalist Revolution in China, 1923–1929*. Cambridge and New York: 1984.

Wilbur, C. Martin, and Julie Lien-ying How. *Documents on Communism, Nationalism, and Soviet Advisers in China 1918–1927: Papers Seized in the 1927 Peking Raid*. New York: 1956.

——. *Missionaries of Revolution: Soviet Advisers and Nationalist China, 1920–1927*. Cambridge, Mass.: 1989.

Wiles, Peter. Editor. *The Soviet Economy on the Brink of Reform: Essays in Honor of Alec Nove*. Boston: 1988.

Williams, Andrew J. "The Genoa Conference of 1922: Lloyd George and the Politics of Recognition." In *Genoa, Rapallo, and European Reconstruction in 1922*. Edited by Carole Fink, Axel Frohn, and Jurgen Heideking. Cambridge: 1991.

——. *Labour and Russia: The Attitude of the Labour Party to the USSR, 1924–34*. Manchester and New York: 1989.

——. *Trading with the Bolsheviks: The Politics of East-West Trade, 1920–39.* Manchester and New York: 1922.

Wohl, Robert. *French Communism in the Making.* Stanford, Calif.: 1966.

Wurm, Clemens A. *Die französische Sicherheitspolitik in der Phase der Umorientierung 1924–1926.* Frankfurt a.M., Bern, Las Vegas: 1979.

Yaroshevski, Dov. B. "The Central Government and Peripheral Opposition in Khiva, 1910–24." In *The USSR and the Muslim World: Issues in Domestic and Foreign Policy.* Edited by Yaacov Roi. London: 1984.

Yermoshkin, Nikolai. "Peaceful Coexistence: A Universal Norm of International Relations." *International Affairs* (Moscow) (1987:6): 71–78.

Zabih, Sepher. *The Communist Movement in Iran.* Berkeley, Calif.: 1966.

Zagladin, N. V. *Istoriia uspekhov i neudach sovetskoi diplomatii: politologicheskii aspekt.* Moscow: 1990.

Zarnitskii, Stanislav V., and A. N. Sergeev. *Chicherin.* Moscow: 1966.

Zimmerman, William. *Soviet Perspectives on International Relations, 1956–1967.* Princeton, N.J.: 1969.

Zurrer, Werner. *Persien zwischen England und Russland 1918–1925: Grossmachteinflüsse und nationaler Wiederaufstieg am Beispiel des Iran.* Bern: 1978.

Index

Compositor: Keystone Typesetting, Inc.
Text: 10/13 Aldus
Display: Aldus
Printer: Haddon Craftsmen
Binder: Haddon Craftsmen